THE CONTEMPORARY
ASIAN AMERICAN
EXPERIENCE

THE CONTEMPORARY ASIAN AMERICAN EXPERIENCE

Beyond the Model Minority

Timothy P. Fong

Holy Names College

Prentice Hall
Upper Saddle River, New Jersey 07458

Library of Congress Cataloging-in-Publication Data

FONG, TIMOTHY P.
   The contemporary Asian American experience : beyond the
model minority / Timothy P. Fong.
     p. cm.
   Includes bibliographical references and index.
   ISBN 0-13-362781-0 (pbk. : alk. paper)
   1. Asian Americans. I. Title.
E184.06F66   1998
973'.0495—dc21   97-33462

Editorial director: *Charlyce Jones Owen*
Editor-in-chief: *Nancy Roberts*
Acquisitions editor: *John Chillingworth*
Production editor: *Edie Riker*
Cover director: *Jayne Conte*
Cover design: *Rosemarie Votta*
Buyer: *Mary Ann Gloriande*
Marketing manager: *Christopher DeJohn*
Editorial assistant: *Pat Naturale*
Cover photo credits top to bottom: Dennie Cody/FPG International; David Young
    Wolff/Tony Stone Images; courtesy of *Asian Week*, the national news weekly for
    Asian Americans; Rich LaSalle/Tony Stone Images.

This book was set in 10/12 New Baskerville by East End Publishing Services
and was printed and bound by Courier Companies, Inc. The cover was
printed by Phoenix Color Corp.

© 1998 by Prentice-Hall, Inc.
Simon & Schuster / A Viacom Company
Upper Saddle River, New Jersey 07458

Printed in the United States of America

10 9 8 7 6 5 4 3 2 1

ISBN   0-13-362781-0

Prentice-Hall International (UK) Limited, *London*
Prentice-Hall of Australia Pty. Limited, *Sydney*
Prentice-Hall Canada Inc., *Toronto*
Prentice-Hall Hispanoamericana, S.A., *Mexico*
Prentice-Hall of India Private Limited, *New Delhi*
Prentice-Hall of Japan, Inc., *Tokyo*
Simon & Schuster Asia Pte. Ltd., *Singapore*
Editora Prentice-Hall do Brasil, Ltda., *Rio de Janeiro*

Contents

PREFACE

This book is intended primarily for college-level courses, but is written in a clear and direct narrative form that can easily reach a broader audience. In *The Sociological Imagination* (1959) C. Wright Mills chides what he calls "socspeak," the complex writing style commonly used in social sciences. Mills complains that in academic circles, anyone who writes "in a widely intelligible way" is belittled for being "a mere journalist."[1] As a sociologist, I know many colleagues who criticize the journalistic writing style for being too simple. As a former journalist, I also know that journalists criticize sociological writing style for being too abstract. Despite these criticisms of each other, sociologists and journalists do share the same common goal: increasing understanding of the issues confronting today's society. Readers will find the journalistic sociology approach in this book refreshing because it combines the rigor of scholarship with the accessibility of journalism. Readers will also better appreciate the significance of the research work of scholars from a variety of academic disciplines.

This book has several major objectives. The first objective is to provide a sound academic background to better comprehend the contemporary history, culture, and social relationships that form the fundamental issues confronted by Asians in America. This book analyzes the interrelationship of race, class, and gender and explores how these factors have shaped the experiences of Asian Americans. The hope is that readers will arrive at a new level of understanding and awareness beyond the simplistic stereotype of the "model minority" through the exposure to important concerns of Asian American groups and communities.

Second, this book is intended to provide a balanced and comparative analysis of the different Asian ethnic groups, newer immigrants, and American-born Asians. While Chinese, Japanese, and Filipinos were among the earliest immigrants from Asia, attention will also be given to new immigrants such as the Koreans, Asian Indians, and Southeast Asian refugees, who have come in large numbers to the United States since1965. With this in mind, chapters in this book are organized by specific issues rather than by specific ethnic group. In addition, this book will be balanced in terms of strong representation of how the various issues pertain to and impact Asian American women.

Third, this book will analyze competing aspects of the Asian American experience. Most of the early research on Asian Americans has focused on the "positive" cultural aspects of a strong work ethic and filial piety, amazing success in education, and enviable economic upward mobility. Since the 1970s, however, an increasing number of Asian American scholars have challenged what they feel is an overemphasis on anecdotal evidence and superficial statistical data. They have focused on issues of prejudice and discrimination, underemployment, educational problems, family and intergenerational conflict, and a host of other social concerns intended to provide a comprehensive picture of the Asian American experience.

Fourth, this book will compare and contrast various theoretical perspectives throughout the text where appropriate. This approach is unique, but necessary given the diversity of issues being covered. For example, the book will discuss different theories on immigration, immigrant adaptation and assimilation, ethnic entrepreneurship, educational achievement, ethnic identity, interracial marriage, and political incorporation, among others. Within this, recent Asian immigrants greatly differ from earlier immigrants in socioeconomic background and adjustment to American society. Clearly there is a need to review traditional concepts and theories, which are primarily based on the previous historical experiences.

Lastly, this book features an up-to-date collection of immigration, demographic, socioeconomic, and educational data on Asian Americans. Liberal use of tables highlights this information and serves as an excellent resource for the general audience, students, and researchers. In addition, an extensive bibliography of books, articles, and reports on Asian American issues is included in the book. This will be extremely useful for student papers and research projects.

I believe this book could not have been written without the help of many others. I first and foremost want to thank all the academic researchers, the journalists, and the community activists who have focused their attention on Asian Americans and Asian American issues. This is evidence of the growth and maturity of Asian American Studies as an academic discipline, the increased attention on Asian Americans in the media, and the importance of the issues raised on the grass-roots level. Together, their works and activities over many years have converged, and have only recently reached a critical mass. Whether directly cited or not, their works and activities are very much the core of this book. It is their insights, their analysis, and their hard work that gives this book life. I would also like to thank my colleagues in the Asian American Studies Department at California State University, Northridge, and the Social Sciences Division at Holy Names College where I have taught while writing this book. Their support and encouragement were invaluable. Special thanks go to Francis Hui and Lena Chang of the Cushing Library at Holy Names College, and to Wei-chi Poon of the Asian American Studies Library at UC Berkeley for their help locating reference materials. My highest praises go to Nancy Roberts, Sociology Editor at Prentice Hall, and Edie Riker, Editorial/Production Supervisor from East End Publishing Services, for their professional guidance on this book. Lastly, this book is dedicated to my wife, Elena Almanzo, the little one on the way, and our community of family and friends.

Timothy P. Fong
Holy Names College

ENDNOTE

1. C. Wright Mills, *The Sociological Imagination* (New York: Oxford University Press, 1959), pp. 218–19.

INTRODUCTION: CHANGING ASIAN AMERICA

VISIBILITY AND INVISIBILITY

The Los Angeles riot that erupted in 1992 following the acquittal of four police officers in the beating of motorist Rodney King prompted a national reexamination of race relations and poverty issues. This time, however, the debate needed to focus beyond just black and white issues. Suddenly, Asian Americans—in this case primarily Korean Americans—could not be ignored in the race relations equation. Throughout the violent uproar, Korean American businesses were the targets of looting and arson. After the smoke had cleared and the ashes cooled, it was discovered that over two thousand Korean-owned businesses were either damaged or destroyed during the riot. Together Korean and other Asian American businesses suffered over $460 million in property losses, nearly half the total of all property losses in the city.[1]

Despite this cataclysmic event, it is clear that precious little is known about Asian Americans in the United States. Just one year before the Los Angeles uprising, a national poll conducted by the *Wall Street Journal* and NBC News revealed some disturbing attitudes toward Asian Americans. A majority of Americans believed that Asian Americans are not discriminated against, and one out of five African Americans even believed that Asian Americans receive "too many special advantages."[2] In August 1993, the *Los Angeles Times* reported results of a survey that found most Southern Californians admired Asian Americans for their work ethic and strong family ties. At the same time, however, the same survey found a large number of people—46 percent—also thought that new Asian immigrants are a burden to the local economy.[3] In 1994, nearly two years after the urban disturbance in

1

Los Angeles, the National Conference of Christians and Jews released the results of another national survey on race relations that also produced troubling opinions of Asian Americans. On the positive side, all groups surveyed supported the notion of cultural diversity. On the other hand, Asian Americans felt the most in common with whites, even though both whites and blacks felt the least in common with Asian Americans.[4] A severe lack of understanding creates conflicting images of visibility and invisibility for Asian Americans in the minds of many in the United States today. Asian Americans are visible only in such stereotypes as "perpetual foreigners," "overachievers," and the "model minority." This often leads to irrational resentment. Recently, a Los Angeles radio talk show host complained about Asian American dominance in women's figure skating. "You know, I'm tired of the Kristi Yamaguchis and the Michelle Kwans!" stormed Bill Handel of station KFI-AM. "They're not American. . . . When I look at a box of Wheaties, I don't want to see eyes that are slanted and Oriental and almond shaped. I want to see American eyes looking at me."[5] The fact that both Yamaguchi and Kwan are not recognized as U.S.-born citizens is evidence of the invisibility of Asian Americas due to widespread ignorance of their distinct histories and contemporary experiences.

The visibility (stereotypes) and invisibility (ignorance) witnessed in the above polls and radio host's outburst speak to the urgency of the problem, and will be a recurring theme throughout this book. Despite this duality, Asian Americans can no longer be considered a marginal minority group. Since 1970 Asian Americans have been the fastest growing population group in the United States. In 1990 Asian and Pacific Islander Americans numbered over 7.2 million, and represented 2.9 percent of the United States population. The Asian American population nearly doubled between 1970 and 1980, and increased 95.2 percent between 1980 and 1990 (see Table I-1). From 1980 to 1990, the percentage of growth by the Asian American population far exceeded that of the Hispanic population, which grew by 51.5 percent. Asian Americans grew at a much higher rate than the African American population (13.2 percent), and grew at a rate over 20 times greater than the non-Hispanic white population (4.2 percent). Demographers project that the Asian American population could be as large as 20 million by the year 2020.[6] The rapid growth in the Asian American population is due primarily to the passage of the 1965 Immigration Reform Act, which ended discriminatory immigration policies that purposely kept down the number of immigrants from Asia. In the 19-year time span between 1941 and 1960, relatively few Asians immigrated to the United States. In just the nine years between 1961 and 1970, over 427,000 immigrants came to the U.S. from Asia. This number increased to over 1.5 million between 1971 and 1980 and reached over 2.7 million between 1981 and 1990. From 1991 to 1994 there were over 1.3 million immigrants from Asia to the United States (see Table I-2).

Table I-1 United States Population, 1980–1990

	1990	1980	Increase %
Total U.S.	248,709,873	226,545,805	9.8
Non-Hispanic White	188,128,296	180,602,838	4.2
African American	29,986,060	26,482,349	13.2
NativeAmerican Indian, Eskimo, Aleut	1,959,234	1,534,336	27.7
Asian/Pacific Islander	7,273,662	3,726,440	95.2*
Chinese	1,645,472	812,178	102.6
Filipino	1,406,770	781,894	79.9
Japanese	847,562	716,331	18.3
Asian Indian	815,447	387,223	110.6
Korean	798,849	357,393	123.5
Vietnamese	614,547	245,025	150.8
Laotian	149,014	47,683	212.5
Cambodian	147,411	16,044	818.8
Hmong	90,082	5,204	1,631.0
Other Asian & Pacific Islander	758,508	357,465	112.2
Hispanic**	21,113,528	13,935,827	51.5
Non-Hispanic & Other Race	249,093	264,015	-5.7

*The percentage of change between 1980 and 1990 in this table is lower than the 107.8 percent found some other published reports. Other reports were based on the count of all Asian Pacific Americans in 1990 but only nine specific Asian American groups in 1980. The 95.2 percent figure cited in this table is more accurate and comparable, and is the percentage change if you count only the nine specific Asian American groups between 1980 and 1990.
**Hispanic includes those "White" and other races.
Source: U.S. Bureau of the Census, *1990 Census of the Population, General Population Characteristics, United States Summary,* CP-1-1, (Washington, DC: U.S. Government Printing Office, 1993), Table 3; U.S. Bureau of the Census, *Asian Pacific Islander Population in the United States: 1980* PC80-1-1E, (Washington, DC: U.S. Government Printing Office, 1988), Table 1.

Table I-2   Asian Immigrants to the United States, Fiscal Years 1941–1994

	All Countries	*Asia**	*%*
1994	804,416	232,449	35.1
1993	904,292	345,425	38.2
1992	973,977	344,802	35.4
1991	1,827,167	342,157	18.7
1981–90	7,338,062	2,738,157	37.3
1971–80	4,493,314	1,588,176	35.3
1961–70	3,321,677	427,642	12.9
1951–60	2,515,479	153,249	6.1
1941–50	1,035,039	37,028	3.6

* Includes Iraq, Israel, Syria, Turkey, and other Southwest Asian countries.
Source: U.S. Immigration and Naturalization Service, *Statistical Yearbook of the Immigration and Naturalization Service, 1994,* (Washington, DC: U.S. Government Printing Office, 1996), Table 1, pp. 25–29.

Who Are Asian Americans?

Lack of understanding of Asian Americans is due in part to the fact that they are an extremely heterogeneous minority group. They are composed of people whose ancestry originates from dozens of countries, who have been in the United States for generations, and those who are only recent immigrants and refugees. They are composed of people who are highly educated, professionally skilled, and relatively affluent. The Asian American population also includes a significant number of people who are completely illiterate, possess little more than subsistence farming skills, and are extremely poor. In addition, who is considered to be Asian is not clearly defined. The United States Census Bureau uses the broad term "Asian and Pacific Islander Americans" in it's population count, which includes native Hawaiians, Samoans, Guamanians, and so forth. The Immigration and Naturalization Service broadly counts Asian immigrants to include people from Southwest Asian countries such as Iran, Israel, and Turkey. As a result, this book must make important distinctions and limitations.

First of all, this book concentrates on the most prominent Asian American ethnic groups in the United States who represent the vast majority the U.S. census category, "Asian Pacific Islander." They are Chinese American, Japanese American, Filipino American, Korean American, Asian Indians, and Southeast Asian refugees, consisting of Vietnamese, Cambodians, Laotian, and Hmong Americans. Second, this book will focus on the Asian American experience as a distinct minority in the continental United States. While I recognize the overall importance of Hawaii in the history of Asian Americans, I will not discuss the

Asian American experience in Hawaii in great detail. Asian Americans are the majority population in Hawaii, and their experience is quite different from other Asian Americans on the mainland. For example, Japanese Americans in Hawaii were not interned during World War II, while over 110,000 Japanese Americans on the mainland were forcibly incarcerated.

Because I do not focus on Hawaii and the Pacific Islander population, I prefer to use the term "Asian American," rather than "Asian Pacific Americans" or "Asian Pacific Islander Americans" in this book. There will be, however, individuals quoted and sources cited throughout this book that do use the "Asian Pacific" terms. Since I focus on the Asian American experience after the 1965 Immigration Reform Act, I generally refer to all persons of Asian ancestry living in the United States as Asian Americans. I do this because the overwhelming majority of Asian immigrants and refugees who have come to the United States after 1965 did so fully intending to settle down and become United States citizens. Despite obvious ethnic and language differences within this broadly defined group, the term "Asian American" *is* significant and meaningful. The above nine groups have been shaped by similar historical experiences in the United States, and today confront a myriad of common issues. This book examines many of these common issues and is intended to show that Asian Americans continue to face prejudice, discrimination, and racially motivated violence that clearly hinder their full and open participation in American society. At the same time, this book is not intended to be only about social problems. The increasing number of highly educated, motivated, and talented Asian Americans is an asset to the United States in terms of economic growth and cultural enrichment. I will highlight these aspects of the Asian American experience as well. Lastly, this book also works to show both the similarities and differences between Asian Americans and other racial, ethnic, and immigrant groups to emphasize that the post-1965 contemporary Asian American experience challenges any easy definition or theoretical analysis.

ORGANIZATION OF THE BOOK

The organization of this book is based on the Asian American Contemporary Issues course I have been teaching for the past several years, and is intended generally to flow sequentially, with each chapter building on information from previous chapters. Chapter 1 starts with a history of the Asian American experience in the United States and discusses the tremendous changes for Asian Americans after 1965. A historical overview is highly instructive to show both the dramatic progress made by Asian Americans, as well as disturbing trends and animosities that continue to this day. Chapter 2 provides a demographic and socioeconomic profile of Asian Americans. This chapter will feature the latest data on settlement patterns, geographic dispersion, ethnic entrepreneurship, as well as a critical analysis of the popular "model minority" image of

Asian Americans today. Chapter 3 examines the highly touted success of Asian Americans in education and highlights several theories for this phenomenon. At the same time, Chapter 3 also looks beyond the generalized statistics and addresses several educational issues confronting Asian Americans in primary school (K–12) through college.

The book then shifts from the classroom to the workplace. Chapter 4 focuses the subtleties of discrimination in the workplace, which, upon close examination, are not so subtle at all. Chapter 5 confronts anti-Asian violence, probably the most important issue to confront Asian Americans today. Key to this chapter is a discussion of four factors that encourage and perpetuate anti-Asian hostility, along with a closer look at the volatile issue of Asian American and African American relations. Because much of the anti-Asian sentiment and violence stems from negative images of Asians in the media, Chapter 6 provides coverage and analysis of stereotypes of Asian Americans in film and other media. The chapter not only offers a historical perspective but also looks at very recent examples, and shows how Asian American media artists and activist groups are trying to raise awareness about these issues.

While certain images of Asian Americans are perpetuated in the media, the realities of Asian American life are constantly changing. Chapter 7 looks at Asian American families and identities, with particular emphasis on diversity and new transformations. Important cutting-edge issues such as identity formation, mental health concerns, interracial marriage, biracial Asian Americans, and gay and lesbian Asian Americans are included in this chapter. Lastly, Chapter 8 addresses the issue of Asian American political empowerment. The chapter begins with an overview of electoral and nonelectoral empowerment efforts by Asian Americans, and ends with an examination of the important role of Asian Americans in several recent national, state, and local elections.

PERSPECTIVE OF THE BOOK

This book focuses on some of the most important issues confronting Asian Americans since 1965. The issues raised here are significant because they are likely to continue to be seen in one form or another in the future. The strength of this book comes from highlighting each of the major issues within a broader historical context and from an interdisciplinary perspective. This book also draws attention to how various issues such as images in the media, anti-immigrant sentiment, and anti-Asian violence interrelate, and analyzes how the concepts of race, class, and gender intersect throughout the Asian American experience.

This book is deeply rooted in many of the ideals first articulated during the founding years of the Asian American Movement following the 1968 student strike at San Francisco State College (now San Francisco State University). One of the most important ideals that emerged from the student strike was the need to make education "relevant." This means taking knowledge from the academic institutions that can be useful to students outside of the classroom walls and beyond the final exam. At the same time, this book is also clearly centered in the "new" thinking on the Asian American Movement as a political force, and Asian American Studies as an academic discipline.

Shirley Hune, professor of urban planning at the University of California at Los Angeles, has written extensively on the changes in thinking about the contemporary Asian American experience. Within this, she has called for "paradigm shifts," which are alterations of commonly held worldviews and values among people. In her article, "Rethinking Race: Paradigms and Policy Formation" (1995), Hune raises the point that race relations in the United States have historically been very narrowly focused. She questions what she calls the "vertical" model of race relations that depicts whites on top of the socioeconomic and political hierarchy, with all other nonwhites flailing below. She prefers to view race relations in a "horizontal" fashion that recognizes not only racial factors but also the importance of class and gender factors that cut across racial lines. "The relations between Asian American small business owners and their non-Asian employees and clientele, new multiracial and multiethnic residential patterns, biracial families, the growing class disparities within racial/ethnic groups, the shift in party affiliation and voting preferences of racial groups from Democrats to Republicans and other indicators give rise to rethinking race relations," Hune writes.[7]

Second, Hune challenges the presumption that race is a relatively fixed biological phenomenon, and that social inequalities experienced by racial minorities are largely determined by biological factors. Instead, Hune draws upon Michael Omi and Howard Winant's "Racial Formation" theory that argues race is in fact an ever changing socially constructed phenomenon. This means race relations are extremely dynamic and are constantly being redefined. Racial formation theory identifies the combination of both micro (discourse, meaning) and macro (government policies, social institutions) levels of contestation that help explain why Asian Americans have experienced periods of relatively calm race relations, other periods of intense hostility, and sometimes heightened racial antagonism against one Asian American group, but not another.[8]

Third, Hune points to the fact that Asian Americans have for the most part been studied separately from one another and that studies on individual groups (i.e., Chinese, Japanese, Filipino, Asian Indian, Korean, and Southeast Asians) are far more numerous than studies that address Asian Americans as a whole. "This approach was a necessary beginning for Asian American Studies as it sought to reclaim its historic place in American history and culture," Hune writes. "However, this paradigm results in descriptions of ethnic-specific experiences that are circumscribed, while assumed to be representative of the entire community."[8] She calls for a new paradigm that explicitly and accurately compares *and* contrasts the diverse Asian American experiences. This new paradigm called for by Hune is seen throughout this book's content and organization.

Fourth, early research on the Asian American experience has often viewed Asian-Americans as victims of racial, economic, and political subjugation in the United States. This image was often perpetuated by earlier Asian American scholars and activists, often as a way of rallying political unity. However, Hune argues that the historic and contemporary Asian American experience has shown a far greater tendency and willingness to confront, organize, and challenge oppressive situations they face. Asian Americans throughout this book were shown fighting back against the glass ceiling, educational discrimination, anti-Asian violence, distortions in the media, and political isolation. At the same time, Hune also acknowledges what she calls "differential power and agency." She recognizes the fact that certain groups of Asian Americans face more hardships and limitations than others, and the difficulties for the poor, the uneducated, the limited English speakers, the noncitizen, and recent immigrants and refugees should not be ignored.[9] Good examples from this book can be seen in detailed descriptions of the garment workers' struggle against Jessica McClintock and the abuses of the garment industry, along with the campaigns aimed at encouraging voter registration and participation among new immigrants.

Lastly, Hune addresses the need to see the new immigrant experience as fundamental to the contemporary Asian American experience. The early evolution of Asian American Studies rejected any connection with Asian Studies, or the study of regions of Asia, in the belief that the Asian American experience was unique and had nothing to do with anything that happened in Asia. Today, many Asian American Studies scholars are acknowledging the importance of analyzing the Asian American experience from a global perspective. This can be seen in the transnational movement of people, capital, consumer markets, interpersonal networks, culture, and technology from Asia to the United States described in various sections in this book. This can also be seen in the dramatic impact Asian immigrants have made in the demographic, social, cultural, and political life in urban and suburban communities across the nation.

Taken together, these "paradigm shifts" are the mainstays for present and future thinking about Asian Americans, and all are addressed in this book. The rapid growth of the Asian American population, the expanded research and scholarship on Asian American issues, and the continued commitment by Asian American artists and activists are the catalysts for tremendous change and progress. The Asian American experience is continuously unfolding and redeveloping, and is extremely dynamic; it is like a story of many themes and subplots, with no easy conclusion. It is also a story full of challenges and promises longing to be told.

ENDNOTES

1. Edward T. Chang, "America's First Multiethnic 'Riots,'" in Karin Aguilar-San Juan (ed.), *The State of Asian America: Activism and Resistance* (Boston: South End Press, 1994), pp. 101, 114.
2. Michael McQueen, "Voters' Response to Poll Disclose Huge Chasm Between Social Attitudes of Blacks and Whites," *Wall Street Journal*, May 17, 1991.
3. Carla Rivera, "Asians Say They Fare Better Than Other Minorities," *Los Angeles Times*, August 20, 1993.
4. Steven A. Holmes, "Survey Finds Minorities Resent One Another Almost as Much as They Do Whites," *New York Times*, March 3, 1994.
5. Sam Chu Lin, "Radio Tirade," *Asian Week*, April 5, 1996.
6. Paul Ong and Suzanne J. Hee. "The Growth of the Asian Pacific American Population: Twenty Million in 2020," in *The State of Asian Pacific America: Policy Issues to the Year 2020* (Los Angeles: LEAP Asian Pacific American Public Policy Institute and UCLA Asian American Studies Center, 1993), pp. 11–23.
7. Shirley Hune, "Rethinking Race: Paradigms and Policy Formation," *Amerasia Journal* 21:1&2 (1995): 29–40.
8. *Ibid.*, pp. 31–32; also see Michael Omi and Howard Winant, *Racial Formation in the United States: From the 1960s to the 1980s* (New York: Routledge and Kegan Paul, 1986).
9. *Ibid.*, p. 33.
10. *Ibid.*, pp. 32–33.

1

THE HISTORY OF ASIANS IN AMERICA

A BRIEF HISTORY OF ASIANS IN AMERICA

Immigration

The historical experience of Asian Americans in the United States is not at all atypical of other minority groups. As a distinct racial minority group, and as immigrants, Asian Americans faced enormous individual prejudice, frequent mob violence, and extreme forms of institutional discrimination. But Asian Americans have not merely been victims of hostility and oppression; indeed, they have also shown remarkable strength and perseverance, which is a testimony to their desire to make the United States their home. Between 1848 and 1924, hundreds of thousands of immigrants from China, Japan, the Philippines, Korea, and India came to the United States. While this period represents the first significant wave, these immigrants were by no means the very first Asians to come to America.

Recent archaeological finds off the coast of Southern California have led to speculation that the West Coast of America may have been visited by Buddhist missionaries from China in the fifth century. While direct evidence of this claim is still being debated, it is known that the Spanish brought Chinese shipbuilders to Baja California as early as 1571, and later Filipino seamen were brought by Spanish galleons from Manila and settled along the coast of Louisiana. Chinese merchants and sailors were also present in the United States prior to the discovery of gold in California in 1848. Most people are unaware that Asian Indians were brought to the America during the late eighteenth century as indentured servants and slaves.[1]

The California gold rush did not immediately ignite a mass rush of Chinese immigrants to America. In fact, only a few hundred Chinese arrived in California during the first years of the gold rush, and most of them were merchants. However, large-scale immigration did begin in earnest in 1852 when 52,000 Chinese arrived that year alone. Many Chinese came to the United States not only to seek their fortunes but also to escape political and economic turmoil in China. As gold ran out, thousands of Chinese were recruited in the mid-1860s to help work on the transcontinental railroad. Eventually more than 300,000 Chinese entered the United States in the nineteenth century, engaging in a variety of work. During this same period Chinese also immigrated to Hawaii, but in far fewer numbers than to the continental United States.[2]

Large capitalist and financial interests welcomed the Chinese as cheap labor and lobbied for the 1868 Burlingame Treaty, which recognized "free migration and emigration" of Chinese to the United States in exchange for American trade privileges in China. As early as 1870 Chinese were 9 percent of California's population and 25 percent of the state's work force.[3] The majority of these Chinese were young single men who intended to work in this country a few years and then return to China. Those who stayed seldom married because of laws severely limiting the immigration of Chinese women and prohibiting intermarriage with white women. The result was the Chinese were forced to live a harsh and lonely bachelor life that often featured vice and prostitution. In 1890, for example, there were roughly 102,620 Chinese men and only 3,868 Chinese women in the United States, a male–female ratio of 26:1.[4] Despite these conditions, Chinese workers continued to come to the United States.

Following the completion of the transcontinental railroad in 1869, large numbers of unemployed Chinese workers had to find new sources of employment. Many found work in agriculture where they cleared land, dug canals, planted orchards, harvested crops, and were the foundation for successful commercial production of many California crops. Others settled in San Francisco and other cities to manufacture shoes, cigars, and clothing. Still others started small businesses such as restaurants, laundries, and general stores. Domestic service such as houseboys, cooks, and gardeners were also other areas of employment for the Chinese. In short, the Chinese were involved in many occupations that were crucial to the economic development and domestication of the western region of the United States.[5] Unfortunately, intense hostility against the Chinese reached its peak in 1882 when Congress passed the Chinese Exclusion Act intended to "suspend" the entry of Chinese laborers for ten years. Other laws were eventually passed that barred Chinese laborers and their wives permanently.[6]

The historical experience of Japanese in the United States is both different yet similar to that of the Chinese. One major difference is that the

Japanese emigrated in large numbers to Hawaii and were not significant in United States until the 1890s. In 1880 there were only 148 Japanese living in the U.S. mainland. In 1890 this number increased to 2,000, mostly merchants and students. However, the population increased dramatically when an influx of 38,000 Japanese workers from Hawaii arrived in the U.S. mainland between 1902 and 1907.[7] The second difference was the fact the Japanese were able to fully exploit an economic niche in agriculture that the Chinese had only started. The completion of several national railroad lines and the invention of the refrigerator car were two advancements that brought forth tremendous expansion in the California produce industry. The early Japanese were fortunate to arrive at an opportune time, and about two thirds of the Japanese found work as agricultural laborers. Within a short time the Japanese were starting their own farms in direct competition with non-Japanese farms. By 1919 the Japanese controlled over 450,000 acres of agricultural land. Although this figure represents only 1 percent of active California agricultural land at the time, the Japanese were so efficient in their farming practices that they captured 10 percent of the dollar volume of the state's crops.[8]

The third major difference was the emergence of Japan as a international military power at the turn of the century. Japan's victory in the Russo-Japanese War (1904–1905) impressed President Theodore Roosevelt and he believed a strategy of cooperation with the Japanese government was in the best interest of the United States. Roosevelt blocked calls for complete Japanese exclusion and instead worked a compromise with the Japanese government in 1907 known as the "Gentleman's Agreement." This agreement halted the immigration of Japanese laborers but allowed Japanese women into the United States. With this in mind, the fourth difference was the fact that the Japanese in the United States were able to actually increase in population, start families, and establish a rather stable community life.[9]

Filipino immigration began after the United States gained possession of the Philippines following the Spanish-American War in 1898. The first Filipinos to arrive were a few hundred pensionados, or students supported by government scholarships. Similar to the Japanese experience, a large number of Filipinos went directly to Hawaii before coming to the U. S. mainland. Between 1907 and 1919 over 28,000 Filipinos were actively recruited to work on sugar plantations in Hawaii. Filipinos began to emigrate to the United States following the passage of the 1924 Immigration Act, which prohibited all Asian immigration to this country and there was a need for agricultural and service labor.[10]

Because Filipinos lived on American territory, they were "nationals" who were free to travel in the United States without restriction. In the 1920s over 45,000 Filipinos arrived in Pacific Coast ports, and a 1930 study found 30,000 Filipinos working in California. These Filipinos were overwhelmingly young, single males. Their ages ranged between 16 and 29, and there were 14 Filipino men for every Filipina. Sixty percent of these Filipinos worked as migratory agricultural laborers, and 25 percent worked in domestic service in Los Angeles and San Francisco. The rest found work in manufacturing and as railroad porters. Unlike the Japanese, Filipinos did not make their mark in agriculture as farmers, but as labor union organizers.[11] Both Filipino farm worker activism and Japanese farm competition created a great deal of resentment among white farmers and laborers.

Koreans and Asian Indians slightly predated the Filipinos, but arrived in much smaller numbers. Between 1903 and 1905 over 7,000 Koreans were recruited for plantation labor work in Hawaii, but after Japan established a protectorate over Korea in 1905, all emigration was halted.[12] In the next five years, Japan increased its economic and political power and formally annexed Korea in 1910. Relatively few Koreans lived in the United States between 1905 and 1940. Among those included about 1,000 workers who migrated from Hawaii, about 100 Korean "picture brides," and a small number of American-born Koreans. The Korean population in the United States during that time was also bolstered by roughly 900 students, many of whom fled to their home country because of their opposition to Japanese rule. Like other Asian immigrant groups, Koreans found themselves concentrated in California agriculture working primarily as laborers, although a small number did become quite successful farmers.[13]

The first significant flow of Asian Indians occurred between 1904 and 1911, when just over 6,000 arrived in the United States. Unlike the other Asian groups, Asian Indians did not work in Hawaii prior to entering the American mainland, but they worked primarily in California agriculture. Similar to the Chinese, Filipinos, and Koreans, they had an extremely high male to female ratio. Of the Asian Indians who immigrated to the United States between 1904 and 1911, there were only three or four women, all of whom were married.[14] Eighty to ninety percent of the first Asian Indian settlers in the United States were Sikhs, a distinct ethno-religious minority group in India. Despite this fact, these Sikhs were often called Hindus, which they are not. Sikhs were easily recognizable from all other Asian immigrant groups because of their huskier build, they wore turbans, and they kept their beards. But like other Asians in the United States at the time, they also worked primarily in California's agricultural industry. Asian Indians worked first as farm workers, and like the Japanese, also formed cooperatives, pooled their resources, and began independent farming.[15] Immigration restrictions, their relatively small numbers, and an exaggerated male–female ratio prevented Asian Indians from developing a lasting farm presence. One major exception can be found in the Marysville–Yuba City area of Northern California, where Asian Indian Sikhs are still quite active in producing cling peaches.[16]

Anti-Asian Laws and Sentiment

The United States is a nation that proclaims to welcome and assimilate all new-comers. But the history of immigration, naturalization, and equal treatment under the law for Asian Americans has been an extremely difficult one. In 1790 Congress passed the first naturalization law limiting citizenship rights to only a "free white person."[17] In 1870, during the period of reconstruction following the end of the Civil War, Congress amended the law and allowed citizenship for "aliens of African nativity and persons of African descent."[18] For a while there was some discussion on expanding naturalization rights to Chinese immigrants, but that idea was rejected by politicians from western states.[19] This rejection is exemplary of the intense anti-Chinese sentiment at the time.

As early as 1850 California imposed a Foreign Miners Tax, which required the payment of $20 a month from all foreign miners.[20] The California Supreme Court ruled in *People v. Hall* (1854), that Chinese could not testify in court against a white person. This case threw out the testimony of three Chinese witnesses and reversed the murder conviction of George W. Hall, who was sentenced to hang for the murder of a Chinese man one year earlier.[21] In 1855 a local San Francisco ordinance levied a $50 tax on all aliens ineligible for citizenship. Since Chinese were ineligible for citizenship under the Naturalization Act of 1790, they were the primary targets for this law.[22]

The racially distinct Chinese were the primary scapegoats for the depressed economy in the 1870s, and mob violence erupted on several occasions through to the 1880s. The massacre of 21 Chinese in Los Angeles in 1871 and 28 Chinese in Rock Springs, Wyoming, in 1885 are examples of the worst incidents. It is within this environment that Congress passed the 1882 Chinese Exclusion Act. The act suspended immigration of Chinese laborers for only ten years, but it was extended in 1892 and 1902. The act was eventually extended indefinitely in 1904.[23] The intense institutional discrimination achieved the desired result: The Chinese population declined from 105,465 in 1880 to 61,639 in 1920.[24]

Anti-Chinese sentiment easily grew into large-scale anti-Asian sentiment as immigrants from Asia continued to enter the United States. During the same period that the Chinese population declined, the Japanese population grew and became highly visible. As early as 1910 there were 72,157 Japanese Americans compared to 71,531 Chinese Americans in the United States.[25] The Japanese farmers in California were particularly vulnerable targets for animosity. One of the most sweeping anti-Asian laws was aimed at the Japanese Americans, but affected all other Asian American groups as well. The 1913 Alien Land Law prohibited "aliens ineligible to citizenship" from owning or leasing land for more than three years. Initially the Japanese Americans were able to bypass the law primarily because they could buy or lease land under the names of their American-born offspring (the Nisei), who were U.S. citizens by birth. The law was strengthened in 1920, however, and the purchase of land under the names of American-born offspring was prohibited.[26]

Several sweeping anti-immigration laws were passed in the first quarter of the twentieth century that served to eliminate Asian immigration to the United States. A provision in the 1917 Immigration Act banned immigration from the so-called "Asian barred zone," except for the Philippines and Japan. A more severe anti-Asian restriction was further imposed by the 1924 National Origins Act, which placed a ceiling of 150,000 new immigrants per year. The 1924 act was intended to limit Eastern and Southern European immigration, but a provision was added that ended any immigration by aliens ineligible for citizenship.[27]

Asian Americans did not sit back passively in the face of discriminatory laws; they hired lawyers and went to court to fight for their livelihoods, naturalization rights, and personal liberties. Sometimes they were successful, oftentimes they were not. In the case of *Yick Wo v. Hopkins* (1886), Chinese successfully challenged an 1880 San Francisco Laundry Ordinance, which regulated commercial laundry service in a way that clearly discriminated against the Chinese. Plaintiff Yick Wo had operated a laundry service for 22 years, but when he tried to renew his business license in 1885 he was turned down because his storefront was made out of wood. Two hundred other Chinese laundries were also denied business licenses on similar grounds, while 80 non-Chinese laundries were approved—even those in wooden buildings. The Supreme Court ruled in favor of Yick Wo, concluding there was "no reason" for the denial of the business license "except to the face and nationality" of the petitioner.[28]

The inability to gain citizenship was a defining factor throughout the early history of Asian Americans. The constitutionality of naturalization based on race was first challenged in the Supreme Court case of *Ozawa v. United States* (1922). Takao Ozawa was born in Japan but immigrated to the United States at an early age. He graduated from Berkeley High School in California and attended the University of California for three years. Ozawa was a model immigrant who did not smoke or drink, he attended a predominantly white church, his children attended public school, and English was the language spoken at home. When Ozawa was rejected in his initial attempt for naturalization, he appealed and argued that the provisions for citizenship in the 1790 and 1870 acts did not specifically exclude Japanese. In addition, Ozawa also tried to argue that Japanese should be considered "white."

The Court unanimously ruled against Ozawa on both grounds. First, the Court decided that initial framers of the law and its amendment did not intend to *exclude* people from naturalization but, instead, only determine who would be *included*. Ozawa was denied citizenship because the existing law simply didn't include Japanese. Second, the Court also ruled against Ozawa's argument that Japanese were actually more "white" than other darker-skinned "white" people such as some Italians, Spanish, and Portuguese. The Court clarified the matter by defining a "white person" to be synonymous with a "person of the Caucasian race." In short, Ozawa was not Caucasian (though he thought himself to be "white") and, thus, was ineligible for citizenship.[29]

Prior to the *Ozawa* case, Asian Indians already enjoyed the right of naturalization. In *United States v. Balsara* (1910), the Supreme Court determined that Asian Indians were Caucasian and approximately 70 became naturalized citizens. But the Immigration and Naturalization Service (INS) challenged this decision, and it was taken up again in the case of *United States v. Thind* (1923). This time the Supreme Court reversed its earlier decision and ruled that Bhagat Singh Thind could not be a citizen because he was not "white." Even though Asian Indians were classified as Caucasian, this was a scientific term that was inconsistent with the popular understanding. The Court's decision stated: "It may be true that the blond Scandinavian and the brown Hindu have a common ancestor in the dim reaches of antiquity, but the average man knows perfectly well that there are unmistakable differences between them today."[30] In other words, only "white" Caucasians were considered eligible for U.S. citizenship. In the wake of the *Thind* decision, the INS was able to cancel retroactively the citizenship of Asian Indians between 1923 and 1926.

Asian Americans also received disparate treatment compared to other immigrants in their most private affairs, such as marriage. In the nineteenth century, anti-miscegenation laws prohibiting marriage between blacks and whites were common throughout the United States. In 1880 the California legislature extended restrictive antimiscegenation categories to prohibit any marriage between a white person and a "negro, mulatto, or Mongolian." This law, targeted at the Chinese, was not challenged until Salvador Roldan won a California Court of Appeals decision in 1933. Roldan, a Filipino American, argued that he was Malay, not Mongolian, and he should be allowed to marry his white fiancee. The Court conceded that the state's anti-miscegenation law was created in an atmosphere of intense anti-Chinese sentiment, and agreed Filipinos were not in mind when the initial legislation was approved. Unfortunately, this victory was short-lived. The California State legislature amended the anti-miscegenation law to include the "Malay race" shortly after the Roldan decision was announced.[31]

World War II and the Cold War Era

For Asian Americans, World War II was an epoch; but the profound impact was distinct for different Asian American groups. For over 110,000 Japanese Americans, World War II was an agonizing ordeal soon after Japan's attack of Pearl Harbor on December 7, 1941. The FBI arrested thousands of Japanese Americans who were considered potential security threats immediately after the Pearl Harbor bombing raid. Arrested without evidence of disloyalty were the most visible Japanese American community leaders, including businessmen, Shinto and Buddhist priests, teachers in Japanese language schools, and editors of Japanese language newspapers. Wartime hysteria rose to a fever pitch, and on February 19, 1942, President Franklin Roosevelt issued Executive Order 9066. This order established various military zones and authorized the removal of anyone who was a potential threat. While there were a small number of German and Italian aliens detained and relocated, this did not compare to the mass relocation of Japanese Americans on the West Coast of the United States.[32]

The order to relocate Japanese Americans because of military necessity, and the threat they posed to security, was a fabrication. There was considerable debate even among military leaders over the genuine need for mass relocation, and the government's own intelligence reports found no evidence of Japanese American disloyalty. "For the most part the local Japanese are loyal to the United States or, at worst, hope that by remaining quiet they can avoid concentration camps or irresponsible mobs," one report stated. "We do not believe that they would be at least any more disloyal than any other racial group in the United States with whom we went to war."[33] This helps to explain why 160,000 Japanese Americans living in Hawaii were not interned. More telling was the fact that Japanese Americans in the continental United States were a small but much resented minority. Despite government reports to the contrary, business leaders, local politicians, and the media fueled antagonism against the Japanese Americans and agitated for their abrupt removal.[34]

With only seven days' notice to prepare once the internment order was issued, and no way of knowing how long the war would last, many Japanese Americans were forced to sell their homes and property at a mere fraction of their genuine value. It is estimated that the Japanese Americans suffered economic losses alone of at least $400 million. By August 1942 all the Japanese on the West Coast were interned in ten camps located in rural regions of California, Arizona, Utah, Idaho, Wyoming, and Arkansas. Two thirds of the interned Japanese American men, women, and children were U.S. citizens, whose only crime was their ancestry; even those with as little as one-eighth Japanese blood were interned. The camps themselves were crude, mass facilities surrounded by barbed wire and guarded by armed sentries. People were housed in large barracks with each family living in small cramped "apartments." Food was served in large mess halls, and toilet and shower facilities were communal. Many of the camps were extremely cold in the winter, hot in the summer, and dusty all year round. The camps remained open for the duration of the war.[35]

After the first year of the camps, the government began recruiting young Japanese American men to help in the war effort. The military desperately needed Japanese Americans to serve as interpreters for Japanese prisoners of war and translators of captured documents. But to the military's incredulity, most American-born Japanese had only modest Japanese language skills and had to take intense training in the Military Intelligence Service Language School before they could perform their duties.[36] It was, however, the heroic actions of the 100th Infantry Battalion, which later merged with the 442nd Regimental Combat Team, that stand out the most among historians. The two segregated units engaged in numerous campaigns and served with distinction throughout Europe. By the end of the war in Europe, for example, the Nisei soldiers of the 442nd suffered over 9,000 casualties, while earning over 18,000 individual decorations of honor. The 442nd was the most decorated unit of its size during all of World War II.[37]

Compared to the Japanese American experience, other Asian American groups fared far better during and after World War II. Changes for Chinese Americans were particularly dramatic. Prior to the war, the image of the Chinese was clearly negative compared to the Japanese. A survey of Princeton undergraduates in 1931 thought the top three traits of the Chinese were the fact they were "superstitious, sly, and conservative," while Japanese were considered "intelligent, industrious, and progressive."[38] Immediately after the bombing of Pearl Harbor, Chinese store owners put up signs indicating they were not Japanese, and in some cases Chinese Americans wore buttons stating, "I am Chinese." To alleviate any further identification problems, *Time* magazine published an article on December 22, 1941, explaining how to tell the difference between Chinese and "Japs." The article compared photographs of a Chinese man and a Japanese man, highlighting the distinguishing facial features of each.[39] Just months later, a 1942 Gallup Poll characterized the Chinese as "hardworking, honest, and brave," while Japanese were seen as "treacherous, sly, and cruel."[40]

Employment opportunities outside of the segregated Chinatown community became available to Chinese Americans for the first time during the war, and continued even after the war ended. Chinese Americans trained in various professions and skilled crafts were able to find work in war-related industries that had never been open to them before. In addition, the employment of Chinese American women increased threefold during the 1940s. Leading the way were clerical positions, which increased from just 750 in 1940 to 3,200 in 1950. In 1940 women represented just one in five Chinese American professionals, but by 1950 this increased to one in three. On another level, Chinese actors suddenly found they were in demand for film roles—usually playing evil Japanese characters. Shortly after the war, writers such as Jade Snow Wong and Pardee Lowe discovered the newfound interest and appreciation of Chinese Americans could be turned into commercial success through the publication of their memoirs.[41]

On the military front, Asian Americans also distinguished themselves. Over 15,000 Chinese Americans served in all branches of the military, unlike the Japanese Americans who were placed only in segregated infantry units and in the Military Intelligence Service. Similarly, over 7,000 Filipino Americans volunteered for the army and formed the First and Second Filipino Infantry Regiments. About 1,000 other Filipino Americans were sent to the Philippines to perform reconnaissance and intelligence activities for General Douglas MacArthur.[42] Equally significant was the War Bride's Act of 1945, which allowed war veterans to bring wives from China and the Philippines as non-quota immigrants. This resulted in a rapid and dramatic shift in the historic gender imbalance of both groups. For example, between 1945 and 1952, nine out of ten (89.9 percent) Chinese immigrants were female, and 20,000 Chinese American babies were born by the mid-1950s. Similarly, between 1951 and 1960 seven out of ten (71 percent) Filipino immigrants were female.[43]

On the broad international front, alliances with China, the Philippines, and India eventually began the process of changing the overtly discriminatory immigration laws against Asians: The Chinese Exclusion Law was repealed in 1943 and an annual quota of 105 immigrants from China was allotted; in 1946 Congress approved legislation that extended citizenship to Filipino immigrants and permitted the entry of 100 Filipino immigrants annually; also in 1946, the Luce-Cellar Act ended the 1917 "Asian barred zone," allowed an immigration quota of 100 from India, and for the first time permitted Asian Indians to apply for citizenship since the *United States v. Thind* case of 1923. Though these changes were extremely modest, they carried important symbolic weight by helping to create a favorable international opinion of the United States during and immediately after the war.[44]

Geopolitical events during the Cold War era of the 1950s and 1960s immediately following World War II continued to have important ramifications for Asian Americans. After the 1949 Communist Revolution in China, about 5,000 Chinese students and young professionals were living in the United States. These "stranded" individuals were generally from China's most elite and educated families, and were not necessarily anxious to return to China because their property had already been confiscated and their livelihoods were threatened. These students and professionals were eventually allowed to stay in the United States.[45] Several other refugee acts in the late 1950s and early 1960s allowed some 18,000 other Chinese to enter and also stay in the United States. Many of these refugees were well-trained scientists and engineers who easily found jobs in private industry and in research universities. These educated professionals were quite distinct from the vast majority of earlier Chinese immigrants because they usually were able to integrate into the American mainstream quickly, becoming the basis of an emerging Chinese American middle class.[46]

The Cold War affected immigration from Asian countries as well, but in a very different fashion. During and after the Korean War (1950–1953), American soldiers often met and married Korean women and brought them home to the United States. Between 1952 and 1960 over a thousand Korean women a year immigrated to the United States as brides of U.S. servicemen. At the same time, orphaned Korean children, especially girls, also arrived in the United States in significant numbers. Throughout the 1950s and up to the mid-1960s, some 70 percent of all Korean immigrants were either women or young girls. While Korea was the site of the actual conflict, large numbers of troops were also stationed in nearby Japan. Even higher numbers of Japanese women married American soldiers, left their home country, and started a new life in the United States. Roughly six thousand Japanese wives of U.S. servicemen annually immigrated to the United States between 1952 and 1960, which was over 80 percent of all immigrants from Japan. These Korean and Japanese war brides and Korean orphans were spread throughout the United States and, as a result, had very little interaction with other Asian Americans already living in this country.[47] These war bride families were, however, a significant part of the biracial Asian American baby boom that will be discussed in greater detail in Chapter 7.

POST-1965 ASIAN IMMIGRANTS AND REFUGEES

Asian immigration and refugee policies have clearly been influenced by a number of factors, including public sentiment toward immigrants, demands of foreign policy, and the needs of the American economy. While World War II and the Cold War years were epochal for Asian Americans, the period since the mid-1960s has proven to be even more significant. An overview of U.S. immigration statistics shows just how important recent immigration reforms and refugee policies have affected Asian Americans.

Official records on immigrants entering the United States did not exist before 1820, but since that time it is quite obvious that the largest number of immigrants to this nation have come from European countries. Between 1820 and 1994 over 37.7 million Europeans immigrated to the United States (see Table 1–1). In contrast, there were only 7.3 million immigrants from Asia during the same period of time. Looking at this figure more closely, however, we find over 5.6 million immigrants from Asia arrived in the United States in the brief period between 1971 and 1994. Though the Chinese and Japanese have the longest histories in the United States, the largest group of Asian immigrants since 1971 has come from the Philippines. Over 1.1 million Filipino immigrants entered the United States between 1971 and 1994. It is also significant to note that over 90 percent of Filipino, Asian Indian, Korean, and Southeast Asian refugees entered the United States since 1971.

Table 1-1   Immigration to the United States by Region, Fiscal Years 1820–1994

Region	Total 1820-1994	Between 1971-1994	% of Immigrants Since 1971
All Countries	61,503,866	16,341,228	26.6
Europe	37,732,981	2,193,839	5.8
Asia	7,334,013	5,641,167	76.9
China*	1,084,567	641,264	59.1
Hong Kong**	360,906	270,358	74.9
India	605,090	564,294	93.3
Japan	494,226	128,842	26.1
Korea	719,149	678,285	94.3
Philippines	1,275,119	1,152,217	90.4
Vietnam	568,577	563,902	99.2
Other Asia	2,226,379	1,755,641	78.8
North America			
Canada and Newfoundland	4,407,840	414,490	9.4
Mexico	5,969,623	3,584,830	60.1
Caribbean	3,139,648	1,049,648	65.3
Central America	1,087,219	830,062	80.0
South America	1,487,918	995,203	66.9
Africa	442,790	366,317	82.7
Oceana	229,468	111,293	48.5
Not specified	267,643	1,228	.5

* Beginning in 1957, China includes Taiwan.
** Data not reported separately until 1952
Source: U.S. Immigration and Naturalization Service, *Statistical Yearbook of the Immigration and Naturalization Service* (Washington, DC: Government Printing Office, 1996), Table 1, pp. 25–29.

This section of the chapter will focus on three broad events that have directly influenced both the numbers and diversity of Asians entering the United States since 1965. These events are (1) the passage of the 1965 Immigration Reform Act (2) global economic restructuring and (3) the Vietnam War.

The 1965 Immigration Reform Act

Why did the dramatic increase in Asian immigration take place? What changes in the law or public attitudes facilitate such a rapid influx of immigrants from Asia? One important reason was the civil rights movement of the 1960s, which brought international attention to racial and economic inequality in the United States—including its biased immigration policies. This attention is the background for the passage of 1965 Immigration Reform Act, the most important immigration reform legislation. This act, along with its amendments, significantly increased the token quotas established after World War II to allow the Eastern Hemisphere a maximum of 20,000 per country, and set a ceiling of 170,000.

This act created the following seven-point preference system that serves as a general guideline for immigration officials when issuing visas: (1) unmarried children of U.S. citizens who are at least 21 years of age; (2) spouses and unmarried children of permanent resident aliens; (3) members of the professions, scientists, and artists of exceptional ability; (4) married children of U.S. citizens; (5) brothers and sisters of U.S. citizens who are at least 21 years of age; (6) skilled or unskilled workers who are in short supply; and (7) non-preference applicants.

United States immigration policy also allowed virtually unrestricted immigration to certain categories of people including spouses, children under 21, and parents of U.S. citizens. These provisions served to accelerate immigration from Asia to the United States. While the primary goal of the 1965 Immigration Reform Act was to encourage family reunification, a much higher percentage of Asian immigrants initially began entering the United States under the established occupational and non-preference investment categories. In 1969, for example, 62 percent of Asian Indians, 43 percent of Filipinos, and 34.8 percent of Koreans entered the United States under the occupational and investor categories. By the mid-1970s, however, 80 to 90 percent of all Asian immigrants entered the United States through one of the family categories.[48] Still, studies clearly show that most post-1965 Asian immigrants tend to be more middle-class, educated, urbanized, and they arrive in the United States in family units rather than as individuals, compared to their pre-1965 counterparts.[49]

The framers of the 1965 law did not anticipate any dramatic changes in the historical pattern of immigration, but it is clear that Asian immigrants have taken advantage of almost every aspect the 1965 Immigration Reform Act. Asians were just 7.7 percent of all immigrants to the United States between 1955 and 1964; this rose to 22.4 percent between 1965 and 1974, and increased to 43.3 percent between 1975 and 1984. The percentage of Asian immigrants remained steady for several years but declined sharply in the late 1980s and early 1990s (see Table 1–2). This decline was due to the sudden increase of mostly Mexicans who were able to apply for legal status following the passage of the Immigration Reform and Control Act of 1986 (IRCA). By the early 1990s, 2.67 million aliens received permanent residence status under IRCA.[50]

This "amnesty" provision was only a part of IRCA, which was fully intended to control illegal immigration into the United States. IRCA also required that all employers verify the legal status of all new employees, and it imposed civil and criminal penalties against employers who knowingly hire undocumented workers.[51] While IRCA closed the "back door" of illegal immigration, another reform, the Immigration Act of 1990, was enacted to keep open the "front door" of legal immigration. Indeed, this law actually authorizes an *increase* in legal immigration to the United States. In response to uncertain economic stability at home, growing global economic competition

Table 1-2   Percent of Immigrants Admitted by Region, *Fiscal Years 1955–1994*

Region	1955–1964	1965–1974	1975–1984	1985-1990	1991-1994
All	100.0	100.0	100.0	100.0	100.0*
Europe	50.2	29.8	13.4	8.9	14.9
North/West	28.6	11.0	5.2	4.0	4.6
South/ East	21.6	18.7	8.1	4.9	10.3
Asia	7.7	22.4	43.3	33.5	33.0
North America	26.4	19.0	14.8	28.8	27.0
Caribbean	7.0	18.0	15.1	12.0	10.4
Central America	2.4	2.5	3.7	7.2	5.9
South America	5.1	6.0	6.6	6.2	5.5
Africa	.7	1.5	2.4	2.6	2.0
Oceania	.4	.7	.8	.5	.5

* May not add to 100 due to rounding.
Source: U.S. Immigration and Naturalization Service, *Statistical Yearbook of the Immigration and Naturalization Service* (Washington, DC: Government Printing Office, 1996), Table C, p. 21.

abroad, and the dramatically changed face of immigration, the 1990 law sent a mixed message to Asian immigrants.

First of all, the law actually authorized an increase in legal immigration, but at the same time placed a yearly cap on total immigration for the first time since the 1920s. For 1992 to 1995, the limit is 700,000 persons, and 675,000 thereafter. While this appears to be an arbitrary limit, it still allows for an unlimited number of visas for immediate relatives of U.S. citizens. This may not have a negative effect on Asian immigration since, as a group, Asians have the highest rate of naturalization compared to other immigrants.[52] Second, the law encourages immigration of more skilled workers to help meet the needs of the U.S. economy. The number of visas for skilled workers and their families increased from 58,000 to 140,000, while the number for unskilled workers was cut in half to just 10,000. This may prove to be a benefit to Asians who, since 1965, have been among the best-educated and best-trained immigrants this nation has ever seen. Third, the 1990 immigration law also seeks to "diversify" the new immigrants by giving more visas to countries who have sent relatively few migrants to the United States in recent years. This program has been popular with lawmakers who want to assist emigrants from Western European countries, at the expense of Asians. For example, up to 40 percent of the initial visas allocated for the diversity category were for Ireland. Noted immigration attorney Bill Ong Hing found sections of the Immigration Act of 1990 "provide extra independent and transition visas that are unavailable to Asians."[53]

The lasting legacy of the civil rights movement on immigration policy was the emphasis on fairness, equality, and family reunification. But the increased emphasis on highly skilled immigrants found in the 1990 immigration law indicates some loosening of those ideals and priorities. It is clear from the above descriptions of Asian American history that the conditions for the post-1965 Asian migrants are quite distinct from pre-1965 migrants. This seemingly obvious observation reflects the fact that international migration is not a simple, stable, nor homogeneous process. Even with this in mind, the most popular frame of reference for all movement to the United States continues to be the European immigrant experience throughout the nineteenth and early twentieth centuries. The popular European immigrant analogy is highlighted in the words of welcome written on the Statue of Liberty:

Give me your tired, your poor
Your huddled masses yearning to breathe free
The wretched refuse of your teeming shore.
Send these, the homeless, tempest-tost to me,
I lift my lamp beside the golden door!

The European immigrant experience, however, is by no means universal, and is only part of what scholars today see as a much broader picture of the international movement of people and capital. Understanding the broader dynamics of global economic restructuring is useful in comparing and contrasting post-1965 Asian immigrants with other immigrants and minority groups in the United States.

Global Economic Restructuring

What makes people want to leave their home country and migrate to another country? The most commonly accepted answer is found within what is known as the push-pull theory. This theory generally asserts that difficult economic, social, and political conditions in the home country force, or push, people away. On the other hand, these people are attracted, or pulled, to another country where conditions are seen as more favorable. Upon closer examination, however, this theoretical viewpoint does run into some problems. Most significantly, the push-pull theory tends to see immigration flows as a natural, open, and spontaneous process, but does not adequately take into account the structural factors and policy changes that directly affect immigration flows. This is because earlier migration studies based on European immigration limited their focus on poor countries that sent low-skilled labor to affluent countries with growing economies that put newcomers to work. The push-pull theory is not incorrect, but is considered to be incomplete and historically static. Recent studies have taken a much broader approach to international migration and insist that in order to understand post-1965 immigration from Asia, it is necessary to understand the recent restructuring of the global economy.[54]

Since the end of World War II, global restructuring has involved the gradual movement of industrial manufacturing away from developed nations such as the United States to less developed nations in Asia and Latin America where labor costs are cheaper. This process was best seen in Japan in the 1950s through 1970s, and accelerated rapidly in the 1980s to newly industrialized Asian countries, namely Taiwan, Hong Kong, Singapore, and South Korea. Other Asian countries such as India, Thailand, Indonesia, Malaysia, and the Philippines also followed the same economic course with varying degrees of success. In the 1990s mainland China has increased its manufacturing and export capacity dramatically, and is steering on the same economic path of other Asian nations.

Among the effects of global restructuring on the United States is the declining need to import low-skilled labor because manufacturing jobs are moving abroad. At the same time, there is an inclining need to import individuals with advanced specialized skills that are in great demand. According to research by Paul Ong and Evelyn Blumenberg (1994), this phenomena is evi-

denced in part by the increasing number of foreign-born students studying at
U. S. colleges.[55] In the 1954–1955 academic year the United States was host to
just 34,232 foreign exchange students; this number increased to over 440,000
in 1994.[56] Over half of all foreign students in the United States are from Asian
countries, and most major in either engineering, science, or business. A 1993
report by the National Science Foundation found that over half of the doctorate degrees in engineering, mathematics, and computer science were earned
by foreign graduate students.[57] Many of these foreign graduate students
planned to work in the United States and eventually gained permanent immigrant status. Companies in the United States have, of course, been eager to
hire foreign-born scientists and engineers. Not only are highly skilled immigrants valuable to employers as workers, many also start their own high-tech
businesses. For example, Subramonian Shankar, is the co-founder and president of American Megatrends Inc., a company that manufactures personal-
computer motherboards and software in Norcross, Georgia. AMI started business in 1985 and now has a work force of 130 people, made up of native-born
Americans and immigrants. "I couldn't have done this in India," Shankar says
proudly.[58]

The medical profession is another broad area where Asian immigrants
have made a noticeable impact. Researchers Paul Ong and Tania Azores
(1994) found that Asian Americans represented 4.4 percent of the registered
nurses and 10.8 percent of the physicians in the United States in 1990. Ong
and Azores estimate that only a third of Asian American physicians and a
quarter of Asian American nurses were educated in the United States. Graduates of overseas medical and nursing schools have been coming to the
United States since the passage of the 1946 Smith-Mundt Act, which created
an exchange program for specialized training. While this exchange was
intended to be temporary, many medical professionals were able to become
permanent immigrants. A physician shortage in the United States during the
late 1960s and early 1970s, coupled with the elimination of racial immigration quotas in 1965, brought forth a steady flow of foreign-trained M.D.s from
Asian countries. A 1975 United States Commission on Civil Rights report
found 5,000 Asian medical school graduates entered the United States annually during the early 1970s. But, under pressure from the medical industry,
Congress passed the 1976 Health Professions Educational Act, which
restricted the number of foreign trained physicians who could enter the
United States. Despite the passage of this law, almost 30,000 physicians from
Asia immigrated to the United States between 1972 and 1985, and data up to
1990 show roughly half of all foreign-trained physicians entering the United
States have come from Asia.[59]

Asia is also the largest source for foreign nurses. In particular, over half
of all foreigns trained nurses come from the Philippines. One 1988 study con-
servatively estimated 50,000 Filipino nurses were working in the United States

at the time. Filipino nurses find work in the United States attractive because they can earn up to 20 times the salary they can make in the Philippines, and their English-speaking abilities make them highly desired by employers. Filipino nurses are also attracted to the United States because of liberal policies that eventually allow them to stay permanently. While most foreign-trained nurses are brought to work initially on a temporary basis, the passage of the Immigration Nursing Relief Act of 1989 allows nurses to adjust to permanent status after three years of service.[60]

The general explanations for the origins of migration found that push-pull theory continues still to have some value today. Opportunities for large numbers of professionals in Asian countries are still difficult and limited, while opportunities and relatively high salaries are available in the United States. Political instability throughout Asia also continues to be an important push factor for Asian immigrants and refugees. At the same time, this immigration process is not totally natural or spontaneous, as witnessed by foreign student and immigration policies encouraging well-trained individuals to come to the United States. Overall, the changing character of the push and pull in terms of the types of migrants entering the United States and the new skills they bring are very much a result of dynamic global economic restructuring. Global economic restructuring is an important context for understanding not only why Asian immigrants have come to the United States but also how well they have adjusted and been accepted socially, economically, and politically. It is important to note that not all Asian immigrants are middle-class and successful professionals; there is also a sizable number of other Asian immigrants, especially refugees, who have found their lives in America extremely difficult. The extreme diversity among Asian Americans is due in large part to the third major event affecting migration from Asia—the Vietnam War.

The Vietnam War and Southeast Asian Refugees

Since 1975 large numbers of Southeast Asian refugees have entered the United States, and today California is the home for most of them (see Table 1–3). Roughly three quarters of all Southeast Asian refugees are from Vietnam, with the rest from Laos and Cambodia. Unlike most other post-1965 Asian immigrants who came to the United States in a rather orderly fashion seeking family reunification and economic opportunities, Southeast Asian refugees arrived as part of an international resettlement effort of people who faced genuine political persecution and bodily harm in their home countries. Southeast Asian refugees to the United States can be easily divided into three distinct waves: the first wave arrived in the United States in 1975 shortly after the fall of Saigon; the second wave arrived between 1978 and 1980; and the third entered the United States after 1980 and continues to this day. The

Table 1-3 States with the Largest Southeast Asian Populations

State	Vietnamese	Cambodian	Laotian	Hmong	Total
California	280,223	68,190	58,058	46,892	453,363
Texas	69,634	5,887	9,332	176	85,029
Washington	18,696	11,096	6,191	741	36,724
Minnesota	9,387	3,858	6,381	16,833	36,459
Massachusetts	15,449	14,050	3,985	248	33,732
Virginia	20,693	3,889	2,5899	7	27,178
Pennsylvania	15,887	5,495	2,048	358	23,788
Wisconsin	2,494	521	3,622	16,373	23,010
New York	15,555	3,646	3,253	165	22,619
Florida	16,346	1,617	2,42	7	20,379

Source: U.S. Bureau of the Census, *1990 Census of the Population, General Population Characteristics, United States Summary* (Washington,.DC: Government Printing Office, 1993), CP-1-1, Table 262.

United States has accepted these refugees not only for humanitarian reasons but also because of a recognition that U.S. foreign policy and military actions in Southeast Asia had a hand in creating much of the calamity that has befallen the entire region.

U.S. political interests in Southeast Asia actually began during World War II, although for years efforts were limited to foreign aid and military advisers. Direct military intervention rapidly escalated in 1965 when President Lyndon B. Johnson stepped up bombing raids in Southeast Asia and authorized the use of the first U.S. combat troops in order to contain increasing Communist insurgency. The undeclared war continued until U.S. troops withdrew in 1973 at the cost of 57,000 American and 1 million Vietnamese lives. The conflict also caused great environmental destruction throughout Southeast Asia, and created tremendous domestic antiwar protests in the United States.[61]

As soon as the U.S. troops left, however, Communist forces in Vietnam regrouped and quickly began sweeping across the countryside. By March 1975 it was clear that the capital of South Vietnam, Saigon, would soon fall to Communist forces. As a result, President Gerald Ford authorized the attorney general to admit 130,000 refugees into the United States.[62] In the last chaotic days prior to the fall of Saigon on April 30, 1975, "high-risk" individuals in Vietnam, namely high-ranking government and military personnel, were hurriedly airlifted away to safety at temporary receiving centers in Guam, Thailand, and the Philippines. This group marked the first wave of Southeast Asian refugees, who would eventually resettle in the United States. The first wave is distinct in that they were generally the educated urban elite and middle class from Vietnam. Because many of them had worked closely with the U.S. military, they tended to be more westernized (40 percent were Catholics), and a good portion of them were able to speak English (30 percent spoke English well). Another significant feature is the fact that roughly 95 percent of the first wave of Southeast Asian refugees were Vietnamese, even though the capitals of Laos and Cambodia also fell to Communist forces in 1975.[63]

Once these first wave refugees came to the United States, they were flown to one of four military base/reception centers in California, Arkansas, Pennsylvania, and Florida. From these bases they registered with a voluntary agency that would eventually help to resettle them with a sponsor. About 60 percent of the sponsors were families, while the other 40 percent were usually churches and individuals. Sponsors were responsible for day-to-day needs of the refugees until they were able find jobs and become independent. The resettlement of the first wave of refugees was funded by the 1975 Indochinese Resettlement Assistance Act and was seen as a quick and temporary process. Indeed, all four reception centers closed by the end of 1975 and the Resettlement Act expired in 1977.

The second wave of Southeast Asian refugees was larger, more heterogeneous, and many believe even more devastated by their relocation experience than the first wave. The second wave of refugees were generally less educated, urbanized, and westernized (only 7 percent spoke English and only about 7 percent were Catholic) compared to their predecessors; at the same time they were much more ethnically diverse than the first wave. According to statistics, between 1978 and 1980, about 55.5 percent of Southeast Asian refugees were from Vietnam (including many ethnic-Chinese), 36.6 percent from Laos, and 7.8 percent from Cambodia. The second wave consisted of people who suffered under the Communist regimes and were unable to leave their countries immediately before or after the new governments took power.[64]

In Vietnam, the ethnic-Chinese merchant class was very much the target of resentment by the new Communist government. Many of the Chinese businesses in Vietnam were nationalized, Chinese language schools and newspapers were closed, education and employment rights were denied, and food rations were reduced. Under these conditions, about 250,000 left North Vietnam and sought refuge in China. Roughly 70 percent of the estimated 500,000 "boat people" who tried to escape Vietnam by sea were ethnic-Chinese. The treacherous journey usually took place on ill-equipped crowded boats that were unable to withstand the rigors of the ocean or outrun marauding Thai pirates. The U.S. Committee for Refugees estimates at least 100,000 people lost their lives trying to escape Vietnam by boat.[65] Along with the Chinese, others in Vietnam, particularly those who had supported with the U.S.-backed South Vietnamese government and their families were also subject to especially harsh treatment by the new Communist leadership. Many were sent to "reeducation camps" and banished to work in rural regions clearing land devastated by 30 years of war.

The holocaust in Cambodia began immediately after the Khmer Rouge (Red Khmer) marched into the capital city of Phnom Penh on April 17, 1975. That same day the entire population of the capital was ordered to the countryside. After three years it has been broadly estimated between 1 and 3 million Cambodians died from starvation, disease, and execution out of a population of less than 7 million. In 1978 Vietnam (with support from the Soviet Union) invaded Cambodia, drove the Khmer Rouge out of power, and established a new government under its own control. Famine and warfare continued under Vietnamese occupation, and by 1979 over 600,000 refugees from Cambodia fled the country, mostly to neighboring Thailand. In Laos, the transition from one government to another was initially rather smooth compared to Vietnam following the fall of Saigon. After over a decade of civil war, a coalition government was formed in April 1974 that included Laotian Communists, the Pathet Lao. But shortly after Communists took power in Vietnam and Cambodia, the Pathet Lao moved to solidify its full control of the country. It was at this time that troops from both Laos and Vietnam began a military campaign against the Hmong hill people, a preliterate ethnic minority group that lived in the mountains of Laos who were recruited by the U.S. government to serve as mercenaries against Communist forces in the region. The Hmong were seen as traitors to the Communist revolution, and massive bombing raids were ordered against them that included the dropping of napalm and poisonous chemicals. Thousands of Hmong were killed in these fierce assaults, and those who remained had little choice but to seek refuge in neighboring Thailand. While the Hmong were not the only people in Laos who were persecuted, by 1979 roughly 3,000 Hmong were entering Thailand every month, and as late as 1983 an estimated 75 percent of the 76,000 Laotians in Thai refugee camps were Hmong people.[66]

The world could not ignore this massive outpouring of refugees from Southeast Asia, and in 1979 President Jimmy Carter allowed 14,000 refugees a month to enter the United States. In addition, Congress passed the Refugee Act of 1980, which among other things set an annual quota of 50,000 refugees per year, funded resettlement programs, and allowed refugees to become eligible for the same welfare benefits as U.S. citizens after 36 months of refugee assistance (this was changed to 18 months in 1982). The third wave of Southeast Asians are technically not considered refugees, but are in actuality immigrants. This has been facilitated by the 1980 Orderly Departure Program (ODP), an agreement with Vietnam that allows individuals and families to enter the United States. ODP was a benefit for three groups: relatives of permanently settled refugees in the United States, Amerasians, and former re-education camp internees. By the end of 1992, over 300,000 Vietnamese immigrated to the United States, including 80,000 Amerasians and their relatives, as well as 60,000 former camp internees and their families.[67] The resettlement experience, the development of Southeast Asian communities, as well as the influx of Amerasians to the United States will be respectively discussed in greater detail in Chapters 2 and 7.

It is obvious that Southeast Asian refugees/immigrants have been a rapidly growing and extremely diverse group. According to the 1990 census, there were 1,001,054 Southeast Asians in the United States, or 13 percent of the total population of Asian Americans. Individually, the census counted 614,547 Vietnamese, 149,014 Laotians, 147,411 Cambodians, and 90,082 Hmong. Some have argued that these census figures are an undercount of the actual numbers of people from Southeast Asian countries. Researchers point to the fact that the total number of arrivals to the United States from Southeast Asia is roughly the same as census figures. This is an anomaly because the census figure should be about 20 percent larger to reflect the number of American-born Southeast Asians. There are, however, several reasons for this disparity. First of all, new arrivals from Southeast Asia who have little knowledge of the English language may simply not have responded to census questionnaires. This certainly is a general concern for all Asian American groups. Second, and probably most important, it is estimated that between 15 and 25 percent of those from Vietnam, Cambodia, and Laos are actually ethnic-Chinese. It is quite possible that many ethnic-Chinese from Southeast Asia answered the appropriate census question of ethnicity without regard to their nationality. Third, no one is exactly sure how Amerasians identified themselves on the 1990 census, or if they even participated at all. While a factor, it is important to note that most of the Amerasians from Vietnam did not actually enter the United States until after the 1990 census was taken. All references to the Southeast Asian population should keep these considerations in mind.[68]

CONCLUSION

This chapter briefly describes the history and recent growth of the Asian population in the United States. It also highlights the significance of the 1965 Immigration Reform Act, global economic restructuring, and the Vietnam War as three broad events that profoundly impacted both the number and type of migrants who have come to the United States from Asian countries. In order to examine post-1965 Asian Americans comprehensively, it is particularly important to look not only at the rapid growth of the population but also at a multitude of other factors, such as personal history, nativity, length of time in the United States, pre-migration experiences and traumas, education, socioeconomic class background, and gender. The following chapter will detail the social and economic diversity of immigrant and American-born Asians, as well as their settlement patterns and impact on various communities across the United States.

ENDNOTES

1. Shih-shan Henry Tsai, *The Chinese Experience in America* (Bloomington: Indiana University Press, 1986), p. 1; also see Stan Steiner, *Fusahang: The Chinese Who Built America* (New York: Harper & Row, 1979), pp. 24–35; Elena S. H. Yu, "Filipino Migration and Community Organization in the United States," *California Sociologist* 3:2 (1980); 76–102; and Joan M. Jensen, *Passage from India: Asian Indian Immigrants in North America* (New Haven: Yale University Press, 1988), pp. 12–13.
2. Sucheng Chan, *Asian Californians* (San Francisco: MTL/Boyd & Fraser, 1991), pp. 5–6.
3. Ronald Takaki, *Strangers from a Different Shore* (Boston: Little, Brown and Company, 1989), pp. 79, 114.
4. Stanford Lyman, *Chinese Americans* (New York: Random House, 1974), pp. 86–88.
5. Chan, *Asian Californians*, pp. 27–33,
6. Lyman, *Chinese Americans*, pp. 63–69.
7. Yuji Ichioka, *The Issei: The World of the First Generation Japanese Immigrant's, 1885–1924* (New York: The Free Press, 1988), pp. 64–65.
8. Roger Daniels, *Concentration Camps: North America Japanese in the United States and Canada During World War II* (Malabar, FL: Robert A. Kreiger, 1981), p. 7.
9. Bill Ong Hing, *Making and Remaking Asian America Through Immigration Policy, 1850–1990* (Stanford, CA: Stanford University Press, 1993), pp. 28–30.
10. Chan, *Asian Californians*, p. 7.
11. Edwin B. Almirol, *Ethnic Identity and Social Negotiation: A Study of a Filipino Community in California* (New York: AMS Press, 1985), pp. 52–59; and H. Brett Melendy, "Filipinos in the United States," in Norris Hundley, Jr. (ed.), *The Asian American: The Historical Experience* (Santa Barbara: Cleo Books, 1977), pp. 101–128.
12. Takaki, *Strangers from a Different Shore*, pp. 53–57.
13. Chan, *Asian Californians*, pp. 7, 17–19, 37; and Warren Y. Kim, *Koreans in America* (Seoul: Po Chin Chai Printing Co., 1971), pp. 22–27.
14. Joan M/ Jensen, *Passage from India: Asian Indian Immigrants in North America* (New Haven: Yale University Press, 1988), pp. 24–41; and Rajanki K. Das, *Hindustani Workers on the Pacific Coast* (Berlin and Leipzig: Walter De Bruyter & Co, 1923), p. 77.
15. Das, *Hindustani Workers*, pp. 66–67.
16. Bruce La Brack, "Occupational Specialization Among Rural California Sikhs: The Interplay of Culture and Economics," *Amerasia Journal* 9:2 (1982): 29–56.
17. Naturalization Act of 1790, I Stat. 103 (1790).
18. Act of 14 July 1870, 16 Stat. 256.
19. Roger Daniels, *Asian Americans: Chinese and Japanese in the United States* (Seattle: University of Washington Press, 1988) p. 43.
20. Chan, *Asian Californians*, p. 42.
21. Robert F. Heizer and Alan F. Almquist, *The Other Californians: Prejudice and Discrimination under Spain, Mexico, and the United States to 1920* (Berkeley: University of California Press, 1971), p. 129.

22. Takaki, *Strangers from a Different Shore*, p. 82.
23. Lyman, *Chinese Americans*, pp. 55–85.
24. Takaki, *Strangers from a Different Shore*, pp. 111–112.
25. Juan L. Gonzales, *Racial and Ethnic Groups in America*, second edition (Dubuque, Iowa: Kendall/Hunt Publishing Co., 1993), p. 136; and Juan L. Gonzales, *Racial and Ethnic Families in America*, second edition (Dubuque, Iowa: Kendall/Hunt Publishing Co., 1993), p. 3.
26. Chan, *Asian Californians*, pp. 44–45.
27. Hing, *Making and Remaking Asian America*, pp. 32–39.
28. *Yick Wo v. Hopkins*, 118 U.S. 356 (1886); and Lyman, *Chinese Americans*, p. 79.
29. *Takao Ozawa v. United States*, 260 U.S. 178 (1922); Heizer and Alquist, *The Other Californians*, pp. 192–193; and Ichioka, *The Issei*, pp. 210–226.
30. *United States v. Bhagat Singh Thind*, 261 U.S. 204 (1923); Jensen, *Passage from India*, pp. 255–260; and Gurdial Singh, "East Indians in the United States," *Sociology and Social Research* 30:3 (1946): 208–216.
31. Megumi Dick Osumi, "Asians and California's Anti–Miscegenation Laws," in Nobuya Tsuchida (ed.), *Asian and Pacific American Experiences: Women's Perspectives* (Minneapolis: Asian/Pacific American Learning Resource Center, University of Minnesota, 1982), pp. 1–37; and Takaki, *Strangers from a Different Shore*, pp. 330–331.
32. William Petersen, *Japanese Americans* (New York: Random House, 1971), pp. 66–100; Roger Daniels, *Concentration Camps, U.S.A.* (New York: Holt, Rinehart & Winston, 1971), pp. 75, 81–82; and Jacobus tenBroek, Edward N. Barnhart and Floyd W. Matson, *Prejudice, War, and the Constitution* (Berkeley: University of California Press), pp. 118–120.
33. Cited in Commission on Wartime Relocation and Internment of Civilians, *Personal Justice Denied* (Washington, DC: Government Printing Office, 1982), pp. 52–53.
34. Takaki, *Strangers from a Different Shore*, pp. 379–392.
35. Commission on Wartime Relocation and Internment of Civilians, *Personal Justice Denied*, p. 217; tenBroek, Barnhart, and Matson, *Prejudice, War, and the Constitution*, pp. 155–177, 180–181; and Daniels, *Concentration Camps: North America*.
36. Chan, *Asian Californians*, p. 101.
37. Petersen, *Japanese Americans*, p. 87.
38. Cited in Marvin Karlins, Thomas L. Coffman, and Gary Walters, "On the Fading of Social Stereotypes: Studies of Three Generations of College Students," *Journal of Personality and Psychology* 13 (1990): 4–5.
39. *Time*, December 22, 1941, p. 33.
40. Cited in Harold Isaacs, *Images of Asia: American Views of China and India* (New York: Harper & Row, 1972), pp. xviii–xix.
41. Chan, *Asian Californians*, pp. 103–104; and Lyman, *Chinese Americans*, pp. 127, 134.
42. Takaki, *Strangers from a Different Shore*, pp. 357–363, 370–378; Manuel Buaken, "Life in the Armed Forces," *New Republic* 109 (1943): 279–280; and Bienvenido Santos, "Filipinos in War," *Far Eastern Survey* 11 (1942): 249–250.
43. Harry H. L. Kitano and Roger Daniels, *Asian Americans: Emerging Minorities*, second edition (Englewood Cliffs, New Jersey: Prentice Hall, 1995), p. 42, Table 4–2; and Monica Boyd, "Oriental Immigration: The Experience of Chinese, Japanese, and Filipino Populations in the United States," *International Migration Review* 10 (1976): 48–60, Table 1.
44. Chan, *Asian Californians*, pp. 105–106.
45. Diane Mark and Ginger Chih, *A Place Called Chinese America* (San Francisco: The Organization of Chinese Americans, 1982), pp. 105–107.

46. Chan, *Asian Californians*, pp. 108–109.

47. *Ibid.*, pp. 109–110.

48. Hing, *Making and Remaking Asian America*, Appendix B, pp. 189–200; Table 9, p. 82.

49. Hing, *Making and Remaking Asian America*, pp. 79–120; Luciano Mangiafico, *Contemporary American Immigrants: Patterns of Filipino, Korean, and Chinese Settlement in the United States* (New York: Praeger Publishers, 1988), pp. 1–26; James T. Fawcett and Benjamin V. Carino (eds.), *Pacific Bridges: The New Immigration from Asia and the Pacific Islands* (Staten Island, NY: Center for Migration Studies, 1987); and Herbert R. Barringer, Robert W. Gardner, and Michael J. Levine (eds.), *Asian and Pacific Islanders in the United States* (New York: Russell Sage Foundation, 1993).

50. U. S. Immigration and Naturalization Service, *Statistical Yearbook of the Immigration and Naturalization Service, 1993* (Washington DC: Government Printing Office, 1994), p. 20.

51. Roger Daniels, *Coming to America* (New York: HarperCollins Publishers, 1990), pp. 391–397.

52. U.S. Immigration and Naturalization Service, *Statistical Yearbook of the Immigration and Naturalization Service, 1994* (Washington DC: Government Printing Office, 1996), p. 126, Chart O.

53. Hing, *Making and Remaking Asian America*, pp. 7–8.

54. Paul Ong, Edna Bonacich, and Lucie Cheng (eds.), *The New Asian Immigration in Los Angeles and Global Restructuring* (Philadelphia: Temple University Press, 1994), pp. 3–100; and Edna Bonacich, Lucie Cheng, Norma Chinchilla, Nora Hamilton, and Paul Ong (eds.), *Global Production: The Apparel Industry in the Pacific Rim* (Philadelphia: Temple University Press, 1994), pp. 3–20.

55. Paul Ong and Evelyn Blumenberg, "Scientists and Engineers," in Paul Ong (ed.) *The State of Asian Pacific America: Economic Diversity, Issues & Policies* (Los Angeles: LEAP Asian Pacific American Public Policy Institute and UCLA Asian American Studies Center, 1994), pp. 113–138. It is important to note that I am distinguishing between foreign exchange students who are overseas nationals from Asian American students who happen to be foreign born.

56. *Ibid.*, p. 173; and U.S. Department of Commerce, *Statistical Abstract of the United States, 1995* (Washington DC: Government Printing Office, 1995), p. 188, Table 295.

57. Cited in *Statistical Abstract, 1995*, p. 619, Table 997.

58. Michael J. Mandel and Christopher Farrell, "The Immigrants: How They're Helping to Revitalize the U.S. Economy," *Business Week*, July 13, 1992, pp. 114–120, 122.

59. Paul Ong and Tania Azores, "Health Professionals on the Front–Line," in Paul Ong (ed.), *The State of Asian Pacific America: Economic Diversity, Issues & Policies*, pp. 139–164.

60. Paul Ong and Tania Azores, "The Migration and Incorporation of Filipino Nurses," in Ong et al. (eds.), *The New Asian Immigration in Los Angeles and Global Restructuring*, pp. 166–195; and Mangiafico, *Contemporary American Immigrants*, pp. 42–43.

61. Literature on the Vietnam conflict is voluminous. For an excellent and readable overview see Stanley Karnow, *Vietnam: A History* (New York: Penguin Books, 1991).

62. The quota for refugees under the 1965 Immigration Reform Act was only 17,400, so President Gerald Ford instructed the attorney general to use his "parole"

power to admit the 130,000 refugees. The use of parole power was also used to bring European refugees to the United States during the 1950s. For more detail, see Hing, *Making and Remaking Asian America,* pp. 123–128, and Paul J. Strand and Woodrow Jones, Jr., I*ndochinese Refugees in America: Problems of Adaptation and Assimilation* (Durham, NC: Duke University Press, 1985).

63. Chan, *Asian Californians,* p. 128; and Chor-Swan Ngin, "The Acculturation Pattern of Orange County's Southeast Asian Refugees," *Journal of Orange County Studies* 3:4 (Fall 1989–Spring 1990): 46–53.

64. Ngin, "The Acculturation Pattern of Orange County's Southeast Asian Refugees," p. 49; and Ngoan Le, "The Case of the Southeast Asian Refugees: Policy for a Community 'At-Risk,'" in *The State of Asian Pacific America: Policy Issues to the Year 2020* (Los Angeles: LEAP Asian Pacific American Public Policy Institute and UCLA Asian American Studies Center, 1993), pp. 167–188.

65. For more details see Strand and Jones, *Indochinese Refugees in America*; Barry L. Wain, *The Refused: The Agony of Indochina Refugees* (New York: Simon & Schuster, 1981); and U.S. Committee for Refugees, *Uncertain Harbors: The Plight of Vietnamese Boat People* (Washington D.C.: Government Printing Office, 1987).

66. Chan, *Asian Californians,* pp. 121–138; Kitano and Daniels, *Asian Americans: Emerging Minorities,* pp. 170–191; U.S. Committee for Refugees, *Cambodians in Thailand: People on the Edge* (Washington, D.C.: Government Printing Office, 1985); and U.S. Committee for Refugees, *Refugees from Laos: In Harm's Way* (Washington, D.C.: Government Printing Office, 1986).

67. U.S. Committee for Refugees, *Uncertain Harbors,* pp. 19–20; and Ruben Rumbaut, "Vietnamese, Laotian, and Cambodian Americans," in Pyong Gap Min (ed.), *Asian Americans: Contemporary Trends and Issues* (Thousand Oaks, CA: Sage Publications, 1995), p. 240.

68. Ruben Rumbaut and J. R. Weeks, "Fertility and Adaptation: Indochinese Refugees in the United States," *International Migration Review* 20:2 (1986): 428–466; and Rumbaut, "Vietnamese, Laotian, and Cambodian Americans," pp. 239–242.

2

EMERGING COMMUNITIES, CHANGING REALITIES

VISIBILITY AND INVISIBILITY

An April 1996 issue of *Newsweek* reported the results of a poll that found 54 percent of American voters said new immigrants hurt their communities. The same poll found only 21 percent who said immigrants were a benefit to their communities.[1] As a largely immigrant population, Asian Americans are keenly aware of anti-immigrant sentiment and are very much affected by changes in immigration laws. The previous chapter showed the large numbers of immigrants and refugees coming from Asia since 1965, and it is no surprise that the result has been increased visibility of Asian Americans across the United States. This visibility has brought heightened concern about the impact of Asian Americans on the social, cultural, economic, and political landscape in a number of states and local regions. A great deal of attention and animosity in recent years has been primarily focused on undocumented (illegal) immigrants. Although the vast majority of Asian immigrants enter the United States legally, the public image of Asian newcomers was dramatically altered with news of the cargo ship *Golden Venture* in June 1993. The wayward freighter ran aground along the coast of New York carrying almost 300 Chinese men and women who were being smuggled into the United States. Many of the passengers panicked for fear of arrest and deportation, and 10 died trying to escape from the shipwreck. It was not long before stories of smuggling rings bringing in "hundreds of thousands" of Chinese to the United States illegally were reported in the news media, and this helped to create the atmosphere for state and federal lawmakers to crack down on illegal immigration.[2]

This was most dramatically seen the following year with the passage of statewide Proposition 187 in California, which called for the denial of public health, education, and social services to undocumented aliens in the state. In addition, Proposition 187 allowed the police, nurses, doctors, schoolteachers, and social workers to verify the immigration status of anyone "reasonably suspected" of being in the United States illegally. The ballot initiative passed by a wide 60 percent to 40 percent margin, but its implementation has been held up in various court battles. Although immigration advocates warned that Proposition 187 was a precursor to much larger attacks on legal immigrants, several exit polls found 47 percent of Asian American voters in California supported the initiative because they felt they had nothing to fear since they had come to the United States legally.[3] But it was not long before calls for greater limitations and control of legal immigration began being heard. Immigration control was a hotly debated topic during the 1995–1996 congressional session as lawmakers attempted to reduce the number of legal immigrants entering the United States drastically by eliminating visa categories for adult children and siblings of newly naturalized U.S. citizens, making it more difficult for companies to hire skilled foreign workers, and cutting the number of political refugees admitted annually. "It's a state of emergency for Asian and other immigrants of color," exclaimed immigration advocate Eric Mar during a protest in front of the Federal Building in San Francisco. Mar also led a seven-day hunger strike to draw attention to the anti-immigrant movement in Congress. "It takes a drastic action to raise awareness about the politicians' scapegoating and serious attacks on immigrants," he said.[4] Ironically, calls for stricter immigration limits were conducted even as Immigration and Naturalization Service was reporting a decline in the overall numbers of new immigrants to the United States for the fourth year in a row.[5]

As a result, much of the political debate has centered on the visible costs versus the seemingly invisible benefits of large numbers of immigrants in the United States. For example, Social Security Administration figures show elderly legal immigrants make up 30 percent of all elderly receiving Supplemental Security Income (SSI). There is nothing illegal about elderly immigrants on SSI who have been in the United States for more than five years, but they do represent the fastest growing group of people receiving this government benefit. Critics charge that these immigrant recipients are abusing the system and often come from families that can afford to take care of them.[6] One of the most widely cited studies on the negative costs of immigration was conducted by Donald Huddle, an economist at Rice University in Houston (1993). The study was sponsored by the Carrying Capacity Network, an organization that calls for drastic reductions in the number of immigrants entering the United States. Huddle and his student researchers lumped illegal and legal immigrants together and argued that they are a net drain on the local, state, and U.S. economy because they use more in public services than they pay in taxes.[7]

The negative implications of immigrants from these two reports have been challenged by University of Maryland professor, Julian L. Simon (1995). Simon agreed that government expenditures for what is commonly called welfare, such as Aid to Families with Dependent Children (AFDC), Supplemental Security Insurance, and Medicaid, are indeed about $150 per person greater for immigrants. However, these expenditures are only a very small part of total government social outlays for both immigrant and native-born citizens. Simon calculated Social Security and Medicare payments are by far the most expensive government transfer programs, and they pertain more to natives than to immigrants. Taking Social Security and Medicare with public schooling, unemployment compensation, and welfare all together, Simon estimated $2,200 per person, per year is spent on legal immigrants, $1,690 is spent for illegal immigrants (who are not eligible for most of the programs above), while $3,800 is spent on natives. Simon also highlights the fact that if refugees are excluded from his assessment, the rate of welfare use for new immigrants would be even less. Not only are fewer government expenditures spent on immigrants, Simon also found post-1970s immigrant families actually paid more taxes than American-born native families. This is especially true the longer immigrants live in the United States. In short, Simon concludes that immigrants are *not* a drain on the U.S. economy. Simon punctuated his conclusions by citing a poll of top economists that found 80 percent believed that twentieth-century immigrants have had a "very favorable" impact on the U.S. economy. In fact, 63 percent of these economists favored more immigration would be better for the United States, while none believed there should be fewer immigrants.[8]

Simon is also highly critical of the Huddle report and its conclusions. He contends Huddle's research was fundamentally flawed because of weak data gathering methods and broad general assumptions that only served to bias Huddle's results. According to Simon, Huddle overstated the use of public services by immigrants, underestimated the amount of taxes paid by immigrants, exaggerated the loss of jobs by natives to immigrants, and virtually ignored the positive stimulation of the economy by immigrant entrepreneurs and workers. Simon has been particularly outspoken about the fact that Huddle's work has been so widely and uncritically publicized in the media. Simon contends that Huddle's conclusions lack any scientific merit or rigor, and would not stand up to close review by academic peers. Indeed, Simon has challenged Huddle to defend his conclusions before a "science court" of economists in a letter published in the *New York Times*.[9]

Several other recent studies show that legal and illegal immigrants contribute far more in taxes than they cost in government services. Economist Jeffery S. Passel of the Washington DC–based Urban Institute (1994) calculated various taxes paid by immigrants that were left out by Huddle and found immigrants contributed at least an extra $50 billion into the U.S. economy than Huddle estimated.[10] Another study focusing specifically on the impact of immigration on California was conducted by the Tomas Rivera Center in Claremont, California (1996). Rather than using a one-year snapshot to determine the effects of immigrants on the economy, this study uses a long-range premise that most immigrants will spend a large part of their lives in the state and will pay their fair share of taxes over that span of time. It found that legal immigrants returned, on average, an estimated net surplus of $24,943 to the state over a lifetime, while illegal immigrants employed over a lifetime return an average of $7,890.[11] Lastly, a report by the Center for New West, a Colorado-based independent research organization (1996), concluded that immigrants have a positive effect on the California economy and the state benefits from immigrant skills, work ethic, and contacts in foreign markets. The report runs counter to anti-immigrant sentiments and said the state's economy has been transformed from a dependency on aerospace and defense contracting to a new economy invigorated by multicultural diversity and free trade. Among its many charts and figures, the report cites the fact that California has 57 of the top 100 fastest growing exporters in the United States.[12]

Armed with this kind of information, Asian American political leaders and many other immigration support groups were active in fighting against some of the harshest aspects in the 1996 immigration reform proposals. By April both houses of Congress passed their versions of immigration reform, but neither included limits on legal immigration. The issue created interesting allies on both the Senate and House sides of Congress. For example, leading the charge for immigration restrictions in the Senate were Republican Alan Simpson from Wyoming and Democrat Dianne Feinstein from California. Senators against immigration restrictions included conservative Orrin Hatch from Utah and liberal Ted Kennedy from Massachusetts. Texas Senator Phil Gramm, whose wife is Korean American, offered a deeply personal as well as solidly economic argument in favor of maintaining the current levels of legal immigration. "The American dream is not going to fade, and not going to die, on my watch on the Senate floor," stormed the fiery conservative Republican. "I do not want to tear down the Statue of Liberty. There is room in America for people who want to work."[13]

With this background information in mind, this chapter is intended to provide a demographic and socioeconomic profile in Asian Americans. The first part of this chapter will focus on the settlement patterns, community formation, and diversity of Asian American newcomers. In addition, the wide geographic dispersion and suburbanization of Asian Americans today is a major feature that was not seen in the past. The second part will closely examine the highly publicized and highly prominent phenomenon of Asian ethnic entrepreneurship. In urban areas across the nation some Asian American groups have become quite successful starting their own businesses by finding interesting and unusual economic niches in which they sometimes dominate. The third part of this chapter will look closely at the socioeconomic status of Asian Americans, both immigrants and U.S.-born. Summary statistics tend to provide a very positive picture and Asian Americans have been dubbed by many as the "model minority." However, this section will also provide a detailed analysis of the model minority image of Asian Americans and a critical reevaluate of this concept. The statistics and analysis formed in this chapter will serve as important background for all the chapters that follow.

SETTLEMENT PATTERNS

The settlement patterns of various post-1965 Asian Americans are distinct from each other, as well as from the pre-1965 Asian Americans. This can be seen when examining some important demographic characteristics and the emergence of new Asian American communities.

Nativity and Geographic Distribution

The recent influx of immigrants and refugees from Asia is evident by the extremely high percentage of foreign-born Asian Americans. According to the 1990 census, 65.6 percent of all Asian Americans are foreign-born (see Table 2-1). This statistic is in stark contrast to the 7.9 percent foreign-born among the

Table 2-1 Percentage of Foreign-Born Asian Americans by Ethnic Group

Group	Percentage
U.S.	7.9
Asian or Pacific Islander	63.1
Asian	65.6
Chinese	69.3
Filipino	64.4
Japanese	32.3
Asian Indian	75.4
Korean	72.7
Vietnamese	79.9
Cambodian	79.1
Laotian	79.4
Hmong	65.2

Source: U.S. Bureau of the Census, *1990 Census of the Population, Asians and Pacific Islanders in the United States* (Washington, DC: Government Printing Office, 1993), CP-3-5, Table 1.

Table 2-2   Asian Americans Who Do Not Speak English "Very Well,"
5 Years Old and Over

| | Percentage | | |
Group	All	Native	Foreign-born
U.S.	6.1	2.3	47.0
Asian or Pacific Islander	38.4	11.4	51.3
Asian	39.8	12.2	51.4
Chinese	50.4	15.0	63.1
Filipino	24.2	6.3	32.2
Japanese	25.2	8.5	58.7
Asian Indian	23.5	10.0	26.6
Korean	51.6	12.0	62.3
Vietnamese	60.8	34.3	65.1
Cambodian	70.0	55.3	71.9
Laotian	67.8	53.1	69.9
Hmong	76.1	72.8	77.1

Source: U.S. Bureau of the Census, *1990 Census of the Population, Asians and Pacific Islanders in the United States* (Washington, DC: Government Printing Office, 1993), CP-3-5, Table 3.

general U.S. population. While the overall percentage of foreign-born Asian Americans is high, it does vary considerably by group. Only 32.3 percentage of Japanese Americans are foreign-born, while 79.9 percent of Vietnamese Americans are foreign-born. A high percentage of foreign-born within a group generally means a high percentage of individuals who are not fluent in the English language. The 1990 census found 39.8 percent of all Asian Americans over the age of 5 did not speak English "very well," compared with just 6 percent of all native-born Americans over the age of 5 who do not speak English "very well" (see Table 2-2). Despite being a largely foreign-born population and self-stated concerns about English language proficiency, Asian immigrants have had the highest rate of naturalization of any group since 1971 (see Table 2-3).

Asian Americans have historically clustered in California and Hawaii, but today Asian Americans are found in significant numbers across the United States. According to the 1990 census, seven out of the top ten states with the largest Asian American population are actually outside the West Coast region (see Table 2-4). The state with the largest Asian American population is California, followed by New York, and then Hawaii. Although the

Table 2-3   U.S. Naturalization by Decade, 1962–1994

Region	1961–1970	1971–1980	1981–1990	1991–1994
Europe	62.4	30.8	15.4	12.0
North America	20.9	28.1	26.2	26.7
South America	2.2	5.3	6.5	8.0
Asia	12.9	33.5	48.8	49.1
Other	1.5	2.3	3.2	4.2

Source: U.S. Immigration and Naturalization Service, *Statistical Yearbook of the Immigration and Naturalization Service 1994,* (Washington, DC: Government Printing Office, 1996). p. 126, Chart O.

number of Asian Americans living in Hawaii is relatively small compared to California, Asian Americans do represent 61.8 percent of the island state's population. Many people are surprised to learn that Texas, Illinois, and New Jersey are home to almost a million Asian Americans. Like nativity, the geographic distribution of Asian Americans does vary by individual group. For example, 75.9 percent of Japanese and 70.5 percent of Filipino Americans

Table 2-4   States with the Largest Asian and Pacific Islander American Population, 1990

State	1990 Population	% of State	% of U.S. Asian/PI Population
California	2,845,659	9.6	39.1
New York	689,760	3.9	9.5
Hawaii	685,236	61.8	9.4
Texas	319,459	1.9	4.4
Illinois	285,311	2.5	3.9
New Jersey	272,521	3.5	3.7
Washington	210,958	4.3	2.9
Virginia	159,053	2.6	2.2
Florida	154,302	1.2	2.1
Massachusetts	143,392	2.4	2.0

Source: U.S. Bureau of Census, *1990 Census of the Population, General Population Characteristics, the United States* (Washington, DC: Government Printing Office, 1993), CP-1-1, Table 262.

Table 2-5　Asian Pacific Islander American Regional Distribution, 1990

Group	West	Midwest	Northeast	South
U.S.	21.2	24.0	20.4	34.8
White	20.0	26.0	21.1	32.4
Black	9.4	19.1	18.7	52.8
American Indian, Eskimo, Aleut	47.6	17.2	6.4	28.7
Asia or Pacific Islander	55.7	10.6	18.4	15.4
Chinese	52.4	8.1	27.0	12.4
Filipino	70.5	8.1	10.2	11.3
Japanese	75.9	7.5	8.8	7.9
Asian Indian	23.1	17.9	35.0	24.0
Korean	44.4	13.7	22.8	19.2
Vietnamese	54.3	8.5	9.8	27.4
Cambodian	57.7	8.8	20.5	13.1
Laotian	51.0	18.6	10.7	19.6
Hmong	55.0	41.3	·1.9	1.8
Hispanic	45.2	7.7	16.8	30.3

Source: U.S. Bureau of the Census, *1990 Census of Population, General Population Characteristics, The United States* (Washington, DC: Government Printing Office, 1993), CP-1-1, Table 253.

live on the West Coast. About half of all Chinese, Vietnamese, Cambodians, and Hmong Americans live in the West, while less than half of Laotians, Koreans, and Asian Indian Americans live in the West. Asian Indians are particularly well dispersed with only 23.1 percent living out West, 35.0 percent in the Northeast, 17.9 percent in the Midwest, and 24.0 percent in the South (See Table 2-5).

New Communities

As with other racial minority groups, Asian Americans have historically been marginalized and segregated from both rural communities and urban cities due to pressures from the dominant society. But complex patterns can be seen in the post-1965 era and new dynamic communities have emerged. One pattern is the increased visibility of Asian Americans in large cities across the country. While Asian Americans generally congregate in major metropolitan

Table 2-6 U.S. Cities with the Largest Asian and Pacific Islander American Population, 1990

State	City	Population	% of City's Population
NY	New York	512,719	7.0
CA	Los Angeles	341,807	9.8
HI	Honolulu	257,552	70.5
CA	San Francisco	210,876	29.1
CA	San Jose	152,815	19.5
CA	San Diego	130,945	11.8
IL	Chicago	104,118	4.6
TX	Houston	67,113	3.7
WA	Seattle	60,819	11.8
CA	Long Beach	58,266	13.6

Source: Asian & Pacific Islander Center for Census Information and Services, *Ten Years of Growth: A Demographic Analysis on Asian and Pacific Islander Americans* (Asian/Pacific Islander Data Consortium-ACC15: San Francisco, 1992), Table US-4B.

centers such as San Francisco, Los Angeles, and New York, other lesser-known cities have also become quite popular. Table 2-6 shows that in 1990 San Jose and San Diego have the fifth and sixth largest Asian American populations in the nation. Chicago, Illinois, with over 100,000 Asian American residents, has the seventh largest population of Asian Americans and is the midwest hub for the group, while Houston, Texas, is the major southern city with the largest Asian American population.

Reflecting the diversity of the Asian American population since 1965, even the cities of San Francisco, Los Angeles, and New York have witnessed dramatic changes taking place (see Table 2-7). The two largest Asian ethnic groups in New York City are Chinese and Asian Indian Americans. However, most people don't realize that more Chinese Americans live in New York City (238,919) than in San Francisco (127,140), and that more Asian Indians live in New York City (94,590) than in the next nine cities with the largest Asian Indian population combined (85,167). There are more Filipino (87,625) and Korean Americans (72,970) concentrated in Los Angeles than Chinese (67,196) and Japanese Americans (45,370). Southeast Asians have tended not to cluster themselves in the major cities like San Francisco, Los Angeles, and New York. The city with largest population of Vietnamese Americans is San Jose (41,303); the largest population of Laotian Americans is in Fresno, Cali-

Table 2-7   U.S. Cities with the Largest Asian American Population by Ethnic Group, 1990

Chinese City	Pop.	*Korean continued* City	Pop.
New York (NY)	238,919	San Jose (CA)	7,207
San Fran. (CA)	127,140	Philadelphia (PA)	6,969
L.A. (CA)	67,196	Cerritos (CA)	6,513
Honolulu (HI)	44,841	San Fran. (CA)	6,240
San Jose (CA)	31,112	Torrance (CA)	5,888
Oakland (CA)	27,672		
Chicago (IL)	22,295	*Filipino*	
Monterey Park (CA)	21,971	City	Pop.
Alhambra (CA)	21,303	L.A. (CA)	87,625
Sacramento (CA)	18,904	San Diego(CA)	63,381
		Honolulu (HI)	44,932
Japanese		New York (NY)	43,229
City	Pop.	San Fran. (CA)	42,652
Honolulu (HI)	106,522	San Jose (CA)	38,169
L.A. (CA)	45,370	Chicago (IL)	27,443
New York (NY)	16,828	Daly City (CA)	25,092
Hilo (HI)	13,299	Vallejo (CA)	20,186
Torrance (CA)	13,017	Long Beach (CA)	17,329
Pearl City (HI)	12,763		
San Fran. (CA)	12,047	*Asian Indian*	
San Jose (CA)	11,794	City	Pop.
Kaneohe (HI)	10,752	New York (NY)	94,590
Waimalu (HI)	10,666	L.A. (CA)	17,227
		Chicago (IL)	16,386
		Houston (TX)	11,615
Korean		San Jose (CA)	10,672
City	Pop.	Jersey City (NJ)	7,361
L.A. (CA)	72,970	Philadelphia (PA)	6,293
New York (NY)	69,718	Edison (NJ)	6,076
Honolulu (HIA)	15,063	Fremont (CA)	5,577
Chicago (IL)	13,863	Dallas (TX)	3,960
Glendale (CA)	9,445		

Table 2–7 (continued)

Vietnamese		Hmong	
City	Pop.	City	Pop.
San Jose (CA)	41,303	Fresno (CA)	16,556
L.A. (CA)	18,674	St. Paul (MN)	11,499
Houston (TX)	18,453	Merced (CA)	4,749
San Diego (CA)	17,060	Sacramento (CA)	4,270
Garden Grove (CA)	15,001	Stockton (CA)	4,195
Santa Ana (CA)	14,878	Minneapolis (MN)	4,126
Westminster (CA)	11,376	Milwaukee (WI)	3,330
San Fran. (CA)	9,712	La Crosse (WI)	1,914
New York (NY)	8,400	Wausau (WI)	1,885
Stockton (CA)	6,672	Linda (CA)	1,818

Cambodian		Laotian	
City	Pop.	City	Pop.
Long Beach (CA)	17,468	Fresno (CA)	7,751
Stockton (CA)	10,212	San Diego (CA)	6,261
Lowell (MA)	6,475	Sacramento (CA)	4,885
L.A. (CA)	4,257	Stockton (CA)	4,045
Philadelphia (PA)	4,026	Seattle (WA)	2,819
San Diego (CA)	3,918	Oakland (CA)	2,529
San Jose (CA)	3,765	Minneapolis (MN)	2,325
Fresno (CA)	3,712	Portland (OR)	2,135
Tacoma (WA)	3,323	Visalia (CA)	1,923
Modesto (CA)	3,132	Modesto (CA)	1,853

Source: Asian & Pacific Islander Center for Census Information and Services, *Ten Years of Growth: A Demographic Analysis on Asian and Pacific Islander Americans* (Asian/Pacific Islander-Data Consortium-ACC15: San Francisco, 1992), Tables US-T5-T10, T12-T13, T15.

fornia (7,751); and the largest Cambodian American population is in Long Beach, California (17,468)

Another pattern is Asian American suburbanization. This is the movement of Asian American communities away from traditional urban centers into middle-class suburban settings. The result of two decades of large-scale immigration from Asia has seen the emergence of new "Chinatowns," "Manilatowns," "Koreatowns," and "Little Saigons" in suburban areas across the country. The best examples of the suburbanization of Asian Americans can be seen in areas

Table 2-8   Counties With the Largest Asian and Pacific Islander American Population, 1990

State	County	Population	% of Total Population
CA	Los Angeles	954,485	10.8
HI	Honolulu	526,459	63.0
NY	Queens	238,336	12.2
CA	Santa Clara	261,466	17.5
CA	Orange	249,192	10.3
CA	San Francisco	210,876	29.1*
CA	San Diego	198,311	7.9
CA	Alameda	192,554	15.1
IL	Cook	188,565	3.7
NY	Kings	111,251	4.8

* San Francisco is both a city and a county.
Source: Asian & Pacific Islander Center for Census Information and Services, *Ten Years of Growth: A Demographic Analysis on Asian and Pacific Islander Americans* Asian/Pacific Islander Data Consortium-ACC 15: (San Francisco, 1992), Table US-4B.

surrounding Los Angeles, San Francisco, and New York. All three cities have long been the ports of entry and initial settlements for most Asian immigrants. But this pattern has been altered as relatively affluent and well-educated immigrants, and established American-born Asians, are bypassing the traditional urban centers and moving directly into outlying communities. Table 2-8 shows the U.S. counties with the largest Asian American populations and is an indicator of the spread of Asian American communities outside of the core cities.

During the 1980s the San Gabriel Valley, a region just east of downtown Los Angeles, was the scene of demographic shifts so dramatic that it surprised even experienced demographers. Once the domain of white middle-class homeowners, the Asian American population more than doubled in well-to-do communities such as San Marino, Hacienda Heights, and Diamond Bar. Easily the most notable location in the area is Monterey Park, which has a population of 60,000 residents and is 57 percent Asian. Monterey Park's population is largely immigrant Chinese and has earned the titles of "America's First Suburban Chinatown," and "The Chinese Beverly Hills."[14] In Orange County, California, known mostly as the bastion of affluent and conservative whites, Asian Americans make up just over 10 percent of the population. Asians by far outnumber other racial minority groups in Orange County, which is the home of the largest concentration of Vietnamese Americans in the United States. The city of Westminster in Orange County, population 53,000, has a very active Vietnamese commercial district and signs on the freeway direct visitors to this "Little Saigon."[15]

Similar changes are witnessed around the San Francisco Bay Area. According to the 1990 census, nearby Santa Clara and San Mateo counties both have Asian populations of roughly 17 percent. Santa Clara County, anchored by Stanford University and the high-tech mecca, Silicon Valley, can actually boast of a larger Asian American population than San Francisco. In San Mateo County, Filipinos are the largest Asian American ethnic group, and most live in Daly City. Daly City's population of 92,000 is 43.8 percent Asian—almost two thirds of whom are Filipinos—and is known as "Adobo City," named after the finest Filipino delicacy.[16] In both Santa Clara and San Mateo counties, commercial thoroughfares show a strong Asian presence that was once found only in the major metropolitan cities. Chinese-owned shops, supermarkets. and restaurants abound, hundreds of Filipino-run stores can be seen, and the number of Korean and Asian Indian businesses have increased by the score.

Flushing, New York, is technically not a suburban Asian American community because it is located in the New York City borough of Queens. However, Asian immigrants and entrepreneurs have quickly turned the previously quiet area into a bustling residential and commercial alternative to Manhattan's historic Chinatown, which is much more crowded and expensive. The area has become so popular that of the 512,719 Asian Americans who live in New York City in 1990, about half (238,335) live in Queens. On weekends, thousands of Asian Americans flock to Flushing to eat, shop, bank, do business, and many believe this robust activity has revitalized an area that was previously in economic decline. More recently, another new Chinatown has blossomed in Brooklyn, New York. Chinese immigrants were attracted to the area because of low rents and an opportunity. One of those Chinese immigrants is Danny Tsoi, who arrived in Manhattan in 1977. His first job was in a Chinese restaurant in old Chinatown, but after a series of jobs he moved to Brooklyn in 1989 and opened his Ocean Palace Seafood restaurant. "When I first came here," he says, "my friends told me 'Danny, you're stupid to waste your money.' Now they tell me, 'Danny you're smart.'"[17]

Most Asian Americans live in urban or suburban areas in various states, but there are important exceptions. Three quarters of California's 46,892 Hmong population live in the state's Central Valley agricultural regions in and around Fresno, Merced, Sacramento, and San Joaquin counties. Initially, the Hmong and other Southeast Asian refugees were scattered across the country by the U.S. government in hopes they would have an easier time assimilating into American life if they were physically isolated from one another. But many of the Hmong and other Southeast Asian refugees did not like the cold weather and separation, and migrated out west or to other warm-weather states. "My people never hear of snow before," explains Hmong refugee Na Vang. "We arrive at night in some place like Minnesota, wake up in the morning and suddenly whole world is white."[18] Still, two conspicuous clusters of Hmong refugees continue to make their homes in concentrated areas of Minnesota and Wisconsin

ETHNIC ENTREPRENEURSHIP

The dramatic increase of the Asian American population throughout the United States is highlighted by the proliferation of Asian American–owned and–operated business enterprises. The latest available government figures show Asian American businesses have increased remarkably compared to other racial minority groups in terms of numbers and sales in the 1980s (see Table 2-9). Asian American businesses grew from 187,707 in 1982 to 355,331 in 1987, an increase of 89.9 percent. By comparison, the number of black-owned businesses during this same period increased just 37.6 percent, and the number of businesses owned by American Indians and Alaska Natives

Table 2-9   Asian American Owned Business Enterprises, 1982–1987

	1987		1982	
Group	Firms (number)	Receipts ($1,000,000)	Firms (number)	Receipts ($1,000.000)
Black	424,165	19,800	308,260	9,600
American Indian/ Alaska Natives	21,338	911	13,557	485
Asian	355,331	33,125	187,707	12,663
Chinese	89,717	9,610	48,827	4,309
Filipino	40,412	1,914	23,359	747
Japanese	53,372	3,837	43,529	2,116
Asian Indian	52,266	6,715	23,770	1,660
Korean	69,304	7,683	30,919	2,670
Vietnamese	25,671	1,361	4,989	215
Other Asian/Pacific Is.	24,310	2,005	12,298	937
Hispanic	422,373	24,700	233,975	11,800

Source: U.S. Department of Commerce, *1987 Economic Census: Survey of Minority-Owned Business Enterprises* (Washington, DC: Government Printing Office), MB87-1 (1990), MB87-2, MB87-3 (1991).

Table 2-10 Asian American Self-Employment Persons 16 Years Old and Over by Ethnic Group and Foreign-born, 1990

Group	Self-Employed All	Foreign-born
U.S.	6.97	6.84
Asian or Pacific Islander	6.66	7.12
Asian	6.77	7.13
Chinese	6.74	6.97
Filipino	3.17	3.18
Japanese	7.04	7.69
Asian Indian	6.13	6.23
Korean	16.99	18.10
Vietnamese	5.72	5.81
Cambodian	4.11	3.65
Laotian	2.04	2.01
Hmong	2.23	2.21

Source: U.S. Bureau of the Census, *1990 Census of the Population, Asians and Pacific Islanders in the United States* (Washington, DC: Government Printing Office, 1993), CP-3-5, Table 4.

increased 57.7 percent. Growth in the number of Hispanic-owned businesses rivaled Asian Americans with an increase of 80.5 percent. In 1987 Asian Americans owned nearly as many businesses as African Americans and Hispanics, even though both have much larger populations. Between 1982 and 1987, the sales generated from Asian-owned businesses shot up from $12.6 billion to $33.1 billion, a 162 percent increase. This exceeds the 105 percent increase by black-owned businesses, the 87.3 percent increase by American Indian and Alaska Native–owned businesses, and the 110.3 percent increase in sales generated by Hispanic-owned businesses. According to the 1990 census, however, Asian Americans are not overrepresented in terms of business ownership compared to the national average. Of all people in the United States 16 years and older, about 7 percent are self-employed. Among Asian Americans the percentage of self-employment is 6.8. By far the Asian American group with the highest percentage of self-employment is Korean Americans. The census shows almost 17 percent of Korean Americans are self-employed. Filipinos, on the other hand, have a relatively low self-employment rate of just 3.2 percent. Among Southeast Asian refugees, self-employment is

5.7 percent for Vietnamese, 4.1 percent for Cambodians, and just around 2 percent for Laotian and Hmong Americans (See Table 2-10)

Ethnic entrepreneurship, in general, and Asian American entrepreneurship, in particular, are not new phenomena. Certain ethnic groups in the United States have historically shown a noticeable propensity toward self-employment. Among Eastern European/Middle Eastern immigrants, Jews, Armenians, Syrians, and Lebanese are most noted for their business acumen. Among Latinos, Cubans have a much higher self-employment rate compared to Mexicans and Puerto Ricans. Black immigrants from the Caribbean have shown a far greater percentage of small business enterprises than American-born blacks. In addition, Chinese and Japanese Americans have a long history of self-employment.[19] Today, however, post-1965 Asian American business owners do stand out from other racial minority groups and do have some unique characteristics that are important to note. First, according to a U.S. census, 81.8 percent of self-employed Asian Americans are immigrants. This statistic is dramatic compared to the fact that immigrants represent only 9 percent of these self-employed in the United States.[20] Second, according to the U.S. census report, *Characteristics of Business Owners, 1992*, Asian Americans have a wider variety of sources from which to raise the capital necessary to start their own business. Personal savings; borrowing from relatives, friends, or prior business owners; as well as commercial bank loans were the methods used to raise start-up funds.[21] Lastly, according to University of Southern California sociologist Edward Park, many Asian American high-technology entrepreneurs start their businesses with venture capital raised from overseas investors. Park cites one study that estimates that between 1985 and 1990, $1.7 billion of venture capital from Asia was invested into new high-technology start-up firms in California's world-famous Silicon Valley region.[22]

The types of Asian American businesses range from highly successful international high-technology research and manufacturing firms, to professional business and medical offices, to small-scale street vendors, restaurants, mom-and-pop grocery stores, as well as hotel and motel operations. Most Asian American businesses are rather modest, if not marginal, family operations. This is evidenced by the fact that although Asian American businesses accounted for 2.6 percent of all business in the United States, they brought in only 1.7 percent of the sales receipts.[23] Most people are familiar with the ubiquitous Chinese or Japanese restaurant, but in recent years some Asian Americans have found other, sometimes unusual, economic niches in which they cluster and often dominate. For example, Korean Americans in New York and Los Angeles were the leaders in importing and selling wigs to African American women throughout the 1970s. In recent years, Korean Americans have expanded their business interests considerably and now own the majority of green groceries (produce markets) in New York; they own a large number of liquor stores and grocery stores in many parts of Los Angeles, and have a strong business presence in Atlanta, Georgia, and Chicago, Illinois, among other places.[24]

Asian Indians have become very involved in the hotel and motel business throughout the continental United States. Many of these operations are owned by Gujarati Indians, an ethnic group originally from the northern Indian state of Gujarat. In 1987, the *Wall Street Journal* reported that 28 percent of all motels in the United States were owned by Asian Indians, and these operations range from cheap inner-city residential hotels to well-known chain franchises found along interstate highways. Unpaid family labor, especially among the women, is a central element in keeping these businesses viable. Wives, sisters, and daughters of the owners often do all of the daily cleaning and laundry chores in these hotels and motels. Franchising is also a very popular way for Asian Indians to work for themselves. They are often found behind the counters of 7-11 stores, behind the Plexiglas partitions in various brand-name gas stations and mini-markets, and behind the wheel of taxicabs.[25]

Among Southeast Asian refugees, Vietnamese women have found a niche as manicurists. It has been estimated that about 30 percent of the roughly 22,000 nail salons in the United States are owned by Vietnamese. In some areas, such as Los Angeles, 80 percent of nail salons are Vietnamese owned and operated. This type of work has become popular because it requires little or no business experience, it is an easy skill to learn, English-speaking proficiency is not necessary, it takes only a small investment of money to get started, and the licensing process is fairly simple. In addition, the average yearly earnings plus tips for an individual manicurist is around $20,000 to $24,000.[26] Manicurists typically start off by renting space in beauty and hair-styling shops, or work for an established nail salon. The goal for many manicurists is to open a family-run business. "You can net $40,000 to $50,000 a year," explains Anna Magren, editor of the trade publication, *Nails Magazine*. "With this you can hire your family, it's not as expensive as a franchise, and it's yours." Of course distributors of nail care and beauty supplies are extremely pleased with the rapid expansion of Vietnamese manicure salons because it has served to dramatically increase the sales of their specialty products. "Many shops are open 12 hours a day, seven days a week, and it's fast work," Magren beams.[27]

Recently, Cambodian refugees have come to dominate the doughnut shop industry in California. "Cambodian people may speak very little English, but they know how to run a doughnut shop," says Ning Yen, a doughnut entrepreneur who fled Cambodia in 1980. According to a 1995 report in the *Wall Street Journal*, Cambodian Americans and their families run at least 2,450 doughnut shops, overtaking the once omnipresent Winchell's Donut Houses chain. Winchell's now operates just 120 doughnut outlets in California, and they are beginning to franchise out to many Cambodian Americans. The undisputed founder of the Cambodian doughnut phenomena is Ted Ngoy, the former Cambodian ambassador to Thailand, who came to the United States as a refugee in 1975. He was initially hired as a manager-trainee in a Winchell's doughnut shop, and after two years of hard work and saving Ngoy purchased his own business in La Habra, California. In a few years Ngoy built a chain of 32 stores across the state, hired and trained many fellow Cambodian refugees, and loaned them money to start their own businesses. Today Ngoy is no longer directly involved in the doughnut business and has returned to Cambodia to work on government reform. In the meantime, Ning Yen has taken over a multimillion dollar doughnut supply company, B&H Distributors Inc., which serves mostly Cambodian clients across the United States and is making plans to expand its business to Asia.[28]

Whatever their characteristics, or the type of business they are in, self-employment assures a life of hard work and long hours, with no guarantees of success. There have been several attempts to explain why many groups have the relative high percentage of self-employment while others do not. One perspective is the cultural theory that argues that certain groups have innate cultural values similar to the Protestant work ethic and are compatible with the spirit of capitalism.[29] This perspective, however, has been criticized by social scientists for a number of reasons. The most basic criticism is that there is tremendous diversity among various entrepreneurially oriented groups. Indeed, as we saw above, there is no consistency in terms of geographic location or religio-cultural background for who has a tendency to start a small business and who does not.

For Asian Americans, the most common cultural explanation seems to focus on Confucian values as the reason for business success both in the United States, as well as the recent emergence of Pacific Rim countries. There is, however, a great deal of diversity and mixture within and throughout Asian countries. For example, Buddhism was founded during the sixth century B.C. in northern India and spread out to central and eastern Asia. Confucianism became the official state philosophy in China in the second century B.C. and spread across Korea to Japan. Catholicism was brought to both the Philippines after it became a colony of Spain in the early sixteenth-century, and it was introduced to Vietnam after French colonialism in the late nineteenth-century. Moreover, Christian missionaries were quite successful in converting many Koreans, although they were much less successful in other parts of Asia.

Without denying the importance of cultural and religious influences, it is difficult to draw any firm conclusions about Asian American propensity toward entrepreneurship solely on cultural factors. For example, why are Chinese Buddhists generally more active in small business, but Laotian Buddhists are less likely to do so? Similarly, why are Catholic Vietnamese starting businesses more than Catholic Filipinos? Among Koreans, is the Protestant ethic the more dominant cultural influence or is the Confucian ethic more dominant? These types of questions have led other social scientists to look beyond just a cultural explanation of the Asian Americans and their entrepreneurial experience and move toward examining the social situation. Researchers who study Asian Americans have noticed that many Asian American businesses are found in inner-city locations that are devoid of major market chain stores. As a result, these Asian Americans have formed what is known as a "middleman" niche for themselves that no one else is willing or able to fill. The middleman minority theory has been used by James Loewen in his book, *The Mississippi Chinese: Between Black and White* (1971), to examine Chinese American grocery store owners in Mississippi at the turn of the century, and by Edna Bonacich and John Modell in their book, *The Economic Basis of Ethnic Solidarity: Small Business in the Japanese American Community* (1980), to examine Japanese American farmers in California prior to World War II.[30] Today, however, the best example of this phenomena is seen with Korean American–owned stores operating in predominantly black communities in urban centers across the nation.

Under this theory, "middleman minorities" play a buffer role between large corporations and marginalized populations. Middleman minority merchants are necessary and are encouraged because they are able to sell goods and products of the corporations to people who ordinarily would not have easy access to the merchandise. According to sociologist Edna Bonacich, middlemen minorities are forced into the self-employment situation because they know societal "discrimination" limits their opportunities to do much else in the mainstream economy. Korean American sociologist Pyong Gap Min has argued against the middleman minority theory and finds little evidence that U.S. corporate interests encourage Korean Americans to start small businesses. In addition, he believes Korean Americans choose to start their own business and are not coerced to do so. Min surveyed Korean American merchants in Atlanta and found that a high percentage of Korean American immigrants are educated and held white-collar jobs in their home countries. Min also found Korean Americans' perception of their own labor market "disadvantages" (primarily language) was the main reason for starting a business over anything else, including awareness of host society discrimination. In short, Min believes Korean Americans make an economic and rational choice to enter self-employment.[31]

Whether by coercion or choice, the situations faced by immigrants in a new society appears to be far more a factor in starting up small businesses than cultural factors. But this still doesn't explain why some Asian American groups tend to have higher self-employment rates than others, nor does it explain why other "disadvantaged" groups (e.g., other racial minorities) have not taken the self-employment option more so than they currently do. More recently, other social scientists have looked at the clustering of large numbers of Asian American businesses that together form ethnic "enclave economies." Enclaves appear to function quite well separate from, but also in competition with, the local mainstream economy. The positive aspects of the enclave economy are most developed by Alejandro Portes and Robert Bach (1985) in their research on Cubans in Miami, Roger Waldinger (1985) in his research on immigrant enterprise, and Min Zhou (1992) in her study of New York's Chinatown.[32]

This theory contends that enclaves develop through the transplantation of a significant number of people from the professional and entrepreneurial classes who migrate (either through immigration or as refugees) into the United States. For example, in her book, *Chinatown: The Socioeconomic Potential of an Urban Enclave,* Zhou contends that Chinese immigrants with high levels of education, professional skills, and some capital find operating a small business within an enclave is preferable to working in the mainstream economy. This is particularly true for those with no English-speaking ability but also for those who do speak English. Success within the enclave is dependent on several factors: First, there is an ethnic population and consumer market large enough to support a number of ethnic businesses; second, enclave businesses do tend to pay workers less and make them work longer hours, thus providing themselves with a competitive edge; third, ethnic solidarity within the enclave forms the basis for a mutually beneficial relationship between ethnic business owners and workers. In the enclave, the owner–worker relationship is viewed more like an apprenticeship than as exploitation. Ethnic enclave workers gain valuable work experience that will eventually lead to their own business, often with the help of their employer. In addition, the ethnic enclave businesses provide jobs and opportunities for less privileged immigrant workers who would likely face even greater discrimination and "dead-end" work outside in the mainstream labor market.[33]

This theory, however, is not without its critics. Sociologists Jimy Sanders and Victor Nee (1987) and economist Don Mar (1991) have acknowledged that ethnic enclaves do provide entry-level jobs, but they question whether or not these usually low-paying jobs truly offer immigrant workers the long-term opportunities for upward mobility that enclave theorists claim. More broadly, critics of the enclave economy charge that the theory diverts attention away from the problems facing less educated, non–English-speaking immigrant workers.[34] Data from the 1990 census shows over 22.3 percent of all Asian Americans 25 years and older have less than a high school education, and of these people, 89.7 percent are immigrants.[35] Whether these immigrant workers are in an enclave or not, critics contend, their wages and opportunities are extremely limited. Through these criticisms, it does appear that individual human capital is an important factor to consider. Human capital is often referred to as personal factors or achieved characteristics. For example, education, skills (either professional or technical), work experience, and English language proficiency are usually regarded as the most important and easily transferable human capital characteristics. As a general rule, the higher the level of education and skills available to the individual, the smoother his or her transition into the social and economic mainstream of the United States. This is true both for self-employment as well as for wage earners.[36]

It is also necessary to understand ethnic entrepreneurship from a broader structural perspective and show its connection with global economic restructuring. In their book, *The New Asian Immigration in Los Angeles and Global Restructuring*, editors Paul Ong, Edna Bonacich, and Lucie Cheng contend that the arrival of many educated, middle-class and above Asian immigrants and their resulting ethnic entrepreneurship are not merely a local phenomenon, but are very much a part of the fluid flow of people, skills, and financial capital brought together by a dramatically changing global economy. "The large-scale immigration from Asia after 1965 not only coincided with economic restructuring, but was affected by and contributed to these structural changes," the editors write in their introductory chapter. "As their numbers grow and their influence increases, Asian immigrants are not merely filling the positions that are being created as a result of restructuring. They are helping reshape the economic landscape by creating new and alternative ventures."[37] At the same time, it is important to remember that only a small percentage of Asian Americans own their own businesses. Indeed, most Asian Americans, like most other Americans, earn their money by working for someone else. For this reason we must look beyond self-employment to examine how well Asian Americans are doing socially and economically.

SOCIOECONOMIC PROFILE

In February 1992, the U.S. Commission on Civil Rights produced a report entitled, *Civil Rights Issues Facing Asian Americans in the 1990s.* The report was immediately lampooned in an April 26, 1992 article, "Up from Inscrutable," published in *Fortune* magazine. The article began by stating: "Easily the strangest document produced by the U.S. Commission on Civil Rights in recent years is its just-released report on the predicament, if that is the word, which we doubt, of Asian Americans." The article went on to cite general statistical data indicating that Asian Americans, as a whole, are more educated, have better jobs, and have higher family incomes than the average American. "So what's the problem?" the reporter asked incredulously.[38] Like many people, this reporter's image of Asian Americans was of an untroubled "model minority" whom other racial minority groups should emulate if they want to "succeed." A closer and more critical examination of the data, however, shows tremendous diversity among various Asian ethnic groups, as well as some important invisible factors, that raises serious questions about exactly how well Asian Americans really are doing in terms of their socioeconomic status.

The "Model Minority Myth"

The emergence of Asian Americans as the model minority became prominent in 1966 when two articles in national magazines praised the achievements of the two largest Asian American groups at that time. The first article, "Success Japanese-American Style," was written by sociologist William Petersen and published in the *New York Times Magazine* on January 9, 1966. The article lauded Japanese Americans for overcoming harsh racial antagonism and internment to successfully enter into the American mainstream. That same year, Chinese Americans were also highly commended for their good behavior and economic success in the article, "Success Story of One Minority Group in the United States," published in the *U.S. News and World Report.*[39] Numerous other articles published since that time have also focused on the virtues and accomplishments of Asian Americans, especially in terms of exceptional educational achievements and phenomenal economic upward mobility. While flattering, the model minority image has proven to be more of a burden than a break-through for Asian Americans.

The 1992 report by the U.S. Commission on Civil Rights discussed four ways in which the model minority myth is indeed harmful to Asian Americans. First, the model minority image diverts from very real and very serious social and economic problems that plague many segments of the Asian American popula-tion. Second, it distracts public attention away from continued, often times overt, racial discrimination faced by Asian Americans. Third, the model minority stereotype places undue pressure and anguish on young Asian Americans who think they have to achieve in school. This has been linked with mental health issues for teenagers and even suicides. Fourth, the model minority image serves to fuel competition and resentment between groups, particularly among other racial minorities, who are told if Asian Americans can succeed why can't they?[40]

Many have argued that the emergence of the model minority stereotype in the mid-1960s, and its persistence into the 1990s, has had important political and public policy ramifications. Attention to Asian American success first appeared at a time of increasingly militant "black power movement," which called for increased government intervention to remedy historical and contem-porary racial discrimination. But the quiet self-sufficiency of Asian Americans has often been held up in contrast to active African American calls for greater government action and support for social service programs. According to the 1966 *U.S. News and World Report* article: "At a time when it is being proposed that hundreds of billions be spent to uplift Negroes and other minorities, the nation's 300,000 Chinese-Americans are moving ahead on their own, with no help from anyone else."[41] Since that time, conservative political pundits, includ-ing some African Americans, have used the model minority image to show that the United States is the land of opportunity and contend that government pro-grams such as welfare and affirmative action are unnecessary. Conservatives claim that all racial minority groups can succeed just like Asian Americans if they work hard, don't cause trouble, and assimilate into mainstream American life.

Given the political and public policy attention surrounding the model minority stereotype, it is necessary to see if the image is indeed true. At the heart of the model minority claim are several general statistics that are used as "facts" proving Asian American "success." It is obviously important to look closely at the evidence in order to better judge its validity. The three most commonly cited statistics that are used to "prove" that Asian Americans are the model minority are educational achievement, employment status, and median family income.

Education

Summary statistics do show that Asian Americans are a highly educated group. According to the 1990 census, 37.7 percent of all Asian Americans 25 years of age and over have completed at least four years or more of college education. This figure far exceeds the national average of 20.3 percent for all people who have completed four years of college or more. Educational

Table 2-11 Educational Attainment, 25 Years Old and Over, 1990

Group	4+ College
U.S.	20.3
Male	23.3
Female	17.6
Whites	21.5
Male	25.0
Female	18.4
Black	11.4
Male	11.0
Female	11.7
Not Asian or Pacific Is.	19.9
Male	22.8
Female	17.2
Asian or Pacific Is.	36.6
Male	41.9
Female	31.8
Asian	37.7
Male	43.2
Female	32.7
Hispanic	9.2
Male	10.0
Female	8.3

Sources: U.S. Bureau of the Census, *1990 Census of the Population: Education in the United States* (Washington, DC: Government Printing Office, 1993), CP-3-4, Table 1; *1990 Census of the Population, Asians and Pacific Islanders in the United States* (Washington, DC: Government Printing Office, 1993), CP-3-5, Table 3.

achievement for Asian Americans does, however, differ among males and females. Just over 43.2 percent of Asian American males completed four years of college or more compared to 32.7 percent of Asian American females. This pattern reflects the national trend as 23.3 percent of all men and 17.6 percent of all women in the United States have completed four years of college or more (see Table 2-11). While impressive, it is quite evident that educational achievement by Asian Americans is far from uniform. Table 2-12 shows only 17.4 percent of Vietnamese, 5.7 percent of Cambodians, 5.4 percent of Laotians, and 4.9 percent of Hmong, 25 years old or over earned a four-year college degree or more.

Table 2-12 Asian American Educational Attainment by Sex, Ethnic Group, and Foreign-born, 25 Years Old and Over, 1990

Group	4+ College	Foreign-Born
Chinese	40.7	38.7
Male	46.7	45.4
Female	34.9	32.4
Filipino	39.3	42.3
Male	36.2	39.3
Female	41.6	44.5
Japanese	34.5	35.1
Male	42.6	60.0
Female	28.2	22.2
Asian Indian	58.0	58.5
Male	65.9	66.2
Female	48.7	49.0
Korean	34.5	34.4
Male	50.6	47.4
Female	23.3	25.5
Vietnamese	17.4	17.5
Male	22.3	22.7
Female	12.2	12.1
Cambodian	5.7	5.6
Male	8.6	8.5
Female	3.2	3.1
Laotian	5.4	5.0
Male	7.0	6.6
Female	3.5	3.4
Hmong	4.9	4.8
Male	7.0	6.8
Female	3.0	3.0

Source: U.S. Bureau of the Census, *1990 Census of the Population, Asians and Pacific Islanders in the United States* (Washington, DC: Government Printing Office, 1993), CP-3-5, Table 3.

Employment

High rates of education generally translate into better employment opportunities. Table 2-13 clearly shows how various Asian American groups, both men and women, are well represented in the managerial and profes-

Table 2-13 Asian American Occupational Distribution by Sex and Foreign-born, 16 Years and Over, 1990

Group	Managerial	Professional	Technical Sales	Administrative Support/ Clerical
U.S.	12.3	14.1	15.5	16.3
Male	14.6	13.4	16.6	7.5
Female	10.1	14.8	14.4	24.6
Foreign-born	9.9	12.3	13.3	12.0
Asian and Pacific Is.	12.6	18.1	17.9	15.4
Male	15.4	21.6	20.3	10.5
Female	10.0	14.9	15.6	19.8
Foreign-born	12.0	18.3	18.1	13.9
Asian	12.9	18.5	18.1	15.2
Male	15.7	22.3	20.8	10.6
Female	10.0	15.2	15.6	19.4
Foreign-born	12.1	18.5	18.1	13.9
Chinese	15.1	20.7	17.6	13.5
Male	17.5	27.2	20.3	8.7
Female	12.9	14.8	15.2	18.0
Foreign-born	14.3	19.6	17.3	12.3
Filipino	10.3	16.4	15.6	21.0
Male	11.9	13.4	16.4	17.4
Female	9.3	18.5	15.0	23.6
Foreign-born	10.2	17.8	15.0	20.7
Japanese	17.5	19.4	16.6	17.8
Male	24.2	22.8	20.3	10.0
Female	12.1	16.7	13.5	24.2
Foreign-born	21.3	17.8	16.9	11.9
Asian Indian	14.0	29.6	20.0	13.2
Male	18.9	38.5	23.7	9.8
Female	8.1	19.3	15.7	17.2
Foreign-born	14.1	30.0	19.9	13.0
Korean	12.0	13.5	26.8	10.3
Male	16.9	18.3	33.2	7.1
Female	8.3	9.8	21.9	12.7
Foreign-born	12.1	13.4	27.1	9.7

Group	Managerial	Professional	Technical/ Sales	Administrative Support/ Clerical
Vietnamese	6.1	11.5	17.7	11.8
Male	5.7	14.1	19.2	8.0
Female	6.7	8.1	15.8	16.6
Foreign-born	6.1	11.6	17.7	11.6
Cambodian	4.0	5.8	12.6	10.7
Male	4.9	6.8	12.0	8.1
Female	3.0	4.7	13.3	13.8
Foreign-born	4.0	5.8	12.4	10.6
Laotian	1.8	3.3	6.9	8.2
Male	2.0	3.4	6.2	6.2
Female	1.5	3.1	7.9	11.0
Foreign-born	1.7	3.2	6.8	8.2
Hmong	3.4	9.4	7.3	11.6
Male	3.9	10.5	7.6	9.8
Female	2.6	7.4	6.8	14.8
Foreign-born	3.5	9.7	7.4	11.4

Group	Service	Farming/ Forestry/ Fishing	Precision Prod./Craft/ Repair	Operative/ Laborers
U.S.	13.2	2.5	11.3	14.9
Male	11.3	4.2	21.0	22.5
Female	15.1	0.8	2.1	7.6
Foreign-born	18.1	3.8	12.0	18.6
Asian and Pacific Is.	14.8	1.2	8.0	12.1
Male	15.2	2.0	12.9	14.9
Female	11.9	0.5	3.6	9.6
Foreign-born	7.8	0.5	3.9	6.5
Asian	14.6	1.1	7.8	11.9
Male	15.1	2.0	12.5	14.4
Female	14.2	0.4	3.7	9.7
Foreign-born	15.6	0.1	7.9	13.0
Chinese	16.5	0.4	5.6	10.6
Male	21.6	0.6	8.7	9.8
Female	11.9	0.2	2.8	11.3
Foreign-born	18.5	0.3	5.8	11.8

Table 2–13 *continued*

Group	Service	Farming/ Forestry/ Fishing	Precision Prod./Craft/ Repair	Operative/ Laborers
Filipino	16.8	1.5	7.4	11.0
Male	17.6	2.6	13.7	16.8
Female	16.2	0.7	3.0	7.0
Foreign-born	17.1	1.5	7.0	10.9
Japanese	11.1	2.7	7.8	6.9
Male	10.2	5.1	14.2	9.8
Female	11.9	0.7	2.7	4.6
Foreign-born	17.5	1.9	5.9	7.1
Asian Indian	8.1	0.6	5.2	9.4
Male	7.3	0.9	7.8	11.6
Female	9.0	0.2	2.1	6.8
Foreign-born	7.9	0.6	5.2	9.4
Korean	15.1	0.7	8.9	12.8
Male	11.3	1.1	14.3	13.9
Female	18.0	0.4	4.9	12.0
Foreign-born	14.6	0.6	9.3	13.2
Vietnamese	15.0	1.4	15.7	20.9
Male	12.9	2.3	20.5	22.9
Female	17.7	0.3	9.4	18.2
Foreign-born	14.7	1.4	15.9	21.0
Cambodian	17.9	1.7	17.2	30.0
Male	18.9	2.2	21.5	30.8
Female	16.7	1.2	12.3	29.0
Foreign-born	17.9	1.6	17.3	30.2
Laotian	14.6	1.5	19.8	43.9
Male	14.6	1.8	22.7	45.2
Female	14.8	1.1	15.9	41.9
Foreign-born	14.6	1.5	19.8	44.1
Hmong	20.0	2.3	13.9	32.1
Male	21.5	3.4	16.5	31.1
Female	17.4	0.4	9.3	33.9
Foreign-born	20.0	2.2	13.7	32.1

Source: U.S. Bureau of the Census, *1990 Census of the Population, Asians and Pacific Islanders in the United States* (Washington, DC: Government Printing Office, 1993), CP-3-5, Table 4.

sional occupation ranks. Overall, 12.3 percent of all Americans 16 years and older are employed in managerial occupations, while 14.1 percent are in professional specializations. For Asian Americans in these same categories, the percentage is 12.9 and 18.5 percent, respectively. A gender breakdown shows 14.6 percent of men 16 years and older are managers and 13.4 percent are professionals compared to 15.7 percent managers and 22.3 professionals for Asian American males. For all women, 10.1 percent are managers and 14.8 percent are professionals, compared to 10.0 percent managers and 15.2 percent professionals for Asian American women. As with educational attainment, Asian Americans show a great deal of diversity. Japanese Americans have the highest percent of managers at 17.5 percent, while Asian Indians have the highest percentage of professionals, with 29.6 percent. At the same time Laotians show only 1.8 percent managers and 3.3 percent professionals.

Statistics show there are more Asian Americans on the upper occupational levels, and there are also fewer Asian Americans at the other end of the occupational spectrum. Among all Americans 16 years and older, 14.9 work as operators and laborers compared with just 11.9 percent for all Asian Americans. This, of course, is not to say that there is no Asian American working class. As stated above, there is a significant number of Asian Americans who lack education and English language fluency, and it is these people who find themselves in low-wage employment. A study by Paul Ong and Suzanne Hee (1993) found that 12 percent of Asian American males earned less than $6.00 an hour, compared to 9 percent of non-Hispanic white males. In addition, 20 percent of Asian American males earned less than $15,000 a year, compared with 14 percent of non-Hispanic white males. This situation is much higher for Asian American women, 21 percent of whom earn less than $6.00 an hour and 39 percent earn less than $15,000 a year. However, Asian American women appeared to do better than non-Hispanic white women. Ong and Hee found 22 percent of non-Hispanic white women earned less than $6.00 an hour, while 41 percent earned less than $15,000 a year.[42]

Family Income

Asian Americans, on average, do enjoy a higher family income compared to all other Americans. The 1990 census found the median family income was $41,583, compared to $37,152 for whites, $22,429 for blacks, and $25,064 for Hispanics. Like everything else, the median family income does vary for each Asian American group. Japanese Americans had the highest median family income of $51,550, compared to Hmong Americans who have an average family income of just $14,327. It is important to note that although Asian Americans generally have a higher median family income than the average American, they also have a higher rate of poverty.

The 1990 census shows 11.4 of all Asian American families living below the poverty level. The poverty rate for whites was just 7.0 percent, for blacks 26.3 percent, and for Hispanics 22.3 percent. By contrast, only 3.4 percent of

Table 2-14 Median Family Income and Poverty Status by Asian American Ethnic Group, 1990

Group	Median Family Income	Percent Below Poverty
U.S.	$30,056	10.0
White	$37,152	7.0
Black	$22,429	26.3
Asian & Pacific Is.	$41,251	11.6
Asian	$41,583	11.4
Chinese	$41,316	11.1
Filipino	$46,698	5.2
Japanese	$51,550	3.4
Asian Indian	$49,309	7.2
Korean	$33,909	14.7
Vietnamese	$30,550	23.8
Cambodian	$18,126	42.1
Laotian	$23,101	32.2
Hmong	$14,327	61.8
Hispanic	$25,064	22.3

Sources: U.S. Bureau of the Census, *1990 Census of the Population, Asians and Pacific Islanders in the United States* (Washington, DC: Government Printing Office, 1993), CP-3-5, Table 5; *1990 Census of the Population, Social and Economic Characteristics, Metropolitan Areas* (Washington, DC: Government Printing Office, 1993), CP-2-1B, Tables 6–7, 9–10.

Japanese, 5.2 percent of Filipino, and 7.2 percent of Asian Indian American families live below the poverty level. People might be surprised to learn that even more established Asian American groups such as the Chinese and Korean American families have poverty rates of 11.1 percent and 14.7 percent, both above the national average. At the same time, all Southeast Asian refugee groups suffered extremely high rates of poverty. Among Vietnamese American families the poverty rate was 23.8 percent. This figure is comparable to blacks and Hispanics. However, 32.2 percent of Laotian, 42.1 percent of Cambodian, and 61.8 percent of Hmong Americans live below the poverty line (see Table 2-14).

Because of the mass exodus following the Vietnam War, Congress passed the Refugee Act of 1980, which formalized a policy for refugees and regularized assistance for the resettlement of Southeast Asian refugees. Basic refugee assistance included food, shelter, clothing, mental health services, English language and vocational training, and job placement for up to 36 months (reduced to 18 months in 1982). After this period of refugee assistance "time expired" refugees became eligible for welfare just as U.S. citizens. Southeast Asian refugees were, of course, encouraged to find work and avoid welfare. However, many refugees arrived in the United States with few possessions and the often lacked both transferable vocational and English language skills. As a result, many found adjustment to the United States very difficult. What also made their adjustment particularly arduous was the fact that many faced tremendous hardships leaving their home countries. One 1985 study found 83.3 percent of Cambodian refugees were separated from their families, and 56.3 percent had lost at least one family member. Among Vietnamese refugees, 39.5 percent had lost family members and 30 percent were assaulted during their escape.[43]

But between 1986 and 1992, federal funding for refugee assistance declined 27 percent, which only served to channel Southeast Asians and others into state welfare systems more rapidly.[44] For example, in 1991, it was estimated that the welfare-dependency rate of Southeast Asians in the first 12 months of their resettlement was 45 percent for Vietnamese, 44 percent for Laotians (including Hmong), and almost 100 percent for Cambodians. Southeast Asians, however, were not the only ones affected by reductions in refugee assistance. By comparison, the welfare utilization rate for other immigrant groups, many of whom were admitted to the United States as permanent residents under various refugee acts, was equally high. For example, welfare utilization was 45 percent for Afghans, 34 percent for Iranians, 30 percent for Ethiopians, and 50 percent for immigrants from the former Soviet Union.[45] High rates of poverty and welfare dependency among Southeast Asians is a major factor for the widely bifurcated socioeconomic portrait of Asian Americans.

Beyond the Model Minority

Many people look at general statistics and conclude that Asian Americans either do not face any discrimination relative to other racial minority groups or, if they did, they have overcome them. This image is not completely false for some Asian Americans, but is a rather deceptive overstatement for all Asian American groups. Detailed statistics on Asian American education, employment, and median family income show the difficulty in creating a clear picture of the average Asian American. Even among those relatively successful Asian American groups, several factors must be taken into consideration before any broad assumptions can be made. Many have argued that socioeconomic "success" for Asian Americans can be understood only within the context of: (1) a high percentage of urbanization; (2) more wage earners per family; and (3) comparing per capita income instead of median family income. By examining these factors we find that most Asian Americans are indeed advantaged relative to blacks and Hispanics, but are still disadvantaged relative to whites.

First of all, national statistics of median family incomes are a very poor indicator of relative Asian American success. This is because they compare Asian Americans who tend to live in urbanized areas that naturally have a higher cost of living with whites who live in the same areas, but also with whites who live in lower cost of living regions across the country. A much better comparison would be to compare Asian American family incomes with white family incomes in the same city. With this in mind, 1990 census figures from five cities that have large Asian American populations clearly show how misleading national statistics can be. The median family income for whites was $38,833 in Chicago, $40,549 in Houston, $44,000 in Los Angeles, $42,726 in New York, and $47,547 in San Francisco. By contrast, median family income for Asian Americans was $31,986 in Chicago, $32,643 in Houston, $37,360 in Los Angeles, $33,445 in New York, and $38,294 in San Francisco.[46]

Second, relatively high family incomes among Asian Americans are very much due to the fact that Asian American families tend to have more workers in the household. The 1990 census showed 45.6 percent of all American families had two workers, and 13.4 percent had three or more workers. Among Asian Americans, 45.7 percent of families had two workers, and 19.8 percent had three or more workers. The small difference between all Americans and Asian Americans with two workers in the family is due to the fact that Southeast Asian refugees tend to have fewer dual income families. For example, only 40 percent of Vietnamese American families have two workers, but 21.3 percent of Vietnamese American families do have three workers or more. Filipino and Asian Indian Americans have the most workers in their families. The 1990 census figures show 48.2 percent of Filipino American families have two workers, and 29.6 percent have three workers or more. Among Asian Indian American families, 51.8 percent have two workers, and 17.8 percent have three workers or more (see Table 2-15).

Third, given the considerations above, it would be more accurate to look at per capita income instead of median family income to test Asian American success. In addition, given the undeniable fact that Asian Americans are a relatively well-educated group that tends to live in high-cost urban areas, one would expect fairly high per capita incomes. In the same study by Paul Ong and Suzanne J. Hee cited above, the researchers found that a clear disparity between education-to-income can be seen when looking at statistics on hourly wages for individual Asian American men and women. Despite higher overall levels of education, Ong and Hee found the average hourly wage for Asian American males was $15.40, compared to $15.90 for white males. The researchers found that while highly educated Asian American men made less money than less educated white men, highly educated Asian American women did earn more than less educated white women. Average hourly wages for Asian American women was $12.10, but only $11.10 for white women. It is important to note that even though Asian American women have a higher average education compared to white males, they earned significantly less

Table 2-15 Workers in Family, 1990

Group	1 Worker	2 Workers	3 or more Workers
U.S.	28%	45.6%	13.4%
Asian & Pacific Is.	26.2	45.7	19.8
Asian	26.2	45.7	19.8
Chinese	25.5	47.6	19.0
Filipino	18.1	48.2	29.6
Japanese	33.2	42.9	15.3
Asian Indian	27.7	51.8	17.8
Korean	31.8	44.8	15.9
Vietnamese	25.1	40.0	21.3
Cambodian	20.7	27.7	13.5
Laotian	18.7	35.7	18.9
Hmong	28.0	15.4	6.7

Source: U.S. Bureau of the Census, *1990 Census of the Population, Asians and Pacific Islanders in the United States* (Washington, DC: Government Printing Office, 1993), CP-3-5, Table 4.

money.[47] The results of this study are confirmed by the U.S. Census Bureau, which reported that the 1990 per capita earnings of all Asian Americans was $13,420, while the per capital average for all whites was $15,270. Full-time employed Asian American males had a median per capita income of $26,760, which is lower than the $28,880 earned by white men. Even when looking only at males with four years of college education or more, salaries of Asian American males were not equal. In his group, Asian American males earned $34,470 in 1990, which is below the $36,130 earned by white males. In dollars and cents, even though Asian Americans invest in education in hopes of achieving a higher standard of living, this strategy appears to have only limited returns.[48] The reasons behind this seemingly odd disparity in income levels will be discussed thoroughly in Chapter 4.

CONCLUSION

Seeing Asian Americans only as a "model minority" may seem complementary at first, but it serves only to unfairly homogenize an extremely diverse group of people. The model minority myth completely ignores important historical and socioeconomic realities about Asian Americans. The notion that Asian Americans are the model minority is somewhat similar to the European immigrant analogy described in the previous chapter. The European immigrant analogy views success in terms of poor immigrants who work hard to pull themselves up by their own "bootstraps" and advance socially and economically in the United States. Within this narrow context, the model minority label may seem valid. However, a more critical perspective on the Asian American experience recognizes the role of broader structural forces and policy changes that served to encourage the immigration of highly educated and well-to-do Asian immigrants, as well as the arrival of desperately poor Asian refugees to the United States. It is clear that those immigrants and refugees with the most human capital advantages are, along with their children, doing the best socially and economically. These immigrants and refugees not only support their own families but also contribute greatly to the overall U.S. economy. Asian American immigrants and refugees with the fewest human capital advantages are, along with their children, generally doing worse socially and economically than any other group in the United States.

This chapter has also shown that the post-1965 Asian immigrants are generally more geographically dispersed, better educated, and better off economically than pre-1965 Asian immigrants. At the same time, ample evidence shows that inequality persists even for Asian Americans with the highest levels of education and skills (human capital). Ongoing anti-immigrant sentiment described at the beginning of this chapter shows the contributions and achievements of Asian Americans are not often appreciated. This chapter has also shown that the model minority image of Asian Americans is a dubious concept that does more harm than good. The model minority image serves to distract attention from less affluent and less educated segments of the Asian American population, minimizes the negative impact of discrimination and inequality confronted by Asian Americans, places undue pressure and anguish on young Asian Americans, and creates tremendous resentment against Asian Americans. These issues will be addressed in much greater detail in the chapters ahead.

ENDNOTES

1. John Leland and John McCormick, "The Quiet Race War," *Newsweek,* April 8, 1996, p. 38.
2. Bill Wong, "Human Cargo," *Asian Week,* April 26, 1996.
3. Ignatius Bau, "Immigrant Rights: A Challenge to Asian Pacific American Political Influence," *Asian American Policy Review* 5 (1995): 7–44.
4. Quoted in Bert Eljera, "Mixed Reactions on Immigration Moves," *Asian Week,* March 29, 1996.
5. For details see U.S. Immigration and Naturalization Service, *Statistical Yearbook of the Immigration and Naturalization Service, 1994* (Washington, DC: Government Printing Office, 1996), Table 1, pp. 25–29.
6. Ramon G. McLeod, "Elderly Immigrants Swell Welfare Roles," *San Francisco Chronicle,* April 20, 1996.

7. Donald Huddle, *The Cost of Immigration* (Washington, DC: Carrying Capacity Network, 1993).
8. Julian L. Simon, *Immigration: The Demographic and Economic Facts* (Washington, DC: The Cato Institute and the National Immigration Forum, 1995).
9. Julian L. Simon, "Studies on Immigrants Prove They'd Rather Give Than Receive," in "Letters to the Editor," *New York Times*, February 26, 1994.
10. Jeffery S. Passel, "Immigrants and Taxes: A Reappraisal of Huddle's 'The Cost of Immigrants'" (Washington, DC: Program for Research on Immigration Policy, The Urban Institute, January 1994), p. 6.
11. "Why They Count: Immigrant Contributions to the Golden State" (Claremont, CA: Tomas Rivera Center, 1996).
12. Joel Kotkin, *California: A Twenty-First Century Prospectus* (Denver, CO: Center for the New West, 1996).
13. Quoted in Louis Freedberg, "Feinstein Fails to Limit Legal Immigration," *San Francisco Chronicle*, April 26, 1996.
14. Timothy P. Fong, *The First Suburban Chinatown: The Remaking of Monterey Park, California* (Philadelphia: Temple University Press, 1994).
15. Chor-Swan Ngin, "The Acculturation Pattern of Orange County's Southeast Asian Refugees," *Journal of Orange County* 3:4 (Fall 1989–Spring 1990): 46–53.
16. Dexter Waugh and Steven A. Chin, "Daly City: New Manila," *San Francisco Examiner*, September 17, 1989.
17. Quoted in E. S. Browning, "A New Chinatown Grows in Brooklyn," *Wall Street Journal*, May 31, 1994.
18. Quoted from Frank Viviano, "Strangers in the Promised Land," *Image*, August 31, 1986, pp. 15–21, 38.
19. Ivan Light, *Ethnic Enterprise in America* (Berkeley: University of California Press, 1972); Thomas Sowell, *The Economics and Politics of Race: An International Perspective* (New York: Quill, 1983); and Alejandro Portes and Ruben G. Rumbaut, *Immigrant America: A Portrait* (Berkeley and Los Angeles: University of California Press, 1990).
20. U.S. Bureau of the Census, *1990 Census of the Population, Asians and Pacific Islanders in the United States* (Washington, DC: Government Printing Office, 1993), p. 110, Table 4.
21. U.S. Bureau of the Census, *Characteristics of Business Owners, 1992* (Washington, DC: Government Printing Office, 1992), Tables 9, 14, 17. Asian Americans represented 94.3 percent of the category "Other minority-owned businesses."
22. Edward Jang-Woo Park, "Asians Matter: Asian American Entrepreneurs in the Silicon Valley High Technology Industry," in Bill Ong Hing and Ronald Lee (eds.), *Reframing the Immigration Debate* (Los Angeles: LEAP Asian Pacific American Public Policy Institute and UCLA Asian American Studies Center, 1996), pp. 155–178.
23. U.S. Department of Commerce, *Survey of Minority-Owned Business Enterprises: Asian Americans, American Indians, and Other Minorities* (Washington, DC: Government Printing Office, June 1991), MB87-3, p. 2.
24. Illsoo Kim, *New Urban Immigrants: The Korean Community in New York* (Princeton, NJ: Princeton University Press, 1981); Edna Bonacich and Ivan Light, *Immigrant Entrepreneurs: Koreans in Los Angeles* (Berkeley and Los Angeles: University of California Press, 1988); Pyong Gap Min, *Ethnic Business Enterprise: Korean Small Business in Atlanta* (New York: Center for Migration Studies, 1988); and Eui-Hang Shin and Shin-Kap Han, "Korean Immigrant Small Businesses in Chicago: An Analysis of the Resource Mobilization Process," *Amerasia Journal* 16:1 (1990): 39–60.

25. James P. Sterba, "Indians in U.S. Prosper in Their New Country, and Not Just in Motels," *Wall Street Journal,* January 27, 1987; and Sucheta Mazumdar, "South Asians in the United States with a Focus on Asian Indians: Policy on New Communities," in *State of Asian Pacific America: Policy Issues to the Year 2020* (Los Angeles: LEAP Asian Pacific American Public Policy Institute and UCLA Asian American Studies Center, 1993), pp. 283–301.
26. Craig Trinh-Phat Huynh, "Vietnamese-Owned Manicure Businesses in Los Angeles," in Hing and Lee (eds.), *Reframing the Immigration Debate*, pp. 195–203.
27. Quoted in Beth Hughes, "Ethnic Formula for Success," *San Francisco Examiner,* January 28, 1990.
28. Jonathan Kaufman, "How Cambodians Came to Control California Doughnuts," *Wall Street Journal,* February 22, 1995; and John Flynn, "Success the Old Fashioned Way," *San Francisco Examiner,* April 30, 1995. *Note:* "Doughnut" is the proper spelling, although "Donut" is the commonly used commercial spelling.
29. Thomas Sowell, *Race and Culture: A World View* (New York: Basic Books, 1994).
30. James W. Loewen, *The Mississippi Chinese: Between Black and White* (Cambridge, Harvard University Press, 1971); and Edna Bonacich and John Modell, *The Economic Basis of Ethnic Solidarity: Small Business in the Japanese American Community* (Berkeley: University of California Press, 1980).
31. See Edna Bonacich, "The Social Costs of Immigrant Entrepreneurship," *Amerasia Journal* 14:1 (1988): 119–128; Pyong Gap Min, "The Social Costs of Immigrant Entrepreneurship: A Response to Edna Bonacich," *Amerasia Journal* 15:2 (1989): 187–194; and Min, *Ethnic Business Enterprise: Korean Small Business in Atlanta.*
32. Alejandro Portes and Robert Bach, *Latin Journey: Cuban and Mexican Immigrants in the United States* (Berkeley: University of California Press, 1985); Roger Waldinger, "Immigrant Enterprise and the Structure of the Labor Market," in Bryan Roberts et al. (eds.), *New Approaches to Economic Life* (Manchester: Manchester University Press, 1985), pp. 66-88; and Min Zhou, *Chinatown: The Socioeconomic Potential of an Urban Enclave* (Philadelphia: Temple University Press, 1992).
33. Zhou, *Ibid.*
34. Jimy Sanders and Victor Nee, "Limits of Ethnic Solidarity in the Enclave Economy," *American Sociological Review* 52 (1987): 745-767; and Don Mar, "Another Look at the Enclave Economy Thesis," *Amerasia Journal* 17:3 (1991): 5–21.
35. U.S. Bureau of the Census, *1990 Census of the Population, Asians and Pacific Islanders in the United States,* CP-3-5, Table 3.
36. See Gary S. Becker, *Human Capital: A Theoretical and Empirical Analysis,* second edition (Chicago: University of Chicago Press, 1980); Barry Chiswick, *Income Inequality* (New York: Columbia University Press, 1974); and William A. Scott and Ruth Scott, *Adaptation of Immigrants: Individual Differences and Determinants* (Oxford: Pergamon Press, 1989.)
37. Paul Ong, Edna Bonacich, and Lucie Cheng (eds.), *The New Asian Immigration in Los Angeles and Global Restructuring* (Philadelphia: Temple University Press, 1994), pp. 23–24, 29.
38. "Up from Inscrutable," *Fortune,* April 6, 1992, p. 120
39. William Petersen, "Success Story, Japanese-American Style," *New York Times Magazine,* January 9, 1966, pp. 20–21, 33, 36, 38, 40-41, 43; and "Success Story of One Minority Group in the U.S.," *U.S. News and World Report,* December 26, 1966, pp. 73–78.
40 U.S. Commission on Civil Rights, *Civil Rights Issues Facing Asian Americans in the 1990s* (Washington, DC: Government Printing Office, 1992), p. 19.
41. Peterson, "Success Story," p. 73.

42. Paul Ong and Suzanne J. Hee, "Work Issues Facing Asian Pacific Americans: Labor Policy," *The State of Asian Pacific Americans: Policy Issues to the Year 2020*, pp. 141–152.

43. Ruben Rumbaut, "Mental Health and the Refugee Experience," in Tom C. Owen (ed.), *Southeast Asian Mental Health: Treatment, Prevention, Services, Training and Research* (Rockville, MD: National Institute of Mental Health, 1985), pp. 433–486.

44. Paul Ong and Evelyn Blumenberg, "Welfare and Work among Southeast Asians," in Paul Ong (ed.), *The State of Asian Pacific America: Economic Diversity, Issues & Policies* (Los Angeles: LEAP Asian Pacific American Public Policy Institute and UCLA Asian American Studies Center, 1994), pp. 113–138.

45. Ngoan Le, "The Case of the Southeast Asian Refugees: Policy for a Community 'At-Risk,'" in *The State of Asian Pacific America: Policy Issues to the Year 2020*, pp. 167–188.

46. U.S. Bureau of the Census, *1990 Census of the Population, Social and Economic Characteristics, Metropolitan Areas* (Washington, DC: Government Printing Office, 1994), CP-2-1B, Tables 6 and 9.

47. Ong and Hee, "Work Issues Facing Asian Pacific Americans," pp. 144–148.

48. David G. Savage, "Study Finds U.S. Asians Get More School, Less Pay," *Los Angeles Times*, September 18, 1992.

3

THE RIGHT TO EXCEL: ASIAN AMERICANS AND EDUCATIONAL OPPORTUNITY

VISIBILITY AND INVISIBILITY

Eighteen-year-old Amy Chow from San Jose, California was the team captain of the first U.S. women's gymnastics team ever to win an Olympic gold medal during the 1996 summer games in Atlanta. Chow also became the first American to win an individual event medal in gymnastics when she performed a solid routine on the uneven bars that earned her a 9.837 score and a silver medal. Her athletic accomplishments are all the more stunning given the fact that she battled back and ankle injuries, but she also completed her senior year in high school as a straight-A student taking advance placement English, calculus, and biology classes. Chow was already accepted to Stanford University prior to entering the Olympics, and has future plans to go to medical school and become a pediatrician.[1]

On a different stage, 12-year-old Wendy Guey, a seventh grader from West Palm Beach, Florida looked calm as she stood all alone under the glow of klieg lights and the watchful eye of live CNN cameras. Guey's mother, a teacher, and her father, a nuclear engineer, had complete confidence in their daughter's ability to perform. Guey confidently spelled "vivisepulture" so quickly that the judges had to take a moment to double-check to make sure it was correct before signaling their approval. The room then burst into applause to congratulate the winner of the 1996 Scripps Howard National Spelling Bee. "I knew it as soon as I heard it," Guey said later. The trophy and $5,000 grand prize were awarded to Guey, whose perseverance paid off in her fourth consecutive attempt at the national spelling championship. Wendy is not only a straight-A student who can spell, she also plays the piano and violin, and is a writer for the monthly Florida publication, *Kidzette.* "She's smart. What else can you say," beamed Guey's mother.[2]

Irene Ann Chen was a shy and quiet child who did not show any interest in participating with other children in nursery school. Her lack of social development was a great concern to her parents, who confessed they thought she might be mentally retarded. The parents' fears turned out to be premature and completely unfounded as Chen later went on to win first place in the 1995 Westinghouse Science Talent Search, one of the nation's most prestigious and rigorous high school academic competitions. Chen's award-winning project was an examination of two lymphoma genes that experts believe might eventually help find a cure for cancer. The 17-year-old La Jolla High School (San Diego County) senior grew from being an extremely introverted child to an exceptionally active teenager. She is a member of the school badminton team, and the California Mathematics League, has won medals in the National Latin Exam, and placed third in the Johanna Hodges International Piano Competition. Chen says she plans to use her $40,000 scholarship prize to help pay for her college expenses at Harvard.[3]

Amy Chow, Wendy Guey, and Irene Ann Chen are yet three more high-profile examples of what *Time* magazine has called "The New Whiz Kids." The seemingly phenomenal success of Asian Americans in education from kindergarten through graduate school has humbled other students, impressed their teachers, fascinated researchers, and drawn tremendous media attention. Asian American over achievers were a particularly popular topic in major newspapers and magazines throughout the 1980s. A small sample of these news stories shows the use of provocative titles such as "Confucian Work Ethic" (*Time*, 1983); "A Formula for Success" (*Newsweek*, 1984); "An American Success Story: The Triumph of Asian Americans" (*New Republic*, 1985); "Why Asians Are Going to the Head of the Class" (*New York Times Magazine*, 1986); "When Being Best Isn't Good Enough" (*Los Angeles Times Magazine*, 1987); "The New Whiz Kids" (*Time*, 1987); "The Model Minority Goes to School" (*Phi Delta Kappan*, 1988).[4]

Much of the mainstream media coverage made comparisons between the experiences of Asian American students of the 1980s with Jewish American students of the 1920s and 1930s. During this period, there was noticeable educational mobility among second- and third-generation Jewish Americans, compared to other ethnic groups. For example, by the late 1930s nearly half of all Jewish students in New York City completed high school, a remarkable achievement that only a quarter of all other students were able accomplish at the time. In addition, although Jewish Americans represented just 3.7 percent of the U.S. population at the time, they also represented 9 percent of all college students in the nation.[5]

The recent phenomena of Asian American success in schools is very much a result of the large influx of post-1965 Asian immigrants from Asia and 1975 first wave Southeast Asian refugees who were largely middle-class and educated in their home countries. It is generally the offspring of these immigrants and refugees who are doing so well in school. According to the 1990 U.S. census, almost 38 percent of foreign-born persons from Asia are college graduates, compared to 20.4 percent of all U.S. foreign-born. "Foreign-born professionals have been a double gift to the United States," writes Leon F. Bouvier and David Simcox, authors of the report, *Foreign-born Professionals in the United States* (1994). "They have helped meet the needs of underserved populations and enriched scientific research and education. Moreover, they tend to have children who perform well academically and in many cases will themselves become professionals."[6]

This sentiment is confirmed in the research work of University of Chicago researchers Marta Tienda and Grace Kao. The two researchers conducted a national survey of nearly 25,000 eighth graders and found that Asian, Latino, and black children with immigrant parents indeed outperform other racial minority groups whose parents were born in the United States. The study showed first- and second-generation Asian Americans clearly had the highest achievement levels when compared to third-generation Asian Americans. First- and second-generation Asian American eighth graders tended to have higher grade point averages, and scored about five points higher on standardized reading and math tests than their more Americanized third-generation Asian American peers. Similar, but less spectacular, findings were true for first- and second-generation blacks, primarily immigrants from the Caribbean. Conversely, Latino immigrants did not show significant scholastic improvement compared with third-generation Latinos. However, the first and second-generation Latinos did express a greater desire to graduate from college.[7]

Scholastic Aptitude Test (SAT) scores have often been used as evidence that Asian American are, in fact, the "model minority" when it comes to academic achievement. Results from the 1995 SAT showed Asian Americans scored an average of 956 (out of a total of 1600) on the combined verbal and mathematics sections. This is higher than the 946 average for whites, 744 average for blacks, and 802 average for Mexican Americans (see Table 3-1). Although the high SAT scores for Asian Americans is the result of tallying a low verbal score (418) with a high mathematics score (538), some claim the SAT scores of Asian Americans show the objective and unbiased nature of the test, and the inherent fairness of the U.S. educational system. "Before throwing out in toto America's schools as we have known them, it would be productive to look at how and why these very schools seem to work so well for what can only be considered a most singular and unlikely minority, the Asian Americans," writes Daniel B. Taylor, former vice president of the College Board. In a rather twisted compliment to Asian Americans, Taylor adds, "It is more than a little ironic . . . that American schools seem to serve best the *most inherently alien* of their clientele. . . . 'Miraculous' might be a more apt descriptor."[8] (emphasis mine)

Table 3-1 SAT Average Scores by Race/Ethnicity

Group	1975-1976	1984-1985	1993-1994	1995*
Verbal				
All	431	431	423	428
White	451	449	443	448
Black	332	346	352	356
Mexican American	371	382	372	376
Puerto Rican	364	368	367	372
American Indian	388	392	396	403
Asian American	414	404	416	418
Math				
All	472	475	479	482
White	493	491	495	498
Black	354	376	388	388
Mexican American	410	426	427	426
Puerto Rican	401	409	411	411
American Indian	420	428	441	447
Asian American	518	518	535	538

* Beginning in 1996, the SAT scores were recalibrated. Although 1996 SAT scores are available, they cannot be used in this table because they are not comparable with earlier test scores.
Sources: National Center for Education Statistics, *Digest of Educational Statistics ,1995* (Washington, DC: U. S. Department of Education, Office of Research and Improvements, 1995), Table 125; *The Chronicle of Higher Education Almanac,* September 1, 1995, p. 12.

Although overall educational achievement among immigrant and native-born Asian American is impressive, this does not mean there are no serious issues that need to be confronted and addressed. This chapter will first focus on the contrasting theoretical perspectives that try to answer the vexing question why Asian Americans seem to do so well in school. Second, this chapter will examine some of the most important educational issues for Asian Americans in primary school (K–12). These issues include students with limited English proficiency, parental pressure and stress on young Asian American students trying to live up to the "model minority" image, and racial violence against Asian Americans in school. Lastly, this chapter will highlight the backlash against Asian American educational "success" that emerged on college campuses across the nation. Particular emphasis here will be on alleged quotas in elite colleges and universities that became the biggest issue in higher education throughout the 1980s. It is important to note that all of these issues are closely related to, and often manifest in, all levels of education. For example, the lack of services for limited English proficient Asian American immigrant students in primary school just a few years ago has made it all the more difficult for these students to perform successfully in college today—if they've gotten there at all. Also, alleged quotas against Asian Americans in higher education in the 1980s were ironically revisited again, but this time on the high school level in the 1990s.

WHY ASIAN AMERICANS DO SO WELL IN SCHOOL

There have been many scholarly attempts to explain what appears to be an uncanny Asian American mastery of the American educational system. Theories in this matter can easily be broken down into three general categories: (1) nature, or innate genetic superiority; (2) nurture, or cultural advantages versus cultural disadvantages; and (3) relative functionalism, or a complex combination of primarily both situational and structural forces. All three perspectives have been hotly debated and are by no means limited to just Asian Americans. However, these three perspectives do offer distinct philosophical and practical challenges to education policy in the United States.

Nature/Genetics

For centuries both biological and social scientists have made attempts to "prove" genetic superiority and inferiority of certain racial groups. "Scientific racism" can be traced back to the work of Count de Gobineau, Houston Chamberlin, Madison Grant, Samuel Morton, and many others in the nineteenth and early twentieth centuries. These writers tried to argue that physical differences were a reflection of intellectual differences. In 1849, for example, Morton collected 800 crania from all over the world and attempted to show that cranial size equated intelligence. He filled each cranium with sand, measured the capacity, calculated the average, and came up with the following hierarchy: English (96 cubic inches); Americans and Germans (90 cubic inches); African Americans (83 cubic inches); Chinese (82 cubic inches); and American Indians (79 cubic inches). Because the English had the largest average cranial capacity, Morton theorized, they must be the most intelligent. Conversely, Chinese had a much smaller average cranial capacity, so they must be generally less intelligent. Flawed as Morton's research was, attributing the inferiority of certain racial groups to inherent genetic deficiencies was used to help justify the institution of slavery, the spread of European colonialization throughout the world, and restrictive immigration laws.[9]

This theoretical perspective of genetic superiority/inferiority is not an anomaly of the past, but is a contemporary issue that continues to gain attention. In *Educability and Group Differences* (1973) University of California educational psychologist, Arthur Jensen, speculated that differences in Intelligence Quotient (IQ) scores between blacks and whites was due in substantial part to biological inheritance. Jensen, however, did not stop at looking at just blacks and whites. Although Samuel Morton may have concluded that Chinese were intellectually inferior because of their smaller cranial capacity, Jensen's research found "Orientals" (mostly Chinese) to be highly intelligent. Jensen tested nearly 10,000 children in kindergarten through fourth grade in 21 schools in California and found "Orientals" exceeded all other groups.[10] Since the publication of his book and in other studies, Jensen's work has been thoroughly criticized on many counts. One area of criticism focuses on the methodological flaws in Jensen's research in that he failed to consider important variables such as historical disadvantage, cultural bias, social class, and geography. Another area of criticism comes from Jensen's heavy reliance on IQ test scores that are generally acknowledged to be very ineffective and inconclusive measures of anything that could be considered innate intelligence.

Despite these criticisms, others have followed Jensen's research and tried to control for variables in hopes of presenting better evidence of genetically based intelligence. One of the most notable is Richard Lynn, from the University of Northern Ireland, whose research claims that Chinese, Japanese, and Koreans score higher on standardized IQ tests than whites. For example, in his article, "The Intelligence of Mongoloids: A Psychometric Evolutionary and Neurological Theory" (1987), Lynn cited a number of studies that confirmed his conclusions.[11] The one work that did not agree that Asians had a higher mean IQ score was a six-year study headed by University of Michigan psychologist, Harold Stevenson (1985). Stevenson and his colleagues' research is significant, however, because it carefully compared kindergarten, first-grade and fifth-grade students of similar socioeconomic backgrounds in three similar sized cities—Minneapolis, Sendai (Japan), and Taipei (Taiwan). "This study offers no support for the argument that there are differences in the general cognitive functioning of Chinese, Japanese, and American children," the authors wrote, "Positing general differences in cognitive functioning of Japanese and Chinese children is an appealing hypothesis for those who seek to explain the superiority of Japanese and Chinese children's scholastic achievement, but it appears from the present data that it will be necessary to seek other explanations for their success."[12]

The genetic superiority/inferiority debate has recently been rekindled with the publication of two controversial books, *Race, Evolution and Behavior* (1995), by J. Philippe Rushton, and *The Bell Curve* (1994), by Richard J. Herrnstein and Charles Murray. By far *The Bell Curve* has received the most media attention and critical response with its provocative assertions that (1) 60 percent of every individual's IQ is genetic in origin; (2) IQ is a reliable predictor for social, economic, and educational success or failure; (3) blacks have the lowest average on IQ tests; (4) it is unlikely that environmental factors can account for racial group differences in IQ; (5) any attempts to improve group performance on IQ tests by making environmental changes will fail.

While *The Bell Curve* focuses primarily on blacks and whites, the authors could not avoid studies that looked at Asian IQ scores. Herrnstein and Murray freely cite Lynn's studies that show Asians consistently have higher IQ scores than whites, but they are contradictory about what the findings really mean. On one hand, Herrnstein and Murray believe Asians "probably" have higher IQs because they tend to do better in "visual/spatial" versus verbal abilities. This is exaggerated for non–English-speaking immigrants but tends to be true even for Asian Americans who are monolingual English speakers. According to Herrnstein and Murray, this is why Asian immigrants and Asian Americans tend to abound in fields such as engineering, medicine, and the sciences, rather than literature, law, or politics. On the other hand, the authors acknowledged that the Asian/white IQ differences are small and any general comparisons are subject to error without proper controls. Within this, Herrnstein and Murray agreed with the work of Harold Stevenson that when you do control for socioeconomic differences, the distinctions between Asian and white IQ scores disappear.[13]

Overall, like the work of Arthur Jensen 20 years earlier, *The Bell Curve* created controversy but proved nothing. The book's faulty logic, overreliance on problematic studies, uncritical faith that IQ test scores equate to general intelligence, and ignorance of studies showing the important value of early educational intervention in raising educational performance and achievement levels are all pointed out in numerous reviews.[14] Innate ability is obviously an area of heated argument. A less controversial—and more accepted—reason why Asians and Asian Americans seem to perform well academically is quite simple: Asians work harder.

Data from a 1980 national survey of 58,000 students in 1,015 high schools conducted by the U.S. Department of Education that roughly half of the Asian American sophomores spend five or more hours per week on homework. Only about a third of the white students and a quarter of the black students put as much time into their education as Asian American students. In addition, the survey found that 45 percent of the Asian Americans said they never missed a day of school, and 42 percent said they were never late.[15] A follow-up survey of 25,000 eighth graders, their parents, teachers, and school administrators throughout the nation was conducted in the spring of 1988, and it came up with very similar results. Researchers Samuel S. Peng and DeeAnn Wright (1994) analyzed the follow-up information in detail and concluded that home environments and educational activities account in large part for the difference in student achievement between Asian Americans and other minority students. They found that Asian Americans were more likely to come from stable, two-parent home environments, spent more time at home doing their homework, and spent less time watching television. Asian Americans were also found to be involved in educational activities that are more conducive to learning outside of school (e.g., language, art, music), and took part in more educational activities (e.g., visiting the public library and going to

Table 3-2   Percentage or Average Score on Select Variables by Race/Ethnicity

Variable	Asian	Hispanic	Black	White	Native American
Demographics					
% living with both parents	79.4	65.2	38.8	68.2	53.5
% of parents with > BA+	22.2	5.5	5.5	13.9	4.2
% with income < $15,000	17.8	37.5	47.0	18.1	40.1
Discipline					
Hours per week doing homework	6.8	4.7	5.2	5.7	4.7
Hours per week watching TV	20.6	22.0	26.7	20.3	22.7
Additional Lessons/Activities					
% having outside lessons	65.6	44.6	45.1	61.6	42.6
% having outside activities	91.5	79.9	83.2	91.1	78.4
Educational Expectations/Pressure					
Number of years of education	16.70	15.25	15.24	15.32	15.11

Source: Samuel S. Peng and DeeAnn Wright, "Explanation of Academic Achievement of Asian American Students," *Journal of Educational Research* 87:6 (1994): 349, Table 2. Reprinted with permission of the Dwight Reed Educational Foundation. Published by Heldref Publications, 1319 Eighteenth St. N.W., Washington, DC 20036-1802.

museums) than other minority students. Lastly, Peng and Wright found that Asian American parental expectations were the highest of any other group. The average Asian American parents expected their child to complete 16.7 years of education, which means education beyond a baccalaureate degree. The researchers highlighted the fact that about 80 percent of Asian American parents expected their children to have at least a bachelor's degree compared with 62 percent of white, 58 percent of black, and only half of the Hispanic parents (see Table 3-2).[16]

Nurture/Culture

Studies show that Asian Americans do work harder, so the question now becomes *why* do Asian Americans work harder? A great deal of attention has been focused on Asian cultural values that places a high priority on education, hard work, and family honor as the main reason for Asian American academic success. Anthropologists William Caudill and George DeVos (1956) described how Japanese American students excelled in school, despite the overt prejudice and discrimination they faced during World War II. The authors attributed the strength and persistence of Japanese culture, as well as strong parental involvement, as the two main reasons for this phenomena. Similarly, sociologist Betty Lee Sung also expressed the importance of culture in academic success. "Chinese respect for learning and for the scholar is a cultural heritage," Sung writes in her book, *The Story of the Chinese in America* (1967). "Other minorities have not had the benefit of this reverence for learning."[17]

Research conducted by Nathan Caplan, Marcella H. Choy, and John K. Whitmore (1989, 1991) focused on recent Southeast Asian refugees, and their conclusions serve to further reinforce the cultural argument. The University of Michigan team surveyed 6,750 Vietnamese, Laotian, and Chinese-Vietnamese in five urban areas (Orange County, Seattle, Houston, Chicago, and Boston). The survey population represented the second wave of refugees from Southeast Asia and generally had limited exposure to Western culture, had virtually no English language proficiency, and often arrived in the United States with little more than the clothes on their backs. From the large sample, 200 nuclear families and their 536 school-age children were randomly chosen to be part of more intensive interviews.[18]

The researchers concentrated on the children's academic achievements, including grade point averages (GPA) and standardized test scores. Despite the fact that many of the Southeast Asian children faced traumatic situations leaving their home countries, faced language barriers, and often lived in poverty after they arrived in the United States, their grades and test scores were generally superior to other American students. It was found that 27 percent of the Southeast Asian immigrant students had an GPA in the A range, and 52 percent were in the B range. Just 17 percent of the GPAs were in the C range and only 4 percent had a GPA below a C. On standardized tests, 27 percent of the Asian immigrant students scored in the top ten in math.[19]

However, the researchers did not believe that the high GPAs and test scores occurred in a vacuum. Caplan, Choy, and Whitmore credit Asian cultural values that are deeply rooted in Confucian and Buddhist traditions for the success of Southeast Asian immigrant students. Central to these traditions, they argue, is the family. The researchers found that both the parents and the children have a strong sense of collective obligation to the entire family. One example the researchers cite is how homework time served as a mutually satisfying family affair in many of the Southeast Asian households studied. After dinner, the table is cleared and parents encourage their children to study. In most of these cases, older siblings helped younger siblings along with doing their own homework. The researchers were also impressed by the fact that Southeast Asian high school students spent an average of three hours and 10 minutes on their homework during the weeknights, while Southeast Asian junior high school students averaged two hours and five minutes of homework a day during the school week.[20]

Caplan, Choy, and Whitmore also found that Southeast Asian students seemed to have a high sense of completion gratification, which the researchers attribute to traditional Asian culture. At the same time, both the parents and children believed that learning came from hard work and effort, rather than from innate intelligence. This attitude differs considerably from findings in a 1992 U.S. Department of Education study, *Hard Work and High Expectations: Motivating Students to Learn.* The study concluded that most American students attributed academic achievement with intelligence and that success in school is easy if you are smart. Conversely, if you do not do well in school you must not be smart and, therefore, there is no use in trying. Most students said they preferred to be seen as smart rather than as hardworking because if you have to put a lot of effort into your work, it is a sign of being a slow learner.[21]

The cultural perspective is the most commonly cited and easy to understand reason for Asian American academic achievement. However, the cultural perspective does have its own controversial aspects. The most important is the logical extension in the cultural argument: If Asian Americans have the "right" cultural values, does it mean that other minority groups are culturally "deficient"? This prickly side of the cultural argument can be divided into two types. First, there is cultural deficiency based on *socioeconomic* status, known as the "culture of poverty." This was the thesis focused upon by Edward Banfield in his book, *The Unheavenly City* (1970), in which he argues that "lower class" culture includes having an extreme present-orientation rather than a future outlook on life, lack of self-discipline, and a heightened sense of hopelessness and powerlessness. People in this "culture" tend to do poorly in school, are unable to maintain steady employment, and live in poverty. While the culture of poverty may be a phenomena with a long history of prejudice and discrimination for some groups, this is not the center of Banfield's work.[22]

The other type of cultural deficiency argument is based on the idea that *certain groups* of people either lack the right kind of cultural values, or they accentuate the wrong parts of their culture, which would inhibit their social, economic, and educational mobility. A key proponent of this notion is prominent neoconservative African American economist Thomas Sowell. This argument was forwarded in his book, *Ethnic America* (1981), where he writes, "cultural inheritance can be more important than biological inheritance, although the latter is more controversial." In terms of education, for example, Sowell believes history shows that Chinese, Japanese, and Jews have different attitudes toward educational achievement than Mexicans, blacks, and Puerto Ricans. At the same time, some aspects of culture are best kept under wraps. He writes: "Some groups (such as Jews and the Japanese) have enjoyed and maintained their own special culture, but without making a public issue over it (as blacks and Hispanics have)." Although Sowell makes a point that cultures are neither "superior" or "inferior," he does believe they need to be flexible and appropriately adapted to different circumstances. Some cultural groups, according to Sowell, are more adept at this than others. Sowell's arguments have remained unchanged over the years and are highlighted in his more recent publication, *Race and Culture* (1994).[23]

Relative Functionalism

Attitudes and values are clearly emphasized within the cultural perspective, but is this enough to explain Asian American educational achievement? The cultural perspective has been criticized for being ahistorical, relying too heavily on stereotypes, and lacking in any acknowledgement of social context. With this in mind, two Asian American psychologists, Stanley Sue and Sumie Okazaki, have developed a third theoretical perspective they call "relative functionalism." Relative functionalism does not deny the influence of culture, but it does add other *structural* factors that also deserve attention. In their article, "Asian-American Educational Achievements: A Phenomenon in Search of an Explanation" (1990), Sue and Okazaki contend that Asian American educational achievement is a result of limited opportunities in noneducational areas. Within this, the greater the limitations in noneducational areas, the more important education becomes. This is particularly true for groups that are culturally oriented toward education and have a history of academic success.[24]

Relative functionalism takes a broad interdisciplinary approach to explain Asian American educational achievement and draws from the work of sociologist Stephen Steinberg, education specialist Bob Suzuki, and anthropologists John Ogbu and Maria Matute-Bianchi. Sue and Okazaki first cite from Steinberg's book, *The Ethnic Myth* (1981), because he significantly undermines the thesis that certain ethnic groups succeed because they possess innately superior cultural values. Steinberg argues that socioeconomic class factors in the home country, economic necessity, and historical accident in the new host country converge to move ethnic groups up or down the economic and educational ladder. In the chapter, "The Jewish Horatio Alger Story," Steinberg examines the Jewish experience in the United States in the 1880s during the industrial revolution.

Steinberg agrees that thousands of Eastern European Jews arrived in the United States materially poor. At the same time, however, many Jewish immigrants were literate and brought with them a variety of occupational skills that corresponded remarkably well to the needs of an expanding American economy. These factors gave Jewish immigrants an advantage over other immigrants in the labor market and in public school at the time. Steinberg asserts that literacy was a valuable asset for Jewish immigrants because (1) it facilitated the acquisition of a new language; (2) being literate obviously helped Jews enter into business and more lucrative occupations that required an ability to read and write; and (3) literacy provided an educational head start for Jewish children. "In terms of their European background, Jews were especially well equipped to take advantage of the opportunities they found in America," writes Steinberg. "It is this remarkable convergence of factors that resulted in an unusual record of success."[25]

This analogy parallels the situation for highly educated and skilled middle-class Asian American immigrant experience to the United States since 1965. In addition, the types of skills brought by Asian immigrants do tend to be science and technically oriented, which allow them the best opportunities for gainful employment and upward mobility in a highly competitive, postindustrial economy. This attention to education, and to professions that are in demand, does not go unnoticed in the children of immigrants.

With this idea as a foundation, Sue and Okazaki next refer to Bob Suzuki's provocative article, "Education and the Socialization of Asian Americans: A Revisionist Analysis of the 'Model Minority' Thesis" (1977), where he posits that Asian Americans pursue a narrow education and professional training because of their "status as a minority group." In other words, Asian Americans gravitate to quantitative fields such as engineering, medicine, and the sciences, because of their own perceived (whether conscious or not) limitations. These limitations may be language, in the case of Asian immigrants, or racial, as in the case for more assimilated Asian Americans. In short, Suzuki believes that Asian Americans excel in education because it will get them a better job, higher income, and status, and they would have difficulty in other avenues for advancement because of discrimination. Suzuki's thesis contradicts Herrnstein and Murray's argument that Asians and Asian Americans are genetically more inclined to enter the science and technical fields. Suzuki also challenges the widely accepted idea that Asian Americans do not face discrimination, have achieved middle-class status, and have almost completely assimilated into the American mainstream.[26]

But the fundamental question arises, "Why don't other racial minority groups adopt education as a means of socioeconomic mobility?" Sue and Okazaki confront this question by stating that different minority groups have different historical and contemporary experiences. It is here they cite the work of John Ogbu and Maria Matute-Bianchi (1986), who have forwarded the idea that individuals and groups develop "folk theories" of success. For example, it is generally assumed that if one works hard and gets a good education, one will get a good job and succeed. This belief, however, is not uniformly shared by everyone. Folk beliefs are influenced by a variety of factors such as past history of success, past history of discrimination, availability of successful role models, cultural values, and the like. As a result, some may develop a folk belief that "it doesn't matter how hard I work or how much education I receive, I will still be discriminated against." Sue and Okazaki contend that different racial minority groups have different folk beliefs about education. They cite the work of Roslyn Arlin Mickelson (1990), who found that African Americans generally believe in the importance of education, but they are less likely than whites to believe in the value of education in their own lives. Sue and Okazaki argue that the folk belief for Asian Americans may very well be: "If I study hard, I can succeed, *and* education is the best way to succeed" (emphasis theirs).[27] Sue and Okazaki's relative functionalism theory takes into consideration the complex factors of class (Steinberg), race (Suzuki), and socio-historical context (Ogbu and Matute-Bianchi) in their analysis of Asian American academic achievement.

Criticisms of Sue and Okazaki's relative functional theory was published in the August 1991 issue of the *American Psychologist*, including a sharp rebuttal by Richard Lynn. One writer, David Fox, from the California School of Professional Psychology and the Loma Linda University School of Medicine, even advanced a theory that Asians and Jews excel in education because their native languages are read and written from right to left. According to Fox, right-to-left writing leads to increased and flexible cerebral functioning that affects intellectual performance. Sue and Okazaki dismissed Fox's views as "speculative," highlighted many of the "problematic" assumptions of Lynn's genetic research, and maintained that relative functionalism is an "important consideration" in the debate over Asian American educational achievement.[28]

EDUCATIONAL ISSUES FACING ASIAN AMERICANS

Theoretical questions aside, the relative "success" of Asian Americans in education does give the impression that Asian Americans do not face any significant educational and personal issues. However, limited English proficiency, parental pressure and stress, and racial violence in school are three issues that are especially acute for Asian American students. These three issues impact all Asian Americans from all socioeconomic lines to some degree or another. Of course, limited English proficiency is particularly important to the increasing number of Asian immigrant students entering public schools across the country.

Limited English Proficiency (LEP)

As early as 1982 the U.S. Department of Education estimated there were 3.6 million school-aged limited English proficient (LEP) students across the nation. Another report projected a 35 percent increase in the number of LEP students by the year 2000.[29] Asian Americans are not the majority of LEP students in the United States, but because of the large influx of Southeast Asian refugees and continued immigration from Asia, there is an overrepresention of Asian American LEP students based on their percentage in the population. In California, for example, Asian Americans are less than 10 percent of the state's population, but already make up a third of the LEP students in the state.[30] The 1990 U.S. census figures show that 5.8 percent of Asian Americans between 5 and 17 years of age do not speak English "very well," while only about 1 percent of all Americans between 5 and 17 do not speak English "very well." Southeast Asian youngsters between 5 and 17 had by far the highest per-

Table 3-3 Asian Americans Between 5 and 17 Years of Age Who Do Not Speak English "Very Well"

Group	% Who Do Not Speak English "Very Well"
U.S.	1.0
Asian/Pacific Islander	5.7
Asian American	5.8
Chinese	5.8
Filipino	2.4
Japanese	2.5
Asian Indian	3.4
Korean	5.4
Vietnamese	12.3
Cambodian	23.9
Laotian	20.6
Hmong	35.9

Source: U.S. Bureau of the Census, *1990 Census of the Population, Asians and Pacific Islanders in the United States* (Washington, DC: Government Printing Office, 1993), CP-3-5, Table 3.

centage of not speaking English "very well" compared to the national average. A relatively high 12.3 percent of Vietnamese between 5 and 17 did not speak English "very well." This figure seems modest compared with the 35.9 percent of Hmong, 23.9 percent of Cambodians, and 20.6 percent of Laotians (see Table 3-3).

The most important legal precedent related to the rights of all LEP students goes back to the *Lau v. Nichols* (1974) U.S. Supreme court case. The case involved a San Francisco student, Kinney Lau, who was failing school because he could not understand the language of instruction. A class action lawsuit was filed in 1970 on behalf of Lau and about 1,800 other Chinese American students. At the time of the case, the San Francisco Unified School District was serving over 100,000 students, 16,574 of whom were Chinese American. Almost 3,000 Chinese American students in San Francisco were in need of special help in English, but the district only had fewer than two dozen remedial teachers who were fluent in both Cantonese and English. The suit originally lost in a federal district court but was appealed all the way to the U.S. Supreme Court. In 1974 the high court ruled unanimously to overturn the lower court's decision, finding that the San Francisco Unified School District failed to provide equal opportunity for LEP students. After the Lau decision, the impact on LEP students has been mixed. The primary problem has been inconsistent implementation and enforcement of programs intended to benefit immigrant students.[31]

Certainly there have been success stories of remarkable acquisition of English as a second language by some Asian American immigrant and refugee students. This was the case for A-Bo, who immigrated from Taiwan to San Jose, California, when she was 15 years old. She had been an exceptionally gifted student in her home country but was immediately placed in an English as a Second Language program because of her inability to read and write English. Fortunately, A-Bo was very well educated in all basic subjects prior to entering the United States, and she was able to learn very quickly. Her advanced knowledge of mathematics was obvious and she soon started helping her teacher solve problems. Within just one year she became quite comfortable in English and even joined the debate team. A-Bo's success can be explained by studies that show students with a strong educational background in their own primary language (speaking, reading, and writing) can more readily transfer that information, and this forms a solid foundation for learning a new language.[32]

This example, however, cannot be generalized and may be misleading because there is a great range of educational experience among Asian immigrant and refugee students, and their own abilities to acquire a second language. It is important to remember that not all Asian American immigrant children come from well-educated, urbanized, middle-class and above families, nor do all Asian Americans glide effortlessly through school. Indeed, many Asian American immigrant children, especially those who come from families at the lower end of the socioeconomic levels, face considerable educational and acculturation challenges throughout their educational careers. Nonetheless, many LEP students face tremendous struggles, whatever their backgrounds.

The case of Shia-chi is illustrative of this fact. Shia-chi was also 15 years old when she arrived in Los Angeles from Taiwan. Her parents were well-to-do owners of a clothing factory in Taipei who sent Shia-chi to live with an aunt in order to have a good education in the United States. Shia-chi was not an exceptional student in Taiwan, and her solo relocation to the United States only exacerbated her academic troubles and low self-esteem. Even though she took three years of English in Taiwanese school, Shia-chi was unable to speak, read, or write adequately enough and was unable to adjust to her new situation. She did attend English as a Second Language classes but continued to have difficulty mastering a new language. Although Shia-chi graduated from high school, she is considered "LEP-forever" and ill-prepared for the rigors of college, and lacks the language skills needed for meaningful employment.[33]

The situation for many recent Southeast Asian refugee LEP students is especially critical. Not only have they had to confront the traumas of leaving their home countries, many young recent refugees have had limited formal education in their home countries, or had their educations interrupted by long periods languishing in temporary relocation camps. Equally important is the fact that the sudden arrival of refugees to the United States caught public school officials completely unprepared. For example, in 1987 the state of California reported a need for 217 Cambodian bilingual teachers, but there were none to be found. As late as the 1990–1991 school year several local school districts were failing to meet the needs of refugee students, who were an increasingly large portion of their student population. In Fresno, California, several thousand Southeast Asian refugees have resettled and the school district was suddenly faced with a 19 percent Asian American student body. Roughly 80 percent of Fresno's Asian American students were classified as LEP, nearly all of them were Southeast Asian. During the 1990-1991 school year, nearly 10,000 Southeast Asian LEP students attended school without a certified bilingual teacher.[34]

Similar situations also occurred during the same time in Providence, Rhode Island, and Lowell, Massachusetts, two other locations where the numbers of Southeast Asian refugees grew rapidly. In Providence, approximately 12 percent of public school students were Asian American, 96 percent of whom were Southeast Asian. Across the district, there was not a single Southeast Asian ESL/bilingual education teacher or counselor to serve over 1,400 students. The case in the Lowell school district was only slightly better. Approximately 26 percent of Lowell's student population was Southeast Asian, but only 4 percent of the teachers were of Southeast Asian ancestry. The above cases, all cited in the U.S. Commission on Civil Rights 1992 report on Asian Americans, prompted a stern call for action. "Our investigation has revealed that these needs of Asian American LEP students are being dramatically underserved," the report stated. "They need professional bilingual/bicultural counseling services to help them in their social adjustment and academic development."[35]

Parental Pressure and Stress

The research of Peng and Wright cited earlier touched upon the fact that Asian American parents have higher academic expectations for their children compared with other parents. Although high expectations are important in encouraging excellence, excessive high expectations can create undue pressure and unhealthy levels of psychological and emotional stress on young students. One case involved a 17-year-old Korean high school student who was reportedly beaten by her father because her grade point average dropped below a perfect 4.0. The father was arrested for child abuse and pled not guilty.[36] This is an extreme example, of course, but several studies have shown many Asian American parents commonly express their displeasure when their children bring home anything less than a straight-A report card.[37] When one Asian American student showed her parents a report card with all A's except for one B, the parents focused only on the B grade and chastised their child for not working to work harder. The student became resentful of the fact that she brought home a report card of which any other parent would be proud.[38]

For many Asian American children growing up in traditional Asian families, filial piety—respect and obedience toward one's parents—is expected. Although more acculturated Asian American parents do allow their children greater independence and freedom than immigrant Asian parents, studies show that Asian American parents do tend to exercise more control over their children's lives than non-Asian parents. Parental control may extend as far as choosing what courses to take in school, what school they should go to, what their college major should be. In addition, Asian American parents are far more controlling of their children's social lives. A 1992 survey of high school seniors found only 40 percent of Asian American students dated at least once a week, compared with 64 percent of whites, 52 percent of blacks, and 58 percent of Hispanics.[39] Asian American parents use guilt and shame rather than physical abuse to keep their children in line and to reinforce the fact that their children have strong obligations to the family. Their children often feel extremely self-critical and alienated when they fail in their parents' eyes.[40] In some cases, young Asian Americans become so distraught they may attempt suicide. This is what happened to young Paula Yoo, whose parents saved her just before she slit her wrists with a razor blade. "I wasn't class valedictorian and yes, I flunked calculus," Yoo wrote in a very personal essay published in *A Magazine*. "I was stupid because I didn't make all A's. I was absolutely convinced I was destined for failure."[41]

Conversely, Asian American parents feel extremely responsible for their children's success in school and in their future careers. Their children's successful academic achievements are a direct reflection of their own parenting abilities. If their children do well in school, then they have been good parents; if their children do poorly in school, then the parents are to blame because they didn't do enough. A volatile situation may erupt when the young student's desires do not match his or her parents' high and sometimes rigid expectations. A good example of this can be seen in Audrey Teoh's experience after she told her father she didn't want to study engineering like he wanted her to. After a heated argument, Teoh's flustered father finally said, "You have given up!" She sadly recalls the way her father said those words "just made me feel so small." For his part, Teoh's father believes his "lifetime of experience" gives him the right to tell his daughter what is best for her. At the same time, the episode did leave Mr. Teoh very distraught. He asks, "Was I too strict on my children? Do I overreact? I really have no reference by which to compare my child-rearing methods, and I will never really know for sure what I'm doing is right."[42]

Some Asian American parents not only will pressure their children to excel in school, but also may go through extreme hardships to ensure the very best educational opportunities. One Chicago-area study found more than eight out of ten Asian American parents said they would sell their house and give up their own future financial security to support their children's education. Only three out of ten white parents were willing to make this sacrifice.[43] In Fullerton, California, Sunny Hills High School is recognized as one of the truly elite public schools in the United States. The school has been nicknamed "high pressure high" and is known for its zero dropout rate, the fact that students compete for A+ grades, and as a place where all-night study sessions are considered a badge of honor. Sunny Hills High has also seen a dramatic increase of Asian American students in recent years. In 1985, whites represented 72 percent of the student population, while Asian Americans represented 18 percent. Today, the Asian American student population at Sunny Hills High is around 50 percent, while the white population has declined to 40 percent. Korean Americans are the largest Asian ethnic group at Sunny Hills, and many Korean parents pay a steep price—sometimes as high as $1 million—to buy a home within Sunny Hills' boundaries. Other parents are known to stay in Korea but send their children to live in Fullerton and attend the school. Still other parents borrow addresses from people who live within the district in order to make their children eligible. "There are Korean parents here who don't even speak English but know the SAT (Scholastic Aptitude Test) cutoff to get into Stanford," exclaims astonished English teacher, Kimberley Stein. "When I was in high school, my parents didn't even know what the SAT was."[44]

Asian American parents not only sacrifice but also are willing to fight for their children's education. In San Francisco, an extremely contentious situation emerged at the city's academic preparatory school, Lowell High. Lowell High School was founded in 1856 and is the oldest public high school west of the Mississippi River. Lowell High is also the only public school in San Francisco where students must pass a rigorous test in order to be enrolled. In 1978, the National Association for the Advancement of Colored People (NAACP) sued the San Francisco Unified School District (SFUSD), charging racial segregation. A U.S. district judge issued a consent decree in 1983 after an agreement was reached between the two parties that no ethnic group exceed more than 45 percent of enrollment at any one school. Chinese American parents long denounced the enrollment cap because it forced a limit on the number of Chinese American students who could go to Lowell High. Since 1978, the Chinese American student population has grown to 25 percent of the SFUSD, which makes it the largest single racial group in the district and an important constituency to reckon with. Chinese American parents became especially outraged in 1993 when they learned that higher entrance standards were placed on their children applying to Lowell relative to other groups. The initial plan required Chinese American students to score 66 out of 69 points on a scale that was based on a combination of grade point average and standardized test scores in order to gain admission to the school. Meanwhile, 59 was the cutoff score for whites, and 56 for African Americans and Hispanics. The following year, the Chinese American Democratic Club (CADC) filed a class action lawsuit against the California Board of Education and the San Francisco Unified School District challenging the 1983 consent decree.[45]

The lawsuit created a firestorm of debate within the Chinese American community. On one hand, Roland Quan, vice president of the Chinese American Democratic Club, argued that the admission criteria for all students should be based solely on merit; that simply means those with the highest point totals should be accepted to Lowell High regardless of race. "Opportunities and success based on individual dedication and hard work are the hallmark of America," Quan said. "Unfortunately, the public education system in this country sets its standard at mediocrity."[46] On the other hand, long-time civil rights activist, Henry Der, looked beyond the issue of individual merit and standard test scores. "Chinese Americans are too hung up on these basic-skills test scores," he argued. "(T)he difference between a student who scores a 59 and another who scores a 64 is practically negligible. There's nothing magical about these point scores. . . . There's such an inordinate amount of pressure being placed on these Chinese kids by their parents to get into Lowell that when they get rejected, they feel so debased."[47]

Der prefers to focus attention on the broader issue of educational fairness and equity in a society stratified by both race *and* class. He contends that a strict merit-based system serves only to perpetuate inequality among students who are forced to attend inferior schools, who have limited English skills, and who are poor. Der conducted a study of the Chinese students in San Francisco and found that three quarters of Chinese applicants to Lowell High School in 1993 lived in the most affluent parts of San Francisco. Der contends these students have more options in terms of school choice, access to alternative schools, and associations with high-achieving students than most other students. "Asian Americans can and should acknowledge internal class differences that impede low-income Asian Americans from achieving success," Der writes. "To the extent that low-income Asian students are bused or assigned to other low-income racial minority schools, the educational needs of all low-income racial minorities deserve the highest public priority and diverse set of remedies."[48]

The arguments of both Quan and Der were apparently taken into consideration when the San Francisco school board voted in a new admission policy for Lowell High School. In February 1996, the city school board voted unanimously to use a single cutoff score of 63 out of 69 be applied to all ethnic groups beginning in the 1996–1997 school year. However, in order to comply with court-monitored desegregation, the new policy allows for up to 30 percent of the incoming class to be reserved for low-income students. Students in this group will be allowed to enter Lowell even if they score less than

63 points, but no student will be admitted if they score below 50. The new admissions policy at Lowell High is generally acknowledged to be a compromise offer, and not everyone is completely happy. Roland Quan of the CADC complemented the board for moving "in the right direction," but made it clear that his organization, which represents the parents suing the school district, will continue on with their lawsuit.[49]

The stress created by parental pressure is significant, but it is by no means the only source of conflict for Asian Americans in school. Another cause comes from the school environment itself. This leads to the third major educational issue facing Asian Americans. A major survey of eighth-, tenth-, and twelfth-grade students in 1992 found a high percentage of Asian Americans students did not feel safe in school and often witnessed fights between different racial/ethnic groups. Just under 16 percent of Asian American students surveyed did not feel safe in school. This figure is second only to black students (16.1 percent), but is higher than Hispanics (14.7 percent) and whites (8.6 percent). Over 30 percent of Asian American students often witnessed fights between different racial/ethnic groups, which was second only to Hispanics (31.9 percent), but higher than blacks (22.2 percent) and whites (20.9 percent).[50]

Racial Tensions and Violence in Schools

Daily verbal and physical clashes have, unfortunately, become a part of life for many Asian American youngsters. Although anti-Asian sentiment and violence will be covered in greater detail in Chapter 5, special attention on racial tension and violence in schools is placed here. Because Asian Americans are racially different, sometimes speak with an accent, are viewed as perpetual foreigners, and are seen as clannish overachievers by jealous schoolmates, they have become targets of harassment and bigotry. Incidents occur against immigrant and U.S.-born Asian Americans, and in crowded inner-city schools as well as in seemingly secure suburban schools. Glen Chun, an 18-year-old fourth-generation Chinese American, was accosted by a group of teenagers from the same high school that he attended. Chun was called a "gook" and told to "go back to where you came from," then was chased and beaten to the ground. The incident took place in Marin County, California, a woodsy, upscale middle-class area most known for its liberal attitudes and location just north of San Francisco. Chun was not seriously hurt—a sprained wrist, bruises and cuts on his face—but he was clearly shaken by the event. He claimed there was "no provocation" on his part, and he could not recall any other racial incidents except, "I did hear racial slurs like 'chink' during my junior year."[51]

As part of a May 1995 Asian Pacific Heritage month celebration, students were asked to write an essay entitled, "Growing Up Asian in America." One of the winning essays was written by Vinesh Viswanathan, 11, from Redwood Middle School in Saratoga, California, another middle-class suburban community. Viswanathan wrote about how he used to be bullied in school because he was "humble and meek." Fortunately, he was able to find a friend who was willing to stand up for him. But Viswanathan recalled one night after dinner watching the television program, *The Simpsons,* when one of the characters made fun of the Hindu god, Ganesh, because of his elephant head. "This provided my classmates a good weapon to use to ridicule me the following day at school," Viswanathan recalled. "I was so depressed that I came home complaining to my mom about how unfair life is." He ended his essay with a plea for television producers not to insult minorities' ways of life, heritage, or religious beliefs.[52]

Incidents of taunting and fighting are frequently dismissed by school administrators either because of their insensitivity, or because they do not want to raise the specter of serious racial problems on their campuses. This was the case for Betty Waki, an Asian American teacher at Sharpstown Senior High School in Houston, who was shocked when she received material filled with racist and anti-Asian remarks. She promptly reported the incident to the principal, who suspended the two students found responsible for three days. But the students' parents appealed the punishment to the district superintendent, who reduced the principal's suspension and ordered the two students be placed on four-hour detention and assigned them to write a 300-word essay.[53]

Often incidents like this are dismissed as just a "prank" by school and local government authorities, or as a "phase" by the parents of the offenders. Because of this, communities have found that it sometimes takes a major organizing effort to force change away from entrenched denial by school administrators and some parents. A fight between two Chinese American brothers and at least 10 Latino students at San Gabriel High School in Alhambra, California, a suburb of Los Angeles, sparked months of activities aimed at raising attention to racial conflicts in school. A group of 225 Asian American students from San Gabriel High signed a petition denouncing the incident and claiming that they were often victims of harassment. The Los Angeles County District Attorney's office initially declined to file any criminal charges in the incident, but the case was reinvestigated due to pressure by the Chinese American Parents and Teachers Association (CAPTA) and Los Angeles County Supervisor, Mike Antonovich. Four students were eventually charged with two counts of misdemeanor battery on school property.[54]

Over the next several months, more violent episodes erupted, including fights, a shooting, and a stabbing. Alarmed Asian American and Latino leaders held meetings and rallies to raise attention to the problems of racial tensions on campus. Although some school board members denied any problem existed, representatives of the Chinese American Parents and Teachers Association and the League of United Latin American Citizens (LULAC) would not be appeased. The two groups demanded improvements in multicultural education and the promotion of Asian Americans and Latinos to high-ranking district positions. "It is historic that Asians and Latinos are getting together at the grass-roots level," said Jose Calderon, a father of two sons in the Alhambra School District. Calderon rejected claims by school administrators that the fights were due to the "machismo" of the students and charged there was a "real separation" between Latino and Asian students in the school.[55] If these matters are allowed to continue without intervention by school administrators and parents, Asian American students may decide to take matters into their own hands. This was seen in a recent incident at Arcadia High School, not far from San Gabriel High. In this case, six Asian American students were arrested on assault charges after a fight with several white students. *The Los Angeles Times* reported that a "bounty" had been placed on the heads of the white students in retaliation for allegedly beating up an Asian American student sometime earlier.[56]

The above recent incidents confirm what was highlighted in three of the most often cited studies on immigrant students in public schools. The research of John Willshire Carrea (1988), Laurie Olsen (1988), and Ruben G. Rumbaut and Kenji Ima (1988) all found racial and ethnic hostility, as well as anti-immigrant sentiment, to be a part of the social environment in many schools and communities.[57] Although most of the abuse toward immigrants is from other students, sometimes teachers also openly express their antagonism and bigotry. In addition, there are serious conflicts between native-born and foreign-born students of the same racial and/or ethnic group. American-born Asian Americans often look down upon, and want to disassociate themselves from, immigrant "FOB" (fresh off the boat) students. The immigrants, of course, are not immune nor ignorant of these attitudes around them. "Almost every student in our sample reported the first school year included incidents of being called names, pushed or spat upon, deliberately tricked, teased and laughed at because of their race, language difficulties, accent or foreign dress," Olsen writes. "Comments like, 'they look down at us,' 'they think we are going to take over,' 'they wish we'd go back where we came from,' or 'they think we are taking their jobs and money' were most common."[58]

These sentiments are very much related to what was the most horrific example of racial violence against Asian Americans in schools. This incident, however, did not come from another student or a teacher. It came from an outside intruder wearing military camouflage clothing and armed with an AK-47 style assault rifle, who opened fire into a schoolyard full of children in Stockton, California. On the morning of Tuesday January 17, 1989, a day after the Martin Luther King, Jr. holiday, Edward Patrick Purdy came to the Cleveland Elementary School and shot off 105 rounds into a playground filled with children on recess break. Five children were shot and killed, and 31 others were wounded. Of the children who died, the oldest was 9 and the youngest was 6. Five of the children were Cambodian and one was Vietnamese. After a few minutes of mayhem, Purdy heard police sirens rushing to the scene. He then dropped his rifle, pulled out a 9-mm pistol, and killed himself with a single shot in the head.[59]

For several years prior to the killings, the city of Stockton witnessed a large increase in the number of Southeast Asian refugees. At the time of the shooting, about one out of six residents in Stockton were born in Southeast Asia, making it one of the highest proportions of Southeast Asian refugees in the country. The Cleveland Elementary School's enrollment was over 70 percent Southeast Asian and was a reflection of the broader changes in the community. An October 1989 report to the California State Attorney General concluded that Purdy "focused a particular dislike on Southeast Asians," and the selection of Cleveland Elementary School for the site of the attack was not a random choice. Indeed, Purdy had once attended Cleveland Elementary School, which was by 1989 "dominated by Southeast Asian children, the offspring of those who were the current target of his resentment."[60]

The Stockton schoolyard killings are an extreme example of how anti-immigrant and anti-Asian resentments infiltrate into the primary and secondary schools. Unfortunately, the same types of attitudes have also reached deep into higher education in both overt and covert ways. Foremost among them have been concerns of alleged quotas against Asian American applicants to the most elite and prestigious college campuses in the country.

BACKLASH IN HIGHER EDUCATION

In March, 1992, a small group of Asian American students at Pomona College, an expensive and exclusive liberal arts college in Claremont, California, unveiled a banner that read: "Asian American Studies Now!" That evening, under the cover of darkness, the banner was defaced and altered to read: "Asian Americans die Now!" This message of hate shook the tiny campus and, in one swift move, undermined six years of work by Asian American students to bring an Asian American perspective to the college community and into the general curriculum. This incident is indicative of a backlash that had been brewing against the increasingly conspicuous presence of Asian Americans on college campuses throughout the United States for several years.

Another notable incident occurred in December 1987 at the University of Connecticut (UConn) when four Asian American couples boarded a bus to attend a formal dance. The couples were humiliated by taunts and threats, and were spat upon, by a rowdy group of four male students sitting in the back of the bus throughout the ride. Two of the students reported the terrible episode to campus police, university administration, and the local law enforcement authorities, but felt they were given the "run around." The incident was given attention only when the two students threatened to contact the press. Eventually, one of the offending students was expelled from the school for one year. The other student, a star football player, was mildly punished and was still allowed to play for the football team. The handling of the case so enraged Asian Americans on campus that one Asian American faculty member, Paul Bock, staged a one-person demonstration at UConn's commencement in May 1988 holding a picket sign reading, "Please Reduce Institutional Racism at UConn." Professor Bock also held an eight-day hunger strike to draw attention to what he felt was continuing anti-Asian sentiment on campus.[61]

Bock later resigned his position at UConn and formed the Asian American Council of Connecticut. In 1990 Bock filed a complaint with the U.S. Department of Education's Office of Civil Rights (OCR), charging that Connecticut illegally excluded Asian Americans and American Indians from a program to recruit and retain minority students and faculty. The OCR ruled in Bock's favor in 1993, and the Connecticut Board of Governors for Higher Education agreed to comply with recommended changes. Asian American leaders across the nation applauded the OCR's ruling, and said the decision sets an important precedent against many colleges that exclude Asian Americans for stereotypical reasons. "Connecticut had the worst record against Asian Americans in higher education of any state," Bock said.[62]

Alleged Quotas in Higher Education

Elite universities and colleges across the nation have historically welcomed a small number of the most privileged young people from Asian countries. The goal of these foreign students was to obtain the best education available and return to their home countries as government officials, educators, business, military, and church leaders. Following World War II, many foreign graduate students in the United States, especially those studying in science and engineering fields, chose to stay in this country because of the opportunities for gainful employment in industry and in research universities. Their skills were in great demand during the Cold War era competition with the then Soviet Union. Since the late 1970s, Asian Americans have made tremendous inroads into the most prestigious centers of post-secondary education. Today, Asian Americans make up less than 3 percent of the U.S. population, but they are more than 5 percent of all college students in the United States. This makes Asian Americans the only major racial group to be overrepresented in college relative to its general population (see Table 3-4). In some of the nation's finest institutions of higher education, the percentage of Asian Americans is very high relative to the national average. At Harvard University, for example, Asian Americans made up 18 percent of the undergraduate population in 1996. In California, where Asian Americans represent almost 10 percent of the state's population, the percentage of Asian American undergraduate enrollment is even more impressive. As early as 1981 Asian Americans at the University of California, Berkeley, represented 21.5 percent of the undergraduate class, while whites represented 65.0 percent of the class. By 1996, the scale was tipped and Asian Americans made up 40 percent of the undergraduates at UC Berkeley compared to 31 percent white.

Table 3-4   Enrollment in Institutions of Higher Education by Race/Ethnicity, 1993

Group	% Enrollment	% of U.S. Population
White	75.5	75.6
Black	10.7	12.1
Hispanic	7.6	8.5
Asian Am.	5.3	2.9
Native Am.	0.9	0.8

Sources: National Center for Education Statistics, *Digest of Educational Statistics 1995* (Washington, DC: U.S. Department of Education, Office of Research and Improvement, 1995) Table 201 and U.S. Bureau of the Census, 1*990 Census of the Population Characteristics, United States Summary* (Washington, DC: Government Printing Office, 1993), CP-1-1, Table 3.

Despite these seemingly positive statistics, it was not long ago that American-born Asian students confronted subtle discrimination policies that had the very real effect of limiting their numbers and participation. A major controversy erupted in 1983 when the Asian American Students Association at Brown University (AASA) issued a statement claiming "a prima facie case of racial discrimination against Asian Americans."[63] The primary focus of the group's charge was the clear decline in the admissions rate of Asian American applicants to Brown relative to the university as a whole. The AASA had been monitoring Brown University admissions since 1979 and was deeply disturbed by several findings. Chief among them was the fact that in 1975 the admit rate for Asian Americans at Brown was 44 percent, but by 1983 the admit rate for Asian Americans was just 14 percent. During this same period, the number of Asian Americans applying to Brown increased eight and a half times. The AASA's report also found that Asian American and white applicants were comparable in their academic qualifications, and saw no reason to "justify such a drastic decrease in the admit rate."[64]

Across the country, UC Berkeley professor L. Ling-chi Wang happened to be scanning the university's fall 1984 admissions figures and was taken aback by what he saw. To his surprise, Wang found that the absolute numbers of first-year Asian Americans dropped from 1,303 in 1983 to 1,031 in 1984. This drop of 21 percent was quite an anomaly considering the numbers and percentages of Asian American freshmen at Berkeley had been rising steadily for several years, and this was projected to continue through 1990. Wang began casually reviewing admissions figures after attending several meetings in which disparaging comments were made about the number and quality of Asian American students at UC Berkeley. "I began to feel very uncomfortable that all these people from different departments are saying things about

Asians," Wang admitted. "(S)ome English department professor said that we should do something about these Asian students who are really deficient in the English language."[65] What began as an uneasy feeling quickly gathered momentum and became one of the most heated controversies in higher education in years.

Soon the specter of quotas against Asian Americans spread across the country. "I don't want to say it was a conspiracy, but I think all of the elite universities in America suddenly realized they had what used to be called a 'Jewish problem' before World War II, and they began to look for ways of slowing down the admissions of Asians," Wang told the *New York Times*. "As soon as admissions of Asian students began reaching 10 or 12 percent, suddenly a red light went on."[6] The "Jewish problem" Wang refers to is the restrictive quotas placed on Jewish Americans at a number of elite colleges and universities from the 1920s through to the 1950s. During this period of time, the percentage of Jewish admissions dropped and even the most qualified Jews were excluded from faculty positions in higher education. As greater media attention began to focus on the Asian American admissions issue in the mid-1980s, universities such as Yale, Princeton, Cornell, Stanford, UCLA, among others, came under close scrutiny and even federal investigation.

Not surprisingly, no university admitted to any conscious wrongdoing or deliberate quotas against Asian Americans. However, Brown University acknowledged a "serious problem," and Stanford found "unconscious bias." In 1989, UC Berkeley chancellor, Ira Michael Heyman, publicly apologized for admissions policies that caused a decline in Asian American undergraduate enrollments. "It is clear that decisions made in the admissions process indisputably had a disproportionate impact on Asians," Heyman said to a gathering of Asian American leaders. "That outcome was the product of insensitivity. I regret that occurred."[67] In 1993 UCLA was cleared of any wrongdoing by the U.S. Department of Education's Office of Civil Rights, but the school was ordered to offer admission to five Asian Americans students who were unfairly denied entrance into the Mathematics Department.[68] Investigations at Ivy League schools like Harvard and Princeton found admission rates for whites were indeed higher than for Asian Americans. The differences, however, were not interpreted as bias. In both cases, the lower admission rate for Asian Americans was due primarily to high admission rates to legacy students (children of alumni) and athletes, which are not illegal. Harvard and Princeton argued that legacy privileges are necessary because they serve the institutional goal of obtaining financial and service support from alumni.

A report from the U.S. Department of Education, Office for Civil Rights agreed that if children of alumni are rejected by Harvard, alumni "affection" with the college may decline. If children of alumni were admitted, however, alumni "involvement" will be "renewed." This relationship is deemed crucial to a private, tuition-driven institution of higher education. The discrepancy between white and Asian American admits to Harvard was not extremely high, but did vary from year to year. For example, in 1983 the admission rates ranged from just 1.8 percent higher for whites (16.9 percent) than for Asian Americans (15.1 percent), to 6.3 percent higher for whites (17.6 percent) than for Asian Americans (11.3 percent) in 1990. However, admissions differences between whites and Asian Americans disappeared at Harvard when legacies and athletes were removed from the statistical analysis. These findings were verified in the research work of Stephen S. Fujita and Marilyn Fernandez (1995) using a rigorous and sophisticated statistical analysis.[69]

An even more dramatic case of special privileges given to children of alumni occurred at Princeton University. Between 1981 and 1985 the admission rate for legacy students at Princeton was approximately 48 percent, compared with a 17 percent overall admission rate for whites and 14 percent rate for Asian Americans. A 1985 internal student–faculty investigation at Princeton found in four out of the five years between 1981 and 1985 Asian American applicants were rated higher than whites in terms of academic qualifications, but were rated "below average" in terms of the school's nonacademic criteria (legacy, athletics, affirmative action, extracurricular activities). Like most elite private universities, Princeton based its admission decisions not only on objective factors like grades and test scores but also on subjective and arbitrary factors, which, again, are not illegal and not deemed as an indicator of bias.[70]

Problems with Subjectivity

How poorly do Asian Americans rate in terms of the "subjective," nonacademic criteria? In their article "Diversity or Discrimination? Asian Americans in College," John H. Bunzel and Jeffrey K. D. Au (1987) cited one study of 30,000 Asian American and white high school sophomores and 28,000 seniors that found minimally lower participation differences in sports and artistic activities among Asian Americans and whites. For varsity athletics, the participation rates of Asian Americans was 30 percent compared to 34 percent for whites. Similarly, 9 percent of Asian Americans participated in debating and drama, compared to 13 percent of whites. At the same time, Asian Americans tended to participate more than whites in other extracurricular activities like honorary clubs, school newspapers, and specific subject matter clubs (i.e., science club, math club, history club, French club, etc.). This was also the case for participation in social, ethnic, and community organizations. Bunzel and Au concluded there was no evidence to "support the common stereotype that Asian Americans have significantly lower rates of participation in extracurricular activities than do Caucasians."[71] This conclusion is confirmed in a more recent survey of high school seniors that found Asian Americans are, indeed, quite active in school and community-related extra-curricular activities (see Table 3-5).

Table 3-5   Percent of High School Seniors in Extracurricular Activities by Race/
Ethnicity, 1992

Activity	White	Black	Hispanic	Asian	Native American
Athletics					
Inter scholastic team sport	30.8	32.3	25.8	28.3	30.4
Inter scholastic ind. sport	20.9	21.2	14.9	21.6	20.7
Intermural team sport	22.3	25.8	20.8	24.9	27.9
Intermural ind. sport	12.5	16.7	14.0	14.7	18.2
Performance					
Cheerleading	7.4	10.6	6.7	5.1	11.9
Band/ Orchestra	19.6	24.4	16.9	17.7	16.8
Play/Musical	16.1	15.9	10.6	13.7	14.0
School					
Student gov.	15.4	16.7	14.7	14.6	14.3
Honor society	19.6	14.0	12.5	27.2	13.6
Yearbook/ Newspaper	19.7	14.3	16.8	18.9	21.2
Service clubs	13.6	13.6	14.4	19.3	11.6
Academic clubs	25.8	20.7	22.6	32.3	17.7
Community					
Religious	31.4	33.7	26.9	30.4	14.6
Youth groups	22.5	23.3	18.5	26.4	22.1
Community Service	11.1	12.1	10.9	14.0	9.2

Source: National Center for Education Statistics, *Digest of Educational Statistics ,1995* (Washington DC: U.S. Department of Education, Office of Research and Improvement, 1995) Tables 140 and 142.

Bunzel and Au's report also found other forms of racial stereotyping against Asian Americans by some university officials. Comments like Asian Americans lack an appreciation for a "well-rounded liberal education," were made. Bunzel and Au heard statements like Asian Americans lack an interest in "public service," indicating a perception of greater selfishness and career-orientation among Asian Americans compared to whites, which is not confirmed in the survey cited above. When Bunzel and Au asked administrators why Asian American admission rates tend to be so low, the frequent response was that Asian Americans were an "overrepresented minority" relative to their national population. Within this, admissions officers also acknowledge that "diversity" on their campuses was an important goal. This line of thinking is dangerous for three reasons. First and foremost, this statement shows an obvious ignorance of the tremendous social, economic, and ethnic diversity among Asian Americans, which has already been detailed in this and in earlier chapters.

Second, the notions of diversity and overrepresentation are selectively applied against Asian Americans. For example, there was never any talk about limiting the numbers of children of alumni at elite private universities such as Harvard or Princeton, even though they represent only a small percentage of the U.S. population. The Asian American Students Association at Brown University directly confronted this stereotype in its original 1983 report: "(T)ry limiting the number of alumni sons and daughters in the University to their overall national representation. The point here is not that we wish to cut (the number of) alumni children, but that this argument which Brown used to justify limiting acceptance of Asian Americans is invalid and inconsistent. . . . Indeed, such an argument for limiting admissions to reflect the national population levels only reinforces the idea that there exists an unwritten quota for Asian Americans at Brown."[72]

Third, and easily most controversial, conservative politicians and pundits saw the admissions controversy as a convenient vehicle to dismantle liberal affirmative action policies. Conservatives argued that admissions policies should be based only on merit, and framed the issue as Asian Americans fighting against blacks and Hispanics over limited space in the nation's most prestigious universities. "(A)ffirmative action discriminated against Asian-Americans by restricting the social rewards open to competition on the basis of merit," wrote conservative political columnist, George Will. "(I)t is lunatic to punish Asian-Americans for their passion to excel."[73] This argument may seem persuasive at face value, and is precisely the same argument used by Chinese American parents in the Lowell High School controversy in San Francisco. However, Asian American leaders in higher education flatly rejected eliminating affirmative action, and rejected the idea that the issue was a competition between racial minority groups. They said the real issue was that changes in, and subjective interpretations of, admission policies at various universities were used primarily to benefit whites. "I am not opposed to the use of additional criteria to bring in promising students, especially those who were currently underrepresented," wrote L. Ling-chi Wang. "(But) the admission of larger numbers of whites under various color-blind, but protected, categories in fact account for the disparity between white and Asian American students at UC-Berkeley and other elite private institutions."[74]

By the early 1990s admissions policies at many college and university campuses were reviewed and changed in response to challenges raised by Asian Americans. Constant vigilance must be maintained, however, to prevent any repeat of past problems. "If Asian American admissions should suddenly rise at a university," concluded Bunzel and Au, "it would be essential for all to understand that such an increase is not the result of 'unfair advantages' being given to Asian Americans, but rather the effect of unfair disadvantages being removed."[75]

Broad Enrollment Trends in Higher Education

Although the focus of this section has been on the rights of Asian American students in elite universities, it is important to remember that many Asian Americans do not fit the model minority stereotype. Indeed, many Asian Americans are from poor and working-class backgrounds who must struggle for access to a basic college education necessary to survive in a competitive job market. Their road is far afield from the students in elite institutions of higher education described above. For example, the San Francisco Bay Area has one of the largest concentrations of Asian Americans and is the location of two of the most prestigious universities in the United States. But while Asian American enrollments are high at both UC Berkeley and Stanford universities, they pale compared to City College of San Francisco (CCSF)

CCSF is a two-year community college that serves 86,000 full-time and part-time students through an associate of arts program and the city's adult education system. About half of the students at CCSF are Asian American. Lower-income students are drawn to the publicly funded community college that charges only about $50 per academic semester. Students are most interested in attaining general education credits to transfer to a four-year college, obtaining job training or retraining, and learning English as a Second Language (ESL). In fact, the largest single block of Asian American students are enrolled in ESL classes.[76] According to the latest available figures from the California Post Secondary Education Commission, there are far more Asian American students in the Community College system, and in the California State University system, relative to the University of California system (see Table 3-6). A recent special report on Asian Americans in the California State University system (CSU) also highlighted the need to address ESL needs of immigrant students. "While the issue of ESL support for students is a major concern on all CSU campuses, response to the needs of ESL students are just being initiated on many campuses and have not yet been addressed by others," the report states. "With notable exceptions, campuses of the CSU have not approached the language skill needs of immigrant students in a systematic manner that reflects the increased presence and importance of these students in the CSU."[77] The high numbers of immigrant students entering the CSU with limited English proficiency is very much related to the lack of programs in K–12 to help these students improve their English language skills. Other serious issues raised by the CSU report included problems in campus climate and racial harassment, the need to diversify and incorporate multi-

Table 3-6   Total College in Enrollment in California Public Colleges and Universities*
by System and Race/Ethnicity, Fall 1995

Group	University of California	California State University	Community Colleges
White	71,421	143,448	493,497
Black	6,548	20,674	73,040
Hispanic	19,967	57,019	209,191
Asian Am.	48,328	58,321	156,809
Native Am.	1,496	3,360	12,832
Other	2,610	8,376	16,582
Nonresident	6,699	9,803	48,066
No Response	6,737	24,975	40,594
Total	163,704	325,976	1,050,611

* Includes full-time, part-time, and graduate students. Does not include enrollment in private, independent, or proprietary institutions.
Source: California Postsecondary Education Commission, May 7, 1996.

cultural and international perspectives into the curriculum, the need to examine the underrepresentation of Asian American faculty and administrative/management positions, and the need for greater outreach to, and retention of, underrepresented Asian American groups.

In his article, "Trends in Admissions for Asian Americans in College and Universities" (1993), L. Ling-chi Wang finds these enrollment patterns to be representative of the socioeconomic realities within the Asian American population, and the class hierarchies present in higher education. That is, students from upper-middle-class and above families tend to be drawn to the elite public and private universities. More often than not, students from poor, working-, and middle-class backgrounds head for the options that best suit their academic abilities, career aspirations, and their family's financial abilities to pay.[78]

CONCLUSION

This chapter has shown that the superachieving Asian Americans in education is a prominent but superficial image that needs to be analyzed in much more detail. Attention to Asian American "whiz kids" continues today, and is still drawing as much scorn as it draws praise. In May 1996, the owner of the Cincinnati Reds baseball team, Marge Schott, made negative remarks about

Asian American students published in an issue of *Sports Illustrated*. Schott said she didn't like "those Asian kids," because "they come here . . . and stay so long and then outdo our kids. That's not right."[79] Schott was soon banned from baseball for two years for this and other statements, including compliments to Adolf Hitler. Schott's indiscreet comments were obviously ignorant, but they may be reflective of what many people believe: Asian American students are perpetual foreigners, all of whom excel in school, and they are a threat to "our" kids. Various degrees of this belief have been acted upon, as witnessed in the racial violence and antagonism against Asian Americans in schools, and in the complicated enrollment controversies involving Asian American students at the high school and university levels.

This chapter focused on a variety of important educational issues facing Asian Americans from primary school to postsecondary education that runs counter to Schott's assertions. The success of Asian Americans in education has been, and continues to be, a complex and vexing issue for educators and social scientists. This notwithstanding, this chapter has shown that both race and class are important factors in understanding the relative success and difficulties faced by Asian Americans student in all levels of education. It is true that many Asian Americans have achieved amazingly well in school and have a great deal to be proud of. At the same time, this should not take away from those Asian Americans who work extremely hard to accomplish what they have, and who must continue to struggle to make it through. Asian Americans, like most Americans, generally believe in education as the key to get ahead, believe in hard work and meritocracy, and believe that people should recognize their accomplishments as a positive attribute. The experiences of Asian Americans described in this chapter challenges an uncritical faith in these beliefs.

ENDNOTES

1. Jeff Faraudo, "Silence Is Golden for Reluctant Hero Chow," *Oakland Tribune*, July 24, 1996; and "Chow Takes Silver Medal," *Oakland Tribune*, July 29, 1996.
2. Laura Myers, "Spelling Bee Sweep," *Asian Week*, June 7, 1996.
3. "Science Prodigy Mixes Biochemistry, Music and Laughter," *Oakland Tribune*, March 26, 1995.
4. See "Confucian Work Ethic," *Time*, March 28, 1983; Dennis Williams, "A Formula for Success," *Newsweek*, April 23, 1984, pp. 77-78; David Bell, "An American Success Story: The Triumph of Asian Americans," *New Republic*, July 1985, pp. 24–31; Fox Butterfield, "Why Asian Americans Are Going to the Head of the Class," *New York Times Magazine*, August 3, 1986, pp. 19–24; Linda Mathews, "When Being Best Isn't Good Enough," *Los Angeles Times Magazine*, July 19, 1987, pp. 22-28; David Brand, "The New Whiz Kids," *Time*, August 31, 1987; and Diane Divoky, "The Model Minority Goes to School," *Phi Delta Kappan*, November 1988, pp. 219–222.
5. Joe R. Feagin and Clairece Booher Feagin, *Racial and Ethnic Relations*, fourth edition (Englewood Cliffs, NJ: Prentice Hall, 1994), Chapter 6.

6. Cited in Robert Suro, "Study of Immigrants Finds Asians at Top in Science and Medicine," *The Washington Post*, April 18, 1994.

7. Grace Kao and Marta Tienda, "Optimism and Achievement: The Educational Performance of Immigrant Youth," *Social Science Quarterly* 76:1 (1995): 1–19.

8. Daniel B. Taylor, "Asian-American Test Scores: They Deserve a Closer Look," *Education Week*, October 17, 1990, p. 23.

9. Ruth Benedict, *Race: Science and Politics* (New York: Viking Press, 1959; Thomas F. Gossett, *Race: The History of an Idea in America* (New York: Schocken Books, 1965); and Winthrop D. Jordan, *White Over Black* (Baltimore: Penguin, 1969).

10. Arthur Jensen, *Educability and Group Difference* (New York: Harper & Row, 1973), p. 304.

11. Richard Lynn, "The Intelligence of Mongoloids: A Psychometric Evolutionary and Neurological Theory," *Personality and Individual Differences* 8:6 (1987): 813–844. Also see Richard Lynn, *Educational Achievement in Japan* (London: Macmillan, 1988); and Richard Lynn, "IQ in Japan and in the United States Shows Great Disparity," *Nature* 297 (1982): 222–226.

12. Harold W. Stevenson, J. W. Stigler, S. Lee, G. W. Lucker, S. Kitamura, and C. Hsu, "Cognitive Performance and Academic Achievement of Japanese, Chinese, and American Children," *Child Development* 56 (1985): 718-734.

13. Richard J. Herrnstein and Charles Murray, *The Bell Curve: Intelligence and Class Structure in American Life* (New York: The Free Press, 1994), pp. 272–277, 298–301.

14. Claude Fischer et al., *Inequality by Design: Cracking the Bell Curve Myth* (Princeton, NJ: Princeton University Press, 1996). Also see Russell Jacoby and Naomi Glauberman (eds.), *The Bell Curve Debate: History, Documents, Opinions* (New York: Random House, 1995). Also see reviews by Robert M. Hauser, Howard F. Taylor, and Troy Duster, "Symposium," *Contemporary Sociology* 24:2 (March 1995): 149-161. For one of the best comprehensive reviews of *The Bell Curve*, see Stephen Jay Gould, "Curveball," *New Yorker*, November 28, 1994, pp. 139–149.

15. Samuel Peng et al., "School Experiences and Performance of Asian American High School Students," Paper presented at the Annual Meeting of the American Educational Research Association, New Orleans (April 1984).

16. Samuel S. Peng and DeeAnn Wright, "Explanation of Academic Achievement of Asian American Students," *Journal of Educational Research* 87:6 (1994): 346–352.

17. William Caudill and George DeVos, "Achievement, Culture and Personality: The Case of Japanese Americans," *American Anthropologist* 58 (1956): 1102–26; and Betty Lee Sung, *The Story of the Chinese in America* (New York: Macmillan, 1967), pp. 124–125.

18. Nathan Caplan, Marcella H. Choy, and John K. Whitmore, *The Boat People and Achievement in America: A Study of Economic and Educational Success* (Ann Arbor: University of Michigan Press, 1989); and Nathan Caplan, Marcella H. Choy, and John K. Whitmore, *Children of the Boat People: A Study of Educational Success* (Ann Arbor: University of Michigan Press, 1991).

19. Caplan, Choy, and Whitmore. *Children of the Boat People*, pp. 6–7, 11.

20. *Ibid.*, pp. 105–106.

21. Tommy Tomlinson, *Hard Work and High Expectations: Motivating Students to Learn* (Washington, DC: U.S. Government Printing Office, 1992).

22. Edward Banfield, *The Unheavenly City* (Boston: Little, Brown and Company, 1970).

23. Thomas Sowell, *Ethnic America* (New York: Basic Books, 1981), pp. 284, 295; also see Thomas Sowell, *Race and Culture: A World View* (New York: Basic Books, 1994).

24. Stanley Sue and Sumie Okazaki, "Asian-American Educational Achievements: A Phenomenon in Search of an Explanation," *American Psychologist* 46:8 (1990): 913–920.
25. Stephen Steinberg, *The Ethnic Myth: Race, Ethnicity, and Class in America* (Boston: Beacon Press, 1981), p. 103. The second edition of Steinberg's book (1989) includes a provocative epilogue that focuses on the Asian American experience.
26. Bob H. Suzuki, "Education and the Socialization of Asian Americans: A Revisionist Analysis of the 'Model Minority' Thesis," *Amerasian Journal* 4:2 (1977): 23–51.
27. Sue and Okazaki, "Asian-American Educational Achievements," p. 919.
28. David Fox, "Neuropsychology, Achievement, and Asian-American Culture: Is Relative Functionalism Oriented Times Three?" *American Psychologist* 46:8 (1991): 877–878; and Stanley Sue and Sumie Okazaki, "Explanations for Asian-American Achievements: A Reply," *Ibid.*, pp. 878-880.
29. *The Condition of Bilingual Education in the Nation, 1982: A Report from the Secretary of Education to the President and the Congress* (1982), p. 2; and Rebecca Oxford-Carpenter et al., *Demographic Projections of Non-English-Language-Background and Limited-English-Proficient Persons* (Rosslyn, VA: InterAmerica Research Associates, 1984), pp. 19, 68. Both cited in U.S. Commission on Civil Rights, *Civil Rights Issues Facing Asian Americans in the 1990s* (Washington, DC: Government Printing Office, 1992), p. 76.
30. Leon Bouvier and Phillip Martin, *Population Change and California's Education System* (Washington, D.C.: Population Reference Bureau, Inc., 1987); and U.S. Commission on Civil Rights, *Civil Rights Issues Facing Asian Americans in the 1990s*, p. 77.
31. James Crawford, *Bilingual Education: History, Politics, Theory, and Practice* (Trenton, N.J: Crane Publishing Company, Inc., 1989), pp. 35-37; L. Ling-chi Wang, "Lau v. Nichols: History of a Struggle for Equal and Quality Education," *Amerasia Journal* 2:2 (1974): 16–45.
32. Henry T. Trueba, Lilly Cheng, and Kenji Ima, *Myth or Reality: Adaptive Strategies of Asian Americans in California* (Washington, DC: The Falmer Press, 1993), p. 61–62, 65.
33. *Ibid.*, p. 65.
34. U.S. Commission on Civil Rights, *Civil Rights Issues Facing Asian Americans in the 1990s*, p. 76–80.
35. *Ibid.*, p. 194.
36. John E. Rigdon, "Asian-American Youth Suffer a Rising Toll from Heavy Pressures," *Wall Street Journal*, July 10, 1991.
37. See Laurence Steinberg et al., "Ethnic Differences in Adolescent Achievement: An Ecological Perspective," *American Psychologist* 47:6 (1992): 723–729; Chin-Yau Lin and Victoria Fu, "A Comparison of Child-Rearing Practices American Chinese, Immigrant Chinese, and Caucasian-American Parents," *Child Development* 61:1 (1990): 429–433; Barbara Schnider and Yongsook Lee, "A Model for Academic Success: The School and Home Environment of East Asian Students," *Anthropology & Education Quarterly* 21:4 (1990): 358–377; and Rosina Chia, "Pilot Study: Family Values of American versus Chinese American Parents," *Journal of Asian American Psychological Association* 13:1 (1989): 8–11.
38. Laura Uba, *Asian Americans: Personality Patterns, Identity, and Mental Health* (New York: The Guilford Press, 1994), p. 45.
39. National Center for Education Statistics, *Digest of Educational Statistics, 1995* (Washington, DC: U.S. Department of Education, Office of Research and Improvement, 1995), Table 142, p. 138.
40. *Ibid.*, pp. 38–41, 46–49.

41. Paula Yoo, "Troubled Waters," *A Magazine*, 1:4 (1992): 14, 53–54.
42. Quoted in Sharon Yen-Ling Sim, "Parent's Wishes and Children's Dreams Are Sources of Conflict," *Asian Week*, September 2, 1995.
43. Cited in Jayjia Hsia, "Asian Americans Fight the Myth of the Super Student," *Educational Record*, Fall 1987–Winter 1988, pp. 94–97.
44. Quoted in Jodi Wilgoren, "High-Pressure High," *Los Angeles Times*, December 4, 1994.
45. See the series of articles on Lowell High School: Nanette Asimov, "A Hard Lesson in Diversity," *San Francisco Chronicle*, June 19, 1995; Tara Shioyo, "Recalling Insights—and Slights," *San Francisco Chronicle*, June 20, 1995; Nanette Asimov and Tara Shioya, "A Test for the Best Public Schools," *San Francisco Chronicle*, June 21, 1995.
46. Quoted in "Questions and Answers on Lowell High Series," *San Francisco Chronicle*, June 29, 1995.
47. Gerard Lim, "Lawsuit Over Chinese American HS Enrollment: Class Warfare by the Bay?" *Asian Week*, August 19, 1994.
48. Henry Der, "Clash Between Race-Conscious Remedies and Merit: School Desegregation and the San Francisco Chinese American Community," *Asian American Policy Review* 4 (1994): 65–91.
49, Nanette Asimov, "Single Standard for Admissions at Lowell High," *San Francisco Chronicle*, February 28, 1996.
50. National Center for Education Statistics, *Digest of Educational Statistics*, 1995, Table 138, p. 136.
51. Quoted in May Lam, "Hate Crime Surfaces in Affluent Neighborhood," *Asian Week*, April 2, 1995.
52. Vinesh Viswanathan, "Seeing the Person, Not the Color," *San Francisco Chronicle*, May 17, 1995.
53. Barbara Karkabi, "Betty Waki: Sharpstown Teacher Devoted to Easing School's Racial Tension," *Houston Chronicle*, April 24, 1989.
54. "4 Face Charges in Attack," *Los Angeles Times*, June 6, 1991.
55. Quoted in Irene Chang, "Asian, Latino Activists Seek Ethnic Harmony at Schools," *Los Angeles Times*, September 22, 1991.
56. Denise Hamilton, "6 Accused in Ethnic Fight on Campus," *Los Angeles Times*, February 18, 1995.
57. John Willshire Carrea, *New Voices: Immigrant Students in U.S. Public Schools* (Boston: National Coalition of Advocates for Students, 1988); Laurie Olsen, *Crossing the Schoolhouse Border: Immigrant Students and the California Public Schools* (San Francisco: California Tomorrow, 1988); and Ruben G. Rumbaut and Kenji Ima, *The Adaptation of Southeast Asian Refugee Youth: A Comparative Study*, Final Report to the U.S. Department of Health and Human Services, Office of Refugee Resettlement (January, 1988).
58. Olsen, *Crossing the Schoolhouse Border*, p. 35.
59. The students killed at Cleveland Elementary School were Ram Chun, 8, Thuy Tran, 6, Rathanan Or, 9, Sokhim An, 6, and Oeun Lim, 8.
60. Nelson Kempsky, *A Report to Attorney General John K. Van de Kamp on Edward Patrick Purdy and the Cleveland School Killings* (Sacramento: California Department of Justice, 1989), p. 13.
61. U.S. Commission on Civil Rights, *Civil Rights Issues Facing Asian Americans in the 1990s*, pp. 41–44; also see Sucheng Chan, "Beyond Affirmative Action," *Change* (November–December 1989), pp. 48–51.
62 Quoted in Scott Jaschik, "Affirmative-Action Ruling on Connecticut Called a 'Big Step' for Asian Americans," *The Chronicle of Higher Education*, May 19, 1993.

63. Asian American Students Association of Brown University, "Asian American Admission at Brown University," October 11, 1983, p. 1.
64. *Ibid.*, p. 7.
65. Quoted in Dana Y. Takagi, *The Retreat from Race* (New Brunswick, N.J.: Rutgers University Press, 1992), p. 25.
66. Quoted in Robert Lindsey, "Colleges Accused of Bias to Stem Asian's Gains," *New York Times*, January 21, 1987.
67. Quoted in "UC Berkeley Apologizes for Policy that Limited Asians," *Los Angeles Times*, April 7, 1989.
68. Sandy Banks, "UCLA is Cleared in Bias Case," *Los Angeles Times*, August 27, 1993.
69. U.S. Department of Education, Office for Civil Rights, "Statement of Findings" (for Compliance Review No. 01-88-6009 on Harvard University), October 4, 1990, cited in U.S. Commission on Civil Rights, *Civil Rights Issues Facing Asian Americans in the 1990s*, p. 127; and Stephen S. Fujita and Marilyn Fernandez, "Asian American Admissions to an Elite University: A Multivariate Case Study of Harvard," *Asian American Policy Review* 5 (1995): 45–62.
70. Takagi, *Retreat from Race*, pp. 67–68.
71. John H. Bunzel and Jeffrey K. D. Au, "Diversity or discrimination? Asian Americans in College," *The Public Interest* 87 (Spring 1987): 56.
72. Asian American Students Association of Brown University, "Asian Admission at Brown University," p. 20.
73. George F. Will, "The Lunacy of Punishing Those Who Try to Excel," *Los Angeles Times*, April 16, 1989.
74. L. Ling-chi Wang, "Meritocracy and Diversity in Higher Education: Discrimination Against Asian Americans in the Post-Bakke Era," *The Urban Review* 20:3 (1991): 202–203.
75. Bunzel and Au, "Diversity or Discrimination?" p. 62.
76. Also see Denise K. Magner, "Colleges Faulted for Not Considering Differences in Asian-American Groups," *Chronicle of Higher Education*, February 10, 1993, pp. A-32, A-34.
77. Pacific Americans in the CSU: A Follow-Up Report," a report of the Asian Pacific American Education Advisory Committee (August 1994), p. 12.
78. L. Ling-chi Wang, "Trends in Admissions for Asian Americans in Colleges and Universities: Higher Education Policy," *The State of Asian Pacific America: Policy Issues to the Year 2020* (Los Angeles: LEAP Asian Pacific American Public Policy Institute and UCLA Asian American Studies Center, 1993), pp. 49–60.
79. Quoted in Rick Reilly, "Heaven Help Her," *Sports Illustrated*, May 20, 1996, pp. 77–78.

4

WORKPLACE ISSUES: BEYOND GLASS CEILINGS

VISIBILITY AND INVISIBILITY

In March 1995 the Glass Ceiling Commission released a report that found among the top 1,000 U.S. industrial firms and the 500 largest businesses only 3 percent of senior managers were persons of color, and only 3 to 5 percent were women. The 20-member panel of legislators and business officials formed in 1991 by then-President George Bush was quite blunt about its assessment. "Serious barriers to advancement remain—such as persistent stereotyping, erroneous beliefs that 'no qualified women or minorities are out there,' and plain old fear of change."[1] The term "glass ceiling" refers to an invisible, but very real, barrier for even qualified women and people of color to move upward into managerial ranks (especially upper management) within both private and public institutions.

As we learned in the previous chapters, Asian Americans generally have a high regard for education, have far higher levels of education compared to other groups, and have a "folk belief" that education equates with high income and professional advancement. Yet, despite these attributes and attitudes, Asian Americans are not immune to the limitations of the glass ceiling. One survey of top-level executives in Fortune 500 companies shows that only 0.3 percent of senior executives in the United States are Asian Americans.[2] This survey is consistent with an earlier, and even more broad-based, U.S. Civil Rights Commission report that found U.S-born Asian American men were 7 to 11 percent less likely to be working in any managerial positions compared with similarly qualified white men.[3] General statistics highlighted in Chapter 2 showed a high percentage of Asian American professionals relative to the national average, but it is quite apparent that Asian Americans are disadvantaged relative to white men.

This chapter focuses on the experiences of, and issues confronted by, Asian Americans in the workplace. The one workplace issue that has received the most attention and was raised most frequently by participants in the U.S. Civil Rights Commission's 1989 Roundtable Conferences on the concerns of Asian Americans was the glass ceiling.[4] This chapter will first examine the glass ceiling phenomena as it applies to Asian Americans in a variety of occupational areas. Second, this chapter will highlight the attempts by Asian Americans to fight back against discrimination in the workplace. This section will focus on the important precedent-setting cases of Bruce Yamashita and Rosalie Tung, two Asian Americans who fought their job discrimination cases in court even in the face of seemingly impossible odds. Third, this chapter will look at a much less publicized, but increasingly pressing, problem in the workplace—language discrimination. Since the influx of immigrants from Asia after 1965, greater numbers of Asian Americans whose primary language is not English have entered the work force. Many are feeling held back because of their accents and some employers have gone as far as initiating "English-only" work rules. Lastly, this chapter will focus on the Asian American working class and working poor, and the conditions they face in their struggles to support themselves and their families.

GLASS CEILING

The images of Asian Americans in school are that they are hard working, eager to learn, and achievement-oriented. The educational stereotypes of Asian Americans, however, seem to disappear when they enter the workplace. Among the new images of Asian Americans that have emerged include unfair stereotypes that they are unassertive and passive, not good leaders, have poor social skills, and are too technically oriented. As was discussed in Chapter 1, Asian American efforts in education reap only limited returns in the work world. There are, of course, some notable Asian Americans who have been able to break through the glass ceiling, have excelled in their professions, and have moved into high-profile positions of leadership. Some of them include: Chang-Lin Tien, former chancellor of the University of California at Berkeley; Shirley Young, vice-president of marketing for General Motors; Michael Yamaguchi, U.S. Attorney; and Ginger Lew, U.S. Department of Commerce General Counsel. Numerous Asian Americans have struck out on their own and started their own businesses; not surprisingly, many of them have done so precisely because their careers had been stifled by the glass ceiling or their perceptions of job discrimination. The glass ceiling is one of a variety of workplace concerns for many Asian Americans in all professions and occupations.

Science, Engineering, and High Technology

Areas of employment where Asian Americans would appear to have a very strong foothold and mobility would be in science, engineering, and high-technology fields. Although Asian Americans are less than 3 percent of the U.S. population, they are almost 6 percent of the total engineering work force, and the U.S. Department of Labor projects a 25 percent increase in engineering jobs by the turn of the century.[5] It is estimated that close to one quarter of all scientists and engineers in the U.S. high-technology capital, Silicon Valley, are Asian American. Nationally, over 20 percent of Asian American engineers possess a doctorate degree.[6] Talented individuals in these areas are in great demand, and they are key to maintaining U.S. dominance in an increasingly competitive global economy. On the surface, then, it appears that all is well. On close examination, however, it is not hard to find the phenomena of the glass ceiling in place.

First of all, an analysis of salaries among scientists and engineers by researchers Paul Ong and Evelyn Blumenberg (1994), shows that incomes for Asian Americans with advanced degrees were actually lower than for non-Hispanic whites with the same levels of education. Analyzing the U.S. Bureau of Census, 1990 1% Public Use Microdata Sample, Ong and Blumenberg estimated the median annual earnings by Asian American engineers with a bachelor's degree weres $37,000, compared with $40,800 for whites. The median annual earnings for Asian American scientists with a bachelor's degree were $32,000, compared with $34,600 for white scientists. Individuals with more education, of course, earn more money but a discrepancy is still found between Asian Americans and whites. The median annual earnings for an Asian American engineer with a Ph.D. were $54,000, while non-Hispanic white engineers with a Ph.D. earned $57,200. The same scenario is true for Asian American scientists with a Ph.D. They earned $44,000, or

Table 4-1 Engineers and Scientists, Median Annual Earnings, 1989

	All Education Levels*	Bachelor's Degree	Master's Degree	Ph.D. Degree
Engineers				
Non-Hisp. White	$40,500	$40,800	$49,600	$57,200
Asian Am.	$40,800	$37,000	$45,000	$54,000
Scientists				
Non-Hisp. White	$35,000	$34,600	$40,000	$48,000
Asian Am.	$34,600	$32,000	$40,000	$44,000

* Includes engineers and scientists with less than a Bachelor's degree.
Source: Paul Ong and Evelyn Blumenberg, "Scientists and Engineers," in Paul Ong (ed.), *The State of Asian Pacific America: Economic Diversity, Issues & Policies,* (Los Angeles: LEAP Asian Pacific Public Policy Institute and UCLA Asian American Studies Center, 1994) Table 5, pg. 179.

about 10 percent less than the $48,000 earned by white scientists with a doctorate (see Table 4-1).[7] Ong and Blumenberg acknowledge that part of the salary discrepancy between non-Hispanic whites and Asian Americans in these two professions is the high number of recent Asian immigrants who tend to be paid less than U.S.-born Asians and whites.

Second, several studies show Asian Americans in the high-tech and science occupations confront a glass ceiling that limits the advancement of their careers into managerial positions. A study by the Pacific Studies Center looked at the ethnic and gender stratification of work in Silicon Valley and highlighted a number of interesting points. The study found that whites held 80 percent of the 25,000 management jobs. Asian Americans were well represented in 21.5 percent of the high-tech professionals (i.e., engineers), but were only 12.5 percent among management positions.[8] Another study on Hughes Aircraft in Southern California conducted by UCLA professor William Ouchi found that Asian Americans made up 24 percent of the company's technical staff, but only 5 percent of the managers. Still another study, this one on aerospace giant TRW, found that Asian Americans made up 20 percent of the firm's engineering and science staff, but only 11 percent of the managers.[9] Lastly, a survey of 325 Asian American professionals in Silicon Valley found 80 percent of the respondents perceived Asian Americans to be underrepresented in upper-level management positions. The same survey found 53 percent saying that promotional opportunities were inadequate and 66 percent felt their own chances for promotion were limited because of their race.[10] It is clear from these studies that Asian Americans seem to have little problem getting well-paid employment because of their research and technical expertise, but they are not nearly as welcomed into management and executive positions. As attorney and past-president of the Organization of Chinese Americans, Jim Tso, put it, "today we have the high-tech coolie."[11]

Dissatisfied with being limited to the lab or low-level management, some Asian Americans have decided simply to leave and try to advance their careers elsewhere. "We are beginning to lose them in the technical area in the four-to-seven-year range, when they start to think about promotion," notes Hughes Aircraft vice-president, David Barclay. "And if those promotions are not occurring, they consider moving on."[12] A similar situation is seen at other top research and development centers such as AT&T Bell Laboratories in Murray Hill, New Jersey. Asian Americans are 22 percent of the company's 22,000 employees, but they are leaving at twice the rate of white males. The main reason for this rapid turnover, according to systems engineer David Chai, is the fact that promotions for Asian Americans take three to five years longer than for white males.[13]

Some Asian Americans who felt restricted in their career opportunities have decided to make the big leap and start their own businesses. This was the case with Moon H. Yuen, a former engineer with Bechtel Corporation, who realized he could not move beyond his mid-level management position. After

27 years with the company, Yuen left and formed YEI Engineers Inc., a small independent firm that soon became a competitor with his old employer.[14] Still others are willing to put up a fight. This was the case for Houston, Texas, engineer and attorney, Wei-Chang (Wayne) Liauh. Liauh started working for the giant oil company, Exxon, in 1980 after earning a doctorate in chemical engineering from Pennsylvania State University. He received three merit promotions within three years, but then spent the next eight years in same position. Liauh started studying law in the evenings at the University of Houston, hoping that the degree would help his advancement opportunities at Exxon. When promotions still didn't come, he led a group of Asian American engineers in filing a discrimination complaint. "We do these things because we realize we have no chance in the workplace—sometimes we do these things out of frustration," Liauh said. "You have to prove to yourself you can do certain things the company says you can't."[15]

In the case of immigrant scientists and engineers, a growing number have decided to pack their bags and leave the United States altogether. Taiwan, for example, has been offering high salaries, generous research grants, and other perks to entice overseas graduate students and professionals to come back home. Thousands of scientists and engineers with advanced degrees obtained from U.S. universities have returned to Taiwan within the past several years. This is significant since historically over 90 percent of these highly trained professionals have chosen to remain in the United States. "Most of them can get high-level jobs in Taiwan," said Yaw-Nan Chen, director of Taiwan's science division at its Los Angeles diplomatic mission. "They have some kind of frustration that they do not have an equal chance here."[16]

A special November 1994 issue of *Business Week* reported that over 100 of AT&T Bell Laboratories' prized researchers have returned to Taiwan to begin new careers with greater responsibilities. One such AT&T Bell Labs alumni is Lance Wu, who returned to Taiwan to help head the government's computer research laboratory. One major figure who recently returned to Taiwan is Yuan T. Lee, the Nobel Prize–winning chemist from the UC Berkeley. Lee left his prestigious research position at Berkeley to take on the challenge of running Taiwan's Academia Sinica, an impressive collection of 21 research institutes. Taiwan, and other Asian countries are investing billions of dollars into becoming leaders in high-technology research, development, and production. In Pohang, South Korea, $180 million was spent to build state-of-the-art equipment that would help them compete with any high-technology research center in the world. In Bangalore, India, returning scientists, engineers, and entrepreneurs are quickly creating what many see as the Silicon Valley of South Asia.[17]

Federal and Local Government

There is also evidence that Asian Americans earn lower salaries and are less likely to be in management positions than comparably educated and experienced whites in all levels of government. Employment growth for Asian Americans in state and local government increased 82 percent between 1980 and 1990, and 46 percent between 1982 and 1990.[18] A recent analysis of Asian American mobility within the federal government was conducted by Pan Suk Kim and Gregory B. Lewis (1994). Their work is particularly interesting for two reasons. First, they focused on Asian Americans in federal service when most other studies on employment focused primarily on blacks and whites, and on men and women. Second, they compared Asian American men and women with non-Hispanic white men and women from 1978, 1985, and 1992 federal government employment statistics in order to view changes over time.[19]

As seen in Table 4-2, white males generally held a higher mean grade level (salary scale) than Asian American men in 1992 (10.9 vs. 10.4), and this gap was wider than in 1978 (10.2 vs. 9.8) but narrower than in 1985 (10.5 vs. 9.8). In addition, white males were nearly twice as likely to hold supervisorial

Table 4-2   Characteristics of Asian Americans and White Non-Hispanics in Federal Service, 1978, 1985, 1992

Characteristics	Asian Am. Females	Non-Hisp. White Females	Asian Am. Males	Non-Hisp. White Males
Mean Grade				
1992	7.7	8.1	10.4	10.9
1985	6.9	6.7	9.8	10.5
1978	6.7	5.9	9.8	10.2
% with Supervisory Authority				
1992	7.0	12.0	15.0	27.0
1985	9.0	8.0	15.0	26.0
1978	8.0	6.0	23.0	19.0
Mean Years of Education				
1992	14.4	13.7	15.3	15.2
1985	14.1	13.3	15.2	15.0
1978	13.6	12.9	15.0	14.6
Mean Years of Federal Service				
1992	10.2	12.4	11.6	14.1
1985	9.5	11.0	11.7	13.8
1978	12.5	10.4	12.9	13.2

Source: Pan Suk Kim and Gregory B. Lewis, "Asian Americans in Public Service: Success, Diversity, and Discrimination," *Public Administration Review* 54:3 (May–June, 1994): 285–290, Table 2.

positions than are Asian American men (27 vs. 15). This was a continuation of the situation seen in 1985, but a reversal of the situation in 1978. These factors were true even though the median level of education for Asian American men has always been higher than the median education for white males. One area where Asian American men have consistently been deficient is in the mean years of federal service. This has even declined since 1978 while white males' median years of federal service have increased. This might indicate that Asian American men leave government service at a higher rate than white males.

More detailed analysis by Kim and Lewis clearly found that in 1992 well-educated Asian American men (e.g., those with bachelor's and graduate degrees) generally had higher grades than comparably educated white males, and this has steadily improved since 1978. At the same time, Asian Americans were less likely to be in supervisory positions even if they had the same years of education, federal experience, age, and veteran and handicap status as white men. "In sum," say Kim and Lewis, "as a group, well-educated Asian men face little or no discrimination in achieving high grade positions and salaries, but they are less successful in attaining supervisory or managerial authority."[20]

For Asian American women in federal government employment, however, Kim and Lewis found their status to be, "more complex and troubling." The relative standing of Asian American women in terms of mean grade and supervisory status declined between 1978 and 1992, despite the fact that Asian American women generally had higher levels of education. These discrepancies continued even when adjusting for similar education, seniority, age, veteran, and handicap status. Interestingly, Asian American women with a graduate school education were shown to be 1.9 grades below white women with similar education. This is clearly a significant discrepancy and was a larger gap than what was seen in 1978 and 1985. In addition, Asian American women in 1992 were less likely to hold supervisory positions than white women, even with comparable levels of education and experience. This is a complete reversal of the situation found in 1978 and quite an anomaly considering the general societal trend toward greater equality for all racial minority groups and women. "The most likely explanation is that white women are the group that has gained most from affirmative action in recent years," explain Kim and Lewis. "Asian women have gained on white men, but not as rapidly as white women have, leading Asian women to fall behind relative to white women."[21]

The same general pattern seen in the federal government is also true in local government. In San Francisco, California, where Asian Americans represent 29 percent of the population, studies have shown a lack of advancement opportunities for Asian Americans employed by the city and county. In 1985, 1989, and 1992 the civil rights organization, Chinese for Affirmative Action (CAA), released successive reports intended to analyze employment trends, point out inequities, and offer recommendations for change. In the first two reports, Asian Americans were lacking in administrative positions, professionals were clustered in technical jobs, and specific problems were found with civil service testing system and high-level exempt appointments. The 1992 report offered a mixed review compared with earlier findings. First, the percentage of Asian American administrators increased from 12 percent in 1985 to 13.3 percent in 1992. Slight improvement was also shown with findings that 9 out of 30 major departments employed no Asian American administrators in 1989, compared with just 7 out of 30 in 1992. This positive news, however, was coupled with critical remarks about the fact that the largest city and county departments continued to have the worst promotional records for Asian Americans. For example, the Fire Department had no Asian American administrator despite having a 23.5 percent Asian American representation among its force.[22]

Second, the latest report did show the percentage of Asian American professionals increased slightly from 27 percent in 1985 to 29 percent in 1992. At the same time, Asian American professionals continued to be clustered in the areas of Operations and Finance. These departments include Public Works, Controller, Treasurer, and Tax Collection. The Department of Public Works was highlighted because 53 percent of its professionals were Asian American, but only 10 percent were administrators. In 1992, Asian Americans represented 55 percent of the department's professionals and 23 percent of the administrators. While acknowledging the gains, the report still found fault in the fact that out of a total of 53 departments with professionals on their staff, only 22 departments met the 1990 census work-force parity of 29 percent. In addition, of the 31 larger departments that employed over 30 professionals, only 12 met work-force parity. This figure was actually lower compared with earlier reports, and the study warned, "The overall representation of Asian American professionals must not obscure the fact that Asian professionals are highly underrepresented in many departments or types of work."[23]

Third, the 1992 CAA report found a great deal of fault with San Francisco for not making any significant effort in addressing problems in its civil service system. One major criticism was leveled against policy changes that allowed greater hiring flexibility for managers that the report called, "a double-edged sword." This plan was ideally intended to help bring in more qualified women and racial minorities, but very little progress had been made since its initiation. This change allowed for greater subjectivity and had the potential of being more discriminatory. Another major criticism focused on the need to develop training sessions for panelists on the oral interview boards and appointing officials on how to identify and eliminate stereotypical attitudes that have negative results for Asian American interviewees. Specifically, issues over language, accent, and cultural biases (to be discussed in detail below) needed to be confronted rather than ignored. These criticisms were made in CAA's earlier reports, but by 1992 the civil service had not investigated nor eliminated practices that had greater potential of excluding qualified Asian American candidates for advancement.[24]

Lastly, the report showed that Asian Americans, along with other racial minorities, experienced a decline in the number of high-level exempt appointments to city government. Exempt appointments are positions that do not require civil service examination or approval because they are political appointments selected by newly elected officials once they enter office. Specifically, white exempt administrative representation increased from 77.2 percent in 1988 to 81.5 percent in 1990. Indeed, Asian Americans turned out to be the least likely group to gain an exempt administrative appointment. According to the report, there has been little effort to integrate the ranks of top exempt administrators and that the "old-boys" network is still firmly in place. "This problem of exempt appointments reflects poorly on city leadership," the report states. "The dearth of representation of Asians and other minorities at this level clearly exposes the lack of a serious affirmative action effort on the part of department heads and elected officials."[25]

Although improvements were duly noted, the overall tone of the report was quite stern about what was seen as inadequate opportunities for Asian Americans in San Francisco city and county government. The report stated that deep-seated insensitivity and ignorance of many government officials was a distinct barrier for Asian Americans, and that a commitment to tap into Asian American professional and administrative talent did not appear to be forthcoming in the very near future. "It is a waste of Asian American administrative talent if city government continues to sit on its hands and does not provide a strong, meaningful role for Asian Americans in city management and administration."[26] Since the latest CAA report was published, two high-level Asian American administrators have been hired. In 1995, Bill Lee was appointed chief administrative officer for San Francisco—the most powerful nonelected job in city government. The following year, Fred Lau was appointed police chief of San Francisco. Lau had been with the San Francisco Police Department for 24 years and was the deputy chief for field operations at the time of his appointment.[27]

ASIAN AMERICANS FIGHTING BACK

Confronting the glass ceiling is a major workplace concern for Asian Americans, but this issue does not often gain very much sympathy from non-Asians. One reason for this is the "model minority" stereotype, which plays a large part in maintaining an image that Asian Americans are untroubled and economically successful. Much more attention seems to be placed on how well some Asian Americans are doing relative to other racial minorities in the United States. Another reason why glass ceiling concerns of Asian Americans do not garner much attention is the fact that many believe traditional Asian culture is simply antithetical to Western corporate culture. This is based on broad generalizations about Asian culture that are again used to explain both personal behavior and social results for Asian Americans. "(T)he successful manager has the get-up-and-go to grab the bull by the horns and wrestle it to the ground," explains Frances M. Namkoong, who works for the Mid-America

Consulting Group in Ohio. "In contrast, the Asian is perceived to be passive, non-aggressive."[28]

While most Asian Americans don't deny that Asian and Western cultures differ, they also feel the rapid economic growth in Asian countries clearly contradicts the core of the cultural argument that Asians don't make good managers. Leadership exercised by Asians in the Pacific Rim tends to be much more group-oriented and consensus-driven. Interestingly, this team concept is a growing trend in U.S. corporations as we move into a more competitive economic climate in the twenty-first century. "What is misunderstood is the nature of leadership exercised by Asians," Namkoong adds. "Is the team approach the best way to operate? Certainly the Pacific Rim countries have demonstrated dramatically that the concept has worked for them." The cultural conflict argument in terms of management skills, then, is a moot point.[29]

At the same time, it is not surprising that Western corporate culture does cultivate potential managers among employees who best fit its own image. Because of this, many Asian Americans recognize that they need to be better at promoting and asserting themselves if they hope to get the kinds of employment opportunities they want. Basic advancement strategies such as participating in business-sponsored social events, cultivating mentors, and improving interviewing techniques are all seen as ways to improve the chances for advancement. With this in mind, the University of Illinois at Chicago created a one-year program designed to give foreign-born engineering Ph.D.s a crash course on American culture, with particular emphasis in the ways of American managers. Seminar courses feature a variety of topics including how to make small talk, how to shake hands properly, and how to ask for a raise. Students are even encouraged to follow professional sports, in order to better converse with their colleagues.[30] This type of program is well-meaning and possibly somewhat helpful, but it places all of the responsibility for change on the individual employee only. This does very little to enlighten the corporate or institutional environment about cultural sensitivity or the true benefits of a diversified work force. This sole focus on individual responsibility in the absence of institutional accountability has been criticized by Asian American civil rights leaders. Henry Der, former executive director of Chinese for Affirmative Action in San Francisco, calls for a more activist strategies to break through the glass ceiling.

Der recognizes the fact that hiring and promotional practices are not necessarily rational nor merit-based. He says Asian Americans need to develop strong employee organizations that will serve to guide and monitor the implementation of affirmative action goals. Even with affirmative action policies, or perhaps because of them, Der thinks it is all the more important for Asian Americans to collectively organize and not let their concerns get lost in the competition for entry-level and advancement opportunities. Der also maintains that Asian Americans should make every effort to educate and inform employers about unrecognized biases against Asian Americans. The stereotype that Asian Americans lack necessary managerial and leadership skills, for example, is an unacceptable generalization and should be openly challenged at every opportunity. Finally, Der wants to see Asian Americans "cultivate a heightened sense of social responsibility." This means extending efforts to interact cooperatively with other groups at work to share common experiences, difficulties, and rewards. This is all a part of making plurality and true integration in the workplace a meaningful reality. Der's ideas are not new and are not intended to be adversarial to the employer. However, they do recognize the responsibility for genuine and fundamental change is on both the individual and the workplace.[31]

Two Celebrated Court Cases

Self-improvement and efforts to amicably educate employers about biased attitudes is all well and good, but increasingly Asian Americans are taking the much more decisive step of going to court. Historically, Asian Americans have been reluctant to openly challenge employers through the legal system, and the federal Equal Employment Opportunity Commission reports show that Asian Americans file just one percent of all employment discrimination cases in the United States. At the same time, the EEOC statistics also show a 27 percent increase in the number of discrimination complaints from Asian Americans since 1989.[32] A lawsuit against an employer is an action of last resort primarily because it is a long, drawn-out, expensive, and painful process that, win or lose, could have dire long-term consequences for an individual's career. This is particularly true for employees who continue in their job even after they have filed discrimination charges. In these cases, the work environment is usually quite tense because he or she often feels under extreme scrutiny by supervisors and co-workers, and may be a potential victim of reprisal. In addition, it is extremely difficult to prove intentional discrimination because of its subjective nature and, as a result, the vast majority of cases settle out of court long before anything can be clearly proven, admitted, or resolved.

A settlement out of court is not necessarily bad. It often provides the employee a cash payment while avoiding the risks involved in a jury trial. At the same time, it helps the employer get rid of a problem without admitting any wrongdoing. When an employment discrimination case is successfully followed through to the end, however, the impact is far greater than just the single case. A court or jury decision that finds wrongdoing often serves as an important precedent for similar cases that are waiting to be heard or may emerge in the future. This is what happened with Bruce Yamashita and Rosalie Tung, two of the most celebrated job discrimination cases involving Asian Americans.

In March 1993, Bruce I. Yamashita, a third-generation Japanese American attorney, was finally commissioned a captain in the Marine Corps reserves after a five-year legal battle that sought to prove racial discrimination.

Yamashita had to fight for his commission after being drummed out of the Marine Corps' Officers Candidate School in 1989 because he had shown "leadership failure." His victory resulted in an official apology and, more importantly, an overhaul in the Marine Corps officer-training procedures. In a ceremony held at the House Armed Services Committee room in Washington DC, Yamashita spoke of how much he longed for this moment. "It is with great pride that I wear this uniform today," he said. "It means so much more to me now than ever I could have imagined five years ago." The event was hailed as a decisive occasion by Asian American groups, and another step toward equal opportunity in the U.S. military.[33]

Born and raised in Hawaii, Yamashita claims he did not experience any racism prior to taking the Marine Corps training. But throughout his ten-week officers' training, he was the target of intense racial slurs and harassment. The very first day of the ten-week course Yamashita recalled a staff sergeant telling him, "We don't want your kind here. Go back to your own country!" During his training tour, another sergeant confronted Yamashita about World War II and spat, "We whipped your Japanese ass." Still another sergeant spoke to Yamashita only in broken English and never referred to him by name—only calling Yamashita by the names of well-known Japanese consumer products and automobiles. Just two days before graduation, Yamashita and four other officer-candidates were forced out of the program.[34]

Yamashita pondered for six months before finally deciding to challenge the Marine Corps' decision. During that long period of indecision, Yamashita met with veterans of the Japanese American 442nd Regimental Combat Team, whose military exploits made them one of the most decorated fighting units during World War II. Over four decades after the war's end, both Yamashita and 442nd veterans found out that Japanese Americans still had to prove their loyalty to the United States. Before making his final decision to fight the Marine Corps, Yamashita told a group of 442nd veterans: "If you folks do not support this case, then I will not pursue it. Your sacrifices give me the moral legitimacy to fight back." The veterans, some whom were in tears, told Yamashita he had their support.[35]

Yamashita and his attorneys gathered evidence that showed between 1982 and 1990, a clear "pattern of discrimination" in the officers' training program and that racial minorities were dismissed at a far-higher rate than white candidates. In 1991, after two internal military investigations, the Marine Corps issued a formal apology and offered to allow him to retake the training. Yamashita flatly rejected the offer because it was a denial of the commission he believed he already earned. In 1993 Yamashita was offered an apology and a commission of second lieutenant. Again, he rejected the offer. This time he said the commission was too low and did not recognize the four years that had passed since his dismissal. In addition, the Marine Corps offer was conditional on Yamashita taking an additional six months of officer's training. Yamashita stood firm in his belief that he deserved his commission from the very beginning and did not receive one because of racial discrimination. Later the Pentagon offered Yamashita a commission as captain, which was a rank commensurate with the amount of time he would have earned had he not been dismissed from officer's training. Yamashita decided to accept the commission, although it was in the Marine reserves and not active-duty status. This compromise was acceptable because he retained the right to apply for active-duty status if he wished.[36]

Yamashita wore a crisp green Marine officer's uniform and sported a military-style crewcut at his commissioning. It was clearly an emotional moment when he took his oath of office and had his captain's bars pinned on his collar. Yamashita called the confrontation with the Marine Corps a principled struggle and expressed his hope that abuses that he faced would not happen again. "His commissioning today is a tribute to his dedication, a tribute to his courage," said Japanese American congressman Norman Y. Mineta (D-San Jose), one of many attendees and well wishers at the ceremony. Absent from the event was General Carl E. Mundy, Jr., commandant of the Marine Corps, who was invited to the ceremony but claimed he had a scheduling conflict. Mundy created his own controversy when he appeared on the CBS News program, *60 Minutes*, and said that minorities failed in officers' training because they could not shoot, swim, or use compasses as well as whites. With this difficult chapter in his life behind him, Yamashita has had the opportunity to reflect on what it all means to him. Top among them has been the emergence of a stronger sense of identity. "I was an idiot before all this," he admits. "Before this I was just an American. Now I'm an Asian American."[37]

Another long and hard-fought discrimination case involved Rosalie Tung, a professor who was denied tenure by the University of Pennsylvania Wharton School of Business in 1985.[38] Tung's case is particularly significant because it went all the way to the U.S. Supreme Court and, in 1990, she won a unanimous decision from the Court that set an important precedent for other employment discrimination cases in higher education. The University of Pennsylvania is an highly respected and elite private institution of higher education. It operates 12 schools, including the Wharton School of Business, the oldest business school in the nation. When Tung joined the Wharton School in 1981 she was well regarded for her teaching, publication record, and community service. But when a new person was appointed chair of the management department at Wharton in 1983, her dream job quickly turned into a nightmare. In her charge, Tung stated the new chair began making unwanted sexual advances toward her. When she made it clear to him that she wanted to keep their relationship professional, he became furious and, according to Tung, began a campaign to drive her out of the school. While both Asian American men and women face employment discrimination, the U.S. Civil Rights Commission has acknowledged that Asian American women face the extra burden of sexual harassment on the job. According to the 1992 commission report on Asian American civil rights issues, "the stereotypic expectation of compliance and docility, a formal complaint from an Asian American woman might (be) considered as a personal affront or challenge."[39]

In February 1985 the chair summoned Tung into his office, told her that the personnel committee had denied her tenure, and did not give any reason for the decision. Tung immediately filed a grievance with the University of Pennsylvania, as well as a complaint with the Equal Employment Opportunity Commission. Tung recalls the dean of the Wharton School offered her a cash settlement to drop her EEOC complaint and also threatened to make it difficult for her to find employment elsewhere. He warned her that if she continued with her complaint, they would fight her all the way to the Supreme Court. Tung refused to be intimidated and pursued her actions. The internal grievance commission within the University of Pennsylvania reviewed the personnel files of 13 other faculty members who were granted tenure, found that Tung was indeed discriminated against, and forwarded its report to the EEOC. It was during the grievance commission hearing that Tung learned there were three negative evaluation letters in her file, two of which were written by the chair himself. It was at this point the EEOC issued a subpoena for Tung's personnel file and the file of five other tenured faculty members for their investigation. However, the University of Pennsylvania refused to turn over the files, claiming special privilege for confidential peer review materials and First Amendment principles of academic freedom.

The dean of the school made good on his threat to Tung and the university challenged the subpoena all the way to the U.S. Supreme Court. Tung knew the university was trying to force her into giving up the fight and had the financial resources to do it. "The (university) could afford to drag the victim through years and years of emotional and financial stress and strain," she said. "I could not have survived this ordeal without the strong moral conviction that what I did was right. It would have been easier for me to leave the university quietly with the money offered by the dean of the Wharton School." Tung also knew that stereotypes of Asian women also played a major part in the university's underestimation of her strength and determination. She recalls reading a newspaper article in which colleagues at the University of Pennsylvania described her as "timid, and not one of those loud-mouthed women on campus" and "the least likely person to kick over the tenure-review apple cart." The 1990 U.S. Supreme Court ruling forced the University of Pennsylvania to submit to the EEOC subpoena, thus allowing Tung the opportunity to compare her files with others and to directly challenge any discrepancies or inconsistencies. The decision was both a relief and a vindication for Tung, and for many others who have faced employment discrimination. "I fought the University of Pennsylvania for principle and I'm glad I won," Tung announced to an enthusiastic gathering of supporters shortly after the high court's decision. "I'm glad I fought, and I'm proud of what I've accomplished for myself and other minorities and women in this country."[40]

Tung's court victory has had strong ripple effects throughout the academic world. Its impact may have been felt in finalizing the case of Marcy Wang, an assistant professor in the School of Architecture at UC Berkeley, who sued for sex and race discrimination after she was denied tenure back in 1986. In early 1996, after ten bitter years of legal maneuvering, Wang finally reached a $1 million out-of-court settlement. The university denied any wrongdoing had taken place and said the settlement was offered solely because it would have cost too much money to defend the case in court. UC Berkeley vice-chancellor, Carol Christ, contended that at least ten independent review committees found no direct evidence of discrimination against Wang, and that Wang was denied tenure because of deficiencies in her teaching reviews and research work. Wang disagreed and said she felt "complete and joyful vindication" with the settlement, and plans to continue to "speak out about this kind of discrimination." Her lawyer, Gary Gwilliam, said the university settled because "they knew they were going to lose." He was prepared to bring up several embarrassing issues and incidents that could have potentially affected Wang's case. These included a 1992 report that charged male faculty members in the Architecture Department showed favoritism toward male students over female students and sexual harassment complaints by Asian American women students. "There was no other reason that she (Wang) should not get tenure," Gwilliam told reporters after the settlement was announced.[41] The secretive and subjective nature of faculty tenure is not significantly different from job evaluations found in other occupations in the private or public sector. The cultural stereotypes and irrational judgments seen in both the Yamashita and Tung cases, and the discrimination possibilities seen in the Wang case, are very much part of the workplace environment. Of course, rejection from a job or denial of a promotion is not always the result of discrimination. However, Asian Americans, like other racial minority groups and women, often face that lingering question in their minds about what factors played into their loss of opportunity and mobility.

LANGUAGE RIGHTS

Another issue of particular importance for Asian Americans on the job has to do with language rights. Because there is a large portion of immigrants and nonnative English speakers among the Asian American population, language discrimination is becoming a growing trend and a cause of great concern. Some, including many Asian Americans, believe that the differences in pay and upward career mobility may be understandable because of their lack of English language proficiency. "Communication skills are definitely a problem," admits Yung-Chi Cheng, a professor of pharmacology at Yale University. "My English is very poor. But I have been lucky so far. One way or another people accommodate me."[42]

Concerns over English fluency do have some validity for both employers and employees. Certainly employers want managers and workers who can communicate clearly and without trouble. On the other hand, employees don't want to be unfairly handicapped in a competitive job market. The study conducted by Ong and Blumenberg discussed above did find that Asian American immigrants in the sciences, who have been in the United States for five years or less, earn about 20 to 25 percent less than U.S.-born scientists, and recent immigrant engineers earn about 33 percent less than their U.S.-born counterparts. The earnings gap for immigrant scientists and engineers is not permanent, however, and there does not appear to be any overall earnings gap for immigrant scientists and engineers who have been in the United States for 20 years or more. U.S.-born Asian American scientists actually earned more than their white counterparts, although there didn't seem to be any difference among engineers.[43]

Accent Discrimination

While Asian American immigrants acknowledge their English may not be perfect, they feel that it should not be the only stumbling block in advancing their careers and their other qualities should not be overlooked. This frustration can be found in all fields, of course, and is not limited to professionals. "There is no doubt that communication skills are very important," said Wayne Liauh, during testimony in Houston to the U.S. Commission on Civil Rights. "However, adopting a standard that is unreasonably high may be tantamount to allowing an employment practice that is prejudicial against foreign-born Asian American employees."[44] Ironically, even Asian Americans without accents often confront employers who expect a language problem. One Korean American woman was stunned when she found out an employment counselor placed a note in her file saying, "Chinese but speaks good English." According to the woman, the most troublesome part of this episode is the fact that the counselor did not see a competitive job candidate, but "an Asian woman with a potential language problem."[45]

Discrimination in employment and promotion based on a person's English language proficiency, accent, or the desire to speak another language while at work are all illegal. They are, in fact, covered by Title VII of the 1964 Civil Rights Act prohibiting national origin discrimination. The only exception to language rights protection is in cases where a person is clearly unable to perform the responsibilities of the job because of his or her inability to speak and be understood in English. But since the early 1990s, serious concerns have been raised about subjective assessments of the workers' abilities to communicate, and the impact it has on the workplace. As a result, in 1995 the American Civil Liberties Union (ACLU) of Northern California and the Employment Law Center (ELC) of the Legal Aid Society in San Francisco created a nationwide "Language Rights Hotline" to meet the needs of increased reports of discrimination based on accent and English-only rules.[46]

"We have encountered many people who have been told not to speak any language other than English at work, have been denied credit or insurance because they do not speak English well, or even denied promotions because they have a foreign accent," said ACLU attorney Ed Chen. "Many of these workers are unaware that federal and state laws prohibit discrimination on the basis of language and national origin, yet their legal rights may have been violated."[47] Many attorneys who defend language rights believe the rise in the "official" English or "English-only" movement in the 1980s, along with increased anti-immigrant sentiment in the 1990s, together have fueled the flames of intolerance that has generated a growing number of language discrimination cases. Indeed, language may be used as a less direct way to vent antagonism against immigrants of different races and national origins. "There's a backlash against immigrants . . . that is expressed not in out-and-out racism but in language discrimination," explains Chen.[48]

His words seem to be reinforced by a report from the federal Equal Employment Opportunity Commission (EEOC) showing a dramatic increase of national origin–based employment discrimination cases in which English-only and accent discrimination are counted. In 1993 over 7,300 of these cases were reported. This figure is higher than the total number of similar cases filed during the prior three years.[49] Recently, Asian Americans who have been adversely affected in their jobs because of alleged language problems are successfully challenging their employer's actions. In Seattle, Washington, Cambodian American, Phanna K. Xieng, won a $389,000 settlement against Peoples National Bank for illegally denying him promotions because of his accent. A spokesperson for the bank contended that Xieng's English wasn't good enough to calm down irate customers who were denied credit.[50]

The most publicized case of accent discrimination involved five Filipino American security guards in San Francisco who filed suit against American Mutual Protective Bureau (AMPB) and the United States government in May 1992. The case took on great significance because the five guards were removed from their posts after a Federal Protection Service official in the U.S. Treasury Building complained about having trouble communicating with an unidentified guard over the phone. The official assumed the guard was Filipino and ordered "all the Filipino guards removed from the site." AMPB officials followed orders from the federal government and removed the guards. Attorneys for the guards said AMPB made no attempt to determine whether or not any of the men were actually involved in the phone incident, nor determine whether or not the men were able to perform their jobs.[51]

Until this incident, all of the guards had worked for AMPB for between three to six years and no one had complained about their work performances or their English. All except one of the guards had attended college in the Philippines, where the language of instruction is English. The five guards,

Cayetano Decena, Perfecto Estrada, Teodolfo Loyola, Florentino Ramirez, and Cabrito Rose, were all devastated by their removal. "We felt embarrassed among friends, co-workers and relatives because we were removed for not being able to speak English," said Perfecto Estrada. He added that "(a)ll of us had emotional, mental, and physical distress. We have also suffered from financial hardships and family problems caused by the loss of income." Estrada himself was laid off for six months before he was eventually reassigned to swing, graveyard, and weekend shifts at another post. Of all the guards, Estrada thought he had the least to fear. During his employment at AMPB he was steadily promoted up the ranks to sergeant, then first lieutenant, captain, and eventually to deputy chief. His natural leadership abilities were also reflected in his 28 years of experience in the Philippine military and as a district commander of the Philippine Constabulary highway patrol. "I had worked with AMPB for over five years without any complaints," Estrada said proudly, "I knew I didn't have any problem communicating in English."[52]

In June 1994, a settlement was reached in which the five guards received $87,500 from the U.S. General Services Administration and an undisclosed amount from AMPB. In return, however, no one conceded any wrongdoing. The importance of the case is witnessed by the fact that attorneys from the Asian Law Caucus (ALC) in San Francisco, the ACLU, the ELC, and a private law firm all joined forces on the side of the Filipino American guards. During a press conference following the settlement, Lora Jo Foo, an attorney with the Asian Law Caucus said: "When these five security guards came to ALC in March of 1992 for assistance, we were disturbed that federal government officials could even issue the removal of all Filipinos from the workplace and that [American Mutual Protection Bureau] could obey the order without batting an eye, without questioning the wisdom of the order. Had the [U.S. General Services Administration] ordered the removal of all blacks from the Department of Treasury, I am sure the reaction would have been, 'But that's discrimination; We can't do that.'"[53]

"English-Only" Rules

A second area of language discrimination that is on the rise is in "English-only" rules at work. For Adelaida Dimaranan, a former assistant head nurse with Pomona Valley Hospital Medical Center in Southern California, the evening she was caught speaking her native Filipino language of Tagalog during a dinner break with two co-workers was the beginning of a series of events that would eventually thrust her into the center of national attention. Notes from a staff meeting just four months after the incident reported the head nurse saying, "The use of Filipino language . . . won't be tolerated." Although the hospital denied that a blanket "English-only" rule was ordered, the Filipina nurses worried if they were ever caught speaking Tagolog during breaks, on the phone with families, or informally during meals it might be cause for disciplinary action. This policy was especially difficult for Dimaranan because, as an assistant supervisor, she was expected support the administration. "There was no way I was going to enforce the policy," admitted Dimaranan. "They didn't like that."[54]

Not only did Dimaranan refuse to enforce the policy, she was reprimanded a number of times for continuing to speak Tagolog. According to Dimaranan, this brought on further adverse actions against her. Other assistant head nurses began writing her up on minor infractions that reflected on her work and these began to show up on her performance reports. Dimaranan had received excellent work reviews prior to the Tagolog-speaking incident and had no problems after she was first promoted to assistant head nurse. But after her language troubles began, her reviews were critical and she was said to have "created tensions" and caused "division" among the staff. Based on these work evaluations, Dimaranan was demoted and relocated to another unit in the hospital. Nine nurses who were supervised by Dimaranan signed a letter of support and one of them declared, "I think the supervisors were trying to punish her because she defended herself on the language issue." Just as she fought against what she thought was an unfair English-only work rule, Dimaranan did not take her demotion and transfer quietly. With a 25-year nursing career, 13 years of service to Pomona Valley Hospital, and her dignity to protect, she filed a civil rights lawsuit in both state and federal courts.[55]

The federal Equal Employment Opportunity Commission has held that an English-only work policy is legal if it is justified by a business necessity. However, blanket English-only rules that include worker's breaks or free time are almost always illegal because the business necessity argument cannot be justified. The EEOC also agrees with civil rights advocates who insist the prohibition of speaking a person's native language can create an atmosphere of inferiority, isolation, and intimidation, which could result in a discriminatory working environment. The Dimaranan lawsuit was given a boost when the EEOC decided to intervene on her behalf. On the other hand, an earlier federal court's decision was not favorable in Dimaranan's case. In the *Garcia v. Gloor* (1981) case, the Fifth Circuit found English-only policies were not discriminatory because the employees in this particular instance were all bilingual and could speak English if ordered to do so. The court ruled a person who is fully capable of speaking English and chooses not to do so was not a victim of discrimination. "Mr. Garcia could readily comply with the speaking-English-only rule," the ruling read. "In some circumstances, the ability to speak or the speaking of a language other than English might be equated with national origin, but this case concerns only a requirement that persons capable of speaking English do so while on duty."[56]

Before the case went to trial, the hospital did go on public record opposing English-only work rules. Dimaranan pressed on with her suit, demanded her old job back, and wanted the removal of the negative evaluations from her record. In early 1993 Dimaranan and the hospital reached an out-of-court settlement in which she was paid an undisclosed amount and the hospital admitted no wrongdoing. The Dimaranan case had the potential for setting a legal precedent when employees are free to speak their native language, but she and her lawyers cannot be faulted for accepting a settlement. As discussed earlier in this chapter, there is never any guarantee of winning a lawsuit. To highlight this point, the following year the U.S. Supreme Court refused to hear an appeal by Latino employees at a South San Francisco meat-packing plant who challenged an English-only work policy. The decision left intact a ruling by the U.S. Court of Appeals in San Francisco, and allowed employers to impose English-only rules where and when they see fit. The earlier Court of Appeals ruling declared that English-only work policies were merely an "inconvenience" for workers. To date, the high court has yet to hear a case on English-only work rules, despite a growing number of such cases emerging across the country.[57]

The Dimaranan lawsuit was followed closely by Asian American leaders because English-only rules are not uncommon in hospitals employing large numbers of Filipino nurses. Unions have been active in trying to organize Filipino nurses and the English-only rules are a prime issue. A union representative from the Hospital and Service Employees' Union Local 399 filed a discrimination charge because he was banned from a nursing home in Orange, California, for speaking Tagolog to nurses. Attorneys for Gabriel Espiritu hope the complaint will pressure the Hillhaven Corp.—a Tacoma, Washington, company that owns thousands of nursing homes across the nation—to change a language policy that requires English or the "majority language" of most of the patients to be spoken near patients.

Mark Timmerman, a spokesperson for Hillhaven, claims the policy is not illegal nor discriminatory, and is a business necessity. "Basically, what we ask is that employees not speak a foreign language around patients," Timmerman explained. "We're dealing with patients who are vulnerable emotionally as well as physically." The union counters that the policy is too broad and should not apply to workers who are not speaking with, or providing care to, a patient. In addition, Espiritu found the language policy intimidates nurses and makes it more difficult for him to organize the workers. Espiritu and the union tried to get a court order that would allow him back inside the nursing home, but an Orange County Superior Court judge allowed him to conduct union business only in the break room.[58]

ASIAN AMERICAN WORKING CLASS AND LABOR MOVEMENT

Along with skilled nurses, a growing number of Filipinas are also employed as nursing assistants in convalescent hospitals and as service care workers for homebound elderly and disabled. It is these people who do the basic bathing, bedpan, and lifting work for patients who are unable to care for themselves.

These service workers are often paid minimum wage, receive no benefits, are prone to work-related injury, and face job insecurity. What happened to Natie Llever, a Filipina worker in her sixties, is an example of the difficulties these workers must face. Llever was fired from her job at the Casa San Miguel Convalescent Hospital in Concord, California, after she strained her back lifting a patient. It was this incident that finally prompted the hospital's workers, the majority of whom are Filipinos, to organize and join Service Employees International Union (SEIU) Hospital and Health Care Workers Local 250. Since that time the hospital has been accused of unfair labor practices and a pattern of racial harassment against Filipino workers. The owners of the hospital have recognized the union and are said to be willing to negotiate a contract. However, negotiations have been stalled because of the owners' refusal to rehire 12 Filipino workers who were fired allegedly because they were insubordinant and spoke Tagalog, and for being "too old and sickly."[59]

Relatively little popular attention has been focused directly on the plight of the working poor Asian American women and men in the United States who live below or just above the poverty level threshold. Asian Americans have generally placed a great deal of attention on the glass ceiling problem, a primarily middle-class and professional issue. Recently, increased attention has been drawn to language rights, which does impact both middle- and working-class Asian Americans. Unfortunately, the contributions of the Asian American working class have been largely ignored by the general public and in U.S. labor history. If mentioned at all, Asian Americans were seen as foreign threats to the American workingman and as scabs, who bore the brunt of the mainstream labor movement's wrath. Asian Americans were also seen as the victims of labor's hostile union antagonism, calls for exclusion, and ugly anti-Asian racism. Since a new wave of Asian immigrants has entered the United States since 1965, the labor movement has had to confront changes in the make up of the work force and has recognized the increase in Asian American workers. A 1991 report to the AFL-CIO's Executive Council acknowledged that Asian American communities and the labor movement shared common concerns for "economic and political justice, equal opportunity, and an improved quality of life for all working people." In the addition, the AFL-CIO established a formal support organization for Asian American labor unionists.[60] The result of this effort was the creation of Asian Pacific American Labor Alliance (APALA), which held its founding convention in Washington, DC, on May 1, 1992. Over 500 Asian American unionists from across the nation attended the conference and it was a clear pronouncement of a joint effort to increase the participation between Asian Americans and the American labor movement.[61]

The formal creation of APALA, the first national Asian American labor organization established within the ranks of the AFL-CIO, was long overdue. Asian American workers have historically faced tremendous hardships and exploitation by non-Asian, as well as from Asian employers. As a result, there have been many attempts in recent years to organize Asian American workers in the various sectors in which they are clustered. Important efforts were made to unionize garment workers, hotel and restaurant employees, electronic manufacturing workers, janitors, food processing and cannery laborers, and hospital workers, among many others. These recent efforts by unions have had only modest success, and unionization among Asian Americans remains quite low. The process has been difficult for a number of reasons. First, there has been a general decline in the labor movement since the early 1980s. In the 1960s roughly 35 percent of all U.S. workers were represented by a union. By the early 1990s this figure was reduced to just 17 percent. Second, there continues to be deep-seated stereotypes among some union leaders that Asian Americans are clannish and uninterested in being organized. This creates frustration for the organizers as well as those who need to be organized. Third, because Asian Americans have only recently been welcomed into unions, there are relatively few Asian American union leaders, shop stewards, or organizers. Lack of cultural sensitivity, language fluency, and access to ethnic enclave businesses have proven to be difficult barriers for established unions to overcome in organizing Asian American workers. Many of the workers who are most exploited and most in need of union support are immigrants and are not native English speakers.

Because of these challenges, Asian American labor activists have come together in several communities to help the unionization movement. In the late 1970s and early 1980s the Asian American Federation of Union Members (AAFUM) was formed in San Francisco, and helped to unionize the *Chinese Times* newspaper and Korean American janitors at the San Francisco Airport. The Alliance of Asian Pacific Labor (AAPL) in Los Angeles has been in the forefront of bringing virtually all Asian American union staff and rank-and-file leaders together since the late 1980s. Many of these Asian American unionized workers were activists within their own respective unions but did not have much interaction with each other. It was the AAPL network that helped secure a work site victory for the Aluminum, Brick and Glass Workers Union by getting them in contact with a Vietnamese-speaking organizer from another union who was able to convince newly hired Vietnamese American workers of the merits of collective representation.[62]

Only recently have established unions in New York been seen as reliable partners to many Asian American workers. In 1985 the owners of the Hunan Garden Restaurant in New York's Chinatown fired union workers in an attempt to break the union. When the workers went to their union (Hotel Employees and Restaurant Employees, Local 100) for help, they were frustrated by the lack of attention they were given. As a result, the workers sought help from the New York Chinese Progressive Association, which immediately formed a picket line outside of the restaurant. The picket served two purposes. First, it practically shut down the business for almost a week and, second, it succeeded in embarrassing the union for its inactivity. The union finally addressed grievances of the Hunan Garden workers and helped them

gain reinstatement of their jobs with full back pay. The Hunan Garden workers' victory was the spark that created the Asian Labor Resource Center
(ALRC) in New York, which is made up of Asian American labor activists from
several unions, students, and community organizers. ALRC has been active in
labor support efforts, pro-union education programs, advising in job discrimination cases, and has also sponsored classes on Asian American labor at Cornell University.[63]

Community-Based Labor Organizing

The Hunan Garden incident and the formation of ALRC demonstrate the
importance of community-based labor organizing. Community organizing
campaigns outside the direct auspices of established unions are now increasingly common. According to writer and worker rights advocate Glen Omatsu,
community-based labor organizing has been labeled "pre-union formations"
by labor scholars and union officials. It is generally assumed that community
organizing is just part of a greater labor union movement, and union membership should eventually be the ultimate goal for Asian American workers.
However, Omatsu believes these community organizing efforts may in fact be
"post-union formations" that have emerged because of the decline of the overall labor union movement in recent years and its difficulties in successfully
organizing Asian American workers. "The first trend (pre-union formations)
is national in scope and spotlights workers in high-profile occupations such as
automobile manufacturing, aerospace, and industries with long histories of
labor organizing," Omatsu writes. "The second trend (post-union formations)
deals with a collage of diffuse and localized struggles involving largely
'marginal' workers—new immigrants and refugees, people of color, women,
and employees in the so-called service occupations, light manufacturing, and
'peripheral' industries, like garment work."[64]

    There are a number of examples of community-based organizing
groups, which are part of the second trend of labor organizing and have made
a significant impact on the lives of Asian American workers. One of the most
notable of these is Asian Immigrant Women Advocates (AIWA), based in Oakland, California. AIWA began in 1983 in response to tremendous abuses
within the garment industry in the San Francisco Bay Area. Since that time
AIWA has engaged in a number of activities aimed at educating and empowering Asian immigrant women, as well as community-based organizing efforts
intended to bring about social change. AIWA's philosophy is focused on the
belief that workers know best what they need, and want to improve the quality
of their lives. This worker-centered approach is reflected in AIWA's "Seamstress Survey" that was carried out to find what the priority issues were for the
workers. Over 500 Chinese language surveys were distributed and volunteers
were used to staff phone banks to help explain the questionnaire. Of the sur-

veys sent out, 166 were returned and the results became the basis for AIWA's future efforts. Some of the major findings included:

- English language proficiency was very low among the women workers. Few had ever taken an English language class primarily because they did not have time.
- The respondents varied considerably in age. However, a significant number (26 percent) of the seamstresses were 50 years or older. All of the women had children.
- Over 90 percent of the women stated their husbands worked as unskilled or semiskilled laborers. Their occupations included waiters, busboys, day laborers, and gardeners.
- Wages for the women were generally quite low. A third of the women worked for less than minimum wage and half worked at minimum wage.
- Over half of the respondents (57 percent) worked six days a week or more, and over a quarter (27 percent) were paid by the piece, rather than by a set hourly wage.
- A high percentage of the seamstresses lacked, or were unaware of, basic employee benefits. For example, over 80 percent did not know their hiring and firing procedures, receive sick pay, or have any worker's compensation.
- Over three quarters of the respondents did not receive salary increases, vacation leave, or overtime pay. Almost 70 percent did not get paid holidays or health insurance, and over half did not get any break periods.[65]

Understanding that English language fluency is a basic survival skill, AIWA started workplace literacy classes in the evenings and on Sundays to accommodate working women's schedules. AIWA also sponsors leadership training classes primarily aimed at garment workers. A variety of topics are covered in these training sessions, including (1) the history of Asian immigration; (2) garment industry structure and Garment Workers Justice Campaigns; (3) how to read wages, hours, and deductions on their paycheck; (4) knowing their rights for worker's compensation and state disability insurance; and (5) occupational health and safety issues.[66] Another activity AIWA sponsored was a trip to El Paso, Texas, to attend the First Congress of Working Women. Attendance at this gathering served to establish a network of Latina, African American, Native American, and Asian American working women's rights organizations from across the nation, and to share experiences. "We were all feeling isolated," explained AIWA executive director, Young Shin. "So we got together . . . and talked about the development of a new workers' movement made up of workers who had not been unionized, immigrants, people of color who work in the most marginal sectors of the economy, and workers who are not part of the elite, of any aristocracy of labor."[67]

AIWA's most publicized activity is their role in a national boycott campaign against the Jessica McClintock clothes line. The issue in conflict emerged in mid-1992, when a group of 12 seamstresses from the Lucky Sewing Company came to the AIWA office and complained their paychecks had bounced. The total amount of money owed to the workers was relatively small—just $15,000—but this represented important income to women barely able to make ends meet. AIWA initially confronted the owners of Lucky Sewing, but the company claimed complete bankruptcy and could not pay the workers. Jessica McClintock Inc. had contracted with and paid Lucky Sewing to sew a new line of clothes for sale in major department stores across the country. But after the dresses were made, Lucky Sewing abruptly went out of business and left its workers unpaid. Jessica McClintock Inc., a corporation that grossed $145 million in sales in 1992, denied any responsibility for workers who made their garments, flatly refused to pay the workers' back wages, and defends itself by saying the practice of contracting out work is common throughout the garment industry. AIWA knew that McClintock was not legally liable for the workers' salaries or working conditions, but wanted the company to set a new standard for the industry by making up for the workers' lost wages. AIWA saw McClintock perpetuating the much bigger problem of labor contracting within the garment industry. "Jessica McClintock knows this is not really a money issue," says AIWA's Young Shin. "It's about the working conditions of the workers who sew her dresses. . . . Fundamentally, it's a human-rights issue."[68]

Ironically, Jessica McClintock is generally recognized as a leading role model for working women because of her own personal rags-to-riches story, her work ethic, her philanthropic activities, and her generosity to her corporate employees. Other garment industry leaders such as Esprit, Levi Strauss, Banana Republic, and the Gap, among others, are also known for their socially conscious image, as well as their trendy clothes lines. Unfortunately, the public image belies some of the behind-the-scenes realities. For example, in 1992 Esprit was nominated for a Corporate Conscience Award by the Council on Economic Priorities, but between 1992 and 1993 the Department of Labor (DOL) raided nine sewing contractors in the San Francisco Bay Area that were engaged in illegal labor practices. Four of the contractors cited for their abuses worked for Esprit. In particular, one of these sweatshops contracted by Esprit paid seamstresses only $3.75 an hour with no overtime (minimum wage was $4.25 at the time) and owed the workers $127,000 in back wages.[69] These activities are allowed to continue because brand-name garment industry giants turn a blind eye and a deaf ear to the conditions of the workers who make their clothing. Technically, many apparel companies are "marketeers" who design and sell products, but don't actually own any factories that make the goods. The companies instead hire out to the lowest bidding "contractor" who agrees to sew a certain amount of clothes and deliver them at an agreed upon time. This allows companies like McClintock, Esprit, and others to distance themselves from labor practices on the shop floor.[70]

These corporations know that competition among sewing contractors is fierce. There are over 600 sewing contractors in the San Francisco Bay Area alone, and some of them do bid unrealistically low just to get the job. The work may get done, but workers are overworked and underpaid—if they get paid at all. There are contractors who claim bankruptcy and go out of business, then reappear just months later under another name. Department of Labor investigator Harry Hu recalls one sewing contractor company, Kin Hing, that closed and reopened again with the new name, Hing Kin.[71] Yet another layer of separation away from garment workers comes from apparel industry leaders who say they should be commended, not condemned, because they have been keeping jobs in the United States when the general trend in all areas of manufacturing is to shift jobs overseas where workplace rights are practically nonexistent. Within this, the threat of closing shop and moving to another country is always an available weapon the garment industry uses against its detractors. Garment industry giants also place the final blame on consumers who demand good quality clothes but at affordable prices. There is little more that can be done, they say, but follow the realities of the marketplace.

AIWA insists that exploitation of garment workers does not have to continue and has spearheaded an aggressive campaign to achieve three goals: (1) to educate the public about garment industry abuses; (2) to boycott Jessica McClintock products; and (3) to push for legislative reform. The public education and boycott strategy is seen in pickets held in front of major department stores in 13 cities across the nation, including Los Angeles, New York, Chicago, Boston, Atlanta, and even in front of McClintock's own home in San Francisco. AIWA has also paid for a series of full-page ads in the *New York Times* national edition calling attention to the plight of the 12 unpaid seamstresses, while at the same time highlighting the fact that garment workers earn about $5 to sew a Jessica McClintock dress that retails for $175. A February 14, 1994, *New York Times* ad clearly stated the purpose of the boycott campaign: "Garment manufacturers are now on notice that sweatshop abuses will no longer be tolerated? . . . The campaign will continue until there is justice for the hundreds of thousands of immigrant women who suffer from the endless cycle of abusive sweatshop conditions. Not until Jessica McClintock and other manufacturers sign a Covenant of Fairness giving the women who sew our clothing a shot at fair wages, job security and decent working conditions will we declare victory."[72] Along with the education and boycott campaign, AIWA has actively lobbied for reform laws that would make garment manufacturers jointly liable with contractors for abuses of sewing factory workers. In September 1994, California governor Pete Wilson vetoed such a bill that was passed by both houses of the state legislature. Garment manufacturers, including Jessica McClintock, fought vigorously against the bill. Not surprisingly, industry leaders threatened to move garment production to other states or foreign countries if the bill were passed.[73]

Jessica McClintock also struck back against AIWA and its campaign. In August, 1994, McClintock's lawyers were successful in obtaining an injunction against picketers at her San Francisco boutique and residence. The court ordered protesters to march at least six feet away from the entrance of McClintock's boutique and only two people at a time can march in front of McClintock's home. Similar court motions were heard in other cities where protests have been organized. "Is this justice?" asked an angry protesting seamstress. "She uses profits from our labor to pay expensive lawyers to shut us up."[74] McClintock also paid for a full-page ad in the *New York Times,* defending her position in the dispute and declaring she is the victim of a "blatant shakedown." In addition, McClintock was accused of being behind some rather unseemly tactics intended to divide the Asian American community against the AIWA's efforts. McClintock hired Lynne Choy Uyeda and Associates, an Asian American public relations firm who brought in Asian American students to counter-leaflet at boycott demonstrations in San Francisco and Los Angeles. In addition, the Northern California Chinese Garment Contractors Association—most of whom are McClintock contractors—offered a "charitable gift" to the 12 unpaid seamstresses provided they sign a document stating that the gift is not wages "and the money you are receiving does not represent wages due you from Lucky Sewing."[75] Five of the twelve seamstresses accepted the offer. Lastly, Jessica McClintock made donations to several San Francisco Bay Area Asian American community organizations, "in the spirit of generosity and support." The Asian Women's Shelter returned the check and the Asian Community Health Services said it was going to donate the money back to the community or to the garment workers' cause. "We appreciate the $1,000 check, but I hope that she would focus her efforts on the retribution to garment workers and negotiating a settlement," said Asian Women's Shelter director, Beckie Masaki.[76]

AIWA's direct action tactics and high-profile campaign were highly effective. In March, 1996, AIWA announced it had reached a settlement in its three-year dispute with Jessica McClintock Inc. JMI did not pay any back wages but was willing to donate money to establish a garment workers' education fund for the Lucky garment workers, sponsor scholarships for students and garment workers, provide garment workers with bilingual state and federal publications to better educate them on fair labor standards, and to provide two toll-free numbers (one in English and one in Cantonese) for JMI contractors and employees to facilitate better reporting and compliance with federal labor laws. Lastly, JMI agreed to work with other groups to explore alternative methods for worker wage protection and the viability of an independent industry monitoring program. According to U.S. Secretary of Labor, Robert Reich, the settlement was significant in its call for cooperative efforts by both parties to insure workers' rights as well as to promote awareness of fair labor practices. "I commend both parties for reaching this agreement," Reich said.[77]

AIWA's struggle on behalf of workers has been an inspiration to many across the nation. But for all of their protest efforts, the greatest attention to the plight of garment workers and sweatshop conditions came from a very unexpected source. In April 1996, daytime television talk-show host, Kathie Lee Gifford, was shocked and embarrassed when she found out that the line of clothes bearing her name sold at Wal-Mart stores was being made by underpaid workers in Honduras and New York City. Gifford was particularly upset to learn that some of her garments were made by exploited young teenage laborers. Kathie Lee Gifford, and her husband, sports announcer Frank Gifford, have since become crusaders against sweatshops.[78] Their public denouncements of labor abuses and their celebrity status were utilized successfully by Labor Secretary Reich in his "No Sweat" campaign aimed at eradicating wage and safety violations in sewing shops. Within a few short months this effort resulted in President Clinton announcing an agreement with ten major manufacturers to inform consumers that their clothes were made "under decent and humane working conditions." Among the well-known companies that agreed to these terms included, Liz Claiborne, Nike, L. L. Bean, and Patagonia. Conspicuously absent was Levi Strauss & Co., the world's largest clothes manufacturers, who declined to sign the agreement. A spokesperson for Levi Strauss & Co. complained that the agreement was too vague and inflexible, but did agree that companies should monitor contractors for labor violations. Garment worker advocate groups like AIWA realize that the agreement in and of itself is not perfect, that there are many more manufacturers who have not signed the agreement than have, and that there is still plenty of work that needs to be done to correct the abuses throughout the entire industry.[79]

Nonetheless, AIWA welcomes the attention to an important issue it has been fighting for the last several years. AIWA continues to bring attention to workplace abuses and has begun a new organizing effort. This time AIWA is organizing unskilled and semiskilled workers who assemble computers and circuit boards in high-tech companies in Silicon Valley. The Pacific Studies Center report cited earlier also found Asian Americans represent 41.2 percent of the unskilled workers and 47 percent of the semiskilled workers in the region. "Asian workers have been growing in production work to reflect the growing belief among employers that other nonwhite ethnic groups will be more militant," explains the study's author, Lenny Siegel, of the Pacific Studies Center. According to Helen Kim, an organizer for AIWA, Asian immigrants are more concerned with the use of dangerous chemicals at work than salary issues. "For instance," she says, "the lead used in soldering has a sweet smell that you don't associate with possible danger." One person who had just taken AIWA's workplace literacy classes, was alarmed when she realized her desk was placed next to a barrel labeled "TOXIC." She did not know what the word "toxic" meant until she took the class. Another major campaign may be in the works in the very near future.[80]

CONCLUSION

This chapter has shown a variety of employment issues confronted by Asian Americans. Rather than accepting these conditions passively, Asian Americans are working both individually, and as a group, to challenge some of the workplace practices that directly affect their careers, standard of living, and quality of life. Although most of the media attention has been placed on the primarily middle-class issue of the glass ceiling, this chapter has provided a glimpse of a number of other important issues that impact Asian American men and women from every socioeconomic strata. These issues are noteworthy as the Asian American population continues to grow, mature, and make its mark throughout the work force.

ENDNOTES

1. Robert A. Rosenblatt, "'Glass Ceiling' Still Too Hard to Break, U.S. Panel Finds," *Los Angeles Times*, March 16, 1995.
2. Korn Ferry International, "Korn Ferry's International Executive Profile: A Decade of Change in Corporate Leadership" (1990), Table 61, cited in U.S. Commission on Civil Rights, *Civil Rights Issues Facing Asian Americans in the 1990s* (Washington, DC: Government Printing Office, 1992), pp. 132–33.
3. U.S. Commission on Civil Rights, *The Economic Status of Americans of Asian Descent: An Exploratory Investigation* (Washington, DC: Clearinghouse Publication 95, October 1988), pp. 72–75.
4. U.S. Commission on Civil Rights, *Civil Rights Issues Facing Asian Americans in the 1990s*, pp. 131–132.
5. National Science Foundation, *Women and Minorities in Science and Engineering* (Washington, DC: Government Printing Office, 1990), p. 68; and U.S. Department of Labor, "Projections of Occupational Employment, 1988–2000," *BLS Monthly Labor Review*, November, 1989, pp. 51–59.
6. Paul Ong and Evelyn Blumenberg, "Scientists and Engineers," in Paul Ong (ed.), *The State of Asian Pacific America: Economic Diversity, Issues & Policies* (Los Angeles: LEAP Asian Pacific Public Policy Institute and UCLA Asian American Studies Center, 1994), pp. 169–70.
7. Ong and Blumenberg, "Scientists and Engineers," pp. 177–179.
8. Tom Abate, "Heavy Load for Silicon Valley Workers," *San Francisco Examiner*, May 23, 1993.
9. Ralph Vartabedian, "Aerospace Careers in Low Orbit," *Los Angeles Times*, November 16, 1992.
10. Elisa Lee, "Silicon Valley Study Finds Asian Americans Hitting the Glass Ceiling," *Asian Week*, October 8, 1993.
11. Quoted in Winifred Yu, "Asian-Americans Charge Prejudice Slows Climb to Management Ranks," *Wall Street Journal*, September 11, 1985.
12. Quoted in Stanley Karnow and Nancy Yoshihara, *Asian Americans in Transition* (New York: The Asia Society, 1992), p. 40.

13. Catherine Yang, "In Any Language, It's Unfair," *Business Week* June 21, 1993, p. 111.
14. "A 'Superminority' Tops Out," *Newsweek*, May 11, 1987, pp. 48–49.
15. Quoted in Victoria McNamara, "Battling the Bamboo Ceiling," *Houston Post*, May 31, 1993.
16. Quoted in Vartabedian, "Aerospace Careers in Low Orbit."
17. "Have Skills, Will Travel—Home," *Business Week*, November 18, 1994, pp. 164-165; and J. Madeleine Nash, "Tigers in the Lab," *Time*, November 21, 1994, pp. 86–87.
18. U.S. Equal Employment Opportunity Commission, *Annual Report on the Employment of Minorities, Women and Handicapped Individuals in the Federal Government* (Washington, DC: Government Printing Office, 1990).
19. Pan Suk Kim and Gregory B. Lewis, "Asian Americans in Public Service: Success, Diversity, and Discrimination, *Public Administration Review* 54:3 (May–June 1994): 285–290.
20. *Ibid.*, p. 288.
21. *Ibid.*, p. 289.
22. Henry Der et al., *The Broken Ladder ' 92: Asian Americans in City Government* (San Francisco: Chinese for Affirmative Action, 1992).
23. *Ibid.*, pp. 5–6.
24. *Ibid.*, pp. 10–11.
25. *Ibid.*, p. 9.
26. *Ibid.* p. 3.
27. Clarence Johnson, "2nd Choice Easily Wins Key SF Job," *San Francisco Chronicle*, March 28, 1995; and Susan Sword, "New SF Police Chief Is Widely Respected," *San Francisco Chronicle*, January 9, 1996.
28. Frances M. Namkoong, "Stereotyping Is Holding Asian-Americans Back," *Cleveland Plain Dealer*, May 17, 1994.
29. *Ibid.*
30. "Helping Asians Climb Through Bamboo Ceiling," *Wall Street Journal*, December 13, 1991.
31. Henry Der, "Affirmative Action Policy," *The State of Asian Pacific America: Policy Issues to the Year 2020* (Los Angeles: LEAP Asian Pacific American Public Policy Institute and UCLA Asian American Studies Center), pp. 215–232.
32. McNamara, "Battling the Bamboo Ceiling."
33. Quoted in "Marine Wins Bars After Fight Over Bias," *San Francisco Chronicle*, March 19, 1994.
34. Benjamin Pimentel, "One Man's War Against Marines," *San Francisco Chronicle*, February 5, 1994.
35. *Ibid.*
36. Eric Schmitt, "Asian-American Proves Marine Bias," *New York Times*, January 21, 1994.
37. Quoted in Pimentel, "One Man's War."
38. Tenure is the achievement of permanent status within a university's faculty. Tenure is granted after a period of six to seven years of demonstrated excellence in teaching, research, and university community service, as well as rigorous review by colleagues within one's academic field. When a person is denied tenure, that person is, in essence, fired from his or her faculty position.
39. U.S. Commission on Civil Rights, *Civil Rights Issues Facing Asian Americans in the 1990s*, pp. 155–156.
40. Quotes in "Tung Case Pries Open Secret Tenure Review," an edited version of a speech given by Rosalie Tung at UC Berkeley, April 1990, published in *The Berkeley Graduate*, April 1990.

41. Quotes in Yasmin Anwar, "UC Berkeley Puts to Rest Tenure Suit," *Oakland Tribune*, January 9, 1996, and Peter Fimrite, "$1 Million Deal in UC Bias Suit," *San Francisco Chronicle*, January 9, 1996.

42. Quoted in Susan Katz Miller, "Asian Americans Bump Against Glass Ceilings," *Science*, November 13, 1992, p. 1225.

43. Ong and Blumenberg, "Scientists and Engineers," pp. 177–183.

44. Wayne Liauh, Statement at the U.S. Commission on Civil Rights Roundtable Conference on Asian American Civil Rights Issues for the 1990s, May 27, 1989, cited in U.S. Commission on Civil Rights, *Civil Rights Issues Facing Asian Americans in the 1990s*, p. 132.

45. Quoted in "The Asian American Dream?" *A Magazine* 2:3 (December 1993): 70.

46. Samuel R. Cacas, "Language Rights Hotline Established." *Rafu Shimpo*, February 8, 1995.

47. *Ibid.*

48. Quoted in Catherine Yang, "In Any Language, It's Unfair," *Business Week* June 21, 1993, p. 110.

49. Cacas, "Language Rights Hotline Established."

50. Yang, "In Any Language, It's Unfair," pp. 110–111.

51. Erin McCormick, "Filipino Guards Sue Over 'Accent Discrimination,'" *San Francisco Examiner*, April 15, 1993.

52. Quoted in Richard J. P. Cavosora, "Discrimination Spoken Here," *Filipinas*, July 1993, pp. 16–18, 46.

53. Quoted in Samuel R. Cacas, "Accent Discrimination Case by Five Filipino American Security Guards Is Settled," *Asian Week*, June 10, 1994.

54. Quoted in Sarah Henry, "Fighting Words," *Los Angeles Times Magazine*, June 10, 1990, p. 10.

55. *Ibid.*, pp. 10–11.

56. *Garcia v. Gloor*, 618 Fed.2d 264, 270 (1981).

57. Jim Doyle, "High Court Lets English-Only Job Rules Stand," *San Francisco Chronicle*, June 21, 1994.

58. Quoted in Leslie Berestein, "Nursing Home Rule Starts War of Words," *Los Angeles Times*, February 27, 1995.

59. Abraham F. Ignacio, Jr. and H. C. Toribio, "The House of Pain," *Filipinas*, September 1994, p. 19.

60. Alex Hing, "Organizing Asian Pacific American Workers in the AFL-CIO: New Opportunities," *Amerasia Journal* 18:1 (1992): 141-154.

61. Kent Wong, "Building an Asian Pacific Labor Alliance: A New Chapter in Our History," in Karin Aguilar-San Juan (ed.), *The State of Asian America: Activism and Resistance in the 1990s* (Boston: South End Press, 1994), pp. 335–349.

62. *Ibid.*, pp. 344–346.

63. Hing, "Organizing Asian Pacific American Workers," pp. 146–147.

64. Glen Omatsu, "Expansion of Democracy," *Amerasia Journal* 18:1 (1992): v–xix.

65. Miriam Ching Louie, "After Sewing, Laundry, Cleaning and Cooking, I Have No Breath Left to Sing," *Amerasia Journal* 18:1 (1992): 1–26.

66. "Leadership Training Wraps Up," *AIWA News* (The Newsletter of Asian Immigrant Women Advocates), 10:2 (Fall 1994): 3

67. Quoted in Louie, "After Sewing," p. 20.

68. Quoted in Sarah Henry, "Labor & Lace," *San Francisco Chronicle*, September 5, 1993.

69. Laurie Udesky, "Sweatshops Behind the Labels," *The Nation*, May 16, 1994, pp. 665–668.

70. Richard P. Appelbaum and Gary Gereffi, "Power and Profits in the Apparel Commodity Chain," in Edna Bonacich et al. (eds), *Global Production: The Apparel Industry in the Pacific Rim* (Philadelphia: Temple University Press, 1994), pp. 42–62.
71. Udesky, "Sweatshops Behind," p. 667.
72. "Jessica McClintock Just Doesn't Get It," *New York Times,* February 14, 1994.
73. "Governor Wilson Vetoes Garment Manufacturers' Joint Liability Bill," *AIWA News,* 10:2 (Fall 1994): 7.
74. *Ibid.;* "McClintock Attacks Free Speech Rights," *AIWA News* 10:2 (Fall 1994): 1, 6.
75. "Jessica McClintock Just Doesn't Get It."
76. Yumi Wilson, "Designer's Largesse Questioned," *San Francisco Chronicle,* February 16, 1994; and Steven A. Chin, "Garment Workers Fight for Back Pay," *San Francisco Examiner,* February 16, 1994.
77. Asian Immigrant Women Advocates Letter and Press Release, March 20, 1996.
78. Bill Wong, "Sweatshop Fame," *Asian Week,* June 21, 1996.
79. Victoria Coliver, "Clinton Cuts 'Sweatshop-Free' Deal," *Oakland Tribune,* August 3, 1996.
80. Quotes in Abate, "Heavy Load for Silicon Valley Workers"; and Nina Schuyler, "Asian Women Come Out Swinging," *The Progressive,* May 1993, p. 14

5

Anti-Asian Violence: Breaking the Silence

VISIBILITY AND INVISIBILITY

Anti-Asian sentiments and violence against Asian Americans has a long history in the United States. Individual racists, hate groups, and xenophobic lawmakers together created a hostile environment during the late nineteenth and early twentieth centuries that served to severely limit the numbers of immigrants from Asia and forced most Asian Americans to retreat into segregated communities that were out of harm's way. Since the passage of immigration reforms in 1965 and the influx of refugees after the Vietnam War, the increasing Asian American population has become more and more conspicuous across the nation. This increased visibility in recent years has also created periodic renewals of angry anti-Asian sentiments that is manifested in increasing incidents of violence against Asian Americans. Despite the more positive images of Asian American students, professionals, and business entrepreneurs, there is growing concern over what many see as an ongoing and ugly trend. Asian American leaders commonly cite the brutal 1982 killing of Vincent Chin in Detroit, Michigan, as the crucial incident that raised the issue of anti-Asian violence to the forefront of public attention. Chin was a 27-year-old Chinese American who was bludgeoned to death with a baseball bat by two autoworkers who allegedly blamed Japan for problems in the U.S. economy and thought Chin was Japanese. The two assailants pled guilty to manslaughter, but a Michigan judge sentenced them each to just three years' probation and a fine of $3,780. Shocked by both the senselessness of the killing and the lenient sentence, Asian Americans saw Chin as a martyr whose death galvanized the Asian American community and led to a nationwide call for federal intervention. After intense pressure, the U.S. Department of Justice brought federal civil rights charges against Ronald Ebans, an auto plant supervisor, and his unemployed stepson, Michael Nitz. In June 1984 Nitz was acquitted of the civil rights charge, but Ebans was found guilty and sentenced to 25 years in prison. Two years later, Ebans' conviction was overturned on appeal. The case was retried in Cincinnati because of the tremendous amount of publicity Chin's killing received in Detroit. The second trial ended in April 1987 with an acquittal for Ebans.[1]

The acquittal sent a chill throughout the Asian American community. For many, the message was that Asian Americans are second-class citizens—tolerated as long as they remain a quiet and passive "model minority," but patronized, or worse, when they attempt to exercise their rights. Since that time Asian American activists have called for federal, state, and local law enforcement authorities to keep statistics on reported cases of hate bias incidents, and for laws that would carry stronger penalties for those convicted of hate-related crimes. Recently, the National Asian Pacific American Legal Consortium (NAPALC), an organization made up of Asian American legal and civil rights organizations across the United States, began to document and monitor hate violence incidents. In addition, NAPALC works to educate the Asian Pacific American community, law enforcement, and the general public about the problem of anti-Asian violence. NAPALC published an *Audit of Violence Against Asian Pacific Americans* for the years 1993, 1994, and 1995, and came up with some powerful findings.[2]

First, the 1995 audit found 458 incidents of anti-Asian violence, a 37 percent increase over the 335 incidents reported in 1993. In 1995 and 1994, about 90 percent of the incidents were confirmed to be racially motivated and racism was strongly suspected in the other cases. In 1993, less than half of the reported incidents were categorized as proven because the racial motivation was only suspected and could not be proven (see Table 5-1). Second, most of the cases of anti-Asian violence in 1995 were assaults, harassment, or vandalism. Within this, the 1995 audit also found Asian Pacific Americans were three times as likely to be assaulted (including aggravated assault) than harassed. These findings are consistent with the 1993 results. Third, violence against Asian Pacific Americans most commonly took place in the victim's home, in public areas, or at his or her place of business. All three areas increased sharply compared with reports from the 1993 audit. Lastly, 73 incidents of vandalism were reported in 1995, nearly doubling the 39 cases reported in 1994.

The issue of anti-Asian violence is a major concern for Asian Americans, even though it is met with considerable ignorance and insensitivity among the general public and law enforcement authorities. This is due to the fact that anti-white, anti-black, anti-Semitic, and anti-Catholic hate crimes still clearly dominate government statistics on hate crimes. This is exemplified by the national attention given to the high number of fire-bombings of African American churches across the United States seen in

Table 5-1   Anti-Asian Incidents for the United States, 1993–1995

Incident	1993	1994	1995
Arson	*	2	0
Assault	31	85	93
Aggravated Assault	13	30	35
Firebombings	2	0	1
Harrassment	6	53	31
Hate Mail	11	6	9
Homicide	4	0	2
Police Abuse	11	18	13
Robbery	3	3	25
Sexual Assault	2	1	2
Threats	14	23	61
False Arrest	1	11	1
Vandalism	26	39	73
Other	7	3	0
Unknown	24	178	112
Total**	155	452	458

Source: National Asian Pacific American Legal Consortium, *Audit of Violence Against Asian Pacific Americans* (1993, 1994, 1995)
* Not counted.
** The number for 1993 reflects only proven anti-Asian incidents. There were 180 suspected anti-Asian incidents. The number of anti-Asian incidents for 1995 and 1994 includes those that were suspected and proven to be motivated by anti-Asian bias or prejudice. Approximately 90 percent of the reported incidents were proven to be racially motivated.

recent years. Nonetheless, Asian Americans are keenly aware of the potential for being victims of violence simply because of their racial distinctiveness. This chapter concentrates first on definitions, distinctions, and examples of the types of anti-Asian violence confronted by Asian Americans. It will next take a close look at four factors that encourage and perpetuate anti-Asian sentiment and violence. Lastly, this chapter examines the volatile issue of Asian American and African American relations. Racial violence is not limited to just whites against people of color. In an increasing multiracial and multicultural society, the concerns over antagonism between and among all groups is an issue that must be directly addressed. Particular emphasis will be placed on the high-profile tensions between Korean Americans and African Americans in major urban centers across the nation. The rebellion in Los Angeles in 1992—where predominantly Korean businesses were targeted for looting and arson—is the most prominent example of large-scale interracial conflict involving Asian Americans, but roots of the discontent are complex and deserve special attention.

Anti-Asian Violence

Most Asian Americans have experienced the pain caused by direct verbal abuse, subtle put-downs, unconscious insults, and thoughtless comments, as well as stereotypical portrayals in the mainstream mass media. In addition, Asian Americans are also becoming targeted victims of racially motivated assaults and vandalism. NAPALC acknowledges the harm caused by all of the above and has included all of them in its audit of anti-Asian *hate violence*. In contrast, the 1990 Federal Hate Crime Statistics Act was enacted to develop and implement a uniform system of collecting accurate data on *hate crimes*. A hate crime is defined as a "violation of a criminal or penal statute" in which the primary motivation, actual or perceived, is based on race, ethnicity, national origin, immigration status, religion, gender, sexual orientation, or age. Despite laudable intentions, there are limitations that severely hamper the act's ability to be effective.

First, only 27 percent of police departments around the nation reported bias incidents in 1991, while just over half (53 percent) of Americans lived in cities where the FBI collected statistics in 1992. As of 1995, 11 states did not keep statistics on hate crimes, and police departments in many jurisdictions did not maintain accurate or complete records. Data on hate crimes were not always broken down by race, and often were not broken down by specific ethnic subgroups. NAPALC argues that more detailed information is necessary to better determine patterns of hate violence toward a particular group or groups. As a result of weak record keeping, there is a probable undercount of actual hate crime incidents by both the FBI and NAPALC itself. Second, the mere utterance of racial slurs in and of itself is technically not a crime and, thus, is not reported by the FBI. Within this, the FBI does not consider the racial epithets used during a crime to be enough evidence of a hate crime. A hate crime requires additional evidence that indicates bias motivation. NAPALC rejects this narrow definition and prefers to report on *hate violence*, which includes "any verbal or physical act that intimidates, threatens, or injures a person or person's property because of membership in a targeted group." The NAPALC definition is much more expansive, and is used to show that hate violence is far more common than what the FBI narrowly calls hate crimes. As a result, NAPALC's numbers tend to be higher than government figures.[3]

Verbal Assaults

One high-profile example of what NAPALC would consider hate violence that cannot be classified as a hate crime, occurred when U.S. Senator Alphonse D'Amato (R-NY) mocked Lance Ito, the judge in the O. J. Simpson murder trial, on a nationally syndicated radio program. D'Amato used a phony Japanese accent and pejoratively referred to Ito as "little Judge Ito." The senator's outburst was so outrageous and off-the-wall that the program's talk show host warned him to stop. Judge Ito, a third-generation Japanese American who does not speak with an accent, did not respond to the insults, but D'Amato faced an onslaught of harsh criticism. D'Amato finally offered an insincere half-apology on the Senate floor, saying, "If I offended anyone . . . I'm sorry."[4] Another recent example took place across the country, where San Francisco's interim Housing Authority director, Ted Deinstfrey, found himself in deep trouble after making a flippant comment that many found highly demeaning and offensive. During an informal talk with a dozen staff members about the problems of tenants owning vicious pit bulls, Deinstfrey suggested that one way to get rid of the dogs was to move in more Vietnamese—a reference to the stereotype that Southeast Asian refugees eat dogs. When word got out about the comment, Deinstfrey quickly realized his mistake and apologized. "I did say something that was insensitive," he said. "I'd just as soon not repeat it." Deinstfrey also sent a letter of apology to the Center for Southeast Asian Refugee Resettlement, where executive director Vu-Duc Vuong was generous in his forgiveness. "The guy made a stupid mistake and he owned up to it," Vuong said. "As far as I'm concerned the case is closed."[5]

These two incidents, although common, are rather innocuous. Indeed, they most certainly would not have been reported except for the fact that the two people who made the slurs were public officials who were forced to offer apologies. Other incidents, however, can be far more vicious, threatening, and unforgiving. In a highly publicized incident on May 4, 1990, Jimmy Breslin, a Pulitzer prize–winning columnist for *New York Newsday*, went on a newsroom tirade after being criticized by Ji-Yeon Yuh, a newly hired Korean American female reporter. Breslin spat out a string of obscenities and racist and sexist epithets, calling Yuh a "bitch" and "slant-eyed." Breslin also shouted, "She's a yellow cur. Let's make it racial." Breslin did apologize to the entire staff for his outburst and sent a personal note of apology to Yuh. Although Yuh was not in the room at the time, she was badly hurt by the statements. "I was shocked," Yuh said shortly after the incident. "I've been subjected to racist comments before, by strangers on the street. I'd very much like to forget about it, but I think that's impossible."[6]

Newsday editors reprimanded Breslin and assumed the issue was over. But Yuh and other Asian American journalists complained that Breslin's punishment was a mere slap on the wrist and that his apology was feigned. The Asian American journalists produced a tape of Breslin calling in a radio talk show and making jokes about the incident. At one point Breslin said it would be difficult for him to attend the wedding of his nephew, who was marrying a Korean American. When the editors contacted Breslin at his home to talk about the radio show, he again flew into a tirade and claimed he had free speech rights to say anything he pleased. The editors immediately suspended Breslin for two weeks without pay. The incident triggered a national debate over individual free speech versus the sensitivities to women and people of color in the workplace. *Washington Post* columnist, Tony Kornheiser, defended Breslin's invectives and compared the newsroom with "the inside of a locker room." He added that if everyone were to be fired for shouting taunts, "there won't be anybody left to turn out the lights." On the other hand, *Baltimore Sun* columnist Wiley Hall III argued there are no excuses for Breslin's behavior and "our tolerance for bigotry and stupidity has run out." Many angry Asian American journalists believed that Breslin was not given a harsher punishment because of his notoriety, and because the incident involved an Asian American, rather than an African American. Just prior to the Breslin incident, the Los Angeles Dodgers' general manager Al Campanis was fired from his job after using racist stereotypes to explain why there were so few African American managers in baseball. Indeed, even New York mayor, Ed Koch, thought that Breslin would have been fired if "he had said the same thing about blacks."[7]

A less publicized, but equally disturbing incident involved Shirley Gee, her sister Patricia Seto, and their four young children—ages 7 to 9—on a one-hour airplane ride from Burbank to Oakland following a fun-filled weekend at Disneyland on August 22, 1994. About 20 drunken passengers verbally harassed and threatened the two sisters and their children throughout most of the trip. According to Gee, the offending passengers were returning from a wedding party and were loud, obnoxious, and scaring her children. While Gee kept asking the group to quiet down, the flight attendants continued to serve them beers and peanuts. After Gee finally asked a flight attendant to intervene on her behalf, the group became more belligerent. They began calling Gee and sister "bitches," "gooks," and "whores." Gee recalls trying to cover her children's ears from the racist and sexist verbal barrage, but "I've got only two hands and there were four ears to cover." Gee was told, "You should go back to China," and several of the men threatened to teach her "respect" when they got off the plane. One man fired an imaginary gun in Gee's face twice. The two women continued to complain to the flight attendant but were told, "Look, we're all just trying to get along." Gee, Seto, and their children were also not permitted to change their seats because the plane was full.[8]

When the flight landed in Oakland, Gee and Seto refused to leave with their children until everyone else had left and the police could be summoned to escort them away. Seto's two children were so badly shaken and distraught by the incident that they suffered asthma attacks on the airplane. Both Gee and Seto filed a hate crime report to the police, but were later informed that the district attorney's office would not follow up on the case because there was no evidence of a specific crime. Outraged that there was no criminal statute against this kind of abuse, Gee and Seto filed a $5 million lawsuit against the airlines, the flight staff, and the group of disorderly passengers. Because of the incident, their children suffered nightmares and became afraid to leave their homes for fear the men from the airplane would be waiting. Gee says the emotional scars from the incident will take a long time to heal, and the effects are far deeper than anyone will ever see. "Until then I thought my children and their children would not have to be subjected to the hate crimes (sic) I went through as a child," she says. "I lost hope on that airplane."[9]

Physical Violence

As stated above, reported cases of proven or suspected anti-Asian violence increased from 355 in 1993 to 458 in 1995. In all three years, assaults (including aggravated assaults) were the most common incidents of hate violence. The 1993 audit found 107 proven and suspected cases of assault (30 percent), the 1994 audit found 115 cases of assault (25.4 percent), and the 1995 audit found 128 cases of assault (27.9 percent). NAPALC found the high percentages of assault particularly alarming, especially compared with general figures that show only about 10 percent of reported crimes are against individuals, while 90 percent are aimed at property. According to FBI statistics, for example, assault and aggravated assault represented 36 percent of hate crime incidents in 1992. These figures have led NAPALC to declare the "deadly nature" of hate violence and to cite studies that show hate-motivated assaults tend to result in greater numbers of deaths and personal injuries than other non-hate-motivated assaults. Indeed, hospitalization was required in 30 percent of bias-based assaults, while assaults in general had only a 7 percent hospitalization rate. "In sum," the 1993 NAPALC report states, "anti-Asian violence, like other forms of hate violence, is much more dangerous than similar acts not motivated by hate."[10] Along with reporting anti-Asian hate violence, NAPALC also takes an active role in following some of the most egregious incidents and works with local groups to bring these cases to justice. The following four recent examples are intended to show the personal suffering, the environment of fear created by hate-motivated physical violence, and NAPALC's efforts to publicize and monitor individual cases.

The first example involves the beating of Dr. Kaushal Sharan, an Asian Indian doctor in Jersey City, New Jersey. The initial incident took place in 1987, but the journey to seek justice against his assailants went on for six years and resulted in the first civil rights case brought by the U.S. Justice Department involving an Asian Indian victim. In September 1987, Dr. Sharan was walking home when he was accosted by a group of youths who shouted racial slurs as they beat him unconscious. Earlier that same month, a hate group calling themselves "Dotbusters" (referring to the red bindi worn by Indian women on their foreheads) sent a letter to the *Jersey Journal* proclaiming their desire to remove all Asian Indians from Jersey City. Dr. Sharan survived the attack, but he was seen as another victim of a rash of vandalism and assaults following the letter, including the September 27 killing of Navroze Mody by a gang of 11 youths. Although arrests were quickly made in the Mody case, no bias charges were ever filed by police authorities. No arrests were made after the beating of Dr. Sharan, and anti-Asian Indian violence continued at an alarming rate. In frustration, NAPALC and Asian Indian leaders went to Washington, DC, in 1990 to lobby the U.S. Justice Department to investigate the activities of the Dotbusters, along with another hate group calling themselves the "Lost Boys."

In September 1992, three men were indicted on federal criminal civil rights charges stemming from the Sharan assault. Dr. Sharan and NAPALC became actively involved in monitoring the federal criminal trial, along with gathering broad-based support. An ad hoc National Support Committee made up of South Asian physicians, community groups, and student organizations was formed to add high visibility to Dr. Sharan's case. Unfortunately, the three-week trial ended in a hung jury in early 1993. Pressure was placed on the Justice Department and a retrial against one of the defendants began in May 1993. The government's case, however, was severely weakened by sloppy police work following the initial 1987 incident, and this made it extremely difficult to win a conviction. As a result, the jury acquitted the defendant after a two-week trial. This setback for NAPALC, Dr. Sharan, and his supporters was compounded by the Justice Department's decision not to retry the remaining two defendants. Although Dr. Sharan has never had the satisfaction of seeing justice done in his case, his decision to take an active and public stand on anti-Asian violence with NAPALC has been the model that others have followed.[11]

Another NAPALC case focused on Luyen Phan Nguyen, a 19-year-old Vietnamese American premed student who was murdered in Coral Springs, Florida on August 15, 1992. Witnesses saw Nguyen chased "like a wounded deer" and then beaten by a mob, as dozens of onlookers ignored his cries for help. Nguyen's attackers shouted "chink," "Vietcong," and "sayonara" as they kicked and beat their victim. So severely was Nguyen battered, he never regained consciousness. He died 36 hours later of a cerebral hemorrhage and fractured neck. The killing was a shock to the quiet middle-class suburban community of Coral Springs, but officials tried to downplay the racial aspect of the murder. Investigators close to the case pointed to the fact that the fight started at a party where alcohol was served. E. Ross Zimmerman, defense attorney for one of the accused assailants, also denied any racial motivation. "If a person gets into a fight and the person they're fighting with happens to be a different race, they may use words they regret," he explained.[12] These casual denials about the racial aspects of the slaying outraged Asian Americans across the United States in a way not seen since Vincent Chin's death in 1982. Shortly after the killing made the news, Coral Springs Police Chief Roy A. Arigo said he began receiving telephone calls and letters from many Asian American groups and individuals who demanded the case be vigorously investigated as a hate crime.

At this time NAPALC sent a staff attorney from New York to Florida to offer legal assistance to the Nguyen family, and to monitor the progress of the criminal proceedings. NAPALC also joined forces with the Asian American Federation of Florida and local Vietnamese American community groups to build nationwide attention for the Nguyen case. Seven people were arrested for the killing of Nguyen and charged with second-degree murder. The first person to be tried was Bradley Mills, a 19-year-old country club groundskeeper, whom his attorney insisted was on the scene trying to break up the fight. But the other defendants testified that Mills repeatedly hit and kicked Nguyen and called out to his friends to join the attack. Mills was convicted in 1994 and sentenced to 50 years in prison. Five other defendants were also convicted or pled guilty to second-degree murder charges and received varying sentences including one for life in prison without parole. One defendant was acquitted of all charges. The Nguyen slaying brought the Asian American community together in Coral Springs and across the nation in their collective expression of indignation, anger, and frustration. Asian Americans came in large numbers to witness each court hearing and followed the case closely. The incident also sparked a renewed mistrust that will not easily go away. "My parents used to tell me to be careful," said the victim's friend, Lam Nguyen (no relation). "Now I look at people a lot more. I'm less innocent than I was."[13]

Community organizing and public pressure were also very important in securing a conviction for the murder of Sam Nhem, who was beaten to death on August 14, 1993, in a housing project in Fall River, Massachusetts. Nhem, a 21-year-old father of a four-month-old infant, and a friend were viciously attacked without provocation by a group of young men just outside Nhem's home while the two were taking out trash to a public dumpster following a family barbecue. One of the assailants, Robert Latour, who had been banned from the housing project prior to this incident, hurled racial slurs before he attacked Nhem. Shortly after the murder, Nhem's family car was firebombed. Despite these facts, the district attorney's office did not see any racial motivation and was unwilling to prosecute the case as a hate crime.[14] As a result, a NAPALC attorney visited with Nhem's family and met with a Cambodian community organization, and together they initiated a letter writing campaign calling for the district attorney's office to fully investigate the incident. After Latour and two other men were arrested and charged, NAPALC worked with local prosecutors to look for anti-Asian bias among prospective jurors, none of whom were Asian Americans. In addition, NAPALC and members of the Cambodian community in the area attended the trial of Robert Latour, who was eventually convicted of second-degree murder and battery with the intent to intimidate based on race, and sentenced to life in prison. The Nhem murder galvanized the Cambodian community in Fall River and throughout Massachusetts. Cambodian Americans then began reporting prior and current incidents of racially motivated violence, and it became clear that there was a pattern of anti-Asian activities that were all but ignored by local officials.[15]

The Cambodian American community reported incidents of assaults and batteries, firebombings, random shootings and rock throwing through windows, and fights in schools. Massachusetts has had an exceptionally sordid history with regard to its Cambodian refugee population that is reminiscent of the worst anti-Asian violence during the mid-nineteenth century. Between 1983 and 1987 violence against Cambodian Americans and vandalism to their homes were ongoing problems in Revere, Massachusetts. In September 1987, an 11-year-old white student in Lowell, Massachusetts, screamed racial epithets at a 13-year-old Cambodian American youngster and then pushed him in a canal. The Cambodian American junior high student, Vandy Phorng, could not swim and was washed away by the water's strong current and drowned. In December 1988, a firebomb destroyed several residences and left 31 Cambodian Americans homeless in Lynn, Massachusetts.[16] Increased awareness and anger over these and other incidents of hate violence served to forge a joint effort by NAPALC, the Cambodian Community of Greater Fall River, and the Lawyers' Committee for Civil Rights Under Law of the Boston Bar Association to recognize and report hate-related activities. The collection of statistics is the first step in educating the Asian American community and the general population about the seriousness of anti-Asian violence. According to NAPALC, between 1993 and 1994 reports of anti-Asian hate crimes increased from 39 to 46.[17] In June 1996, the Fall River Housing Authority agreed to a number of demands from the Cambodian American residents. These demands included the establishment of a bilingual hotline to report emergencies and crimes, the hiring of a civil rights officer to monitor hate-motivated violence, the creation of clear eviction proceedings for hate crimes, and cultural sensitivity training for staff.[18]

In Sacramento, California, a serial bomber terrorized the community with what appeared to be racially motivated attacks. A string of firebombings in 1993 damaged a Jewish synagogue, the offices of the National Association for the Advancement of Colored People (NAACP), the Japanese American Citizen's League (JACL), the residence of a Chinese American city council member, and the local office of the Department of Fair Employment and Housing, among others. Tension in the community was heightened when a local television station received a call from someone who claimed credit for the bombings, saying they were done on behalf of the "Aryan Liberation Front." The overt nature of these incidents, the significant destruction of property, and the potential for great loss in human lives prompted immediate action by law enforcement authorities. After an intensive and high-profile investigation, Richard Campos, a 19-year-old self-proclaimed white separatist, was arrested and charged with 12 felony counts. Charges against Campos included arson, possession of a destructive device (Molotov cocktail), and the attempted murder of Sacramento City council member Jimmie Yee and his wife. Campos was a minor at the time of his arrest but was prosecuted as an adult because of the seriousness of the crimes. "The message must go out that Sacramento will never tolerate this type of crime and every suspect will face the full force of the law," said the district attorney, Steve White.[19]

At Campos' home, police found towel fragments that matched the wicks used on Molotov cocktails found at the bomb sites, along with a typewriter that produced letters matching racist hate literature. In addition, several of Campos' former teachers recognized his voice as the caller to the television station, and a witness said he saw someone looking like Campos at the NAACP bombing. After the arrest, a NAPALC representative from San Francisco, along with several local organizations and community groups, came together and formed the Firebombing Trial Coalition. The Coalition attended the Campos' trial and urged the maximum sentence. Past experience has shown an inconsistent record of convictions for anti-Asian violence, and for that reason the Asian Law Caucus—a NAPALC affiliate—and private attorneys filed a civil rights lawsuit against Campos and his parents. On April 20, 1995, Campos was convicted on five criminal charges and sentenced to 17 years in prison. Because of the success in obtaining a criminal conviction, the civil case was dropped. This example again shows that both community pressure and cooperation with law enforcement are necessary to confront hate violence and hate crimes.[20]

CONTRIBUTING FACTORS TO ANTI-ASIAN VIOLENCE

What are the reasons behind anti-Asian sentiment and violence? Is it merely intolerance toward individuals who are physically distinct? Those who focus on these types of incidents point to much broader issues. NAPALC and the U.S. Commission on Civil Rights have identified a number of factors that contribute to anti-Asian violence and hate crimes. Among the most important are (1) increase in anti-immigrant sentiment, (2) economic competition between racial and ethnic groups, (3) "move-in" violence, and (4) poor police–community relations. All of these factors play an important role in hate-related activities against Asian Americans, and they are frequently interrelated.

Anti-Immigrant Sentiment

Chapter 1 described the increase in anti-immigrant sentiment in the United States in recent years. Federal, state, and local politicians have used immigration—and the fact that most immigrants to the United States today are from Asia and Latin America—as hot-button issues to excite voters. In addition,

Congress has made a number of recent proposals intended to halt, or at least reduce, the number of legal immigrants to the United States. Immigrants have also been targeted for deep cuts and even elimination from programs such as welfare, free school lunches, and health care. These sentiments go far beyond political rhetoric and public policy debates. Racial slurs against Asian Americans are quite often coupled with anti-immigrant insults such as "go home" and other obvious inciteful phrases that show animosity against others who are not considered "Americans."

In July 1995, a Japanese American woman in San Francisco was assaulted while walking her dog in the park. Her assailant threw a bag of dog feces at her and yelled, "Go home! Go home!" and "Hiroshima!" In May 1994, right in the middle of heightened racial tension in Sacramento due to the series of bombing incidents, an Asian American man was stabbed with a knife by someone who told police he wanted to "defend our country." Many of these racially motivated, anti-immigrant assaults target anyone who is considered foreign, with no distinction between ethnic groups or national origin. In October 1994, an Asian Indian student in Fairmont, Pennsylvania, was harassed by a group of youths who yelled, "Go home, fucking Iranian, you fucking Asian shit, go home, foreigner."[21] The tragic death of Chinese American Jim Loo in Raleigh, North Carolina, in 1989 is a graphic example of another victim of mistaken identity and misplaced anger. Loo and some friends were playing pool in a bar when they were accosted by two brothers, one of whom said, "I don't like you because you are Vietnamese. Our brothers went over to Vietnam, and never came back." The bar's owner forced the two brothers to leave the bar, but they waited outside until Loo and his friends came out. A fight broke out and Loo was killed. Similarly, the murder of Luyen Phan Nguyen was traced to the fact his attackers had been talking about the Vietnam War, and targeted Nguyen to vent their anger without realizing that Nguyen's father fought with U.S. forces during the war.[22]

Because of racial distinctiveness, all Asian Americans are blindly ascribed the role as "perpetual foreigners" and "the other." This was the case for young Megan Higoshi, a Japanese American Girl Scout who was selling cookies at a local mall in Southern California. Higoshi, dressed in her scout uniform, politely asked a male shopper if he wanted to buy some cookies. The responded man responded curtly, "I only buy from American girls."[23] Shirley Gee is keenly aware of how the anti-immigrant backlash affects Asian Americans and Latinos. "Our communities have watched with growing dread how politicians have crafted the debate in such a way as to blame this nation's, or state's ills on immigrants," she says. Reflecting on the abuse she and her family experienced on the airplane flight, Gee recognizes the general mood of intolerance contributed to her harassment. "The fact that these people felt free to act out their racism with 120 captive passengers on board watching illustrates the permissive climate created by this country's leadership."[24]

Economic Competition

Anti-Asian sentiment and violence is also fueled by economic competition between racial and ethnic groups. This competition manifests itself in two ways. First it results in animosity and jealousy of Asian Americans who many perceive as having achieved status as the "model minority" at the expense of others. In November 1995, Robert Page, a 25-year-old unemployed meat cutter in Novato, California, wrote a note to himself declaring, "What the fuck, I'm going to kill a Chinaman!" Later that morning Page attacked a Chinese American male with an eight-inch knife in a grocery store parking lot, chased him into the store, and then began stabbing him again in front of shocked patrons. Page hated Chinese because in his mind they "got all the good jobs."[25] Second, this competition is also related to anti-immigrant, anti-foreigner tensions described above, and misplaced hostility is once again aimed at Asian Americans in general.

The most obvious example of this type of economic competition and misplaced hostility is seen in what is popularly referred to as "Japan-bashing." Trade imbalance conflicts with Japan, continued high unemployment rates in the United States, along with a growth in well-recognized Japanese name-brand products such as Honda, Toyota, Mitsubishi, Sony, Nikon, Nintendo, and Toshiba have all led to a blind backlash against Asian Americans. The U.S. Commission on Civil Rights 1992 report on Asian Americans specifically addressed the problems created by the model minority and Japan-bashing.[26] However, at the New York press conference to announce the report, concerns over Japan-bashing clearly took center stage. According to Commission Chairman Arthur A. Fletcher, "Japan-bashing is on the rise across this nation, and there are signs that racial animosities toward Japanese Americans and other U.S. residents who trace their origin to many different Asian lands are increasing as well."[27] The commission's report cited the 1982 killing of Vincent Chin by two autoworkers in Detroit as the most obvious example of how Japan-bashing and anti-Asian feelings can lead to deadly consequences, and recommended that political leaders stop using Japan as a scapegoat for all of the economic woes in the United States.

A prime example of this was seen when New Hampshire Democrat John Durkin, a candidate for U.S. Senate in 1990, accused his Republican opponent of being an agent of "the same Japs who planned and carried out a sneak attack on December 7, 1941." The Republican senatorial candidate was so branded because he accepted campaign contributions from a Japanese company. Durkin continued his tirade by adding, "Here we have the Japs, they buy Rockefeller Center and are trying to turn the Rockettes into geishas. That's bad enough. But here they're trying to buy a U.S. Senate seat."[28] Throughout the 1992 presidential campaign trail, Democratic and Republican candidates alike were scoring political points with their calls for protectionist trade legislation against Japan, as well as other "get tough with Japan" themes. The recent upswing in the "Buy American" movement reflects the popular sense of unease that the United States is losing its independence, identity, and economy to Japan.[29] This "Buy American" campaign was reportedly started in 1991 by an Ohio ear surgeon, Dr. William Lippy, who offered a $400 bonus to his employees who purchased a new or used American automobile by July 4. In less than one year, the movement had spread and escalated across the nation.

In Edwardsville, Illinois, Bill Chartrand offered a 2-cent-a-gallon discount to customers who drove American cars. In Greece, New York, the small upstate suburban community voted against buying a $40,000 excavating machine that was made in Japan in favor of a similar piece of equipment made by an American company that cost $15,000 more. The Los Angeles County Transportation Commission rescinded a $122 million contract for new railcars it had just issued following heavy protests by union workers and local politicians. Probably the most publicized example of the Buy American crusade took place in 1992, when the Seattle Mariners baseball franchise announced that a group of investors led by Minoru Arakawa, president of Nintendo of America, was interested in purchasing the team. Local residents and baseball fans rejoiced because Minoru, a 15-year resident of Seattle, offered to keep the financially ailing team in town. At the same time, the competing bidder for the franchise, wanted to relocate the team to a more lucrative market. Baseball owners balked at Minoru's offer, saying they didn't want any "non–North American" ownership of America's national sport. The Japanese American Citizen's League immediately wrote to Baseball Commissioner Fay Vincent, objecting to the spirit and tenor of the owners' rationale. "What is at issue here," the letter stated, "is the underlying sense of racial xenophobia which permeates the dialogue of U.S.-Japan relations."[30]

Without denying problematic elements with some Japanese trade and economic policies, most economists and trade experts are dubious about the merits and long-term wisdom of the Buy American efforts. There is a great deal of attention placed on the American auto industry, but there is concern that U.S. protectionist policies in one area would harm the motion picture, music, apparel, and food industries that enjoy a lucrative market share in Japan. There is also a great deal more interdependence between the United States and Japanese economies than most people would assume. "A General Motors car can have more Japanese components than a Japanese car," explains David B. Friedman, a trade relations expert with the Rand Corp. in Santa Monica, California. This reality came home to the people in Greece, New York, who found out that the "American" company they wanted used engines made in Japan, while the "Japanese" company used engines built in the United States. It is also important to note that the large trade imbalance between the United States and Japan is due in good part due to the fact that Japan is a much smaller country with a much smaller population. Despite this fact, Japan still imports more goods from the United States than any other country except Canada. Most Americans would probably be surprised to learn that Japan is only the third largest holder of investments in the United States, well behind Britain and the Netherlands.[31]

In his book, *The Work of Nations* (1991), economist and former U.S. Labor Secretary, Robert Reich, argues that the answer to improving the overall American economy boils down to (1) a willingness of industries to retool and educate or retrain workers to compete effectively in a rapidly changing global economy; and (2) a commitment by the nation to educate and prepare young people for the jobs in the future. In essence, make America more competitive, rather than wallow in self-pity and finger-pointing. A similar theme comes from journalist James Fallows in his book, *More Like Us: Making America Great Again* (1989). Fallows is a harsher critic of Japan and its economic policies than Reich is, but he nonetheless agrees that reinforcing America's strengths in innovation, entrepreneurship, pioneering spirit, and freedom goes a lot farther than complaining about Japan.[32] So why the continued fear and hate mongering about Japan?

Asian American and civil rights leaders believe racism is at the core of this matter. Would Americans be upset if Canadians purchased the Seattle Mariners and moved them to Vancouver? Does anyone complain that Rupert Murdock, an Australian, owns the Fox Television Network and is one of the largest media moguls in the nation? Are there demonstrations where protesters take sledgehammers to Volkswagen automobiles because Germans don't buy American cars? Was anything said when Mobil Oil was bought out by BP (British Petroleum)? Dennis Hayashi, then national director of the Japanese American Citizen's League in San Francisco, praised the strong stand by the U.S. Commission on Civil Rights against Japan-bashing. "(W)e feel this 'Buy American' campaign that's spreading across the nation is the cutting edge of anti-Asian prejudice that leads to anti-Asian violence."[33]

Move-in Violence

The *1994 Audit of Violence Against Asian Pacific Americans* found a surprisingly high number of cases of hate violence took place in and around the victim's home. Harassment and vandalism were the most common forms of what NAPALC and the U.S. Commission on Civil Rights both call "move-in violence." This form of violence is intended to intimidate individuals and families from living in certain neighborhoods or housing projects. The report, *Civil Rights Issues Facing Asian Americans in the 1990s*, cited several examples of racist literature being distributed in neighborhoods across the country where Asian Americans had recently taken up residence. These neighborhoods ranged from low-income areas that recent Southeast Asian refugees have found affordable to suburban communities favored by middle-class and professional Asian Americans. From there, incidents escalate to verbal taunts, to egg throwing, to shattering windows with rocks or BB guns, to more serious acts of vandalism, to firebombings, to physical assaults, to murder.

The shooting death of 18-year-old Xuyen Nguyen in front of his home on September 18, 1992, brought to light the ongoing dangers faced by many Southeast Asian refugee families in several of San Francisco's low-income housing projects. "I saw it coming," Nguyen's mother told a reporter from the *San Francisco Examiner*. "I think we were attacked because we are Vietnamese." She went on to describe several other incidents of violence and hostility the family quietly endured, including one youth who came to their front door and screamed, "Move! Move! Move!" Other Southeast Asian refugee tenants reported their children were repeatedly harassed and attacked on their way to and from school. Despite these incidents, the San Francisco Housing Authority denied that refugees were victims of racially motivated intimidation. "We're concerned about the possibility of Asian families being targeted but, in fact that's not what we have in front of us right now," explained one housing authority official. "The problem, as I see it, is increasing crime." Housing and police officials also admitted that Southeast Asians were repeatedly victimized because they had a reputation of not reporting crimes.[34]

NAPALC and the local affiliate organization, the Asian Law Caucus (ALC) of San Francisco, viewed the issues and sequence of events very differently. First, it is important to note that the San Francisco Housing Authority began randomly assigning Southeast Asian families into predominantly African American housing projects as part of a "Voluntary Compliance Agreement" following allegations of racial segregation raised by the federal department of Housing and Urban Development. Second, this response to "integrate" the projects was done without any explanation to the established residents who saw Southeast Asians as "intruders" and interpreted their sudden arrival as simply a displacement of needy African Americans. Third, Southeast Asian tenants who were limited-English speakers found the lack of bilingual housing staff only reinforced an environment of isolation and alienation within the projects. Fourth, NAPALC and ALC began receiving complaints from Southeast Asian tenants in the projects, and took about a year to gather enough information to show a distinct pattern of racially motivated harassment and violence. Fifth, even when Southeast Asian tenants did come forth to complain to the housing authority about their situation and conditions, their needs were ignored. For example, immediately after their son was killed, the Nguyens requested a transfer out of their housing unit, but they received no response. Even a letter from the San Francisco Police Department's Hate Crime unit on the Nguyens' behalf sent to the director of the San Francisco Housing Authority failed to elicit a response. As a result, the Nguyens moved out and were forced to find more expensive housing on their own. Lastly, NAPALC and ALC realized the institutional roots and policy blunders, along with individual ignorance and prejudice, all worked together to create a highly volatile situation. The latent effect of this attempt to integrate public housing actually resulted in fewer needy Southeast Asian families in the projects because so many moved away in fear of their lives.[35]

NAPALC and ALC filed a class action lawsuit on behalf of the Southeast Asian tenants who sought increased security, staff training, and improved assignment and emergency transfer policies that would benefit all residents. In addition, the suit sought language assistance and increased support services for new residents. A settlement in the case with the San Francisco Housing Authority and HUD was reached in early 1995, which included public hearings on integration strategies and race relations in public housing. The real benefits of this lawsuit and the hearings that followed were not only to settle the issues raised in San Francisco but also to improve public housing policies across the nation and to insure fair access to all populations in need of low-income housing. A report of findings and recommendations from the San Francisco hearings was submitted in April 1995 and has served as a model for the rest of the nation. This case clearly illustrates that the issues and concerns of low-income Asian Americans is not isolated from the needs of other populations. Rather than just seeing the San Francisco Housing Authority problem exclusively a concern to the Southeast Asian refugees, NAPALC and ALC broadened the focus to where the solutions have important significance for low-income people across the nation.[36]

Poor Police–Community Relations

Both NAPALC and the U.S. Commission on Civil Rights recognize that improved relations between the various Asian American communities and local police is critical in addressing anti-Asian violence and crime. Unfortunately, law enforcement authorities have historically tended to ignore the often small and segregated Asian American communities in major urban centers. In recent years, police departments have attempted to reach out to the growing Asian American population, but sustained efforts are rare. The NAPALC audits and the U.S. Commission on Civil Rights report agreed on three interrelated areas that are crucial in bringing the police and Asian Americans closer together as partners in the community. They are (1) increased sensitivity to anti-Asian violence and the needs of the growing Asian American community, (2) increased representation of Asian Americans in the police force, and (3) confronting police misconduct against Asian Americans.

First of all, most police departments have not been sensitive to the issue of anti-Asian violence. For example, although the Los Angeles County Commission on Human Relations has been collecting statistics on crimes motivated by racial and religious bigotry since 1980, there is still a great lack of awareness about these incidents and how they impact Asian Americans. NAPALC reported a case where a Los Angeles police officer came to the home of a Japanese American woman where her car had been spray painted with racist graffiti. The officer identified the case as a simple vandalism and did not consider it a hate-related incident. Failure to recognize even overt acts of racial violence inevitably breeds distrust and frustration with law enforcement agencies, to the point where Asian Americans lack the faith even to report any crime—including hate incidents.[37] Related to this, police officials have also been slow in responding effectively to the needs of the increasing number of immigrant Asians in urban cities across the nation. These immigrants are clearly hampered by their inabilities to communicate in English, and the need for increased interpreter services is imperative if Asian Americans are to gain access to police services. Some police departments have responded positively and are trying a number of means to better communicate with the Asian American community. Most police departments rely on local Asian American community organizations to provide interpreters on an on-call basis. This system, however, is problematic because volunteers are not always available when needed. Other police departments have begun utilizing a private translation service based in Monterey, California, that has a long list of interpreters for almost any language and quickly connects them with police departments over the telephone at a modest cost. While this service is more reliable than community volunteers, it is not efficient in 911 emergency situations where time is of the essence. Despite these efforts, the need to hire interpreters and bilingual officers is quite obvious.[38]

This leads to the second crucial area for improving police and Asian American community relations. According to the U.S. Commission on Civil Rights, "Asian Americans are noticeably underrepresented among police officers in most law enforcement jurisdictions across the country."[39] This continues to be true even when police departments are under court order to increase the representation of women and racial minorities within their force. Many believe there are persistent stereotypes that Asian Americans are not aggressive enough to meet standard police requirements, aren't interested in law enforcement as a career, and lack English language proficiency. As a result, Asian Americans are not heavily recruited, are discouraged from applying, or are not accepted when they do apply. The lack of bilingual Asian American police officers and staff has long been a great concern to members of the Asian American community. As early as 1973 the San Francisco Police Department was sued for its hiring practices that discriminated against Asian Americans. The suit cited lax recruitment efforts to inform Asian Americans about available positions in the police department, a failure to eliminate arbitrary restrictive requirements for becoming a police officer, and limited promotional opportunities for current Asian Americans on the police force. The lawsuit was a long and bitter legal battle, but was eventually effective in gaining a consent decree in 1979 to establish "goals and timetables" for hiring bilingual Asian American officers. Both NAPALC and the U.S. Commission on Civil Rights contend that the lack of representation is a major factor in why crime is widely underreported within the Asian American communities. A report from the California State Attorney General's office found that between 40 and 50 percent of crimes against Asian Americans go unreported. Some police and sheriff's departments (Oakland, Long Beach, Modesto, and San Diego) estimated that as much as 90 percent of crimes committed against Asian Americans are never reported.[40]

Confronting police misconduct against Asian Americans is the third identifiable area in need of improvement. Harassment and abuse by police is commonly seen as an issue faced by African Americans and Latinos, but this is also a concern for Asian Americans. This is particularly true in New York where Asian Americans reported half of the total number of police brutality cases. This coincided with a 37.5 percent increase in the overall number of complaints filed with the city's Civilian Complaint Review Board (CCRB) in 1994. The majority of these cases involved South Asian American (mostly Asian Indian and Pakistani) taxi drivers who work in the Bronx and Queens boroughs of New York. Incidents include racial slurs, issuing of false traffic summons, and assaults. Many of the drivers believe they are the victims of racist police officers who are intent on forcing them out of business. The drivers also feel they are caught in a vicious cycle of being targeted for retaliation because they have come forward in reporting incidents of intimidation and violence.[41]

Numerous other cases in New York have also drawn attention. In November 1993, Dat Nguyen, a Vietnamese American college student, alleged he was beaten by a New York City police officer. Nguyen, who received stitches on his head and face and was briefly hospitalized, was later charged with assaulting a police officer. This charge was subsequently dropped. In March 1994, Kim Hyunh, a high school student who stands under five feet tall was arrested for disorderly conduct and for assaulting two police officers, one of whom was over six feet tall. These charges were also dropped.[42] In August 1994, Nancy Tong was arrested for a non-moving traffic violation, taken down to police headquarters, and illegally strip searched. Tong sued the NYPD and eventually received an out-of-court settlement. In another case, an NYPD officer was convicted of attempted assault on a Korean American store owner and his brother. During the incident, the officer allegedly called the two brothers "fucking Orientals" and then accused them of resisting arrest. In this case there were witnesses who saw the police officer brutalize the two Korean Americans and contradicted the officers' version of the story.[43] Since 1986 the Coalition Against Anti-Asian Violence (CAAAV) has been in the forefront of highlighting police brutality cases against Asian Americans. CAAAV's activities have been confrontational, as seen in its joint effort with the National Congress for Puerto Rican Rights to close down the Manhattan Bridge in April 1995 to protest racial violence and police brutality. The demonstration focused on bringing attention to the killing of Young Xin Huang, a 16-year-old high school student who was shot in the back of the head by police. Huang's family later agreed to a $400,000 settlement with the city.[44]

Taken together, all these areas show the need for better law enforcement and Asian American community relations. Strategies for outreach and networking directly to the Asian American communities, along with important institutional changes and legal reforms, must be implemented and supported. Three examples of how these efforts are accomplished can be seen through community policing strategies, the creation of Asian American police advisory boards, and the establishment of a special unit dedicated to hate crimes and hate violence. Community policing in San Diego, California, has included the hiring of Asian American community service officers (CSOs) who work with the city's rapidly growing Southeast Asian population. The CSOs work out of a storefront located in the middle of Southeast Asian neighborhoods. Their job is primarily to serve as police–community liaisons who take police reports, help gather information on crimes and gang activity, work to educate the community by attending community functions meetings, and are actively involved in helping to counsel high-risk youth to stay out of trouble. These CSOs are noncommissioned officers, which means they are uniformed and carry badges, but they are unarmed and cannot carry out all of the duties of a commissioned police officer. The CSOs augment their limited police duties with advanced first aid, cardiopulmonary resuscitation (CPR), and emergency preparedness training.[45] A rash of anti-Asian violence in Oakland, California, during the late 1980s prompted the creation of the Asian Advisory Committee, which is made up of representatives from the various Asian American communities, the police department, city council, public schools, and the county district attorney's office, among others. The committee continues to meet monthly, and the focus has expanded beyond interracial tension to other issues important to the various Asian American groups. These issues include crime in the community (including gang activity), problems related to language and cultural differences, community outreach, and Asian American representation throughout the ranks of the Oakland Police Department.[46]

Community policing and Asian Advisory Committees are comprehensive approaches to police–Asian American community relations. The specific issue of anti-Asian violence cannot be directly addressed, however, unless comprehensive statistical data are gathered and assessed. As stated in the beginning of this chapter, the 1990 Federal Hate Crime Statistics Act passed by Congress was intended to serve this purpose, but it is heavily reliant on state and local law enforcement agencies to provide the necessary raw data. However, relatively few police departments have special units that deal specifically with identifying, investigating, and reporting hate crimes. This leaves tremendous discretion to the beat officer who most likely has no training in or sensitivity to this issue. The formation of special hate crime units is also limited by the fact that hate crime laws themselves continue to be divisive and controversial, even among civil rights leaders. Every state in the nation has some sort of criminal hate crime statute and/or provides relevant civil protection because of increased attention on hate-related violence. But some of these laws have been challenged in the U.S. Supreme Court with mixed results. In 1992 the high court unanimously ruled that a St. Paul, Minnesota, hate crime ordinance was unconstitutional on the grounds that it violated free speech rights. The incident involved the prosecution of a white teenager who burned a cross in the yard of an African American family. The following year, the Supreme Court upheld a state of Wisconsin hate crime statute because it provided a penalty enhancement for a criminal act that was motivated by hate, but did not specifically punish hateful thought. NAPALC has been closely following these and other court cases, is supportive of the criminal penalty-enhancement statutes, and believes that these laws will be upheld in court.[47]

The four factors described in this section highlight the extent of anti-Asian sentiment and hate-related violence. The U.S. Commission on Civil Rights and NAPALC have called this a "national problem," and both agree that the greater awareness is the first step to improving the environment of misconception, mistrust, and misplaced hostility against Asian Americans. The Commission and NAPALC also chastised the statements and actions of public officials who consciously play on the politics of division and help to create the environment of hostility against immigrant and native-born Asian Americans. Improving the limited data collecting system on incidents of anti-Asian hate violence and hate crimes is another high priority. Data collecting has improved in recent years, but information is difficult to obtain, often incomplete, and severely limited by widespread underreporting. Because of this, anti-Asian violence will continue to be a major issue confronting Asian Americans for some time to come.

ASIAN AMERICAN AND AFRICAN AMERICAN RELATIONS

It is important to understand anti-Asian violence as part of what many see as a broader trend toward greater verbal, physical, and legislative attacks against many other minority groups in the United States. These groups include immigrants, people of color, religious minorities, women, gays and lesbians, the homeless, the poor, and others. It is these groups who are the targets in the politics of division and the victims of a backlash against those who are considered marginalized "outsiders" from the "mainstream." At the same time, it must be acknowledged that hate sentiment and hate violence are not limited to just whites on nonwhites. Indeed, in recent years there has been a great deal of tensions between various minority groups, including Asian Americans and African Americans in inner-city communities across the nation. These tensions exploded into the public's consciousness during the 1992 urban unrest in Los Angeles, immediately after a jury acquitted four white Los Angeles police officers in the beating of black motorist Rodney King.

The chaos in Los Angeles began on April 29 and lasted four days. Some 30,000 uniformed personnel (including police officers, sheriff's deputies, the California National Guard, U.S. Army soldiers, and specially trained Marines) were eventually sent to the scene to enforce a dawn-to-dusk curfew. In addition, bus service was halted and schools were closed in many parts of the city for several days. Very real fears that the rioting would spread across the city forced the postponement of L.A. Dodger baseball games, and the relocation of the L.A. Lakers National Basketball League playoff games. According to various news reports, 58 people were killed, over 2,000 were injured, more than 12,000 were arrested, and property damage estimates from the riot ran close to the $1 billion mark. An estimated 10,000 stores in Los Angeles were at least partially damaged and burned. Particularly hard hit were the over 2,000 businesses owned by Korean Americans, whose combined property losses alone added up to nearly half of the city's total. Some Korean merchants armed themselves and stayed in their shops for days to prevent looters from coming into their stores. Most of these merchants complained they were forced to defend their own businesses because the police did not respond to their calls for help.

On a national level, the unrest triggered smaller upheavals in several other cities, including San Francisco, Atlanta, Seattle, Las Vegas, and Miami. The days of rage in 1992 focused the nation's attention on the economic, social, and political inequities that divided blacks, whites, and other people of color. Edward T. Chang, professor of Ethnic Studies at the University of California at Riverside, has written extensively on black–Korean American relations and acknowledged that the 1992 riot in Los Angeles was a clear sign of the future of race relations in America. At the same time, Chang's essay, "America's First Multiethnic 'Riots,'" (1994) looks beyond the highly sensationalized stories of conflicts between African Americans and Korean Americans, and recognizes the structural roots of inequality. Chang makes important comparisons and distinctions between the 1992 Los Angeles and the 1965 Watts riots. The uprising in the Watts section of Los Angeles also began with a police incident against a black motorist, and resulted in several days of violence, arson, and vandalism that left 34 people dead, more than 1,000 injured, and 3,800 arrested. Beyond these basic facts, Chang asserts, the similarities between the two largest incidents of urban unrest end.[48]

First of all, the 1965 Watts riot was contained in the low-income areas of South Central Los Angeles, in which 81 percent of the residents were African American at the time. The 1992 Los Angeles riot was also centered in South Central, but the population had shifted to only about 52 percent African American and over 40 percent Latino. The African American population in South Central has been declining precipitously since 1965, including a 20 percent drop between 1980 and 1990. The 1992 riot was clearly more widespread than the 1965 Watts riot. The civil disorder in 1992 quickly spread to other parts of the city, including middle-class neighborhoods. The media may have played up the black versus white, along with the black versus Korean angle, but television cameras showed just as many Latino faces as black faces looting Korean stores. Chang even cites police records showing Latinos made up 45.2 percent of the arrests during the 1992 riot, compared with 41 percent blacks and 11.5 percent whites. The 1965 Watts riot sparked a series of upheavals in cities across the nation over the next two years, all of which were eventually studied in the 1968 Kerner Commission report. The commission concluded that the United States was separated into two nations, one black and one white. Chang's analysis of the 1992 Los Angeles riot found the implications were far beyond black and white, and beyond individual race relations and antagonism.[49]

Second, Chang looked at the broader factors behind the 1992 urban unrest. He describes pressures created by the economic downsizing, or deindustrialization, of South Central Los Angeles that saw hundreds of businesses closing, manufacturing leaving the area, and thousands of jobs being lost. Chang also asserts that the structurally created economic depression in the area is further heightened with the emergence of a popular "neoconservative" ideology throughout the 1980s and into the 1990s. This ideology assumes that all groups have been, or will eventually be, accepted into the American mainstream and will enjoy the fruits of equal opportunity. But this will happen only if they are willing to work hard and pull themselves up by their own bootstraps. In other words, this view sees the persistence of joblessness and poverty found among certain groups as evidence of a lack of individual character and initiative, rather than critical social problems often beyond individual control. The shifting of blame solely on the victims of structurally created inequality leads only to greater frustration and anger among the most disenfranchised people of the nation. At the same time, Korean immigrants, like other Asian Americans, are often held up as examples of the "model minority" and are used to show the "American Dream" of economic prosperity can be achieved through hard work and sacrifice. The question is often asked, if Korean Americans can succeed why can't other groups? Inner-city residents both resent and envy Korean immigrant entrepreneurs because of their "success." But as discussed in Chapter 1, Korean Americans often see themselves as mere economic "survivors." Indeed, for many Korean immigrants, owning a small business is a major step down in social and economic status.[50]

Lastly, Chang acknowledges police department abuses and mistrust in the judicial system as two more areas of brewing discontent, especially within the African American community throughout Los Angeles. The savage beating of Rodney King by four white police officers, which took place on the evening of March 3, 1991, was captured on videotape and shown on national television. Just two weeks later, on March 16, 1991, a store security camera recorded the fatal shooting of 15-year-old Latasha Harlins by a Korean American grocer after a dispute over a $1.79 bottle of orange juice. This videotape was also widely broadcast across the country—sometimes in tandem with the

Rodney King beating—and appeared to be yet another piece of clear evidence of the violence inflicted against African Americans. "Well, at last they see we're not lying," said South Central merchant, Art Washington. "Now the world sees . . . that this stuff actually happens."[51] Unfortunately, African American hopes for justice based on seemingly irrefutable evidence were quickly and unceremoniously dashed. On November 15, 1991, Korean American storeowner, Soon Ja Du, was convicted of voluntary manslaughter, and sentenced to five years of probation for killing Latasha Harlins.[52] African American leaders were shocked by what they considered a lenient sentence, and demanded the resignation of the presiding Superior Court judge, Joyce A. Karlin. Their anger had barely enough time to cool when on April 29, 1992, a jury came out with the not guilty verdicts against the four police officers accused of beating Rodney King. It was then that the bubbling cauldron finally exploded.

In light of these multiethnic and structural factors, Chang is particularly critical of the media for continuing to portray the 1992 Los Angeles riot as "an extension of the ongoing conflict between Korean merchants and African American residents. . . ." He argues that interethnic tensions within the African American community has long historical roots, and that Koreans are certainly not the first group to operate stores in black neighborhoods. Prior to the 1965 Watts riot many of the businesses in the then predominantly African American South Central area were owned by Jews. Many of these Jewish-owned stores were also destroyed during the 1965 Watts riot. After 1965, Chinese, Japanese, and finally Koreans and Latinos became major small business owners in and around South Central Los Angeles. "Although over the years the conflicts in Los Angeles have shifted from one racial group to another, the class-based nature of the struggle has remained consistent," Chang contends. "It is not, therefore, a racial issue, but a class issue involving small businesses and residents."[53] Chang does not deny individual conflict and racial antagonism, but his broader analysis was seldom addressed in the mainstream media. A brief look at black–Korean relations prior to the 1992 Los Angeles uprising shows why it was easy to focus on the more sensationalized individual, racial, and cultural differences that exist between the two groups.

History of Korean–Black Tensions

Beginning in the early 1980s, Asian American–owned businesses began opening in predominantly black neighborhoods in large numbers across the country, and it was not long before isolated incidents of hostility were being reported. Although most of the media attention has focused on black–Korean conflicts, one of the first widely reported incidents took place in 1986 when Sarah Carter got into an argument with Cheung Hung Chan, the owner of a Chinese take-out restaurant in the predominantly black Anacostia neighborhood of Washington, DC. The dispute was minor—a mix-up over a food order—but it ended with Chan chasing Carter out of his restaurant while waving a .38-caliber revolver. Carter returned in less than an hour, but this time she came with Rev. Willie Williams and other residents who set up a picket line outside of the restaurant, vowing to drive Chan and other Asian American–owned business out of the area. Rev. Wilson railed against Asian Americans as "the latest of a series of ethnic groups that have come into our community, disrespected us, raped us economically, and moved out at our expense." The boycott was also a call to residents to "support our own" and pointed to the need for more black-owned businesses in the area. The episode was a prominent news item and seemed to strike a responsive chord in other African American communities as well.[54]

Relations between Korean Americans and African Americans were especially tense in New York throughout the 1980s, where one observer counted at least five organized boycott efforts, each lasting eight weeks or more.[55] By far the most notable and longest boycott effort began in January 1990 in the Flatbush section of Brooklyn, New York. In this case, a scene erupted in the Red Apple Market when customer Ghislaine Felissaint, a Haitian American, said she was grabbed around the neck by a store employee, knocked to the ground, slapped, kicked, and verbally abused. The store employees, however, denied Felissaint's claims and told a very different story. According to their accounts, Felissaint was searching through her purse for an extra dollar to pay for her food, then became belligerent and disruptive when the cashier began helping another customer. The store manager then came out to try and calm Felissaint down. The manager admitted he put his hands on Felissaint's shoulders as he tried to escort her out. When he did so, Felissaint fell to the ground and refused to move. The police and an ambulance were called to the store and Felissaint demanded that store owner, Bong Jae Jang, be arrested. By this time, an agitated crowd had gathered and the employees quickly closed the store. When one of the employees attempted to leave the store, he was pelted with rocks, bottles, and fruits. The employee ran for safety across the street to the Church Street Fruit and Vegetable Store, which happened to be another Korean American–owned business.[56]

A rally began early the following morning in front of both the Red Apple and the Church Street Fruit and Vegetable stores. The protesters called for a boycott of the two stores and demanded that they be closed permanently. The crowd quickly grew larger and more hostile as time went on. Protesters shouted, "Koreans out! Shut 'em down!" and screamed, "Traitor! Traitor!" to customers who entered the stores. Racist rhetoric on leaflets were handed out to bypassers, and the pregnant wife of one of the store owners reportedly had to undergo a medical abortion after she was attacked by a demonstrator.[57] The store owners vowed to stay open and then went to court and obtained a restraining order on May 10, 1990, to keep protesters at least 50 feet away from the business entrances. The New York City Police initially refused to enforce the order, claiming that resentment from the community would create an even greater public safety concern. Tensions from the boycott were by now extremely intense and spreading. On May 13 three Vietnamese American men in Flatbush were attacked by a group of African American youths who allegedly shouted, "Korean Motherfuckers," and "Koreans, what are you doing here?" One of the Vietnamese Americans was in critical condition with a fractured skull after he was beaten with a claw hammer.[58] Finally, on September 17, the New York State appellate court ruled that the police had no discretion in this matter and they were not entitled to make arbitrary decisions whether or not to obey the county court's authority. As soon as the police began enforcing the court order, 13 demonstrators were arrested for disorderly conduct. New York Mayor David Dinkins made a highly publicized visit to both stores a few days later, and it was not long before customers began returning to the markets. Calls for continuing the boycott became more and more muted, although they did continue for several more months until one of the store owners sold out to another Korean American.[59]

In Los Angeles, tense relations between African American customers and Korean American shopkeepers were also witnessed throughout the 1980s. Unlike New York, lines of communication between African Americans and Korean Americans were kept open thanks to the work of the Los Angeles County Human Relations Commission, which was instrumental in helping to establish the Black-Korean Alliance (BKA) in 1985. All efforts to keep the peace were abruptly shattered after the fatal shooting of Latasha Harlins in April 1991. Two months later, a boycott effort began to grow after another African American, Lee Arthur Mitchell, was shot to death by a Korean American during a robbery attempt. The boycott movement was led by Danny Bakewell, the leader of a group called the Brotherhood Crusade. "The basis on which we take issue with Korean Americans . . . is what has been a blatant disregard for African American life as evidenced by some Koreans," said Bakewell.[60] He also complained that Korean American store owners sold inferior goods, followed customers around the store like suspected thieves, treated customers rudely at the checkout counter, and charged excessively high prices. Bakewell also continued to propagate the commonly held belief that Korean Americans succeed because they received unfair advantages in obtaining bank loans that were unavailable to African Americans.

Korean American merchants responded to Bakewell's charges by saying they, in fact, are the ones in most danger and pointed to numerous incidents in which the Korean store owners were robbed, assaulted, and killed. In the 18 months prior to the 1992 L.A. riot, 12 Korean merchants had been killed while working in their stores. "But who cries for these victims?" asked Tae Sam Park, the liquor store owner who shot Mitchell. Park, who suffered three broken ribs in his scuffle with Mitchell during the robbery attempt, added sharply, "I have done nothing other than defend my wife and my business."[61] Korean Americans also argue they are not rude people but are aware that cultural differences may present themselves as rudeness to customers. Polite behavior among Koreans includes maintaining a reserved demeanor, not looking people in the eyes, and placing change on the counter rather than in the customer's hand. In addition, Korean Americans acknowledge that their lack of fluency in English can cause miscommunications and unintentional problems. Most importantly, Korean American merchants do not see themselves as exploiters of the community, but as hardworking immigrants trying to run a small family business. The high prices they charge relative to supermarkets, they say, is due to the fact they cannot buy items in the volume needed to keep prices lower. Finally, there is very little evidence that Korean small business owners receive special treatment from government or corporations to start their stores in low-income neighborhoods. Several studies have mentioned, however, that Korean Americans do save large amounts of capital and borrow from friends or relatives, which does give them a significant advantage when applying for a government or commercial small business loan (see Chapter 2).

In this environment of violence and mistrust, relations between African Americans and Korean Americans quickly went from bad to worse. Tensions became especially high following the release of the song "Black Korea" by popular rap artist Ice Cube that included incendiary lyrics and a tacit warning to Korean American shop owners: "Pay respect to the Black fist, or we'll burn your store right down to a crisp." The light sentence given to Soon Ja Du for killing Latasha Harlins served only to raise animosities between the two groups to even greater heights. On the afternoon of April 29, 1992, the riot in Los Angeles began. It became immediately clear that Asian American businesses, particularly Korean American businesses, were the targets of much of the mob anger and violence. The Asian Pacific Legal Center, a Los Angeles–based civil rights organization, quickly organized a press conference to denounce the acquittals of four LAPD officers in the Rodney King beating. The press conference included members of the Black-Korean Alliance, who called for citywide unity and downplayed the racial antagonism between the two groups. "I think that's overblown," said Eui-Young Yu, director of the Korean American Studies Center at California State University, Los Angeles.[62]

But on the streets of South Central Los Angeles, a different story was being told. "We went after the Oriental stores. . . . Those were the only ones really burned at first," explained Vernon Leggins, a 35-year-old local resident. "I helped, out of anger, not need. This should have happened a long time ago after they killed that little girl (Harlins) . . . over orange juice." Another local resident, Torrey Payne, added: "They burned the Koreans out because of the way the Korean merchants treated people. . . . That's who they're burning, because of that 15-year-old girl." The looting and destruction, of course, were not limited to African Americans. One Latino was asked why Korean stores were being targeted, and he bluntly stated: "Because we hate 'em. Everybody hates them."[63] Over the course of the next few days,

Korean Americans were never so alone, so isolated, and so lost. Not only were they victims of a fury they did not understand, desperate calls to the police and fire departments to help save their businesses went unheeded. Many began to believe they were being sacrificed while emergency services were directed to protect the more affluent—and more white—parts of the city. "Korean American newcomers must feel utterly betrayed by what they had believed was a democratic system that would protect life, liberty and property," wrote Elaine Kim, professor of Asian American Studies at the University of California at Berkeley. Kim gave eloquent voice to what she knew many Korean Americans were feeling in a moving personal editorial published in *Newsweek* shortly after the riot. "The shopkeepers who trusted the government to protect them lost everything. In a sense, they may have finally come to know what my parents knew more than a half century ago: that the American Dream is only an empty promise."[64]

The Aftermath

Days after the riot came an uneasy calm, but residents of South Central Los Angeles began to realize they were unable to get even the most basic of necessities, such as diapers for babies and food for their children. These were items that had been provided by the Korean American–owned stores. People failed to realize that the relative success of Korean merchants was due to the fact that they filled an empty commercial gap in the community. Ironically, the vast majority of Asian business owners in South Central Los Angeles came to the United States following the passage of the 1965 Immigration Reform Act. It was the black-led civil rights movement that helped create this landmark legislation that directly opened the doors for large numbers of Asian immigrants to enter this country. One of the obvious consequences of the riot is the fact that many in the Korean American community now realize they can no longer survive by isolating themselves from the broader community. "The riots taught us it is not enough to work hard," said Ky Chuoen Kim, an economist and president of the Korean American Management Association. The unexpected result of this realization has been an increase of interest among Korean Americans, especially small business owners, to take organized cultural sensitivity classes.[65]

Although professor Edward Chang has argued there are much broader structural concerns that need to be addressed, in the meantime, he agrees that Korean immigrants need to know they are living in a multicultural United States and not monocultural Korea. Indeed, Chang has taught African American and Latino history in the United States in sensitivity seminars. He has also published a book on African American history written in Korean that has been widely read in the United States and in Korea. At the same time, Chang adds, cross-cultural understanding goes both ways. Noting that there are over 800,000 Korean Americans in the United States today, Chang believes it is imperative that people understand who they are. "In the American context, Asian Americans have always been defined primarily as Chinese and Japanese," he explains. "The [L.A.] riots put Koreans officially on the map. It has since become our task to inform the American public who we are, where we stand, and what is our place."[66]

Through education, many have found important similarities especially between Korean and African Americans. Los Angeles writer Itabari Njeri described how Koreans have faced subjugation under Japanese colonial rule, along with the "day-to-day realities of anti-Asian prejudice," while African Americans not only carry the historic memory of slavery but also the status of "America's most stigmatized minority."[67] Another similarity that many were unaware of was the fact that both Koreans and African Americans are overwhelmingly Christian, and that both are strongly faith-based communities. As a result, many attempts have been made by church leaders to bridge the gaps between the two groups. For example, Kaia Niambi Shivers was selected to represent African American Catholic youth during a two-week trip to Korea in the spring of 1992 as part of a Korean/African American Dialogue program. The visit "altered" her life and she wrote a prizewinning essay about her positive experiences in Korea. "I can admit that I wasn't too fond of Korean Americans in my community," wrote Shivers, a resident of Los Angeles. "I now understand that it was lack of communication and cultural ignorance. Koreans are not mean and nasty, and African Americans are not criminals. It was misunderstanding of both groups that widened the gaps between us."[68] Lastly, Korean and Korean American organizations have sponsored programs intended to provide cultural exchange and improve race relations. In 1994 five African American college students were awarded scholarships to attend Yonsei University, in Seoul, South Korea. "I'm looking forward to involving myself in the culture," said Angela Rene Crawford, a senior majoring in economics at UC Berkeley, who stated she plans to create workshops on cultural tolerance in the future. "(T)his is just the beginning of a long, long drive."[69]

CONCLUSION

This chapter describes the serious problem of violence against Asian Americans that is clearly on the rise in the United States. The root causes for these anti-Asian sentiments and violent acts are both structural and individual in nature. At the same time, there are four easily identifiable factors highlighted in this chapter that are lightening rods that serve to exacerbate tensions between Asian Americans and other groups. These four factors are (1) increase in anti-immigrant sentiment, (2) economic competition between racial and ethnic groups, (3) "move-in" violence, and (4) poor police–community relations. As seen throughout this chapter, all of these factors play an important role in hate-related activities against Asian Americans, and they are frequently interrelated.

On numerous occasions, political and community leaders have spoken out mindlessly—or sometimes even consciously—using overgeneralizations and racially tinged rhetoric to fan the fires of anti-Asian hostility. Those who promote disharmony and racial divisiveness must be challenged, and the public must be educated to think beyond the simplistic statements intended solely to incite and scapegoat. Organizations such as the National Asian Pacific American Legal Consortium (NAPALC) have done an excellent job in drawing attention to the problem of anti-Asian violence and helping bring communities together to change the climate of hate, ignorance, and indifference. Unfortunately, if these attitudes are left unchecked for too long, they will only fester and can explode in ways that cannot be controlled. This was the case in the 1990 boycott of Korean stores in New York, as well as in the devastating civil unrest in Los Angeles in 1992.

It is obvious that anti-Asian sentiment and hate violence cannot be viewed in isolation. The complex national issues of unemployment, poverty, and inequality that lie at the root of anti-Asian sentiment will take far more effort and political will to solve than is currently being shown by elected officials. In the meantime, however, individual, small group, and community education and pressure are what it will take to make a difference. "Given the worsening political climate for immigrants and anyone who looks or talks differently," concludes NAPALC in its 1994 audit, "it is critical that everyone who cares about combatting hate violence step forward and speak out against . . . any divisive attempts to pit communities against each other."[70]

ENDNOTES

1. Ebans' conviction was overturned by the Sixth Circuit Court of Appeals in September 1986. A new trial was ordered in part because of prosecutorial misconduct. Evidence of prosecutorial misconduct included references by the prosecutor to impermissible hearsay statements in the closing argument. A new trial was also ordered because critical evidence had not been admitted at the trial court. The critical evidence included tapes of the main witnesses being questioned and potentially coached in their responses. See *United States v. Ronald Ebans* 800 F.2d.1422 (1986 6th Cir.).

2. National Asian Pacific American Legal Consortium, *1993 Audit of Violence Against Asian Pacific Americans* (First Annual Report); National Asian Pacific American Legal Consortium, *1994 Audit of Violence Against Asian Pacific Americans* (Second Annual Report); and National Asian Pacific American Legal Consortium, *1995 Audit of Violence Against Asian Pacific Americans* (Third Annual Report). For more information or to request copies of the audits, contact NAPALC at 1629 K Street, NW, Suite 1010, Washington, DC 20006.

3. National Asian Pacific Legal Consortium, *1994 Audit of Violence Against Asian Pacific Americans*, pp. 3, 7; and *1995 Audit of Violence Against Asian Pacific Americans*, pp. 12–13.

4. Quoted in "D'Amato Apologizes for Spoof of Judge Ito," *Newsday,* April 6, 1995.
5. Quoted in Phillip Matier and Andrew Ross, "'Dog' Comment Bites the S.F. Housing Chief," *San Francisco Chronicle* July 17, 1995.
6. Quotes in Constance Hays, "Asian-American Groups Call for Breslin's Ouster Over Racial Slurs," *New York Times,* May 7, 1990; and Josh Getlin, "Rage and Outrage," *Los Angeles Times,* May 15, 1990.
7. "Tolerance of Bigotry Has Run Out," *Los Angeles Times,* May 11, 1990; and Eleanor Randolph, "In N.Y., the Breslin Backlash: Asians Demanded Ouster after Newsday Tirade," *Washington Post,* May 8, 1990.
8. Quotes in Danielle Cass, "Unfriendly Skies' Slurs Launch Suit," *Oakland Tribune,* October 27, 1994; Karen D'Souza, "Some Foresee Era of Intolerance," *Oakland Tribune,* December 26, 1994; and Peggy Stinnett, "Racism Is in the Air, Literally and Otherwise," *Oakland Tribune,* October 30, 1994.
9. Quoted in Stinnett, "Racism Is in the Air, Literally and Otherwise."
10. National Asian Pacific American Legal Consortium, *1993 Audit of Violence Against Asian Pacific Americans,.* p. 16.
11. *Ibid.,* pp. 9–10
12. Quoted in "Rising Toll of Hate Crimes Cited in Student's Slaying," *Los Angeles Times,* October 10, 1992.
13. National Asian Pacific American Legal Consortium, *1994 Audit of Violence Against Asian Pacific Americans,* p. 5; and quoted in "Rising Toll of Hate Crimes."
14. Sam Cacas, "Fall River Trial Ends with Murder Conviction," *Asian Week,* September 23, 1994.
15. *Ibid.*
16. U.S. Commission on Civil Rights, *Civil Rights Issues Facing Asian Americans in the 1990s* (Washington, DC: Government Printing Office, 1992), pp. 31–32, 63.
17. National Asian Pacific American Legal Consortium, *1994 Audit of Violence Against Asian Pacific Americans,* p. 5.
18. National Asian Pacific American Legal Consortium, *1995 Audit of Violence Against Asian Pacific Americans,* p. 9.
19. "Racist Convicted in Firebombings Faces New Trial," *San Francisco Chronicle,* September 1, 1994.
20. National Asian Pacific American Legal Consortium, *1994 Audit of Violence Against Asian Pacific Americans,* p. 6.
21. *Ibid.,* p. 9; *1995 Audit of Violence Against Asian Pacific Americans,* p. 31
22. Seth Effron, "Racial Slayings Prompt Fear, Anger in Raleigh," *Greensboro News and Record,* September 24, 1989, cited in U.S. Commission on Civil Rights, *Civil Rights Issues Facing Asian Americans in the 1990s* pp. 26–28; and Mike Clary, "Rising Toll of Hate Crimes," *Los Angeles Times,* October 10, 1992.
23. Quoted in Seth Mydans, "New Unease for Japanese Americans," *New York Times,* March 4, 1992.
24. Quoted in Stinnett, "Racism Is in the Air, Literally and Otherwise."
25. National Asian Pacific American Legal Consortium, *1995 Audit of Violence Against Asian Pacific Americans,* p. 32; and Torri Minton, "Quiet Marin Confronts Hate Crimes," *San Francisco Chronicle,* November 29, 1995.
26. U.S. Commission on Civil Rights, *Civil Rights Issues Facing Asian Americans in the 1990s,* pp. 18–24.
27. Quoted in Lynne Duke, "Panel Links Japan-Bashing, Violence," *Washington Post,* February 29, 1992.
28. Quoted in "Opponent Calls Senate Candidate a Japanese Agent," *San Francisco Chronicle,* October 27, 1990.
29. Walter Schapiro, "Japan Bashing on the Campaign Trail," *Time,* February 10, 1992, pp. 23–24.

30. Robert Reinhold, "Buying American Is No Cure-All, U.S. Economists Say," *New York Times,* January 27, 1992; "The Push to 'Buy American,'" *Newsweek,* February 3, 1992, pp. 32–35; Lance Morrow, "Japan in the Mind of America," *Time,* February 10, 1992, pp. 17–21; and Carl Nolte, "Racism Charge Over Mariners Sale," *San Francisco Chronicle,* February 7, 1992.

31. Quoted in Reinhold, "Buying American Is No Cure All"; "Push to 'Buy American,'" p. 32; and Morrow, "Japan in the Mind of America," p. 21.

32. Robert B. Reich, *The Work of Nations* (New York: Alfred A. Knopf, 1991); and James M. Fallows, *More Like Us: Making America Great Again* (Boston: Houghton Mifflin, 1989).

33. Quoted in Sam Fulwood III, "Japan-Bashing Condemned by Rights Panel," *Los Angeles Times,* February 29, 1992.

34. Quoted in Steven A. Chin, "Asians Terrorized in Housing Projects," *San Francisco Chronicle,* January 17, 1993.

35. National Asian Pacific American Legal Consortium, *1993 Audit of Violence Against Asian Pacific Americans,* pp. 10–11; Chin, "Asians Terrorized," January 17, 1993.

36. National Asian Pacific American Legal Consortium, *1994 Audit of Violence Against Asian Pacific Americans,* pp. 6–7.

37. National Asian Pacific American Legal Consortium, *1993 Audit of Violence Against Asian Pacific Americans,* p. 17.

38. U.S. Commission on Civil Rights, *Civil Rights Issues Facing Asian Americans,* pp. 49–53.

39. *Ibid.,* p. 57.

40. State of California, Attorney General's Asian Pacific Advisory Committee, *Final Report* (December 1988), p. 62.

41. National Asian Pacific American Legal Consortium, *1994 Audit of Violence Against Asian Pacific Americans,* p. 12.

42. Samuel R. Cacas, "Vietnamese American Man Charges Police Brutality in Defense Trial," *Asian Week,* September 30, 1994.

43. Tomio Geron, "N.Y.P.D. Settles APA Complaints," *Asian Week,* March 1, 1996.

44. Tomio Geron, "APA Activism, New York Style," *Asian Week,* April 5, 1996.

45. U.S. Commission on Civil Rights, *Civil Rights Issues Facing Asian Americans,* p. 60.

46. "Asian Advisory Committee on Crime" (Oakland Police Department: Community Services Division, 1996).

47. National Asian Pacific American Legal Consortium, *1993 Audit of Violence Against Asian Pacific Americans,* p. 23; *1994 Audit of Violence Against Asian Pacific Americans,* p.10.

48. Edward T. Chang, "America's First Multiethnic 'Riots,'" in Karin Aguilar-San Juan (ed.), *The State of Asian America: Activism and Resistance* (Boston: South End Press, 1994), pp. 101–118.

49. *Ibid.* Also see Tim Ruttin, "A New Kind of Riot," *The New York Review,* June 11, 1992.

50. Chang, "America's First Multiethnic 'Riots,'" pp. 108–109. Also see Edward T. Chang, "New Urban Crisis: Intra-Third World Conflict," in Shirley Hune et al. (eds.), *Comparative and Global Perspectives* (Pullman, WA: Washington State University Press, 1991), pp. 169-178.

51. Quoted in "How Los Angeles Reached the Crisis Point Again, Chapter 5," a *Los Angeles Times* special report, May 11, 1992, p. T10.

52. For details on the shooting and profiles on Latasha Harlins and Soon Ja Du, see Jesse Katz and John H. Lee, "Conflict Brings Tragic End to Similar Dreams of

Life," *Los Angeles Times*, April 8, 1991. For an excellent analysis of the sentence given to Du, see Neil Gotanda, "Re-Producing the Model Minority Stereotype: Judge Joyce Karlin's Sentencing Colloquy in *People v. Soon Ja Du*," in Wendy L. Ng et al. (eds.), *Reviewing Asian America: Locating Diversity* (Pullman, WA: Washington State University Press, 1995), pp. 87–106.

53. Chang, "America's First Multiethnic 'Riots,'" pp. 110–111.
54. Karl Zinsmeister, "Asians and Blacks: Bittersweet Success," *Current*, February 1988, pp. 9–15; quoted in Susanna McBee, "Asian Merchants Find Ghettos Full of Peril," *U.S. News and World Report*, November 24, 1986.
55. Pyong Gap Min, "Problems of Korean Immigrant Entrepreneurs," *International Migration Review* 24 (1990): 436–455.
56. U.S. Commission on Civil Rights, *Civil Rights Issues Facing Asian Americans*, pp. 34–40.
57. Pete Hamill, "New Race Hustle," *Esquire*, September 1990, pp. 77–80; *Ibid.*, p. 36.
58. Hamill, "New Race Hustle," p. 77; and Robert D. McFadden, "Blacks Attack Vietnamese; One Hurt Badly," *New York Times*, May 14, 1990.
59. U.S. Commission on Civil Rights, *Civil Rights Issues Facing Asian Americans*, p. 39; Pyong Gap Min, "Cultural and Economic Boundaries of Korean Ethnicity: A Comparative Analysis," *Ethnic and Racial Studies* 14 (1991): 225–241.
60. Quoted in Solomon J. Herbert, "Why African-Americans Vented Anger at the Korean Community During the LA Riots," *Crisis*, August–September, 1992, pp. 5, 38.
61. Quoted in Rick Holguin and John Lee, "Boycott of Store Where Man Was Killed Is Urged," *Los Angeles Times*, June 18, 1991.
62. Quoted in Lisa Pope, "Asian American Businesses Targeted," *Los Angeles Daily News*, May 1, 1992.
63. Quotes in *Ibid.*, and in Sumi Cho, "Conflict and Construction," in Robert Goodings-Williams (ed.), *Reading Rodney King: Reading Urban Uprising* (New York and London: Routledge, 1993), p. 199.
64. Elaine Kim, "They Armed in Self-Defense," *Newsweek*, May 18, 1992.
65. Quoted in K. Connie Kang, "No Longer 'Work, Work, Work,'" *Los Angeles Times*, October 22, 1994.
66. Quoted in Daniel B. Wood, "As Korean Americans Become Visible, They Seek Understanding," *Christian Science Monitor*, July 27, 1993.
67. Itabari Njeri, "Power Elite Turns Out a Bitter Brew," *Los Angeles Times*, November 29, 1991.
68. Quoted in Wood, "As Korean Americans Become Visible."
69. Quoted in Elisa Lee, "Martin Luther King, Jr. Scholarship Recipients Depart for Seoul," *Asian Week*, June 17, 1994.
70. National Asian Pacific American Legal Consortium, *1994 Audit of Violence Against Asian Pacific Americans*, p. 15.

6

CHARLIE CHAN
NO MORE:
ASIAN AMERICANS
AND THE MEDIA

VISIBILITY AND INVISIBILITY

The door of opportunity is beginning to break open for Asian Americans in the media. They are now expressing their own experiences and sensibilities in books, films, television, theater, art, and music. Asian American writers, performers, and artists are finally gathering a wider and more appreciative audience. Some of the best-known major market breakthroughs include George Takei's portrayal of Lt. Sulu on the original *Star Trek* television series (1966–1969), Bruce Lee's kung-fu classic, *Enter the Dragon* (1972), Maxine Hong Kingston's book, *Woman Warrior* (1976), B. D. Wong's Tony award-winning performance in the Broadway play, *M. Butterfly* (1988), and the recent short-lived television sitcom, *All-American Girl* (1994), starring comedienne Margret Cho.

Many have traced this recent upsurge of attention to the number of feature films imported from Asia that have received critical acclaim and box-office success.[1] These films range from Chinese director Chen Kaige's epic *Farewell My Concubine* (1993), to action films like John Woo's *Hard Boiled* (1992), to comedy-dramas like Ang Le's *The Wedding Banquet* (1993) and *Eat, Drink, Man, Woman* (1994) from Hong Kong, to the redubbed, reedited, and rereleased Jackie Chan movies, such as *Rumble in the Bronx* (1995) and *Supercop* (1996). Vietnamese film director Tran Anh Hung's *The Scent of Green Papaya* (1993) and *Cyclo* (1996) have also received positive reviews in the United States. These recent films from Asia are far more popular and successful than earlier Japanese art and cult films. The recent films, along with glowing performances by Asian actors and actresses, have also spurred interest in Asian American themes and performers. The best example of this is *The Joy Luck*

Club (1993), directed by Wayne Wang, based on the best-selling book by Amy Tan, and distributed by Disney Studios. Another example is the Hollywood film, *Dragon: The Bruce Lee Story* (1993), starring Hawaiian-born actor Jason Scott Lee (no relation) in the title role. "Maybe Asian is the flavor of the month," quips director Wayne Wang. He understands that the "Asian chic" trend may be only temporary, but he remains optimistic. "That taste keeps changing, but now it has coincided with the maturity of talent."[2]

This is quite a contrast from earlier days when most of the images of Asians and Asian Americans in the media were mediated by others. Earlier characterizations were often negative and menacing, and these images are still perpetuated today. Asian American media watchers and critics continue to complain about racist stereotypes that emerge in the mainstream media. Several Asian American organizations recently pressured MGM-UA Home Video to withdraw the sale of a special videotape of World War II–era Bugs Bunny cartoons that contained racist slurs against Japanese. One cartoon, "Bugs Bunny Nips the Nips," has Bugs Bunny spouting racial epithets at Japanese characters who were drawn with slanty eyes, buck teeth, thick glasses, and other exaggerated physical features. Lori Fujimoto, spokesperson for the Japanese American Citizen's League, complained, "It hurts that a large corporation is so insensitive to rerelease this video to children." The studio executives explained they did not endorse these images, but only wanted to show the history of animation.[3] This chapter focuses on how dominant media images have had an important impact on how others see Asian Americans and how Asian Americans see themselves. Particular emphasis in this chapter will be on film, television, theater, and the news media. Although there has been a great surge of important and highly acclaimed literary works written by Asian Americans, it is far beyond the scope of this chapter to try and cover this area. This chapter will first provide an overview of popular images of Asians and Asian Americans in motion pictures, highlighting important gender differences, how they've changed over time, and how they emerged again in the heavily protested film premiere of *Rising Sun* (1993). Next, this chapter will look at Asian Americans on television and feature the recent rise and fall of the program, *All-American Girl* (1994). Third, this chapter will detail the controversies generated by two major theater productions, *M. Butterfly* (1988) and *Miss Saigon* (1990). Lastly, this chapter will also examine Asian Americans in the news media.

HISTORY OF ASIAN AMERICANS IN MOTION PICTURES

Negative images of Asians in the media can easily be traced back to the mid- to late 1800s when Asian migrants first arrived in large numbers to the United States. The common theme of the day was of the "Yellow Peril," or an invasion of faceless and destructive Asiatics, who would eventually overtake the nation and wreak social and economic havoc. In her book, *Romance and the "Yellow Peril"* (1993) Gina Marchetti argues that Hollywood films are not merely harmless entertainment, but "must be understood as linked with other discourses involving race, class, gender, ethnicity and similar pressing social and political concerns."[4] For example, the dominant ideology of Western superiority versus Eastern inferiority eventually led to the passage of the 1882 Chinese Exclusion Law, as well as a multitude of other anti-Asian legislation. Among the most powerful anti-Chinese statements during this period can be seen in writer Bret Harte's poem, "The Heathen Chinee," published in 1870. The immensely popular poem was reprinted across the country. In the poem, Harte describes a "peculiar" Chinese character, Ah Sin, who is wily and sly, but gets caught cheating at a card game. Ah Sin is then attacked and beaten by his white competitor, who yells, "We are ruined by Chinese cheap labour."[5] Similarly, Atwell Whitney's novel, *Almond Eyed* (1878), depicts hoards of Chinese immigrants polluting the environment, degrading American labor, debasing white women, and destroying American society. These types of images continued with the advent of silent films such as *Tsing Fu, the Yellow Devil* (1910), where the sinister Chinese wizard plots revenge against a white woman who rejects his lecherous intentions. The rise of Japan as a military and industrial power following the 1905 Russo-Japanese War was the inspiration for *The Japanese Investigation* (1909), which prominently featured the threat of U.S. involvement in an Asiatic war.[6]

The 1920s and 1930s produced a series of movies that provided highly stereotypical images of "bad" and "good" Asian characters. The personification of evil was seen in the infamous Fu Manchu movies. Fu Manchu was the world-threatening villain originally created in a 1911 short story by British author Sax Rohmer, but this character was soon found in novels, heard on radio programs, and eventually seen on the big screen. Fu Manchu only served to enhance the most negative images of Asians and the Yellow Peril. On one hand, he possessed superhuman intellect and ambition, and on the other, he was subhuman in his immorality and ruthlessness. Contrasting Fu Manchu was the benign and nonthreatening character, Charlie Chan, the cherubic and inscrutable Chinese American detective from Honolulu. This character was again created by another non-Asian, although writer Earl Derr Biggers clearly intended to make Chan a "positive" representation of Chinese. Charlie Chan began as series of novels and quickly made it into the movie houses. Almost 50 Charlie Chan movies were released between 1926 and 1949. Chan was a super-sleuth who solved complex murders, while reciting phoney "Confucious say" proverbs, such as "Bad alibi like dead fish; can't stand the test of time."[7] These popular Asian characters were not only created by whites, they were usually portrayed by whites, as well. All of the actors in the early Fu Manchu movies were whites grotesquely made up to look Asian. The first two Charlie Chan movies hired Japanese American actors for the lead role, but as the films gained popularity they were quickly replaced by white actors who colored their hair jet black and used scotch tape to alter the shape of their eyes. Ironically, Charlie Chan frequently worked with his bumbling number one and number two sons, both of whom were always played by Asian American actors.

Asian and Asian American roles were quite rare in Hollywood, but when one did come up, it was often "scotch tape Asian" actors who got the parts. Paul Muni and Louise Rainer, both Austrian Jews, played the lead roles in the epic *The Good Earth* (1942), the film adaptation of Pearl Buck's classic novel about heroic Chinese peasants. Some rather well-known actors were also given the opportunity to play roles that were simply not available to Asian Americans. For example, Katherine Hepburn played a feisty Chinese peasant woman in *Dragon Seed* (1941) and Marlon Brando played a Japanese interpreter in *Teahouse of the August Moon* (1956). Probably one of the worst portrayals by a scotch tape Asian was done by Mickey Rooney in *Breakfast at Tiffany's* (1961). In this romantic comedy, Rooney plays a Japanese photographer complete with thick glasses, squinty eyes, and buck teeth. Another notable example of a scotch tape Asian can be seen in the movie, *Year of Living Dangerously* (1983), starring Mel Gibson and Sigorney Weaver. In this film, actress Linda Hunt was cast to play the part of a male Chinese photographer.

The casting of a woman actress to play an Asian male character presents yet another media image issue that is not only racist, but highly gendered. Popular media images of Asian males, whether "bad" or "good," have historically been depicted as either uncontrollably lustful or completely asexual. Fu Manchu's lasciviousness toward white women was, of course, never directly acted upon on screen, but the threat was always there. At the other end of the spectrum, Charlie Chan exemplified the completely asexual Asian male character. Although he was said to be married and had a large family, audiences were introduced to only two of his sons. We never get to see his wife and, of course, Chan was never enticed by other women nor were any women enticed by him. In most other instances, Asian American males were depicted as domestic servants, regulated to "women's work," and never having a life outside of catering to whites and doing their jobs. More recently, Asian American males have been seen as nerdy and inept characters, who are clumsy rather than threatening in their attraction to white women. This depiction is exemplified by the Chinese exchange student, played by Gedde Watanabe, in the film *Sixteen Candles* (1984). It would be difficult to think of an Asian American character who didn't lust (unrequited) after women, ignore women all together, or wasn't ignored by women. Even virile Bruce Lee in his mega-hit *Enter the Dragon* was precluded from having any interest in women, unlike his white (John Saxon) and black (Jim Kelly) co-stars. Lee may have been one of the very few celibate action heros in Hollywood.

The recent film *The Ballad of Little Jo* (1993) is worth mentioning because it provides a typical gendered image of the Asian American male with a fascinating twist. In this Western, a young middle-class and educated woman from the East Coast bears an illegitimate child and leaves home in disgrace. She discovers that the rugged, untamed, and ruthless West during the late 1800s is no place for a woman alone. Josephine Monaghan (Suzy Amis) cuts off her hair and disguises herself as a young man named Little Jo. She keeps her true identity from everyone for years, successfully confronting all the dangers and challenges the Wild West has to offer. She eventually purchases some property on the outskirts of town and builds a cabin to live in seclusion. Over time, through hard work and self-sufficiency, Little Jo becomes a respected—although distant—part of the community. The film takes a change in direction when Little Jo saves a Chinese laborer (David Chung) from a group of harassing townsfolk by agreeing to take him home as her houseboy. In the company of another person for the first time, Little Jo cannot for a moment let her guard down for fear of giving away her secret identity. Under this pressure, she initially treats him with contempt, verbally abusing him and forcing him to sleep outside of the cabin like an animal. The gender role reversal is particularly stark with the lean long-haired houseboy acting demurely to scruffy Little Jo. He even tries to win her favor by cleaning, cooking, and baking her favorite fruit pies. Perhaps because of the injustices she has faced, Little Jo slowly begins to treat her houseboy with more civility, then with affection, then eventually with love. He is the only one with whom she shares her secret, and then the two share a secret relationship of their own. The male–female roles between the two outcast lovers becomes somewhat more egalitarian in the privacy of their cabin; but in public, she must maintain her dominant masculine persona, while he maintains a submissive feminine one. Their secret life together lasts for many years until he tragically dies of some unknown illness. Little Jo must suffer alone and in silence over the loss of her mate, and soon she herself becomes extremely ill and dies. *The Ballad of Little Jo* was directed by Maggie Greenwald and is keenly aware of the race and gender dynamics of the era it depicts.

Despite a few notable exceptions, Asian men have most often been depicted as strangely asexual characters. Asian women, on the other hand, have often been depicted as almost completely sexual. The Asian woman's sexuality is based on images of being petite, exotic, and eager to please and serve men. A "bad" element of this stereotype can be seen in the villainous "dragon lady" characters who use their exotic charms to seduce innocent and unsuspecting men for evil purposes. This type of character is best seen in the early films of Ann May Wong produced in the 1920s and 1930s. Wong was born in Los Angeles' Chinatown and started her career as a movie extra. Her big break came playing opposite Douglas Fairbanks, Sr., in the silent classic, *The Thief of Baghdad* (1924). But Wong became most famous for her dragon lady roles as Fu Manchu's daughter in *Daughter of the Dragon* (1931) and in *Shanghai Express* (1932), starring opposite Marlene Dietrich. The "good" version of the sexual Asian woman can be seen in *Sayonara* (1957), starring Miyoshi Umeki. Umeki won an academy award for best supporting actress for her portrayal of a

Japanese woman who falls in love with an American serviceman stationed in Japan after World War II. One scene from the movie has Umeki gently scrubbing her lover's back in a Japanese bathtub. Umeki is so loyal to her man, she commits suicide when she finds she is not allowed to marry the American and live with him in the United States. A similar scenario is seen in *The World of Suzie Wong* (1960), starring Nancy Kwan. Kwan plays a Hong Kong prostitute who falls in love with an American artist, played by William Holden. In the film, Suzie is willing to give herself unconditionally to the white man, but expects nothing in return.

Asian American Studies professor Elaine Kim has written extensively on racial and sexual stereotypes in the media. She argues that these types of images are deeply ingrained in American attitudes, that "it is sometimes difficult to distinguish fact from fantasy or to see members of racial minority groups as individuals." She adds: "We would be hard pressed to think of many portrayals in American popular culture of Asian men as lovers of white or Asian women, but almost every exotic Asian woman character is the devoted sexual slave of a virile white man. The image of the Asian woman as exotic sex object describes the sexual power and significance of the white man at the expense of the Asian man."[8] This is not to say that a few Asian American men have, in fact, distinguished themselves on the big screen in other ways. A popular dramatic actor and romantic lead in early silent films was Sessue Hayakawa. His career faded rather abruptly with the advancement of talking films and the increased anti-Japanese sentiment before, during, and after World War II. However, Hayakawa did return and gave an academy award–nominated performance in *The Bridge on the River Kwai* (1957). The actor Mako was also nominated for an academy award for his bravado work in *The Sand Pebbles* (1966). One of Hollywood's most distinguished cameramen was the late James Wong Howe, who worked on 125 films during his 52-year career in Hollywood. And first-time actor Haing Ngor, a physician from Cambodia, won an academy award for best supporting actor in the powerful film *The Killing Fields* (1987). There were also two notable films that can be considered rather exceptional. One was *Go for Broke* (1951), about the all-Japanese American 442nd Regimental Combat Team and their heroic campaigns in Europe during World War II. The other film was the musical *Flower Drum Song* (1961) based on the 1957 novel by Chin Yang Lee. This was the first and only film that featured Asian Americans in singing and dancing roles. Although both films were heavily burdened with assimilationist sentiments, they provided a different perspective on Asian American life to mainstream audiences.

In response to the general lack of quality roles in Hollywood, young independent Asian American media artists and activists began producing their own film projects. According to filmmaker Renee Tajima (1991), Asian American cinema has gone through two stages of development. The first stage took place in the late 1960s and early 1970s and was sparked by increased ethnic awareness and social consciousness. These early filmmakers were dedicated to highlighting the Asian American experience and changing the distorted images of the past. In 1970 the first Asian American media organization, Visual Communications, was formed in Los Angeles to provide technical and distribution assistance to a new generation of media producers. Visual Communications produced a number of documentaries including *Pieces of a Dream* (1974) and *Cruising J-Town* (1976), as well as a feature film, *Hito Hata: Raise the Banner* (1980). The second stage emerged in the 1980s to the 1990s as a period that Tajima calls "institutionalization, pragmatism, and skills attainment." During this time several other media-related organizations across the country were formed and greater attention was given to art and professionalism over politics, and to expanding the audience. High-quality documentaries such as Loni Ding's *Nisei Soldier* (1983) and *The Color of Honor* (1987), Arthur Dong's *Sewing Woman* (1983) and *Forbidden City, U.S.A.* (1989), Felicia Lowe's *Carved in Silence* (1987), Lisa Yasui's *Family Gathering* (1988), Rene Tajima and Christine Choy's *Who Killed Vincent Chin* (1988), and Steven Okazaki's *Unfinished Business* (1984) and *Days of Waiting* (1990) are just a few examples of films and videos produced during the second-stage period. Feature films also started to emerge during this second stage. Wayne Wang's first film, *Chan Is Missing*, opened in theaters in 1981 and received rave reviews. Other notable films during the 1980s include Peter Wang's *A Great Wall* (1984) and Steve Okazaki's *Living on Tokyo Time* (1987).[9]

More recently, another stage can be added beyond the first two described by Tajima. This stage can be called "mainstreaming" because more inroads are being carved out by Asian American actors, directors, writers, and producers. Certainly Joan Chen has emerged as one of the most highly recognized actresses in Hollywood with starring roles in several major films, including *The Last Emperor* (1987), *Heaven and Earth* (1993), along with some box office flops like *Golden Gate* (1994). Tia Carrere is another recognized actress, who is of mixed Asian Pacific (Hawaiian, Filipino, and Chinese) and Spanish ancestry. While recognized, the roles she's played have been fairly limited and stereotypical. She played the exotic Asian female in *Wayne's World* (1992) and the dragon lady villainess in *True Lies* (1993). Carrere also had a major role in *Rising Sun* (1993), a controversial film that will be discussed in detail in the next section. Jason Scott Lee has emerged as the first Asian American actor cast as a romantic lead with broad major market appeal since Sessue Hayakawa in the early silent screen era, having starred in *Map of the Human Heart* (1992), *Dragon: The Bruce Lee Story* (1993), and *Jungle Book* (1994). The film *The Joy Luck Club* (1993) was generally heralded as a major breakthrough specifically because of its Asian American theme, its mainstream appeal, and also because it was a move away from historical stereotypes of Asian and Asian American women.

Behind the camera, Asian Americans are also making progress. *The Joy Luck Club* provided director Wayne Wang with big-budget experience, and the film's success has opened opportunities for him to direct other Hollywood films. Other filmmakers are branching out in Hollywood and directing films not at all related to Asian or Asian American themes. Ang Lee was the director of the heralded film *Sense and Sensibility* (1995), which was based on the book by Jane Austen. Screenwriter Desmond Nakano directed his first film, *White Man's Burden* (1995), a story about race relations starring Harry Belafonte and John Travolta. Most notably, action-film director John Woo was behind the camera on two recent blockbusters, *Broken Arrow* (1995) and *Face Off* (1997).

The rapid ascent of Asian Americans in the motion picture industry in recent years may also be attributed to the increase of Asian Americans gaining a hold in powerful positions with major studios and production companies. The top executives include Janet Yang, president at Oliver Stone's Ixtlan Productions; Fritz Friedman (of Filipino and Jewish descent), vice-president at Columbia TriStar Home Video; Teddy Zee, executive vice-president at Columbia Pictures; and Chris Lee, senior vice-president of production at Tri Star. In 1992 Friedman and independent producer Wenda Fong formed the "Coalition of Asian Pacifics in Entertainment" (CAPE), with the intention of creating a network for Asian Americans in the film, television, and music industries. "People are so intimidated by Hollywood," says Janet Yang. "It's important to help each other out because it's such a tough business."[10]

The Controversy Over "Rising Sun"

Despite these recent advances, many Asian American media artists and activists contend there is still a long way to go. There is concern that Asian Americans and Asian American themes may be only a passing fancy in Hollywood. More seriously, however, is the movie industry's continued problematic depiction of Asians and Asian Americans. Examples include *Falling Down* (1993), starring Michael Douglas. The film was heavily criticized by Asian Americans for one particular scene that depicted a stereotypically rude Korean merchant who so irritates the Michael Douglas character that he runs amok and winds up destroying the store. *The Shadow* (1994), *Johnny Nmanonic* (1995), and *The Phantom* (1996) are just a few more movies where the villains were evil Fu Manchu–like Asian characters intent on worldwide domination. But the biggest controversy emerged with the heavily criticized release of the big-budget ($40 million) thriller *Rising Sun* (1993), starring Sean Connery, Wesley Snipes, and Harvey Keitel. The film was based on the 1992 best-selling book by Michael Crichton about a beautiful blonde woman murdered by a Japanese businessman. The book was released during a period of sharp tensions between the United States and Japan over trade issues, the fiftieth anniversary of the bombing of Pearl Harbor, and was very reminiscent of the Yellow Peril books written one hundred years earlier. In Crichton's book, the inscrutable Japanese were described as superior in terms of their technology, discipline, and efficiency, but at the same time seen as morally inferior because of their ruthless ambition to take over the U.S. economy, corrupt and predatory business practices, manipulation of trade laws, and lustful behavior toward white women. Although Crichton had never spent more than 48 hours in Japan, he was heavily influenced by the work of writers like Pat Choate (1990), Clyde V. Prestowitz, Jr. (1989), Karl van Wolferen (1989), and others who have argued that Japan is plotting to take over America. It is clear that Crichton wanted his book to be more than a mere murder mystery, as evidenced by the inclusion of an afterword and bibliography at the end of *Rising Sun*. Japanese economic success has not been accomplished "by doing things our way," Crichton writes. "(T)he Japanese have invented a new kind of trade—adversarial trade, trade like war, trade intended to wipe out the competition—which America has failed to understand for several years."[11]

It is within this context that Asian American activist groups began organizing and expressing their concerns immediately after plans for a major motion picture based on Crichton's novel were released. Representatives from the group, Media Action Network for Asian Americans (MANAA), met with the film's production team in early 1993 and requested that they be allowed to view a rough cut of the film. MANAA also wanted the film to begin with a disclaimer stating that it is a work of fiction "not meant to imply that all Japanese people are trying take over America." In this instance, MANAA was seeking a similar disclaimer that was added to director Michael Camino's film *Year of the Dragon* (1984) after a firestorm of protests about its negative depictions of entrenched criminal activity in New York's Chinatown. MANAA emphasized it was neither trying to serve as censor nor attempting to defend Japanese trade, corporate, or government practices. At the same time, however, MANAA was particularly fearful about a possible rise in anti-Asian violence because the portrayals in *Rising Sun* could "fuel racial paranoia, resentment and violence against Asian Americans because of the confusion many Americans have with differentiating between Asian Americans and the fictional images in the media."[12] When the talks broke down, MANAA sent a letter of protest directly to Strauss Zelnick, president and chief operating officer of Twentieth Century Fox, the studio producing the film. In its letter, MANAA again reiterated its demands and this time threatened a high-profile protest upon the release of *Rising Sun* if they were not met. Zelnick rejected MANAA's demands, citing both free speech rights and damage to the film's "commercial potential."[13]

Although the studio and the film's producers did not concede to MANAA's demands, the group's demands did not go completely unheard. The revised movie script did blunt some of the more strident anti-Japanese attacks and the murderer in film was changed from the original book's version. These changes so irked Crichton and co-screenwriter, Mike Backes, that they walked off the project after just seven weeks. *Rising Sun* director Philip Kaufman denied he was influenced by Asian American protests. In a *Los Angeles Times* profile he stated, "I don't think the movie softsells any of the [political] issues at all. In fact, if anything, it opens up discussion." In terms of the movie script that differed significantly from the original book, Kaufman added bluntly, "(Y)ou can't make a movie that lectures or has a bibliography of sources the way the novel does."[14] Despite these changes, MANAA made good on its threat and organized demonstrations in Los Angeles, San Francisco, New York, Chicago, and Washington, DC. In a news conference, MANAA president Guy Aoki complained that Japanese characters in the film were depicted as "ruthless, aggressive people intent on getting their way in business through blackmail, extortion and even murder."[15] These types of portrayals, he added, could contribute to escalating hate crimes against Asian Americans. Even actors in the film were uneasy about the final results. Veteran actor Mako, who played a Japanese executive in the film, had his concerns. "There aren't enough Japanese elements in *Rising Sun*," he said. "What you see is a superficial glimpse." Actor Cary-Hiroyuki Tagawa, who played the film's primary murder suspect, "Fast" Eddie Sakamura, admits there were parts of the film he would liked to have changed. "I think so, only because I've played a lot of stereotypes."[16]

The tangible results of the *Rising Sun* protest are much more subtle than obvious. MANAA never called for a boycott of *Rising Sun*, nor criticized the actors for accepting roles in the film. Instead, MANAA worked to educate both the studio and the movie audience around issues important to Asian Americans, especially increased concern about anti-Asian violence. In this way MANAA has earned grudging respect and credibility in Hollywood. MANAA has shifted its emphasis away from reacting to negative depictions of Asians in film, to working with studios to discuss the need for greater representation of Asian Americans in all areas of the entertainment business and to help producers develop more positive Asian American—themed projects for a larger mainstream audience. Asian American actors and actresses appreciate MANAA's efforts and hope they will eventually lead to the creation of more roles for them to play. Actor Cary-Hiroyuki Tagawa found the protests of the film he starred in to be refreshing. "This was the first nationwide Asian American mobilization since *Year of the Dragon*," he explained. "And in America . . . if you're not rebellious you don't get noticed."[17]

ASIAN AMERICANS ON TELEVISION

The Asian American experience on television parallels what has happened in the movie theaters. Like the movies, network television mirrors the ideology and events of its times. It comes as no surprise that Asian Americans have for the most part been portrayed in predictable stereotypical fashion. The best analytical work on this subject is Darrell Hamamoto's book, *Monitored Peril: Asian Americans and the Politics of TV Representation* (1994). Hamamoto writes, "In the postwar era, television has been the principal medium by which rituals of psychosocial dominance are reenacted daily. . . . Even the most seemingly benign TV programs articulate the relationship between race and power, either explicitly or through implication."[18] Hamamoto found one of the most common roles for Asian American males on television until recently were as domestic servants to whites. Three early television programs of this kind were *Bachelor Father* (1957–1960), starring John Forsythe as a single man caring for his orphaned niece with the help of his "houseboy," played by Sammee Tong. In *Have Gun Will Travel* (1957–1960, 1961–1963) gunfighter Paladin (Richard Boone) had a personal valet, "Hey Boy," played by Kam Tong. When Tong left the show after 1960, he was replaced by another domestic, a woman named "Hey Girl," played by Lisa Lu. Easily the most famous Chinese domestic servant was Victor Sen Yung, who was the character Hop Sing in the *Bonanza* series that ran for 14 years (1959–1973). Even Bruce Lee got his start on television as the faithful houseboy Kato in the show *The Green Hornet* (1966–1967). A Chinese domestic, played by actor Chao-Li Chi, was also seen in the nighttime soap opera, *Falcon Crest* (1981–1990).

Drawing from the Charlie Chan stereotype in motion pictures, Hamamoto cites police detectives as another common role for Asian American males on television. The most recent example is seen in the San Francisco–based show, *Nash Bridges* (1996–present) starring Don Johnson, where Cary-Hiroyuki Tagawa has a reoccurring role as Lt. A. J. Shimamura. Except for Pat Morita starring in his own short-lived series, *Ohara* (1987–1988), all Asian American detectives have played backup roles to white males. For example, Jack Soo as Sergeant Nick Yemana had a secondary role in the program *Barney Miller* (1975–1982). In the popular television show *Hawaii-Five-0* (1968–1980), actors Jack Lord and James MacArthur led a group of Asian American detectives to solve crimes in the aloha state. Actors Kam Fong and Zulu, among others, played the silent background roles, rushing off when orders were given. Steve McGarrett (Lord) and Danny Williams (MacArthur) did all the talking and thinking while their subordinates did all the running around. After the criminals were captured, the Asian American detectives received none of the credit or glory for making the arrest—that was saved for the white men in charge. "Book 'em, Danno" were the famous last words at the end of each *Hawaii Five-0* episode. In the series *Midnight Caller* (1988–1991), actor Dennis Dun played Billy Po, the assistant to the show's lead star, Jack Killian (Gary Cole), a radio talk show host who worked to solve crimes in his spare time. Although Dun is a talented and established stage actor, and his character was much more developed than the standard Asian detective sidekick, his role was clearly the helper to the hero.

The teen-oriented show *21-Jump Street* (1987–1990) featured four hip police undercover officers, among them Dustin Nguyen, who played the character H. T. Ioki. The dashing and handsome Nguyen quickly became a heartthrob of thousands of teenage girls, but the studio highlighted lead actors Johnny Depp, and later Richard Grieco, to carry the show. Both Depp and Grieco quickly moved on to bigger and better acting roles, while Nguyen faded out of the show. Nguyen did reemerge in the made-for-television movie, *Earth Angel* (1991), but he played a stereotypical nerdy Asian American honor student who worked as pet shop cleanup boy. The movie was a breakthrough of sorts because Nguyen's character, Peter Joy, did finally win the affections of a popular all-American girl (Rainbow Harvest) at the end, but only after he helped her with her homework and he was beaten up by the school bully. It is obvious that television did not know what to do with an atypical Asian American male except to regulate him to a typical Asian American role.[19]

Except for the one role in *Earth Angel*, Asian American males have been basically asexual characters. Even the most famous Asian American on television, Lt. Sulu (George Takei), in the orginal *Star Trek* series (1966–1969), was an obvious sexless character. While all the primary male crew members on the starship *Enterprise* had intergalactic encounters with women—human and alien—Lt. Sulu was always left alone. On the other hand, Hamamoto found several examples of Asian American women who were sexually involved with white men. An early example of this is seen in a 1966 episode of the long-running western program *Gunsmoke* (1955–1975), entitled "Gunfighter, R.I.P." In it gunfighter Joe Bascome (Darren McGavin) is seriously wounded helping to protect a Chinese laundryman, Ching Fa (H. T. Tsaing), and his daughter, Ching Lee (France Nuyen), from harassing thugs. The Chinese father is killed, but his daughter takes the gunfighter to her home and nurses him back to health. The couple fall in love and the gunfighter stays to help out the family business. Before too long, however, he is discovered and is reminded that he has already been paid to kill Matt Dillon (James Arness), the marshal of Dodge City. Bascome does not want his Chinese lover to know about his notorious past as gunfighter; so he verbally abuses her and pretends to reject her in hopes she will forget him. The episode concludes when Ching Lee finds $500 left for her by Bascome. She realizes he really loves her after all, and she goes after him. Ching Lee manages to find Bascome but is gravely injured trying to protect him.[20]

Hamamoto also describes a 1979 episode from the series *How the West Was Won* (1978–1979) entitled, "China Girl." The rather twisted storyline focuses on a family who sails from China to settle in the United States in 1869. During the long voyage over, the daughter, Li Sin, played by Rosalind Chao, is raped by the ship's captain and becomes pregnant. Rather than expressing anger and horror at her debasement, Li Sin is instead rather pleased with the idea that her child is half-white and will be an American citizen when it is born. The story then shows the conflict between Li Sin who wants to keep the child and raise it as an American, and her evil Chinese father, who wants the child killed. In the end, Li Sin marries a Chinese man who agrees to adopt the child as his own, and the family moves to Montana to live happily ever after. "In both *Gunsmoke* and *How the West Was Won*, the theme of Asian female sexual possession by the white male Westerner was clearly articulated," Hamamoto writes. "Whether for the purposes of sexual gratification, as in the instance of 'Gunfighter R.I.P.,' or to exert power and assert authority, as seen in the rape of Li Sin by the ship's captain in 'China Girl,' white males are afforded such license as part of their social endowment as the master race."[21]

At the same time, the Asian woman's sexual prowess and uncontrollable attractiveness to white males is often quite blatant, as witnessed in the made-for-television movie epic, *Tai-Pan* (1986), based on the book by James Michener and produced by movie mogul Dino de Laurentis. In this miniseries, Joan Chen plays the China-doll harlot to a British sea trader, played by Brian Brown. Chen also played a similar sexually insatiable role in a 1989 episode from the show, *Wiseguy* (1987–1990). In this particular episode Chen portrays a labor organizer who transforms from a teary-eyed political idealist into a kinky sex kitten while seducing the show's lead character, an undercover FBI agent, played by Ken Wahl.[22]

Asian American women have more recently been seen in a somewhat wider variety of television roles than Asian American men. For example, on the hospital drama, *St. Elsewhere* (1982–1988), France Nuyen played surgeon Dr. Paulette Keim and Kim Miyori played a doctor named Wendy Armstrong. Joan Chen has been seen as a regular on the show *Twin Peaks* (1990–1991), playing the character Jocelyn "Josie" Packard. It is interesting to note that there have also been Asian American actresses on television who are married to white men. For example, in the last year of the hit program *M*A*S*H* (1972–1983), an Asian character was finally featured. In this case it was a woman, Soon-Lee (Rosalind Chao), who eventually married the cross-dressing corporal Max Klinger (Jamie Farr). Their marriage continued into a post-*M*A*S*H* spinoff, *AfterM*A*S*H* (1983–1984). Chao was also seen as a regular in the show *Star Trek: The Next Generation* (1987–1994) and its spinoff *Star Trek: Deep Space Nine* (1993–present). In these shows, Chao plays botanist Keiko Ishikawa, wife of Transporter Chief Miles O'Brian (Colm Meaney). In the hit comedy series *Friends* (1995–present) Lauren Tom had a temporary reoccurring role as the girlfriend of one of the show's main characters, and Ming-Na Wen plays a sharp-talking gallery owner, social butterfly, and love interest in the show *The Single Guy* (1995–present).

Roles for Asian American men, however, have always been extremely narrow on television. Indeed, television has consistently insulted Asian American men, as witnessed by its own version of a scotch-tape Asian in the series, *Kung Fu* (1972–1975). The idea for the show was originally conceived years earlier by Bruce Lee, who desperately wanted to play the lead role. The story line involved a Shaolin priest who escapes China in the late nineteenth century after avenging the death of his mentor, and finds adventure wandering around the American West. It would have been the perfect vehicle for Lee to fully demonstrate his potent martial arts prowess in front of a national audience that wanted more after his debut in *The Green Hornet*. Lee seemed primed for network stardom, especially after his well-received guest appearance on the detective show *Longstreet* (1971–1972), where he played a martial arts instructor. *Kung Fu* was eventually picked up by ABC, the same network that aired *The Green Hornet* and *Longstreet,* but the starring role was given to actor David Carradine. In addition, the character was changed from Chinese to half-Chinese, half-white. Lee was terribly embittered by this rejection and it was at this point he left the United States for Hong Kong to make his mark in Kung Fu movies. Although *Kung Fu* was a personal disappointment for Lee, it did provide an opportunity for a number of Asian American actors in co-starring roles and guest appearances, which were extremely rare up to that time.

The first major television breakthrough for Asian Americans was not a series, but the prime-time made-for-television movie, *Farewell to Manzanar* (1976). The movie, based on the book co-written by Jeanne Wakatsuki Houston and her husband James Houston, was about the experiences of a Japanese American family after the bombing of Pearl Harbor in 1941. The movie followed the Wakatsuki family into the internment camp at Manzanar, focusing on the destruction and divisions wrought by this event. The father, Ko Wakatsuki (Yuki Shimoda), was temporarily separated from his family and was unfairly detained by government agents who accuse him of being subversive and disloyal to the United States. Wakatsuki was eventually allowed to rejoin his family in Manzanar, but was a broken man who drank bootleg sake to forget his humiliation and misery. In this way *Farewell to Manzanar* did not shy away from showing the hardships created by the forceful relocation of over 110,000 Japanese Americans. The movie also showed the controversy that erupted within the camps over the War Relocation Authority's (WRA) questionnaire asking respondents to state their loyalty to the United States. Specifically, question number 27 of the WRA questionnaire asked Japanese Americans to foreswear any form of allegiance to the Japanese emperor, and question number 28 asked if they would be willing to serve in the United States armed services whenever ordered. There was a group of Japanese American dissidents who either refused to answer both questions or responded "no" to both for political reasons. In the movie, however, Ko Wakatsuki pleads to fellow internees to answer "yes" to both answers, arguing that life was still better in the United States than in Japan despite their present situation. Wakatsuki's two sons Richard (James Saito) and Teddy (Clyde Kusatsu) both answer "yes-yes" to the two questions and quickly enlist in the U.S. Army. An interesting subplot in the movie is a love affair between Richard Wakatsuki and a white nurse (Gretchen Corbett). This was the first instance of a mutual Asian American male–white female sexual liaison, but it was short-lived because Richard was soon killed serving with the famous 442nd Regimental Combat Team in Europe. *Farewell to Manzanar* was criticized by some Asian American activists who found that the story overglorified assimilationist ideals, made internment seem like an uncharacteristic accident of U.S. history, and did not focus enough on the dominant role of anti-Japanese racism in the creation of the wartime relocation policy.[23] Nonetheless, *Farewell to Manzanar* received favorable reviews in the mainstream press and provided a showcase for some superb performances, especially by Nobu McCarthy, who was the movie's narrator and played the role of the mother, Misa Wakatsuki.

Asian Americans on TV in the 1990s

Despite the success and attention given to *Farewell to Manzanar*, it wasn't until almost 20 years later that a major prime-time event involving a largely Asian American cast would again be shown on television. In the fall 1994 season, ABC premiered the situation comedy, *All-American Girl*, starring comedienne Margaret Cho. The show was produced by Disney Studios and was loosely based around Cho's stand-up comedy material focusing on her Korean American family living in San Francisco. Cho and the veteran Asian American cast, which included the mother (Jodi Long), father (Clyde Kusatsu), grandmother (Amy Hill), older brother (Tony Award–winning actor, B. D. Wong), and younger brother (J. B. Quon) created a great deal of excitement among Asian Americans who wanted to see the show succeed. "For there to be an all-Asian family in prime time was not even conceivable to the networks a few years ago," gushed co-star B. D. Wong during an Asian Pacific Heritage Month event at Stanford University. "When I grew up and watched TV, I saw no Asians. . . . We weren't thought of as Americans, but as exotics. The existence of this show is really major and an indication of the change in sensibilities to how we're viewed as people."[24] Along with the excitement also came pressure and extremely high expectations. Because only two of the show's writers were Asian Americans, there was tremendous concern whether or not *All-American Girl* would perpetuate or shatter many of the stereotypes about Asians. Many Asian American groups scrutinized the pilot, read scripts, and attended tapings for weeks before the show even reached the airwaves. Aside from the external pressures, there were also internal problems with *All-American Girl*. The original pilot for the show was so bad that it was unceremoniously dubbed "The Joy Less Club" by television critics, and Disney sent it back for revisions. The premiere program that was aired on September 14, 1994, was actually the show's second segment, and it received only lukewarm reviews.[25]

There was also a great deal of disagreement about the show among Asian Americans themselves. Organized Asian American media advocacy groups, such as the Media Action Network for Asian Americans (MANAA), praised the program primarily because it highlighted and validated the existence of Americans of Asian ancestry. "It's basically an affirmation of our existence," said Guy Aoki, president of MANAA. "That's so important, because we've usually been invisible. We've waited so long for an Asian American sitcom."[26] MANAA later honored Cho and the producers of *All-American Girl* at its second annual Media Achievement Awards banquet in late 1994. Asian American viewers, however, were much less enamored. The first major criticism of the show was the poor quality of writing that produced a situation comedy undistinguishable from anything else on television. *"All-American Girl* is a disappointment and commits the biggest show-business sin: it isn't funny," wrote columnist William Wong. "That it is very much in the mold of other TV comedies starring white and black actors means it is banal entertainment, a specialty of commercial television. If Asian Americans were hoping for a TV show that genuinely reflects Asian cultural sensibilities, they'll have to wait for some future show."[27]

Another major criticism was the show's treatment of Asian American men. While the spunky Cho character was a definite change from the meek and exotic Asian woman so often seen in the media, many were aghast that the show perpetuated the negative images of Asian American males. "My main criticism, frankly, was the way Asian men were portrayed," said Deann Borshay, the executive director of the National Asian American Telecommunications Association.[28] Neither the father nor the older brother were very well-developed characters, and in several episodes Cho's attraction to white males over Asian American males was clearly evident. In the opening program, for example, the mother tries to dissuade Cho from dating a white auto mechanic by introducing her to two Asian American men: one was a wimpy-looking graduate student from MIT and the other an accountant with a speech impediment. In a subsequent episode, Cho becomes interested in a handsome Asian American male, but in the end rejects him because she is too "American," while he is too "Asian." Still another source of criticism came directly from many in the Korean American community. They complained that the cast (except for Cho) wasn't Korean, the mother's accent is more Chinese than Korean, and when the Korean language was spoken, it was so badly garbled that native-Korean speakers couldn't understand it. "I felt sort of awkward watching it," explained Wes Kim, a Korean American from Chicago. "It's sort of strange to see this Hollywood conception of what a Korean family is supposed to be like."[29] At best, Korean Americans seemed only moderately enthused about the show. Professor Elaine Kim also expressed "misgivings" about *All-American Girl,* but hoped it might improve with time.[30]

By midseason, however, *All-American Girl* went from bad to worse and the show was clearly in free fall. The show's producer and writers were fired by the studio, and major changes were hurriedly being made. One of the changes was to move the Cho character out of the family house and into her own apartment with roommates. The experiment was intended to target a younger audience of viewers but, if successful, might lead to reduced roles for the rest of the family members. If the experiment didn't work, there was concern the show would be on its way out completely. A furious letter-writing campaign to the studio and the network calling for *All-American Girl* to be renewed for another season was quickly organized by MANAA and other Asian American groups. These last-ditch efforts proved unsuccessful and the show was canceled after just one season.

At the same time all the attention was given to *All-American Girl*, came the premiere of the syndicated miniseries, *Vanishing Son* (1994), which aired on the Fox Television network. *Vanishing Son* featured Russell Wong as Jian-Wa Chang, a human rights activist who is forced to flee mainland China with his brother after the 1989 Tiananmen Square massacre because of their political beliefs. But once in the United States, the brother is killed and Chang is framed for the murder of two federal agents. The show focuses on Chang trying to clear himself, while evading capture and deportation by the U.S. government. *Vanishing Son* was somewhat like a modern-day "Kung-Fu, except the Jian-Wa character was written to be intense, virile, and sexual. This was a major leap for Asian American men in the media, who have been relegated to less than appealing assistant roles up to this point. Being a representative of the Asian community, I'm mindful of the dialogue and care what kind of image is put out there—the quality and integrity," Wong explains. "Jian-Wa's got a lot of energy and sex appeal. He's a passionate guy. It would be unrealistic not to show it."[31]

The miniseries gathered very positive reviews along with a small but dedicated following, and *Vanishing Son* was quickly turned into a mid-season weekly series in 1995. While the weekly series was met with great anticipation and high expectations just like *All-American Girl*, two major questions were also raised. The first question was whether or not a strong Asian male character in a serious role would be acceptable to a large mainstream audience. The second question was whether *Vanishing Son* could smoothly adjust from a well-crafted and well-planned miniseries to the rigorous pace of weekly series, and still maintain its production quality and audience appeal. This would be difficult for any show, especially since the per-episode budget for a weekly program was 30 percent less than the per-episode costs for the original miniseries.[32] Despite the production company's best efforts to keep the show together, it soon became clear that the weekly series could not maintain either the quality or audience it gained from the miniseries. It was not long before *Vanishing Son* was quietly dropped from the network's program list.

The rapid rise and fall of *All-American Girl* and *Vanishing Son* means that Asian Americans still lack a solid presence in the television mainstream. It is true that the most negative images of Asian Americans on television are no longer common, and there have been some improvements in recent years. At the same time, the limited roles and typecasting of Asian Americans are still very apparent. In the Fox Network series, *Voyager* (1995–present), actor Garrett Wang has a regular role playing Ensign Harry Kim. Although Wang's character has more depth and speaking lines than Lt. Sulu in the original *Star Trek*, it seems that almost every spaceship on television has to have a subordinate Asian junior officer on the bridge to be deemed credible. In the made-for-television movie, *Redwood Curtain* (1995), talented actress and singer, Lea Salonga, was praised for her role as an Amerasian orphan (a child of an American GI father and a Vietnamese mother) in search of her father. Depiction of the lost

Amerasian/Vietnam War orphan is possibly the only sympathetic view of Southeast Asian refugees on television. This television movie was unique in that it focused primarily on the Amerasian experience rather than on the white male searching for his long lost child, or the kind and benevolent white woman coming to the aid of a poor orphan. But the theme of closeness and special bonding between an Asian woman and white men was clearly maintained. In this case, the strongest relationships were between Salonga and the adoptive father (John Lithgow), as well as with the biological father (Jeff Daniels). These emotional connections clearly overshadowed any relationship with the adoptive mother (Catherine Hicks) or the biological mother. Indeed, in this movie, the adoptive mother considered the Amerasian adopted daughter to be an ingrate and a threat. The racist, gendered, and stereotypical images of Asian American men and women described so far in this chapter are not unique to the movies or in television sitcoms and dramas. Indeed, they carry over into the theatrical stage as well.

ASIAN AMERICANS IN THE THEATER

Compared with movies and television, Asian Americans have been practically invisible in the mainstream theater stage. Nonetheless, Asian American actors and playwrights have made remarkable strides in a relatively short time both in large Broadway productions as well as in small local theater houses across the nation. According to James S. Moy, author of *Marginal Sights: Staging the Chinese in America* (1993), among the earliest depictions of Chinese in America were in circus performances as either exotics, comic relief, or sideshow freaks. During the intense anti-Chinese period in the late nineteenth century, decidedly negative portrayals of the Chinese were seen in theatrical works such as *Ah Sin!* (1877), written by Mark Twain and Bret Harte, and *The Chinese Must Go* (1879), written by Henry Grimm. As in early motion pictures, the Chinese characters in most of these circus shows and theatrical productions were played by whites. This continued to be the case throughout the first half of the twentieth century. For example, whites were cast in all of the main roles in Eugene O'Neill's play about the adventures of Marco Polo in China, *Marco Millions* (1927). It wasn't until the late 1950s that the first big Broadway play with a large Asian American cast was produced. This was F*lower Drum Song* (1958), which of course served as the basis for the movie musical by the same name. It took almost 20 years before another Asian-themed musical, *Pacific Overtures* (1976), was brought to the Broadway stage. *Pacific Overtures* made a successful run in New York and later toured across the United States.[33]

These mainstream theatrical breakthroughs were few and far inbetween, and by the mid-1970s Asian American actors and writers became understandably impatient. As a result, four independent full-time Asian American Theater groups were formed: The Asian American Theater Company (San Francisco), The Pan Asian Repertory Theater (New York), The Northwest Asian American Theater (Seattle), and The East-West Players (Los Angeles). Many Asian American performers and writers working in theater and Hollywood today received their early training in one or more of these four groups. Their recent emergence in the previously closed world of theater has clearly had a major impact. The controversies around two of the most highly acclaimed plays involving Asian Americans is evidence of this fact. The two plays, *M. Butterfly* (1988) and *Miss Saigon* (1990), caused an unparalleled firestorm among many Asian Americans both in and out of the theater community.

M. Butterfly won the prestigious Tony Award for best play in 1988 and was the runaway theater event of the season. Another Tony Award went to the play's star, B. D. Wong, for "Best Featured Actor." With all this attention, playwright David Henry Hwang suddenly became the toast of Broadway. *M. Butterfly* was based on the true story of a French diplomat who carried on a 20-year love-affair with a person he thought was a female Chinese opera singer, who instead turned out to be a male Chinese government spy. The title of the play was drawn from Puccini's famous opera, *Madame Butterfly* (1904), about a tragic love story between Pinkerton, an American naval officer stationed in Japan, and Cho-Cho-San, a local Japanese woman. Pinkerton returns to the United States shortly after initiating the affair and leaving Cho-Cho-San pregnant with his child. While he is away, she pines for his return and rejects all other Japanese suitors in order to remain faithful for her lover's eventual return. Pinkerton does return to Japan three years later, but this time with his white wife. Pinkerton's mission was not to reunite with Cho-Cho-San but only to retrieve the child he had abandoned three years earlier. His traumatic arrival and unceremonious rejection is such a humiliating blow to Cho-Cho-San that she commits ritualistic suicide. The opera *Madame Butterfly* clearly articulates the white male fantasy stereotype about dominance over the submissive Asian woman. It is also a metaphor of the traditional colonial and neo-colonial attitude demonstrating Western superiority over the East. Playwright David Henry Hwang, who wrote a number of plays produced by several local Asian American theater companies, was well aware of these themes and in *M. Butterfly* sought to subvert the imagery in no uncertain terms.

Early in the play, the French diplomat, Gallimard (John Lithgow), tells the Chinese opera singer/male spy, Song Liling (B. D. Wong), how much he enjoyed the beauty of love and the purity of sacrifice seen in Puccini's opera *Madame Butterfly*. Song chides the diplomat, telling him, "It's one of your favorite fantasies, isn't it? The submissive Oriental woman and the cruel white man." Gallimard is taken aback by the blunt remark and does not know how to respond. Song presses the point and asks the diplomat to reverse the roles. What if a blond homecoming queen falls madly in love with a Japanese businessman who treats her with contempt? What if the Japanese businessman leaves for three years, and the homecoming queen spends the entire time praying for his return, only to kill herself when she learns he has remarried?

"Now, I believe you would consider this girl to be a deranged idiot, correct?" states Song flatly. "But because it's an Oriental who kills herself for a Westerner—Ah!—you find it beautiful."[34] This was one of many twists in the *M. Butterfly* story line that differ completely from *Madame Butterfly*. Another comes in the end of the play when Gallimard discovers Song's true identity. This time it is Gallimard who is crushed and humiliated, and it is he who eventually commits suicide. Just before his death, the diplomat cries out in anguish, "Tonight, I've finally learned to tell fantasy from reality. And, knowing the difference, I choose fantasy."[35]

Despite Hwang's complex intentions and clever juxtapositions, the play generated both praise and scorn from many Asian American viewers. The positive and negative reviews generally seemed to fall along gender lines. For example, during a forum held at the 1989 National Conference of the Association for Asian American Studies in New York City, these divergent perspectives were displayed. Chalsa Loo, professor of psychology at the University of Hawaii at Manoa, stated that if Pucchini's opera *Madame Butterfly* reinforces the white male fantasy of superior race power and domination, Hwang's play *M. Butterfly* shows that perpetuation of this white male fantasy will eventually serve as the vehicle for his own destruction. Loo lauded the play as a "revenge fantasy" for Asian American women: "Hwang touched a fantasy and desire for Asian American women to throw the sexist, racist stereotype back in his face."[36] Others, like Williamson Chang, professor of law also at the University of Hawaii at Manoa, were clearly upset with *M. Butterfly*. Chang argued that although the play may have challenged some stereotypes, it also perpetuated may others. "Asians, particularly Asian women, are portrayed as cunning, shrewd, manipulative, and deceptive," he said. "The plot of 'M. Butterfly' is much like that of Pearl Harbor—Asians succeed through deception." Chang also complained that the Song Liling character was yet another media insult to Asian men whose image has historically been invisible and emasculated. "Asian males had a lot to lose," he emphasized. "Was this 'he-woman' Song going to be representative of us in years to come? Will colleagues at the office look at you differently when you show up on Monday morning?" Chang concluded his talk by firmly stating: "Give me Bruce Lee or give me death."[37] At the end of this forum, David Henry Hwang spoke on his own behalf. He stated that he wanted *M. Butterfly* to create confusion among many people and he wanted them to confront a multitude of stereotypes they may have. When asked by an audience member if he was taking a chance that people might get the wrong message, or perceive a message he did not intend, Hwang responded: "(Y)ou try and reach the greatest number of people you can with whatever you feel is important to say, and if people choose to misinterpret that work, then that's that. But at least they're being exposed to it which is better than if they had gone to something which only reinforced their reactionary thinking."[38]

The debate over *M. Butterfly* did not even have time to be settled because the oppression of Asian women, the renewal of the *Madame Butterfly* fantasy, and the invisibility of Asian American males, were again raised in the Broadway musical extravaganza *Miss Saigon*. In this case, however, the production created an even bigger stir among Asian Americans, and the criticisms were far more unified and heated. In 1990, Broadway was buzzing about the planned arrival of the hit musical from London, *Miss Saigon*. It was expected that this musical would easily be a smash in New York and would then stop at several other cities as part of its U.S. tour. The plot for *Miss Saigon* was simple and familiar: A Vietnamese prostitute (Kim) falls in love with a white American soldier (Chris). She becomes pregnant, but the two are separated after the fall of Saigon. Kim faithfully waits for Chris to return and take her and their child away. Chris does return to Southeast Asia three years later with his white wife (Ellen) to look for his abandoned child. Kim kills herself after finding out that Chris has remarried.

The publicity around the *Miss Saigon* tour and its reuse of the *Madame Butterfly* scenario created tremendous protest by Asian American media activists, who vowed to organize demonstrations wherever the musical is performed. Even more complaints were heard when it was announced that the prominent role of the Vietnamese pimp (Engineer) was going to be performed by a white actor. This role belonged to Jonathan Pryce who played the part in London using heavy makeup to make him "look Asian." David Henry Hwang and B. D. Wong, among many others, bitterly criticized the use of a scotch tape Asian, or a white man in "yellow-face," as an insult to every Asian American performer whose choices for roles are already severely limited. As pressure mounted, the Actor's Equity Union tried to bar Pryce from playing the character, but the union quickly backed down when *Miss Saigon* producer, Cameron Mackintosh, claimed his right of artistic freedom and also threatened to cancel the show's U.S. tour.

The controversy escalated even further and Asian American activists were stung by accusations that they were trying to censor the arts. According to B. D. Wong, nothing could be further from the truth. "I resent being labelled a person who somehow thought that artistic freedom was not important," he said in a magazine interview.[39] Although the Actor's Equity Union reversed its decision and allowed Jonathan Pryce to play the role of Engineer, Wong and other Asian American artists felt their high-profile protests were worth the effort for a number of reasons. First, it brought attention to the limited number of prominent roles for Asian American actors, and highlighted the blatant contradictions found in "color-blind" or "nontraditional" casting. In its ideal form, color-blind casting recognizes the fact that there are relatively few roles written for actors and actresses of color to play on the mainstream stage. The informal policy of color-blind casting serves to encourage directors and producers to cast qualified Asian Americans in any role that they ordinarily would not be allowed to play. In reality, however, color-blind casting has only helped Asian Americans land secondary roles as non-Asian characters but has also continued to allow whites to take major roles as Asian characters. "Parts playable by any actor are not open to people of color, but to white actors who move easily from role to role, ethnicity to ethnicity," wrote Dom Magwili, former director of the Asian American Theater Project of the Los Angeles Theater Center in a guest editorial published in the *Los Angeles Times*. He cited the casting of African American actor/singer, Robert Guillaume, as the Phantom in *Phantom of the Opera* to be an excellent, though rare, example of color-blind casting at its best. Magwili then asks wryly: "How about the novel idea for 'Miss Saigon' that Asians play themselves? Not a chance."[40]

Media activists also said their protests against *Miss Saigon* helped those both inside and outside the theater world to realize that the use of scotch tape Asians should be seen as unthinkable as casting a white actor in blackface. The musical *Miss Saigon* did open as planned in 1991, but Pryce performed without yellow-face makeup. In addition, after Pryce left the show and *Miss Saigon* began its U.S. tour, an Asian American actor was eventually cast in his place. Third, and most important of all, was the fact that the Asian American performing community was willing this time to stand up and make noise, when in the past they had not. "It is no wonder that these artists become restless and active," wrote playwright Velina Hasu Houston, in another guest editorial published in the *Los Angeles Times*. "They have to be. They're mad and they won't be silent anymore."[41] George Takei also believes increased activism among Asian American writers and performers, along with greater participation and criticism by the Asian American audience, are two essential ingredients for change. "The other part of my soapbox to the community is that we need to be visible in the audiences as well. . . . (T)here's no reason why we shouldn't be supporting the arts."[42]

The enormous success of *M. Butterfly* and the controversies surrounding *Miss Saigon* have clearly brought greater attention to Asian Americans in the theater world. Since the 1970s Asian American writers and performers had been working tirelessly, but in almost total obscurity. Today, many of their efforts have begun to bear fruit and this is exemplified by the quantity and quality of plays that have been produced in recent years. Among the more notable Asian Americans that have emerged in the theater is prolific Philip Kan Gotanda, who has written a number of plays including, *Yankee Dawg You Die, Fish Head Soup, The Wash, Day Standing on Its Head,* and *The Ballad of Yachiyo*. Another prolific playwright is Velina Hasu Houston, whose works include, *Asa Ga Kimishita* (Morning Has Broken), *American Dreams, Tea,* and *Basic Necessities*. Small venue one-person plays by Jude Narita ("Coming into Passion/Song for a Sansei," and "Stories Waiting to Be Told/The Wilderness Within"), Amy Hill ("Tokyo Bound" and "Beside Myself"), and Lane Nishikawa ("Life in the Fast Lane," "I'm on a Mission from Buddha," and "Mifune and Me"), have inspired audiences in tours across the country. A lavish theatrical adaptation of Maxine Hong Kingston's *Woman Warrior* had a well-received run in Los Angeles and in other major theater cities. In 1993 the Asian American Theater Company and the Berkeley Repertory Theater were awarded a $1.5 million grant from the Lila Wallace/Reader's Digest Fund to help diversify the ethnic makeup of their audience. The two theater groups planned to produce four new Asian American–themed collaborations.[43] The maturation of writers and performers, and the emergence of a more appreciative audience are hopeful signs for the future of Asian Americans on the theatrical stage.

ASIAN AMERICANS IN THE NEWS MEDIA

The types of negative images that have been seen in the movies, television, and theater productions are often a reflection of society's attitudes about Asian Americans. It may be a surprise to some that stereotypical images of Asian Americans, both subtle and blatant, can also be seen in what is supposed to be the most objective and unbiased area of the media—the news. In the summer of 1994, more than 5,000 Asian American, African American, Latino, and Native American journalists came together for the first time in Atlanta, Georgia, for a weeklong conference to discuss bias and racial stereotyping in the mainstream news media. Their conference was dubbed "Unity '94" and focused primarily on the negative coverage of minority communities, but also concentrated on lack of upward mobility for journalists of color into the upper levels of management (glass ceiling). At the conference, the report "News Watch: A Critical Look at People of Color" was released, which confirmed much of what the conference attendees already knew. The report found one controversial political cartoon that used the term "nigger," criticized one television station for depicting Native Americans as "drunks," highlighted how Latinos were most commonly portrayed as "alien," "foreigners," and "illegal," while the terms "invasion," "inscrutable," and "manipulative" were closely associated with Asians.[44]

The Atlanta conference also hosted a panel of Asian American leaders who called for more accurate portrayals in the mainstream media. "Asians are often not seen as real people, but as a stereotype," explained Stewart Kwoh, executive director of the Asian Pacific American Legal Center of Southern California. "(W)e're either demonized or invisible."[45] Kwoh's comments were later reinforced by a content analysis study of major market newspaper articles conducted by Joann Lee, co-director of journalism at Queens College in New York. According to Lee, the largest number of stories on Asian Americans focused on immigration, crime, and gang violence. "Whatever the rationale, crime is clearly a big chunk of the news diet," Lee wrote in the trade journal, *Editor & Publisher*. "(W)hat is clear in many stories about Asians and crime is that Asians more often are portrayed as suspects rather than as victims. It is as though Asians as victims are not as newsworthy as Asians a perpetrators."[46]

Table 6-1   Numbers and Percentages of Newspaper Employees by Race and Job
Category

Group	Supervisors	Copy/ Layout	News Reporters	Photo- graphers	Total
All					55,000
Blacks	562	459	1,062	268	2,980
Hispanics	324	272	883	289	1,768
Asian Am.	158	235	491	204	1,088
Native Am.	61	29	95	39	224

Source: American Society of Newspaper Editors, April 16, 1996, Table B.

Asian Americans are not only stereotyped and marginalized in the news, but in the newsrooms as well. According to a 1996 report by the American Society of Newspaper Editors, 1,088 Asian Americans represent one fifth of one percent (0.02 percent) of the total work force of 55,000 (see Table 6-1). The only Asian American editor of a major newspaper was William F. Woo at the *St. Louis Post-Dispatch*. Woo lost his position in early 1996, but the high-profile position he had held was exceptional even in newspapers located in areas with large Asian American populations. The *San Francisco Chronicle*, for example, has only 2.7 percent Asian American representation in the news staff even though it is based in an area that is over 25 percent Asian American. In March 1996, the *Oakland Tribune*, which serves one of the most ethnically diverse communities in the United States, abruptly fired long-time employee and nationally recognized columnist, William Wong. *Tribune* management called Wong's termination an unfortunate part of the newspaper's "restructuring" efforts.[47] Wong was one of just four Asian American columnists writing for a daily metropolitan newspaper, and local community leaders and media advocacy groups quickly organized to protest the move. Their actions included a letter-writing and phone-calling campaign, a call for a boycott of *Tribune* advertisers, as well as a noisy picket line outside of the newspaper's office.[48] Within the *Tribune* itself, a spontaneous demonstration erupted in the newsroom and staff members began chanting, "We want Bill." The following day signs asking "Where's Bill?" were seen on reporters' desks and someone covered Wong's computer terminal with a black cloth.[49] Unlike the *San Francisco Chronicle* and the *Oakland Tribune*, the *Seattle Times* has aggressively recruited journalists of color for years and now has one of the most diverse news staffs in the nation. The *Seattle Times* boasts of a news staff that is 14.6 percent Asian American, including two in supervisorial positions.[50]

In contrast to print journalism, television news would appear to be a place where Asian Americans are well represented. This is because of high-profile personalities like former *CBS Evening News* anchorwoman, Connie Chung. But according to the Federal Communications Commission, Asian Americans represented less than 1 percent of broadcast personnel in 1995. The FCC also breaks down various positions by gender as well as race, and it was found that there were more Asian American women than men in both the management (221 to 181) and professional categories (579 to 347).[51] A relatively high number of Asian American women are commonly seen on television news in the glamorous news anchor positions in several major television markets across the United States. Asian American males are sometimes seen as field reporters chasing down a story, but are hardly ever anchoring a news broadcast. This situation on television news may seem innocuous, but it very much reflects and maintains racialized and gendered media images about Asian Americans. Today it is not difficult to notice that on a number of television stations where Asian American women are anchors, they are usually paired up with a white male.

This issue has always been quietly discussed among Asian Americans in the broadcast industry, but it was first brought out into the open in an article by San Francisco–based writer, Ben Fong-Torres (1986). In it, Fong-Torres interviewed several Asian American broadcast journalists who spoke candidly about what they all knew was going on. Most agreed that media images of both Asian men and women are carried into the television newsroom, but, according to anchorwoman Wendy Tokuda, "In this profession, they work for women and against men." Images of Asian American women being exotic and alluring help keep them in front of the camera, whereas images of Asian American men work to keep them off camera. Explaining the image of Asian American men, Tokuda explains, "They're either wimpy—they have real thick glasses and they're small and they have an accent and they're carrying a lot of cameras—or they're a murderous gangster." Veteran San Francisco television news field reporter Vic Lee acknowledges these stereotypes very much work against him, saying, "I've told my wife, if I'm fired here there're only a couple of cities I can go to get a job based on how well I do my work, not how I look or what color my skin is." Referring to the infamous Vincent Chin incident, Lee admits, "You might as well forget Detroit. They *killed* a guy just 'cause he looked Japanese."[52] The gender dichotomy among Asian Americans in broadcast journalism has hardly changed since the Fong-Torres article.

Neither has the fact that both Asian American women and men in the news media often confront the issue of a glass ceiling, and this is a major reason why there is a high rate of turnover in the profession. A survey of current and former Asian American journalists conducted by Alexis Tan (1990) found the top four most likely reasons for leaving journalism were lack of advancement opportunities, need for other challenges, better opportunities in another field, and difficulties with management. When current journalists were asked about the likelihood of leaving the profession within the next five years, 35.7 percent answered "likely" and "very likely." On a more positive note, the two top reasons for current Asian American journalists to enter the field were excitement of the job and the chance to help the community. [53]

With this in mind, the Asian American Journalists Association (AAJA) was formed in 1981 to enhance opportunities for Asian Americans in the profession, provide scholarships to young Asian Americans wanting to major in journalism in college, and to help news organizations provide better and more in-depth coverage of Asian Americans. According to former AAJA executive director, Diane Yen-Mei Wong, Asian American journalists face unique challenges and additional burdens in their job. Because of their visibility, Asian American journalists are compelled to make themselves available as resources to the community. This may entail attending a great deal of non-work-related functions such as appearing at fund-raisers, hosting events, and speaking in panel discussions. Wong acknowledges this is because there are a limited number of Asian American journalists, editors, and producers. The few who exist are all under pressure to serve as educators to their supervisors and peers. Without the presence of Asian Americans in the newsroom, Wong says, even more stories about Asian Americans would go out to the public that contain harmful stereotypes and insensitive reporting. Lastly, although journalists are expected to be generalists, Asian American journalists are often called upon to represent, as well as cover, all Asian American groups. This notion assumes Asian Americans are just one homogeneous entity, which they are not. Wong encourages Asian American journalists (most of whom are Chinese and Japanese Americans) to lobby for news organizations to hire and train individuals from diverse Asian American population groups. [54]

CONCLUSION

This chapter has shown how stereotypes about Asians and Asian Americans have made their way into various forms of the media. These stereotypes and negative images have historic roots and are very reflective of the racialized and gendered attitudes in the mainstream society. The images of Asian Americans in the media are significant and meaningful because they influence how others see Asians. Today these images are much less overtly sinister and diabolical compared to before, but subtle negative stereotypes still remain and can emerge in the most unexpected ways. American figure skating champion Kristi Yamaguchi's capture of a gold medal during the 1992 Winter Olympics is an interesting case in point. Many observers of her spectacular performances at the Olympics assumed she would reap huge benefits in the form of major endorsement contracts. However, Yamaguchi never really cashed in on the endorsements the way a lot of people expected. It was her misfortune to compete in the Olympics during a period of intense anti-Japanese sentiment in the United States, and to win a gold medal on exactly the fiftieth anniversary of President Franklin D. Roosevelt's signing of Executive Order 9066 (February 19) authorizing the mass removal of over 110,000 people of Japanese ancestry into internment camps.[55] This historical coincidence was an uncanny reminder of the persistent image of Asian Americans as perpetual foreigners. This despite the fact that Yamaguchi's family has lived in the United States for generations, and even though Yamaguchi gave a rousing free-skate performance to the music of "Yankee Doodle Dandy" while dressed in a red, white, and blue costume.

The March 9, 1992, issue of *Business Week* confirmed corporate sponsors' unease with her Japanese heritage in an article entitled, "To Marketers, Kristi Yamaguchi Isn't as Good as Gold."[56] Advertisers simply didn't know what to do with Yamaguchi. She did not quite fit the ideal wholesome fresh-faced girl-next-door type sponsors look for in a figure skater, but neither was she the exotic, erotic, and sexual Asian fantasy woman stereotype. Ironically, one of her earliest and most lucrative contracts was with an optical company that promised to change one's looks and self-image with colored contact lenses. To Yamaguchi's credit, she has never publicly complained about her endorsement situation and is earning good money as a professional ice skater. Nonetheless, many agree that her ability to profit even more handsomely from her hard work and achievements was considerably diminished primarily because of conflicting images of her by others, as well as her lingering ambiguous status in the United States.

The negative images of the Asian American male are even more profound. It is for this reason that actor Jusak Yang Bernhard and casting director Paul G. Bens created a line of greeting cards featuring Asian American male "hunks." This project was intended to provide the public with a different image of Asian American men than what they typically get in the media. The greeting card idea follows up Bernhard and Bens' distribution of the "Asian American Player's Guide," a free directory of over 200 Asian American men and women that was sent to executives and producers nationwide. Both Bernhard and Bens cite the casting controversy involving the Broadway musical *Miss Saigon* as the motivation for their efforts. According to Bernhard, the greeting cards are selling well and were intended to make a bold statement. "It's so new to see Asian men in a different light," he explains. "The whole media thing which has been presented shows Asian men as evil and submissive or nerdy. . . . I want people to get angry."[57]

Benhard and Bens' campaign may have had an impact in Hollywood. Miramax has recently bought the rights to produce a new series of Charlie Chan films, but this time the Chan of the 90s will be a hip, slim, smart, and sexy action hero. Miramax has already signed Russell Wong, best known for his role in the syndicated television series *Vanishing Son*, to play the lead role. Wong will play Charlie Chan's grandson in the updated version, although it has not yet been decided what his first name will be. Some Asian American media activists are appalled at the resurrection of a racist stereotype, while others are at least willing to give the studio the benefit of a doubt. "I think it is possible to reinvent a stereotype," said playwright David Henry Hwang. "I hope they create something better."[58] Hwang's play *M. Butterfly* was his own attempt to reinvent a stereotype of another kind, and it was met with both scorn and praise. The planned Charlie Chan movies and the discomfort generated shows that media images are by no means merely benign forms of entertainment.

Indeed, this chapter has focused on the broad trends of how the popular media thinks of and sees Asians and Asian Americans, and how Asian Americans see themselves. These images are constantly in flux and they can change very rapidly. However, if you understand the context for how and why Asian Americans have been portrayed in the media, you will also understand why there is a need for constant vigilance. Asian Americans, of course, are not merely victims of media ignorance and manipulation. They have often struggled, and continue to struggle, against externally imposed racialized and gendered images and work to recapture and re-create their own self-images and identities. This chapter has shown that media depictions are an important part of the highly complex process of identity formation. The following chapter will focus on other important elements that work to influence and help create self-identity.

ENDNOTES

1. See Richard Corliss, "Pacific Overtures," *Time*, September 13, 1993, pp. 68–70; Damon Darlin, "The East Is Technicolor," *Forbes*, November 8, 1993, p. 318; Ester Wachs Book, "The East Is Hot," *Far Eastern Review*, December 23, 1993, pp. 34–35; and "The China Syndrome," *Mirabella*, March 1994, pp. 58, 60, 62.
2. Quoted in Corliss, "Pacific Overtures."
3. Quoted from "Gouw Gets Warner Bros. to Pull Offensive Cartoon," *Asian Week*, February 17, 1995.
4. Gina Marchetti, *Romance and the "Yellow Peril": Race, Sex, and Discursive Strategies in Hollywood Films* (Berkeley: University of California Press, 1993), p. 7.
5. Cited in Ronald Takaki, *Strangers from a Different Shore* (Boston: Little Brown and Company, 1989), p. 105.
6. Kidotj Farquhar and Mary L. Doi, "Bruce Lee vs. Fu Manchu: Kung Fu Films and Asian American Stereotypes in America," *Bridge: An Asian American Perspective* 6:3 (Fall 1978): 23–40.
7. *Ibid.*
8. Elaine Kim, "Asian Americans and American Popular Culture," *Dictionary of Asian American History* (Chicago: University of Chicago Press, 1986), pp. 99–114.
9. Renee Tajima, "Moving the Image: Asian American Independent Filmmaking 1970–1980," in Russell Leong (ed.), *Moving the Image: Independent Asian Pacific American Media Arts* (Los Angeles: UCLA Asian American Studies Center and Visual Communications, Southern California Asian American Studies Central, Inc., 1991), pp. 10–33.
10. Philip W. Chung, "Beyond Asian Chic," *A Magazine*, Summer 1994, p. 22.

11. Michael Crichton, *Rising Sun* (New York: Ballantine Books, 1992), p. 93; also see Pat Choate, *Agents of Influence* (New York: Alfred A. Knopf, 1990); Clyde V. Prestonowitz, *Trading Places: How We Are Giving Our Future to Japan and How to Reclaim It* (New York: Basic Books, 1989); and Karl van Wolfen, *The Enigma of Japanese Power* (New York: Alfred A. Knopf, 1989).
12. "MANAA's Official Statement on the Movie 'Rising Sun,'" March 1993. Also see Jane Galbraith, "Group Takes 'Rising Sun' Protest Public," *Los Angeles Times,* April 7, 1993; and Guy Aoki and Philip W. Chung, "'Rising Sun,' Hollywood and Asian Stereotypes," *Los Angeles Times,* May 3, 1993.
13. Letter from Straus Zelnick to Guy Aoki, March 23, 1993.
14. Quoted in Gene Seymour, "When Simple Isn't Good Enough," *Los Angeles Times,* July 25, 1993.
15. Quoted in David Ferrell and K. Connie Kang, "'Rising Sun' Opens to Charges of Racism," *Los Angeles Times,* July 31, 1993.
16. Quotes in "The Dark Side of the Sun," *Entertainment Weekly,* August 6, 1993, pp. 26, 29.
17. Quoted in Elaine Dutka, "Asian Americans: Rising Furor Over 'Rising Sun,'" *Los Angeles Times,* July 28, 1993.
18. Darrell Y. Hamamoto, *Monitored Peril: Asian Americans and the Politics of TV Representation* (Minneapolis: University of Minnesota Press, 1994), p. 3.
19. *Ibid.,* pp. 28–29.
20. *Ibid.,* pp. 39–42.
21. *Ibid.,* p. 46.
22. *Ibid.,* pp. 191–193.
23. Raymond Okamura, "Farewell to Manzanar: A Case of Subliminal Racism," in Emma Gee (ed.), *Counterpoint: Perspectives on Asian America* (Los Angeles: UCLA Asian American Studies Center, 1976), pp. 280–283.
24. Quoted in Jefferson Graham, "Actor's Chance to Part a Racial and Cultural Curtain," *USA Today,* September 13, 1994.
25. Ray Richmond, "ABC Gives Innovation 'All-American Try,'" *Los Angeles Daily News,* September 14, 1994.
26. Quored in Benjamin Pimentel, "'All-American Girl' Stirs Debate Among Asians," *San Francisco Chronicle,* November 1, 1994.
27. William Wong, "A Disappointing 'All-American Girl,'" *Oakland Tribune,* October 9, 1994.
28. Quoted in J. K. Yamamoto, "Cho Watch," *San Francisco Bay Guardian,* December 7, 1994.
29. Quoted in Pimentel, "'All-American Girl.'"
30. *Ibid.*
31. Quoted in Jeff Yip, "A Heroic Leading Role for One Asian 'Son,'" *Los Angeles Times,* March 25, 1995.
32. Carlos Mendez, "'Vanishing Son': No Plans to Disappear," *Asian Week,* February 3, 1995.
33. James S. Moy, *Marginal Sights: Staging the Chinese in America* (Iowa City: University of Iowa Press, 1993), pp. 7–48, 94–103.
34. Henry David Hwang, *M. Butterfly* (New York: Penguin Books, 1988), Act 1, Scene 6, p. 17.
35. *Ibid.,* Act 3, Scene 2, p. 90.
36. Chalsa Loo, "M. Butterfly: A Feminist Perspective," in Linda A. Revilla et al. (eds.), *Bearing Dreams, Shaping Visions: Asian Pacific American Perspectives* (Pullman, WA: Washington State University Press, 1993), pp. 177–180.

37. B. C. Chang Williamson, "M. Butterfly: Passivity, Deviousness, and the Invisibility of the Asian American Male," in *Ibid.*, pp. 181–184.

38. "A Conversation with David Henry Hwang," in *Ibid.*, pp. 185–191.

39. Quoted in Steven A. Chin, "The World of B. D. Wong," *Image*, September 5, 1993, pp. 6–10, 31.

40. Dom Magwili, "Makibaka! Asian-American Artists Should Struggle—and Not Be Afraid," *Los Angeles Times*, August 13, 1990.

41. Velina Hasu Houston, "It's Time to Overcome the Legacy of Racism in Theater," *Los Angeles Times*, August 18, 1990.

42. Quoted in Jan Breslauer, "After the Fall," *Los Angeles Times*, January 13, 1991, Calendar Section.

43. Erika Milvy, "Asian American, Berkeley Rep Join Hands," *San Francisco Examiner/Chronicle*, November 21, 1993, Datebook Section, pp. 21–22.

44. Center for Integration and Improvement of Journalism, *News Watch: A Critical Look at Coverage of People of Color* (San Francisco: San Francisco State University, 1994).

45. Quoted in David K. Li, "Don't Stereotype Asians, Panel Tells Journalists," *Oakland Tribune*, August 1, 1994.

46. Joann Lee, "A Look at Asians as Portrayed in the News," *Editor & Publisher*, April 30, 1994, p. 46.

47. Tim Graham, "A Letter from the Editor of the Oakland Tribune," *Oakland Tribune*, April 1, 1996.

48. Aletha Yip, "Talk of the Town," *Asian Week*, March 29, 1996.

49. Benjamin Pimentel and Charles Burress, "Oakland Tribune Fires Respected Columnist Wong," *San Francisco Chronicle*, March 26, 1996.

50. Stanford Chen, "It's a Matter of Visibility," *Quill*, April 1993, pp. 33–34.

51. U.S. Federal Communications Commission, "1995 Broadcast and Cable Employment Report" (Washington, DC: Government Printing Office, June 12, 1996).

52. Ben Fong-Torres, "Why There Are No Male Asian Anchors," *San Francisco Chronicle*, July 13, 1986, Datebook Section, pp. 51–55.

53. Alexis Tan, "Why Asian American Journalists Leave Journalism and Why They Stay" (San Francisco: Asian American Journalists Association, 1990).

54. Diane Yen-Mei Wong, "Will the Real Asian Pacific American Please Stand Up?" *The State of Asian Pacific America: Policy Issues to the Year 2020* (Los Angeles: LEAP Asian Pacific American Public Policy Institute and UCLA Asian American Studies Center, 1993), pp. 270–273.

55. Tim Fong, "Yamaguchi's Gold Won't Deter Hate Crimes," *San Jose Mercury News*, February 25, 1992.

56. Laura Zinn, "To Marketers, Kristi Yamaguchi Isn't as Good as Gold," *Business Week*, March 9, 1992, p. 40.

57. Quoted in Elisa Lee, "Asian American Men Bare More Than Greetings in 'Double A' Cards," *Asian Week*, November 11, 1994.

58. Somini Sengupta, "Charlie Chan, Retooled for the 90's," *New York Times*, January 5, 1997.

7

MORE THAN "FAMILY VALUES": ASIAN AMERICAN FAMILIES AND IDENTITIES

VISIBILITY AND INVISIBILITY

The diversity of Asian Americans makes it extremely difficult to speak about any one generalizable Asian American "family" or "identity." Yet, it is not uncommon to hear that the success of Asian Americans has everything to do with their "family values" so deeply rooted in the rich cultural resources brought from their Asian homelands. Asian family values, it is said, work to enhance Asian American self/ethnic identity and group cohesion in the United States. This is especially true with regard to Asian American educational and economic achievements, even when referring to second- and third-generation Asian American families. The strength of the Asian American family, self/ethnic identity and group cohesion, is often held out as a lesson for other minority groups to envy and emulate, and is closely related to the model minority stereotype. By implication, the lack of success among other racial minority groups is directly attributed to a weakness in their family values and cultures.

The favorable comparisons of Asian American family values with other groups persists despite the fact there is relatively little solid research on Asian American families. Sociologists interested in Asian Americans have tended to focus on race relations issues and broader socio-historical experiences, but have given only cursory attention to Asian American families. At the same time, sociologists interested in families have failed to conduct much research on Asian Americans. In this area of specialization, sociological research has historically suffered from weak methodologies, been heavily biased toward white and middle-class norms, and has maintained strongly held myths, stereotypes, and oversimplifications about racial minority families.[1] Similarly, most psychological studies on Asian American families and cultural identity are also lacking. Most of the studies that do exist focus on Chinese and Japanese Americans, and cannot be considered reliable nor generalizable due to small sample sizes and a lack of replication. " There has never been a time when many researchers systematically examined the structure, function, and variety of Asian American families," writes psychologist Laura Uba (1994). "Consequently, the empirically based picture of Asian American families is fragmented and incomplete."[2] Because of these limitations, the purpose of this chapter is to look beyond the superficial and static "model minority" image of the Asian American family and identity type. It is much more realistic to examine the more dynamic nature of contemporary Asian American "families" and "identities."

With this in mind, this chapter will first examine contemporary Asian American families as fluid and adaptive, rather than just rigid and imbedded cultural phenomena. It is important to note that Asian American families have, in fact, not shown any one consistent pattern throughout their history in the United States. Instead, Asian American families have experienced continuous change in response to the social and structural challenges they've faced. The experiences of the post-1965 Asian Americans is no exception. Second, this chapter will focus on Asian American identities and mental health issues. There is a popular image that Asian Americans are generally well adjusted and do not face significant mental health problems. But as increasingly large numbers of Asian American immigrants and refugees enter the United States, they are challenged to cope in a new social and cultural environment. Pressures to make a living, to conform, to adjust to dramatically changing family roles, and to raise children can and do lead to increased identity and mental health problems. Lastly, this chapter will examine new and emerging Asian American families and identities. Emphasis in this section will be placed on interracial marriages and the natural results of these unions—biracial Asian Americans. This section will also look at family and identity creation, and/or re-creation, among Asian American gays and lesbians.

ASIAN AMERICAN FAMILIES

Assimilation has been the key sociological concept in explaining the experiences of racial minority families. In his book, *Assimilation in American Life* (1964), sociologist Milton Gordon describes Anglo-conformity as the historical pattern of assimilation of ethnic and racial minorities in the United States. This means every effort has been made to "Americanize" both minority groups and immigrants by demanding that they surrender all aspects of their culture and adopt the values of the dominant society. Ideally, of course, this should also be the long-term goal of all minorities. The Anglo-conformity perspective has been challenged by more contemporary social scientists, but it still serves as the foundation for many academic and popular beliefs about minority group status, upward mobility, and family values. This can be seen in a brief review of research on African American, Chicano (Mexican American), and Asian American families.

It is not surprising to find the largest body of literature on racial minority families centers on African Americans, given the black-white focus on race relations in the United States. Although the numbers of studies and types of research on African Americans is significant compared with other groups, sociologist Walter Allen (1978) identified three basic ideological perspectives in a survey of studies conducted on this group. They are (1) the cultural deviant approach, which views African American families as dysfunctional and pathological compared to white, middle-class norms; (2) the culturally equivalent approach, which maintains the success of African American families only in relation to white, middle-class norms; and (3) the culturally variant approach, which views the African American family as different, but legitimate and functional.[3] The first two perspectives are clearly rooted in Anglo-conformity, while the third perspective is an attempt to challenge this basic ideology. The culturally deviant approach, rooted in the thesis that the experience of slavery destroyed African American culture and family life, has been the most dominant perspective in social science literature. Two issues makes this thesis highly controversial. First is its tendency to place inordinant attention on low-income inner-city African Americans and generalize these descriptions for the entire group. Second is its assumption that the passage of sweeping laws ending racial discrimination in employment and housing passed during the 1960s is ample evidence of equal opportunity for everyone in the United States today. According to this perspective, it is the historical legacy of slavery that continues to haunt African Americans rather than any *de facto* racism or economic inequality existing today. In the last 20 years, however, important research has emerged taking the cultural variant approach. From this perspective, researchers have sought to show the development of a rich and vital African American family life *despite* the abuses of slavery. At the same time, new research also highlights the continued existence of race and class inequality and discrimination in the United States that serves to perpetuate socioeconomic differences between black and white families.[4]

Research on Chicano families has witnessed similar treatment. The early social science literature on Chicano families has also taken a cultural deviant approach, and found "traditional" ways of Mexican American culture as a serious problem. From this perspective, *machismo*, or rigid male dominance, was viewed as the most dysfunctional cultural tradition in the Chicano family. Chicano men were seen as irresponsible, preoccupied with sex and alcohol, and violent, compared with Chicanas who were viewed as helpless, submissive to a fault, and hopelessly abused. Since the 1970s, scholars have taken a more critical approach to examining Chicano culture and families, and have expanded their focus to look at external structural factors and their impacts on the Chicano family. "What was once labeled culturally deficient family patterns may now be viewed as family strategies that serve as solutions to constraints imposed by economic and social structures in the wider society," writes sociologist Maxine Baca Zinn. "Although themes of patriarchy remain, the nature of male dominance is different from that described in earlier studies."[5] More contemporary research on Chicano families has found greater range of experiences and more sharing of power than previously assumed.

Compared with African Americans and Chicanos, relatively little research has been done on Asian American families. The two primary reasons for the dearth of research on Asian American families has to do with their historically small population and their more contemporary image of not being a "problem" group.[6] Early research on Asian Americans (primarily Chinese and Japanese Americans) has complemented the group for its ability to preserve its "positive" traditions and values, despite its long history of prejudice and discrimination. Traditional Asian culture has been positively associated with the middle-class Protestant ethic, which encourages self-discipline, sexual conservatism, achievement orientation, thrift, as well as a high level of respect for authority and social control. Asian culture is seen as perhaps being overly strict, but over time it can acceptably blend with more liberal Anglo American patterns. In this regard, a culturally equivalent approach has been the most common explanation for why Asian Americans enjoy success compared to other racial minorities.[7]

Researchers have also pointed to several specific features of Asian American families as evidence of their cultural strength and continuity. Chief among them is the strong nuclear family unit. The census figures for 1990 show that 84.6 percent of Asian Americans under 18 are living in two-parent households, compared to the national average of 73.0 percent. Similarly, statistics also show low rates of divorce. In 1990 the average divorce rate in the United States was 8.3 percent. For all Asian Americans, the divorce rate was just 3.7 percent. Ironically Japanese Americans, who are considered the most assimilated of the Asian American groups, had the highest overall divorce rate at 5.4 percent. At the other end of the spectrum, Asian Indians had the lowest divorce rate at 2.1 percent (see Table 7-1).

Another highly touted feature of Asian American families is their strong commitment to the extended family. This can be examined in a number of ways. Asian Americans have larger household sizes compared to the total U.S. average. Table 7-2 shows that Asian Americans tend to have fewer one- and two-person households but have more households with four persons or more. Larger household size for Asian Americans is due for the most part to living arrangements that include relatives outside of the nuclear family unit. The 1990 census found 17.4 percent of Asian American households live with one or more subfamilies. This figure represents extended family households, including those with related members 15 years or older other

Table 7-1 Asian American Household and Family Characteristics ,*1990*

Group	% Under 18 Living with Two Parents	% over 15 Divorced
All	73.0	8.3
Asian Pacific Americans	83.6	3.8
Asian Americans	84.6	3.7
Chinese	81.6	2.8
Filipino	80.9	4.4
Japanese	86.1	5.4
Asian Indian	91.8	2.1
Korean	89.0	3.8
Vietnamese	76.6	2.9
Cambodian	71.0	2.5
Laotian	82.6	2.4
Hmong	86.2	1.7

Source: U.S. Bureau of the Census, *1990 Census of the Population, Asians and Pacific Islanders in the United States* (Washington, DC: Government Printing Office, 1993), CP-3-5, Tables 1 and 2.

than spouse, children, parents, or parents-in-law. By contrast, just 7.5 percent of all households in the United States live in this type of arrangement (see Table 7-3). The large and extended Asian American households are a reflection of three factors. First, there is the tendency of these households to have more adult children living at home while they are completing their educations. Second, there are also more elderly relatives living with their families. Third, larger-sized Asian American households are also due to the fact that established families often host newly arrived immigrant relatives for a period of time. It is no surprise to find an even higher percentage of Southeast Asian families living in large and extended households. This is due to a combination of the factors just stated as well as their economic conditions, recent migration to the United States, refugee status, and high fertility rates.

Another possible indicator of the strength of Asian American extended family structures is the generally low rate of poverty found among single-female-headed households with children under 18. Asian American women who find themselves divorced, widowed, or separated from husbands can

Table 7-2 Asian American Household Size by Ethnic Group, 1990

Group	% of 1 Person	% of 2 Persons	% of 3 Persons	% of 4 Persons
All	24.4	31.8	17.3	15.1
Asian Pacific American	16.1	22.0	18.6	20.6
Asian American	16.3	22.0	18.4	20.7
Chinese	17.6	23.9	19.1	20.0
Filipino	12.4	19.2	18.1	20.2
Japanese	22.8	31.1	17.6	15.7
Asian Indian	12.1	18.6	19.8	27.8
Korean	14.3	21.0	21.0	26.1
Vietnamese	10.2	15.6	16.7	19.1
Cambodian	4.1	8.4	11.8	18.8
Laotian	4.5	8.4	14.0	18.7
Hmong	2.5	4.8	7.3	9.6

Group	% of 5 Persons	% of 6 Persons	% of 7 or More Persons
All	7.0	2.5	1.6
Asian Pacific American	11.6	5.8	5.5
Asian American	11.5	5.7	5.3
Chinese	10.7	4.9	3.8
Filipino	14.6	8.1	7.4
Japanese	5.6	1.6	0.07
Asian Indian	12.6	5.4	3.6
Korean	11.7	4.1	2.0
Vietnamese	15.1	10.5	12.8
Cambodian	18.9	14.8	23.2
Laotian	20.2	13.8	20.3
Hmong	12.1	13.6	50.1

Source: U.S. Bureau of the Census, *1990 Census of the Population, Asians and Pacific Islanders in the United States* (Washington, DC: Government Printing Office, 1993), CP-3-5, Table 2.

Table 7-3 Asian American Select Living Arrangements by Ethnic Group, 1990

Group	% with One or More Subfamily Members	% with Related Members 15 and Over Other Than Spouse, Children, Parents, or Parents-in-Laws of Householder	% Total
All	2.6	4.9	7.5
Asian Pacific American	5.7	11.8	17.5
Asian American	5.6	11.8	17.4
Chinese	5.4	10.5	15.9
Filipino	9.2	16.8	26.0
Japanese	2.3	4.4	6.7
Asian Indian	5.4	11.1	16.5
Korean	4.2	7.9	12.1
Vietnamese	6.1	21.9	28.0
Cambodian	9.8	20.8	30.6
Laotian	8.5	18.7	27.2
Hmong	9.3	20.2	29.5

Source: U.S. Bureau of the Census, *1990 Census of the Population, Asians and Pacific Islanders in the United States* (Washington, DC: Government Printing Office, 1993), CP-3-5, Table 2.

often rely on their parents or other relatives for support. The 1990 U.S. census found over 42 percent of all female-headed households with children under 18 lived below the poverty level. For Asian Americans, 34.7 percent of female-headed households with children under 18 lived below poverty level. A breakdown by individual Asian American groups provides some highly interesting information. For example, only 17.9 percent of Japanese American female-headed households with children under 18 lived below the poverty level. Among Filipino American female headed households with children under 18, only 19.9 percent lived below poverty level. At the same time it is important to note that recent Southeast Asian refugee groups, whose extended family structures have often been fractured due to their migration experiences, had extremely high rates of poverty among female-headed households with children under 18. Within this category, the 1990 census figures show the poverty rates for Vietnamese, Cambodian, Laotian, and Hmong Americans in this category were 57.6 percent, 71.4 percent, 63.6 percent, and 76.0 percent, respectively (see Table 7-4).

Table 7-4 Asian American Female-Headed Households and Poverty Rates, 1990

Group	% of Female-Headed Households	% of Female-Headed House-holds Below Poverty
All	20.2	42.2
Asian Pacific Americans	11.2	35.6
Asian Americans	10.7	34.7
Chinese	7.8	28.3
Filipino	13.8	19.9
Japanese	11.0	17.9
Asian Indian	3.9	35.1
Korean	10.5	30.4
Vietnamese	15.8	57.6
Cambodian	25.4	71.4
Laotian	11.0	63.6
Hmong	13.3	76.0

Source: U.S. Bureau of the Census, *1990 Census of the Population, Asians and Pacific Islanders in the United States* (Washington, DC: Government Printing Office, 1993), CP-3-5, Table 5.

Changing Roles of Asian American Families

Any examination of contemporary changes in Asian American families must first and foremost look at the diverse immigrant population among Asian Americans and the changing roles of Asian American women since 1965. Only after the passage of the 1965 Immigration Reform Act has the gender balance between Asian American men and women reached parity. The earliest immigration laws in the late eighteenth and early nineteenth centuries described in Chapter 1 worked to perpetuate a distinct gender imbalance among Asian Americans—especially Chinese, Filipino, and Asian Indian Americans. This did not begin to change until the end of World War II. Along with their dramatic increase in numbers, a high percentage of Asian American women also work outside of the home. The 1990 U.S. census figures show that labor force participation among Asian American women 16 years and older is 60.0 percent, compared to 56.8 percent for all women. A detailed look at Asian Americans shows a considerable range of labor force participation among Asian American women. For example, a remarkable 72.3 percent of Filipinas work outside the home compared with just 19.9 percent labor force participation among Hmong women. Figures on Japanese and Korean American women are interesting because they both show an overall labor force participation of just 55.5 percent. But if you look just at U.S.-born Japanese American women—most Japanese Americans are born in the United States—the percentage of labor force participation increases to 65.6 percent. Labor force participation for Japanese immigrant women is just 40.8 percent. The percentage of Korean American women may be artificially low because the census does not count Korean American women who work in their family business and they are usually unpaid labor. A survey conducted by sociologist Pyong Gap Min (1992) found 70 percent of Korean American women in New York worked outside of the home.[8]

The general figures on labor force participation include full-time as well as part-time workers; however, there is a separate breakdown for women who work 35 hours or more. These data are important to examine because they show a higher percentage of Asian American women work more hours, as well as work outside of the home. The 1990 census found 69.7 of Asian American women work 35 hours or more, compared to 64.3 percent of all women in the United States. Filipina Americans again top this category with 74.5 percent working 35 hours or more. Chinese and Japanese American women fall closely behind, with over 69 percent of both groups working full-time or more. It is interesting to find that women in three out of the four Southeast Asian groups also have a higher than average full-time employment record compared to the national average (see Table 7-5).

Labor force participation and full-time employment have both positive and negative consequences for working women. On the positive side, women without husbands must work to earn a living and those who are married can enjoy the benefits of a two-paycheck household. In addition, the challenge of the job and the social contacts with other workers are as important for women's attachment to paid work as it is for men. The fact that a woman is earning a significant income can, in some cases, create a more egalitarian marital relationship over the traditional or authoritarian family structure. This tends to be the case for the more educated, second- and third-generation Asian American professionals.[9] On the other hand, as with all other dual-earner families, conflicts can, and often do, arise. When both the wife and husband work, there is precious little time for each other, their children, or household tasks. This is particularly true for working-class families in which one or both the parents may be working more than one job or working irregular hours. In a survey of Chinese American high school students in New York, Betty Lee Sung (1987) found 32 percent of the students did not see their fathers for days at a time, and 21 percent of the respondents experienced the same situation with their mothers. Sung also found that 21 percent of the respondents did not see their fathers all week, while 17 percent did not see their mothers all week. Not surprisingly, a common complaint among parents Sung heard in her research was that they did not have any time to spend with their children. Many of her respondents worked in garment factories or restaurants that are open seven days a week and late into the evening.[10]

Table 7-5   Percentage of Asian American Women 16 Years and Over in the Labor Force, 1990

Group	% of Women in Labor Force	% at Work 35 or More Hours
All	56.8	64.3
Asian Pacific Americans	60.1	69.5
Asian Americans	60.0	69.7
Chinese	59.2	69.2
Filipino	72.3	74.5
Japanese	55.5	69.1
Asian Indian	58.6	65.8
Korean	55.5	67.3
Vietnamese	55.8	66.5
Cambodian	37.3	67.9
Laotian	49.5	72.9
Hmong	19.9	56.6

Source: U.S. Bureau of the Census, *1990 Census of the Population, Asians and Pacific Islanders in the United States* (Washington, DC: Government Printing Office, 1993), CP-3-5, Table 4.

As with all other groups, Asian American women still bear most of the responsibility for cooking, domestic chores, and child rearing even in dual-earner families. Min's New York study found high levels of stress and marital conflict among Korean American wives who spent 75.5 hours a week working a job and doing housework, which was 12 more hours a week than their husbands worked.[11] Within some of these families, domestic violence may erupt. "The Korean man who beats his wife tends to adhere to a rigid stereotyped model of normative Korean masculine behavior, a role requiring that he do hardly any household tasks and make all important family decisions," writes Young Song in, *Silent Victims: Battered Women in Korean Immigrant Families* (1987), the only book dedicated to the subject of domestic violence within Asian American families. "The battered Korean women are found to be responsible for all household chores. . . . A Korean man might hit his wife because she did not have dinner ready when he came home."[12] Most experts agree that spousal abuse is probably a common but highly underreported crime. It is estimated that three million people, mostly women, are severely assaulted each year by their spouses. Although domestic violence against women exists in all social classes and among all races and ethnicities, there are no reliable statistics on the number of battered Asian American women. However, in a sample of 150 Korean immigrant women interviewed by Song for her book, 60 percent reported experiences of abuse. The most common incidents of abuse involved being hit with a closed fist and being slapped with an open hand. In 24 percent of these cases, women reported being choked by their spouses. Song also found 24 percent of the women spoke of weekly abuse, while 37 percent endured abuse at least once a month.[13]

Another area of stress for both Asian American immigrant and refugee families is the dramatic role shifts they encounter after they arrive in the United States. Nazli Kibria's book, *Family Tightrope: The Changing Lives of Vietnamese Americans* (1993), provides excellent insight into these role shifts for Vietnamese American families. She describes the traditional Vietnamese family as an extended structure that is based on hierarchical Confucian principles of the dominance of males over females, and elders over the young. This kind of organizational form works to instill a strong sense of individual dependence on the larger family unit. Clinging to the safety and security of traditional values is one way Vietnamese families try to endure the dramatic relocation away from their homelands. At the same time, Kibria found the patterns of family roles and authority are constantly being challenged in the United States. She describes older women often exercising considerable power in their households, especially when they work outside the home. In some cases, Vietnamese American refugee women begin to assume the primary role as family "breadwinner" because female-dominated service sector jobs are more easily available for Vietnamese American women than low-skill jobs sought by Vietnamese American men. It should be noted that this gender-reversal situation may be temporary, as the husband takes time to obtain educational or technical training that will eventually enable him to gain more skilled employment. Nonetheless, tensions arise as the traditional role of the male as the primary breadwinner for the family is often undermined in the United States by economic necessity. Although the economic well-being of Vietnamese American families has risen over time, this is often due to a pulling together of resources between the husband, wife, and perhaps other wage earners in the family. Along with changing gender relations, Vietnamese families confront major shifts in authority roles between old and young. Kibria described many Vietnamese families in which the children and younger adults have grown up in the United States and today possess greater language skills, educational opportunities, and job training skills than their parents.[14]

Mun Kee Ly, his wife Bik Yong, and their family are a good example of the authority shifts seen among refugee families described by Kibria. The Lys owned a dry goods shop in a small town near Saigon, but after the Communist takeover of Vietnam in 1975, they had to give up their business and were forced to relocate to Ho Chi Minh City to work in a plastic bag factory. It took the family three years to scrape together the resources necessary to purchase passage out of Vietnam. They were among the first group of "boat people" who left Vietnam in 1978 and, by spring 1979, the family settled in Sacramento, California. Mr. Ly was fortunate to find work as a prep cook in a Chinese restaurant, while Mrs. Ly became a manicurist. Together they worked long and hard to support their family, but they wish they could do more. Their inability to speak and understand English is frustrating for both of them, but especially Mr. Ly. "It really upsets me that I can't speak English better," he says through a translator. "If I could speak English, I could do anything." It is clear that the parents have lost their positions of authority in the family when Mr. Ly adds, "I like to speak English, but my kids don't know how to teach us. Sometimes when we speak English and we say the wrong thing, they reprimand us so we don't feel like trying anymore." As a result, it has been the younger generation in the Ly family that has taken on much greater responsibilities within the family. The burdens are heavy for the oldest child in refugee families, and this is especially true for females.[15]

This is the case for the Ly's oldest daughter, Pam, who was just nine years old when her family escaped from Vietnam. Since that time, she has been the primary caretaker of both her parents, her three younger male siblings, and her younger sister. "I have to do everything," she says with a sigh. Her responsibilities include translating for her parents, balancing the family checkbook, and even mowing the lawn. Pam Ly did graduate from college, but she was not allowed to go away for school, unlike her younger brothers. She works as an office assistant at an insurance company and hopes someday to have a professional job where she wears business suits and carries a briefcase. In the meantime, her career goals are secondary to the needs of the family. "I used to have a lot of anger and resentment," she explains. "I think I've always accepted my role. I just never expected it to be so much."[16]

ASIAN AMERICAN IDENTITY AND MENTAL HEALTH

According to psychologist Stanley Sue (1993), the general perception of Asian Americans is of a group that is relatively free of adjustment and mental health problems. But "stressors" created by dramatically changing roles within Asian American families, as well as societal challenges to individual and ethnic identity, can lead to mental disorders. Asian Americans are not, of course, unique in that all groups experience mental health issues. However, the key concern is to pinpoint the nature and extent of mental health disorders, as well as specific Asian American subgroups that are at higher risk for mental illness.[17] It should be mentioned that there have not been any large-scale studies that specifically identify the rate of mental disorders among Asian Americans. Research on Asian American identity and mental health are scarce because of the expense of conducting such a project on a relatively small, yet highly diverse population. At the same time, smaller-scale studies of individual Asian American groups consistently find significant mental health problems that are failing to be addressed. "Asian Americans apparently have stressors facing them that most Americans do not," writes Laura Uba in her comprehensive book, *Asian Americans: Personality Patterns, Identity, and Mental Health* (1994). Uba's in-depth review of studies found the combination of minority status/racism, cultural conflicts, immigrant status, and refugee experiences as the sources of stress that are distinct from other Americans.[18] Both Sue and Uba recognize the need for much more research on the rapidly growing Asian American population.

Asian American Ethnic Identity

Identity generally refers to a person's sense of belonging in society based on his or her social experience. In today's rapidly changing, increasingly diverse, and highly technological world, many people feel isolated and find it extremely difficult to establish any solid sense of identity. One way of maintaining a sense of identity is to define oneself based on ethnic characteristics. Ethnic identity not only impacts thoughts, beliefs, and behavior, but it also serves as the basis of how a person is viewed by others. In 1971, psychologists Stanley Sue and Derald Sue developed a personality structure for interpreting Asian American identity. Drawing from ethnic culture and American white racism, and highly influenced by assimilation theory, their four classifications were labeled: traditionalist, assimilationist, bicultural, and marginal. The traditionalist usually represented recent immigrants who held close to their Asian cultural heritage. On the other side, assimilationists were those who chose to fully adopt American values and behavioral norms as their own. Those in this category tend to have little ethnic identity and generally associate with people outside of their own ethnic group. Bicultural Asian Americans are those who maintain, and move freely in, both Asian and American cultural spheres. Ethnic identity for these individuals is high, yet they also participate well within the broader American cultural milieu. Lastly, those who are marginal reject both Asian and American cultures and are left isolated, alienated, and alone.

This seminal framework by Sue and Sue became the basic reference for many social science researchers, including the work of psychologist Harry Kitano and historian Roger Daniels. In their book, *Asian Americans: Emerging Minorities* (1995), Kitano and Daniels diagram their own Asian American four-part identity/assimilation model that is very much like the Sue and Sue presentation. In it, they chart out: "Cell A: High Assimilation, Low Ethnic Identity," which is similar to the assimilationist; second, "Cell B: High Assimilation, High Ethnic Identity," is similar to the person who is bicultural; third, "Cell C: Low Assimilation, Low Ethnic Identity," is similar to the person who is considered marginal; and lastly, "Cell D: Low Assimilation, High Ethnic Identity," is similar to the traditionalist (see Figure 7-1).

These two models are very simple and easy to understand, but they have also been criticized for being somewhat static and lacking the ability to explain how ethnic identity is developed. Laura Uba was careful to point out

FIGURE 7–1   Identity/Assimilation Model

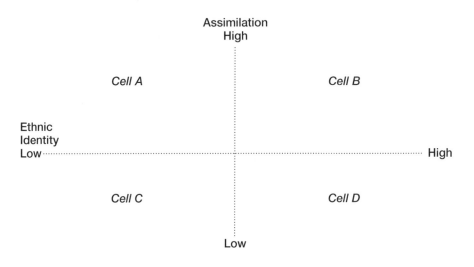

Source: Harry H. L. Kitano and Roger Daniels, *Asian Americans: Emerging Minorities,* second edition (Engle-wood Cliffs, NJ: Prentice Hall, 1995), p. 199.

that the development of ethnic identity is a highly complex phenomenon and can vary greatly from one individual to another. Consciousness, adoption, and adhibition (application) of ethnic identity will often ebb and flow within an individual over time depending on his or her situation and environment. Uba highlighted a number of factors that can account for individual differences in ethnic identity. These factors are formulated externally and are considered contextual; at the same time, these factors are often subject to internal interpretations within the individual. First of all, Uba recognizes that experiences with racism are the "root" of individual differences in ethnic identity. Confronting the harsh realities of racism may cause a person to enhance ethnic identity, or it may cause him or her to reject and deny any ethnic affiliation. Second, it should be no surprise that Uba also identified nativity (foreign-born vs. American-born) and generational differences as important factors in creating and maintaining ethnic identity. It is generally expected in the assimilationist model that the first generation of Asian immigrants would have a greater sense of ethnic identity, while subsequent generations would become much more assimilated into the dominant society, and have less and less ethnic identification.[19]

It is interesting to note, however, that some studies have found a reawakening of ethnic identification within some third-generation Asian American groups. This variation of the assimilationist pattern is not unique and has also been observed among European groups by historian Marcus L. Hansen. From his book, *The Problems of the Third Generation* (1938), emerged "Hansen's Rule" that says in essence: What the second generation tries to forget, the third generation tries to remember.[20] A very good example of how racism, nativity, and generational difference have affected ethnic identity among one Asian American group can be found in psychologist Donna Nagata's book, *Legacy of Injustice: Exploring the Cross-Generational Impact of the Japanese American Internment* (1993). In it, she describes how the forced relocation during World War II continues to haunt Japanese Americans generations later.

The most striking finding from Nagata's work is the legacy of silence between the second-generation Japanese Americans (Nisei) who wanted to forget the internment camp experience, while the third-generation Japanese Americans (Sansei) wanted to remember and learn from the internment experience. Nisei parents who were interned during the war wanted to be seen as Americanized and wanted to separate themselves from their first-generation immigrant (Issei) parents. After the war, the Nisei hoped to protect their children from any further racial humiliation and tended de-emphasize anything distinctly Japanese, while encouraging their children to Americanize to the greatest extent possible. It was not unusual for the Japanese American Sansei, who were coming of age in the 1960s and 1970s, to first learn the details of the internment camp experience in college and only then begin to develop their own sense of ethnic identity and ethnic pride. Nagata sent out a 20-page survey to some 700 Sansei across the United States as part of her research and asked them a number of questions about their family histories. She learned that in most cases any conversations about the camps between the different generations of Japanese Americans were very rare, lasting no more than 15 minutes. Despite this pattern of denial, the children of these Nisei were more likely to develop a stronger ethnic identity, associated more with other Japanese Americans, and have distinct feelings about their vulnerable minority status than those Sansei whose parents were not interned.[21]

Along with external factors, there are also internal factors that affect the development of ethnic identity. Uba describes how Asian American ethnic identity is affected by differences in cognitive development. Some of these cognitive differences are obviously age specific; that is, younger children are simply too immature to understand the complexities of ethnicity. More common differences, however, have much more to do with the sophistication of a person's thinking processes and his or her abilities to integrate divergent experiences and information. Another internal factor Uba describes is the individual's selective attitude toward different aspects of ethnicity. For example, someone may reject notions of male dominance within Asian American culture yet, at the same time, maintain language and ceremonial traditions. Another internal factor described by Uba is one's ability to appropriately evaluate the salience of ethnicity. This means individuals can consciously invoke ethnic identity on a selective basis. At home one may have strong ethnic affiliation, but at work or at school one's ethnicity is kept much more subdued.[22]

Residential area obviously has a great influence on the development of ethnic identity. If one lives in an area dominated by large numbers of co-ethnics such as a Chinatown, Koreatown, Little Saigon, and the like, he or she will have a much higher degree of salience of his or her ethnic identity over an Asian American raised in a predominantly white suburban neighborhood. Asian American ethnic identity is even further complicated by multiplicity of ethnic identities possible. For example, a Filipino American whose parents are immigrants from the Philippines can be identified as a Filipino, a Filipino American, an Asian American, perhaps even Hispanic, or simply as an American, along with many other nonethnic choices. Uba points out that the degree to which an individual Asian American identifies with other Asian American groups has a great deal to do with how the other Asian Americans are perceived.[23] During World War II, many Asian American groups made a point not to be identified with Japanese or Japanese Americans. This was especially true after 1942 when Japanese Americans were ordered by the U.S. military into internment camps. Similarly, many Asian Americans did not want to be identified with Koreans or Korean Americans during the L.A. riot in 1992.

Stressors on Asian American Mental Health

Along with these differences and distinctions in the development of ethnic identity, Uba and others have described several "stressors" commonly faced by Asian Americans. These stressors individually and collectively can have a negative impact on ethnic identity and serve as the cause for mental health problems. Prominent stressors for many Asian Americans are their experiences with racism and awareness of their minority (numerical and social) status. Sociologist Joe R. Feagin (1994) defined racism as "an ideology that considers a group's unchangeable physical characteristics to be linked in a direct, causal way to psychological or intellectual characteristics, and that on this basis distinguishes between superior and inferior racial groups."[24] Asian Americans, along with African Americans, Native Americans, and Mexican Americans, have historically been viewed as the *inferior* racial groups in the United States because of their physical distinctiveness. Today, some Asian Americans also experience a type of racism with a unique twist. They are often the target of a great deal of hostility by others who perceived them as a group that is as doing "too well" in terms of their social and economic status. In either case, experiences with racial antagonism, as well as awareness of physical differences and minority status, may serve to create a sense of anger, frustration, and self-hate among some Asian Americans. These symptoms, of course, can fester and build into severe identity and mental health problems.

In the early 1970s, writer Frank Chin conducted an experiment in his classroom at San Francisco State College (now University). Chin asked his students to fold a piece of paper in half and on one side list what they thought were their "American" qualities and on the other side their "Chinese" qualities. He found that students listed everything that was interesting, creative, adventurous, sexy, and fun as American. Everything on the Chinese side was dull, uncreative, inhibiting, old-fashioned, and repressive. Chin argues that these students were victims of self-contempt and humiliation. "(T)he cliche 'blending East and West,' encourages you to say, 'Well, what are my Chinese parts? What are my American parts?'" he writes. "And what you break down, you break down according to the lines of the stereotype."[25] The findings of Chin's anecdotal experiment has been repeated in a larger and more recent study by Jean Phinney (1989), who found that more Asian Americans preferred to be Euro-American than Asian American. This negative sense of ethnic consciousness was higher than that of either African Americans or Latino Americans. Phinney raises several reasons for these rather surprising findings including: (1) Asian Americans tended to internalize negative "oriental" stereotypes and images; (2) Asian Americans were especially threatened by anti-Asian sentiment; (3) Asian Americans had limited experience with ethnic holidays and did not have strong ethnic identification.[26]

Cultural and generational conflicts are additional stressors on Asian Americans identified by researchers. Although some social scientists have argued there are some important culturally equivalent elements between middle-class Western and Asian culture, Asian American scholars also point to important differences. The most common cultural and generation conflict among Asian Americans centers around the issue of individualism. In the United States, the notion of the independent, spontaneous, outspoken, and aggressive rugged individual is highly valued, whereas in Asian cultures filial piety (obligation to one's parents), modesty, and respect for others are highly regarded. Some broader social issues specifically related to complex cultural and generational conflict have already been discussed in earlier chapters. Chapter 3 described the enormous pressures on young Asian American students to excel in school, and how this can create distress within the family if the student's wishes or talents don't match their parents' expectations. Chapter 4 described how cultural conflict is often seen as an issue in the workplace, and the problems it can create for both the individual and the organization.

The adoption of American values can often become a mixed blessing for Asian Americans, especially when it creates a schism in terms of customs and attitudes on individualism between the different generations in the family. "Asian American families are more hierarchical and undemocratic; freedom and creativity are squelched by Confucian strictness," explains Elaine Kim, professor of Asian American Studies at UC Berkeley. "These are cliches, of course, but also true in a sense."[27] It is not surprising that Asian American women are doubly hampered by the conflict of their parents' high expectations, as well as their strongly held gender-based cultural traditions. The story of Jennifer Ng is a case in point. By most standards, Ng would be considered an image of a successful and well-assimilated Asian American woman. She emigrated from Hong Kong as a child in 1973, grew up in Manhattan, graduated from an exclusive private college in upstate New York, and found a good corporate job as an investment consultant. Yet, for all her efforts and hard work, Ng still hears from her mother: "You better stop being so independent, so outgoing. That's why you have a problem finding a husband." Ng is exasperated that her mother insists that she stay "quiet" and "not express your opinions."[28] Asian American women often feel torn between a sense of independence encouraged by American society, and the sense of obligation to their parents and their parents' cultural values.

In their article, "Invisible Americans: An Exploration of Indo-American Quality of Life," (1995–1996) Snehendu B. Kar et al., surveyed 264 Asian Indian parents and 224 Asian Indian college students. They measured a number of attitudes and experiences, including intergenerational dynamics and areas of conflict and congruence. The researchers found 39 percent of Asian Indian parents reported that the behavior of their children was a major cause of conflict in the family. The greatest source of intergenerational tension within Asian Indian families was clearly around dating and marital preferences of the younger generation. Traditional Asian Indian parents believe dating and marriage concern the whole family and are not matters of individual choice. Among the college-aged children, 52.6 percent of Asian Indian women and 40.9 of Asian Indian men responded that dating preferences were the major conflict issue with their parents. Other major conflict areas highlighted in the survey were quite interesting. More Asian Indian women (13.2 percent) had conflicts over education compared to Asian Indian men (6.8 percent). This may be an indicator that the women are unhappy about not being given the same opportunities as men. Conversely, more Asian Indian men (15.9 percent) expressed dissatisfaction with their careers, compared with women (7.9 percent). This may be an indicator that the men were pushed into careers that were not of their own personal choosing. One of the most significant findings of the survey was that nearly twice as many younger generation Asian Indians reported depression and suicidal tendencies, compared with the Asian Indian parents (12 percent to 6.5 percent).[29]

Racism, cultural and generational conflicts over independence, and gender roles are very important stressors confronted by Asian Americans. At the same time, there is a general consensus among Asian American mental health experts that Southeast Asian refugees are at the highest risk to these and other even more severe stressors. According to Ngoan Le, deputy director of Planning and Community Services with the Illinois State Department of Public Aid, refugees need to be viewed separately from immigrants primarily because of the impetus and conditions for leaving their home countries. He argues that the decision by refugees to come to the United States was based on survival, and the traumas many experienced escaping from their country of origin cannot be underestimated.[30] This sentiment is underscored by sociologist Ruben Rumbaut's study, "Mental Health and the Refugee Experience" (1985). In his survey of refugees in San Diego County, California, Rumbaut found over 73 percent experienced a realistic fear of being killed during their frantic flights to freedom. Many of them, of course, knew of family members who had died, while many have lost touch with friends and relatives and do not know if they are dead or alive.[31]

The mental and physical health problems experienced by the refugees were compounded by extended stays in refugee camps in various first asylum countries in Southeast Asia (e.g., Thailand, Malaysia, Hong Kong) prior to migrating to the United States. Refugees often stayed in these camps for months and sometimes years before they were permanently relocated to the United States or another country. The quality of these refugee camps varied greatly, with some being little more than prisons that merely served to segregate refugees and offered little in the way of amenities and/or social services. Refugees who had the most traumatic escape experiences and who stayed in these camps the longest, tended to have the most difficulties adjusting to their new lives in the United States. Symptoms of mental and emotional distress common among refugees include insomnia, eating disorders, moderate to severe depression, culture shock, and, ironically, homesickness. Rumbaut's survey found that the Cambodians and the Hmong had significantly higher numbers of chronic problems that obviously developed prior to their migration to the United States. Post-traumatic stress syndrome is found among many adult and children Cambodian Americans who survived the mass killings and destruction of their country following the fall of Phnom Penh to the Khmer Rouge forces in 1975. Reported cases of healthy Hmong American males who suddenly died in their sleep (known commonly as Sudden Death Syndrome) were also attributed to refugee-related stress.[32]

Once refugees arrive in the United States and become settled, new sources of stress emerge. The primary stressors for many in the United States are unemployment, underemployment, and poverty. Economic mobility for some Southeast Asian refugees has been achieved but is directly related to a number of human capital factors including English language fluency, education, and professional training. The best example is clearly the Hmong refugees, who were from the rural highlands of Laos and over 70 percent of whom were illiterate in their own language. Their abilities to transfer their agrarian skills to an urban economy have been extremely difficult. Even Southeast Asian professionals are often forced to work well below their skill levels because their foreign credentials are not accepted in the United States. A similar case exists for a large number of former military personnel whose skills are not easily transferable to civilian life.

Underutilization of Services

Despite these and other stressors described above, the utilization of mental health services by Asian Americans remains quite low. Stanley Sue cites a five-year study conducted in the 1980s that found Asian Americans were just 3.1 percent of the clients in the Los Angeles County Mental Health System, even-though they were 8.7 percent of the county's population.[33] Some might say that this is evidence of the relative well-being of Asian Americans. Both Sue and Uba have argued to the contrary and have written extensively on a number of areas that need to be addressed in order to increase the utilization of mental health services among Asian Americans. They include (1) the lack of accessibility and availability of mental health services; (2) the need to confront the general unwillingness and the cultural stigma among Asian Americans to use these services; (3) the need for culturally appropriate mental health services and culturally sensitive mental health professionals.

Accessibility and availability to mental health services include basic factors such as the financial costs of the services and location of service providers that will meet the needs of those in the Asian American community. Asian Americans on limited incomes simply cannot afford private providers and must rely on public or nonprofit service providers if they are to get any help at all. Many mental health experts have argued for locating small community-based outpatient mental health clinics close to where potential clients reside as an essential part of creating a less intimidating environment for the use of these services. Within this, greater outreach to Asian American communities via the ethnic media (newspapers, television shows, radio programs) and the churches can be useful in helping many of those who are unaware of the mental health services and their benefits.

Outreach to the Asian American community may also be an important element toward confronting many of the entrenched cultural stigmas against seeking mental health services. "Many Asian Americans attach a stigma to mental disorders because they think that revealing problems or dealing with problems by seeking professional help are signs of personal immaturity, weakness, and a lack of self-discipline," writes Uba.[34] Although strong family cohesion is often upheld as the distinguishing feature of Asian American families, this close bonding can inhibit families and individual family members from getting the help they need. According to Uba, some of the ways Asian Americans typically try to relieve psychological problems is to "keep busy," don't "think too much," or simply "accept and endure one's problems."[35] At the same time, it is important to note that these types of attitudes are neither universal nor static. Awareness and use of mental health services by Asian Americans do increase over time. A study on second-, third-, and fourth-generation Japanese Americans found decreasing stigmas and increasing acceptance of mental health services depending on the level of the individual's acculturation.[36] Experience shows a sharp increase in the use of mental health services when the facility is specifically targeting Asian American clients, utilizes Asian American therapists, and employs bilingual and bicultural personnel.

There is a great need for culturally appropriate mental health services and culturally sensitive mental health professionals. The most dramatic example of this could be seen immediately after the 1989 schoolyard shootings in Stockton, California. The incident that left 5 children dead and 30 wounded, mostly Southeast Asian refugees, shocked this small rural community and the nation as a whole. In response, over 120 mental health clinicians came to Stockton to help grieving families and distraught residents. But the situation called for a great deal of sensitivity to the refugees' historical and cultural experiences that goes well beyond formal individual or group therapy practices. "You can't treat some of the Cambodians who have gone through the holocaust of the Killing Fields the same way you would someone who has not suffered long-term stress," says local county psychologist Robert Trahms. Many of the mental health workers in Stockton needed bilingual interpreters to help distinguish culturally normal behavior—such as speaking with spirits and ancestor worship—from psychotic delusions. Two days after the massacre, the Stockton Unified School District brought in Dr. Steve Shon, a psychiatrist who heads California's Refugee Mental Health Project, to help coordinate all the necessary mental health and social services to the Southeast Asian community. Shon was especially concerned that the shootings might provoke reoccurring episodes of post-traumatic stress disorder among the refugees, and so he had school psychologists, public health nurses, and social workers monitor families of all the slain and wounded children. In addition, mental health workers distributed information printed in various Southeast Asian languages that referred refugees to the county's Transcultural Mental Health Clinic and provided a number for a multilingual hotline.[37]

Many of the schoolchildren who survived the shooting began suffering a number of maladies including headaches, hallucinations, and fears of evil spirits. There were young students who had to be escorted to the bathroom and from class to class because they were afraid the shooting might happen again. In an attempt to help ease student anxiety, parents asked the school to allow a Buddhist monk to perform a purification ceremony. In addition, other religious leaders were also brought to the school to pray for the dead and call on good spirits to watch over the school and the community. "This is what you encourage them to do—things that are part of their experience to help them reduce anxiety, feel better about what's going on—whether it's going to see the monk, taking herbal medicines, giving offerings—these kinds of rituals and routines they've been used to all their lives," Dr. Shon explains. Along with this, Shon also recognizes a place for professional intervention, especially in the case of severe depression and other extreme emotional and psychological trauma. "I think that when you think there's only one way, that's always dangerous," he adds.[38]

The tragedy in Stockton underscores the challenges faced in bringing together mental health services and Asian American communities. Many Asian American mental health professionals and researchers have long advocated changes in the mental health field that would make services more accessible and available, confront cultural stigmas and unwillingness, and provide greater cultural sensitivity and awareness. In cities with large Asian American populations, programs and facilities that target Asian American clients are the models for changing mental health practices. One of the best models is the Asian Community Mental Health Services (ACMHS) in Oakland, California, which has been offering treatment for a variety of mental disorders ranging from depression to schizophrenia to substance abuse since 1974. The center began when a group of Asian American activists came together after realizing mainstream mental health services were inadequate to meet the specialized growing needs of the Asian American population. The services are a mixture of Western psychological techniques combined with an appreciation of Asian American sensibilities and languages. When the ACMHS first opened its doors, it offered counseling in four languages, but now offers services in 12 languages and treats about 525 patients a year. According to Alan Shin, executive director of ACMHS, 85 percent of the clinic's patients are eligible for public assistance and nearly all of their clients are immigrants or refugees. The center operates on a $2 million budget, much of it state and local government contracts and also from charitable contributions. "If the county were doing this kind of service and doing it well, we wouldn't be around," explains Shin.[39]

NEW ASIAN AMERICAN FAMILIES AND IDENTITIES

So far this chapter has focused on the diverse and changing Asian American families and identities. One of the most exciting areas of research in Asian American studies today can be seen in the greater attention given Asian Americans who are interracially married, biracial and multiracial, and also gay and lesbian. They are also part of the ever-expanding Asian American experience, and much of the recent research done on these populations have concentrated on the creation and re-creation of new family and identity structures.

Interracial Marriage

Interracial marriages (marriage between two people of different races) are a growing but still quite small percentage of all marriages in the United States. The 1990 census counted just over 1.1 million interracial couples, which represents only about 1.9 percent of all marriages. Although many people view interracial marriage a phenomenon involving black–white couples, interracial marriages actually involve a wide range of combinations. Indeed, black–white marriages are still quite rare, representing just 21 percent of all interracial marriages, while interracial marriages among whites and "others" make up over three quarters of all the interracial marriages in the United States. The U.S. census unfortunately does not break down interracial marriage beyond these broad white, black, and other categories. As a result, reliable national figures on Asian American and white interracial marriages are difficult to obtain. Experts generally agree, however, that Asian Americans make up a significant portion of this "other" category.

Prior to the 1965 Immigration Reform Act, Asian American interracial marriage was a relatively rare, although not an unheard of, phenomenon. For example, the earliest recorded interracial marriages included Yung Wing, the first Chinese national to graduate from Yale University, who married a white woman, Louise Kelloge, in 1877. Chinese pioneer woman Lalu Nathoy arrived in the United States in 1872 and, after years of struggle, married Charlie Bemis in 1898. She became better known as frontier woman Polly Bemis. Interracial marriages between Chinese and blacks were also recorded in Mississippi in the late nineteenth and early twentieth centuries. There were also small communities of Filipino men married to white women in urban Chicago, as well as Asian Indian men married to Mexican American women in rural California during the early part of the twentieth century.[40]

Asian interracial marriages began to take on new prominence after World War II. This time the vast majority of these marriages involved U.S. armed services personnel stationed in Asia and native Japanese and Korean "war brides." Between the mid-1940s and the mid-1970s, approximately 100,000 women from Japan and Korea entered the United States as wives of U.S. servicemen. According to researcher Bok-Lim Kim (1972, 1977), these marriages tended to be happy and successful because the wives lived on U.S. military bases that served to insulate them from the poverty and strife in their home country. These war bride marriages also remained stable because the wives were able to maintain their own social networks outside of the base. However, Kim found that troubles began when these interracial couples relocated to the United States. Cultural differences between the couples and adjustment difficulties for the immigrating women were obviously two of the most common issues to arise between couples in these marriages. Frequent antagonism from both sides of the family, and scorn from some outsiders who object to interracial marriages, were two common external factors that created a great deal of tension for the couple. Two thirds of the couples in Kim's study had either separated or divorced within three years of their arrival to the United States.[41]

At the same time, some other studies showed that if these couples survive the initial pressures placed on their marriages, they will be successful, well-adjusted, and generally no different from any other marriages.[42] Obviously research on the relative failure and/or success of these war bride marriages of the 1940s through the 1960s is mixed because the available studies all tend to be anecdotal and have sample sizes too small to be definitive. Despite these limitations, the war bride experience is very important to examine with regard to the increased attention on Asian American interracial marriages in more recent years.

Interest in Asian American interracial marriage reached a peak in the 1980s and early 1990s, especially in the popular media. The realities of Asian and Asian American women dating and marrying usually white males no longer seemed odd, but rather common and acceptable. By this time thousands of American servicemen were bringing home more war brides from the Philippines and Vietnam to join the mix of earlier war brides from Japan and Korea. What few television and movie images that were offered about Asians at the time generally depicted Asian women as spoils of war, docile, petite, and ever-eager to please men. In response to the Asian–white interracial marriage trend, and the images accompanying it, businesses began to emerge specializing in matching up "mail-order" or "correspondence" brides from Asia (usually from the Philippines) with white males in the United States, Canada, and Australia.[43] Attention to this "new" trend of Asian–white interracial dating and marriage was also raised to an even higher level when the *San Francisco Chronicle/Examiner* Sunday magazine printed a feature story entitled, "Asian Women, Caucasian Men" (1990), that sparked tremendous debate and inspired the greatest number of letters in the magazine's history. Writer Joan Walsh was heavily criticized for what many felt was an article laced with stereotypical images. The magazine's editors certainly contributed to the titillating nature of the story by providing an illustration of a long-haired Asian woman whose arms are wrapped around a blond man, her head resting submissively on his broad shoulders.[44]

Amid all of this mainstream media attention, several studies by Asian American scholars were published that attempted to describe and explain the high rate of Asian–white interracial marriages. Among the earliest research efforts was one conducted by psychologist Harry Kitano and his colleagues. In his article, "Asian-American Interracial Marriage" (1984), Kitano counted 1979 marriage licenses of Japanese, Chinese, and Korean Americans in Los Angeles County, and tabulated how many of them married individuals outside of their own ethnic group. The research found that 49.9 percent of Japanese Americans, 30.2 percent of Chinese Americans, and 19.2 percent of Korean Americans married outside of their own group. Particularly remarkable about Kitano's research were figures showing that only 39.4 percent of Japanese Americans were marrying other Japanese Americans. Kitano's research also found that women in all three Asian American groups outmarried (marriage between two people either from a different race or a different ethnic group) significantly more than Asian American men. In 1979, for example, 79.6 per-

Table 7-6 Percentage of Outmarriages Among Asian and Non-Asian Groups Aged 18-64 and Ethnicity of Spouse, United States, 1980

Group	Out-Marriage	Spouse				
		White	Black	Hisp.	Asian	Other
Chinese	15.7	66.5	2.8	2.3	22.2	6.2
Male	14.4	57.6	1.6	3.0	31.6	6.2
(nb)	37.6	54.5	0.9	2.7	35.1	7.0
(fb)	8.2	61.6	2.5	3.3	27.3	5.2
Female	16.8	72.5	3.6	1.8	15.9	6.2
(nb)	36.8	60.5	3.7	2.1	24.6	9.1
(fb)	11.9	81.8	3.6	1.5	9.2	4.0
Filipino	30.0	74.8	6.4	4.8	6.9	7.2
Male	22.2	68.1	1.4	9.0	10.9	10.5
(nb)	60.4	63.0	1.6	9.2	11.8	14.4
(fb)	12.9	74.0	1.2	8.8	9.8	6.2
Female	35.5	77.6	8.6	2.9	5.2	5.8
(nb)	56.9	66.1	6.1	7.1	8.7	11.9
(fb)	31.4	81.7	9.4	1.5	3.9	3.5
Japanese	34.2	77.7	3.9	1.9	11.9	4.6
Male	21.3	64.4	1.6	3.1	22.3	8.6
(nb)	23.0	59.9	1.7	3.0	25.5	9.9
(fb)	16.2	83.4	1.5	3.5	8.5	3.0
Female	41.6	81.6	4.6	1.5	8.8	3.5
(nb)	24.8	67.7	2.5	2.2	19.8	7.7
(fb)	62.1	88.3	5.6	1.2	3.4	1.4
Asian Indian	15.5	86.8	5.4	1.3	3.2	3.2
Male	15.4	84.0	5.1	2.0	5.6	3.3
(nb)	49.6	83.1	4.6	1.5	3.1	7.7
(fb)	14.1	84.1	5.2	2.1	6.0	2.6
Female	15.5	89.6	5.7	0.7	0.9	3.2
(nb)	82.8	96.1	1.7	0.2	0.2	1.7
(fb)	5.2	73.7	15.6	1.8	2.4	6.6
Korean	31.8	79.3	8.3	1.5	8.7	2.2
Male	7.5	58.4	1.8	1.2	34.3	4.2
(nb)	69.4	39.0	1.3	2.6	48.1	9.0
(fb)	4.2	75.3	2.2	0.0	22.5	0.0
Female	44.5	81.1	8.8	1.5	6.5	2.1
(nb)	66.9	60.8	3.1	2.1	27.8	6.2
(fb)	43.8	82.2	9.1	1.5	5.3	1.8

Table 7–6 *continued*

| Group | Out-Marriage | Spouse | | | | |
		White	Black	Hisp.	Asian	Other
Vietnamese	19.8	84.8	4.3	1.1	6.7	2.8
Male	5.5	75.9	0.0	3.4	13.8	6.9
(nb)	25.0	100.0	0.0	0.0	0.0	0.0
(fb)	5.3	74.5	0.0	3.6	14.5	7.3
Female	28.9	85.9	4.8	0.8	5.8	2.7
(nb)	34.4	75.0	12.5	0.0	0.0	0.0
(fb)	28.9	86.0	4.7	0.8	5.9	2.6

nb = native born
fb = foreign born
Source: Sharon M. Lee and Keiko Yamanaka, "Patterns of Asian American Intermarriage and Marital Assimilation, *Journal of Comparative Family Studies* 21:2 (1990): 287–305, Tables 1, 2, and 3.

cent of the Korean American women counted married outside of their own group. By contrast, 52.7 percent of the Japanese American women counted married outside of their own group, while 56.3 percent of the Chinese American women counted married outside of their own group. It should be noted that these figures on Asian American men and women do not separate Asian interracial marriage from interethnic marriages, although it is clear from Kitano's research that most of these marriages were to non-Asians.[45]

Kitano and his colleagues' work was highly provocative, but was also criticized for its rather crude methodology and limited scope. With this in mind, sociologists Sharon M. Lee and Keiko Yamanaka (1990) conducted research similar to Kitano's, but looked at the entire United States, and added Filipino, Asian Indian, and Vietnamese Americans. Lee and Yamanaka used a 5 percent sampling of 1980 U.S. census data to confirm many of Kitano's findings. For example, Lee and Yamanaka found that 92 percent of all Asian American outmarriages were in fact interracial. The researchers also confirmed that more Asian American women than men outmarried. This was due to the high number of foreign-born Asian American women who interracially married compared to the relatively low number of foreign-born Asian American men who interracially married, although the interracial gender gap between U.S.-born Asian men and women was not nearly as pronounced (see Table 7-6). Based on their detailed research, Lee and Yamanaka also found interracial marriage occurs most often among well-educated and professional Asian Americans. Given the fact that Asian Americans have the highest educational and occupational levels, and have the highest income levels relative to other racial minority groups, it does not come as a surprise that their rates of intermarriage are high as well.[46]

Why Do Asian Americans Interracially Marry?

The two studies above clearly show the high rate of Asian American interracial marriage. Three perspectives on interracial marriage are commonly raised to try and explain the reasons for this phenomenon. The most simple and basic explanation for Asian American interracial marriage is a matter of individual choice. Asian Americans just happen to meet many people of different races, fall in love, and get married. Race is not a factor in these intimate personal decisions. In their book, *Adjustment in Intercultural Marriage* (1977), Wen-Shing Tseng et al. explain intermarriage in general by the fact that some people have the need to be different; that is, they are more adventuresome than others and are always interested in trying and liking something different than the usual choice. Similarly, there are some people who marry someone of another race or ethnic group because that other person possesses a valued attribute that their own culture is not as likely to supply.[47] The problem with this perspective is that it doesn't explain variations in interracial marriages among racial minority groups. If love is indeed color-blind, and individuals exercise free choice in personal decisions, why is the interracial marriage rate for African Americans so low?

Another common explanation of Asian American interracial marriage is closely related to the assimilation theory and the work of Milton Gordon (1964). Gordon argues that marital assimilation, or intermarriage, between members of a minority group to members of the majority group is a positive sign of acceptance by the larger society. Compared to the individual free choice perspective, assimilation theory understands that interracial marriage between Asians and whites would not be taking place in any significant scale unless the larger society was willing to accept it. Sociologist Betty Lee Sung calls marriage between an Asian American and a non-Asian "the ultimate assimilation" and has dedicated a book, *Chinese American Intermarriage* (1990), to the subject.[48] The assimilation perspective does offer a broader insight into interracial marriage, but it also fails to answer some other very important questions. If Asian Americans are so well accepted by the American mainstream, why is it that their interracial marriage patterns are mainly characterized by well-educated Asian Americans with high incomes, and not distributed equally throughout the Asian American population? More importantly, why is it that more Asian American women interracially marry than Asian American men?

An attempt to answer these questions produced by far the most controversial perspective on Asian American interracial marriage. In their article, "Marriage Patterns of Asian Americans in California, 1980" (1990), sociologists Larry H. Shinagawa and Gin Y. Pang reinterpreted the statistical data on Asian American interracial marriage and offered a sophisticated analysis that challenged the individual choice and assimilation perspectives.[49] Shinagawa and Pang focused their attention on hypergamy theory, which tries to explain why in most cultures, women marry men of equal or higher social status, whereas men marry women of less social status. In the United States, for example, only about 33 percent of women with four or more years of college marry men with less education. Conversely, 50 percent of men with four years of college marry less-educated women.[50] Shinagawa and Pang then added to the mix the fact that in a class and racially stratified society like the United States men and women often enter into romantic relationships depending on whether the other person possesses certain tangible and/or intangible resources. Tangible resources include money and a good job; intangible resources include physical appearance (i.e., race) and social status.

Shinagawa and Pang concluded that privileged Asian American women "maximize their status" by marrying the "most advantaged individuals with the highest racial position." In other words, well-educated Asian American women in a professional job can generally choose from one of two marital choices: (1) an Asian American man who has same or higher economic status, but same racial status; or (2) a white male with the same or higher economic status *and* higher racial status. Interracially married men, on the other hand, tend to have spouses who "have lower educational and socioeconomic status although they are higher in racial position." This means that the choices for well-educated, professional Asian American men are generally equal: (1) an Asian American woman with lower or the same economic status and the same racial status; or (2) a white woman with lower economic status but higher racial status. These types of choices help to explain why more Asian American women interracially marry than Asian American men.[51]

The problem with the above studies on Asian American interracial marriage stems from the collection and generalized interpretation of statistical data on a subject that is deeply personal and subjective. It is with this in mind that researchers Colleen Fong and Judy Yung (1995) conducted a number of in-depth interviews with Asian American men and women in the San Francisco Bay Area and asked them about their marital choices. The researchers found that interracial marriage involved a multitude of complex issues, some of which have been described above. A few respondents admitted they married whites for some measure of upward mobility and social status, which is evidence of hypergamy. More commonly, respondents focus on elements of free choice. *Both* Asian American women and men frequently stated they married interracially because they wanted to avoid traditional Asian patriarchy, and were seeking more egalitarian family relationships.

At the same time, Fong and Yung also found that the marital choices of Asian American women and men were not completely free. For example, both Asian American men and women were very much affected by stereotypical sexist and racist media images that surrounded them as they were growing up. This was discussed in detail in Chapter 6. Asian American women admitted negative media images of Asian men were a factor in why they viewed white males as more "attractive" and "exciting." Asian American men said were not affected by erotic media images of Asian women because they saw Asian women more like sisters, rather than sex objects. Asian American men, on the other hand, thought media images depicted white women as more "vivacious," compared to the Asian women they knew who were "too introverted." According to Fong and Yung, "both women and men faulted the opposite sex for the same weaknesses: being overly serious, having pragmatic occupations or narrow interests, being rather lackluster and not a part of the dominant or counter culture." It is interesting to note that interviewees in this study realized the media stereotypes of others, but did not believe they themselves were affected. Most of the interviewees in this study were comfortable with their marital choices because they felt their spouses better reflected their own self-concept, rather than any family or socially imposed image. The work of Fong and Yung shows the complex and multilayered factors involved in interracial marriage.[52]

This issue becomes even more complex as Shinagawa and Pang have continued and expanded their research. In their most recent work, "Asian American Pan-Ethnicity and Intermarriage" (1996), they found between 1980 and 1990 the number of interethnic marriages of Asian and Pacific Islander Americans in the United States (e.g., a Chinese American marrying a Korean American, or a Japanese American marrying a Vietnamese American, etc.) approached or have exceeded interracial marriages. Indeed, increase in interethnic marriages rose from 200 to 500 percent in just 10 years. Some of the reasons for this increase in interethnic marriages are (1) a rise in the number of recent foreign-born Asian Americans who are generally intraethnically (marriage between two people of the same ethnic group) or interethnically married; and (2) the counting of Pacific Islander groups such as Hawaiians, Samoans, Togan, and Chamorran who, because of their geographic location and limited contact with whites, naturally tend to marry intraethnically and interethnically. Given these factors, assimilationist theory would still assume that the more assimilated U.S.-born Asian Americans would maintain a high interracial marriage rate. Shinagawa and Pang were aware of this, and focused their attention on select U.S.-born Asian American groups in California to see if the above interethnic versus interracial marriage patterns continued. Table 7.7 shows that at least with Chinese, Filipino, and Japanese Americans, there is still a significant rise in the number of interethnic marriage (see Table 7.7).[53]

Shinagawa and Pang also looked at five specific Asian American "cohorts" in California that represent various age groupings, as well as their major social and historical influences. The researchers found distinct marriage patterns in the various cohorts. The pre–World War II and World War II cohort (prior to 1946) was a period of high levels of racial hostility and antimiscegenation laws in many parts of the United States. Not surprisingly,

Table 7-7   Marriage Patterns for Select Asian American Groups by Nativity in California, 1980 and 1990

Group	Total			U.S.-born		
	1980	*1990*	*Change*	*1980*	*1990*	*Change*
Chinese/men						
Intraethnic	88.9	75.8	14.7	74.3	57.1	-23.1
Interethnic	4.3	16.7	288.4	8.8	23.9	171.6
Interracial (white)	5.4	6.0	11.1	14.3	15.4	7.7
Interracial (non-white)	1.4	1.5	7.1	2.6	3.6	38.5
Chinese/women						
Intraethnic	86.1	74.3	13.7	71.7	51.4	-27.9
Interethnic	2.5	13.9	456.0	6.4	24.4	281.3
Interracial (white)	9.9	10.4	5.1	18.3	20.9	14.2
Interracial (non-white)	1.5	1.4	6.7	3.6	3.0	16.7
Filipino/men						
Intraethnic	79.3	3.8	6.9	38.4	43.3	12.8
Interethnic	2.5	13.9	456.0	5.9	19.4	228.8
Interracial (white)	11.0	8.0	27.3	36.3	26.4	27.3
Interracial (non-white)	7.2	4.3	40.3	19.4	10.9	43.8
Filipino/women						
Intraethnic	73.4	59.8	18.5	42.3	35.2	16.8
Interethnic	2.5	15.0	500.0	4.7	23.2	393.6
Interracial (white)	5.8	5.5	5.2	19.7	12.0	39.1
Interracial (non-white)	18.3	19.7	7.7	33.3	29.6	11.1
Japanese/men						
Intraethnic	82.9	62.1	25.1	80.5	60.5	-24.7
Interethnic	3.8	21.2	457.9	4.5	20.6	357.8
Interracial (white)	10.7	13.9	29.9	11.8	14.6	23.7
Interracial (non-white)	2.6	3.6	38.5	3.3	4.2	27.3
Japanese/women						
Intraethnic	64.2	48.1	25.1	76.8	50.3	34.5
Interethnic	4.2	20.0	376.2	5.0	22.4	348.0
Interracial (white)	27.5	27.5	0.0	15.6	23.1	48.1
Interracial (non-white)	4.1	4.4	7.3	2.6	4.2	61.5

Source: Calculations by Larry Haijime Shinagawa, Ph.D. based on 5 percent Public Use Microdata Sample (PUMS), U.S. Bureau of the Census, 1990. Copyright 1996, Larry Haijime Shinagawa, Ph.D., Assistant Professor, Department of American Multicultural Studies, Sonoma State University. Used with permission.

this was also a period when there were very few interracial marriages. The post–World War II cohort (1946-1962) and the civil rights era cohort (1963–1974) were times when race relations were liberalized and, of course, the war bride era. These were the periods when Asian American interracial marriages began to increase steadily. The post-1960s cohort (1975–1981) and the Vincent Chin cohort (1982–1990) were periods of higher interethnic marriage. Shinagawa and Pang attributed this current trend to a number of factors including (1) the increased population size and concentration of Asian American communities in California; (2) the growing similarities in socioeconomic attainment and middle-class status among Asian Americans; (3) the bridging of Asian ethnic differences due to a common language and common experiences in the United States together with an increased feeling of Asian ethnic cultural affinity among young Asian Americans; and most importantly, (4) an increased sense of racial consciousness and unity. "This racial consciousness and awareness is especially acute in California," the researchers write. "Race, increasingly more than ethnicity, powerfully shapes the experiences and development of identity among Asian Americans." They conclude that, like whites who mostly marry other whites of different ethnic groups (e.g., an Irish American marrying a German American), Asian American interethnic marriage may soon become the more common phenomenon. If true, this will serve to forge the creation of a more generalized Asian American identity, rather than maintain distinct Asian ethnic identities.[54]

Today, the research on the impact of interracial and interethnic marriage on the Asian American family, identity, and community has just begun. As Asian American intermarriages continue into the future, this type of research may emerge and take center stage. This is beginning to happen for biracial Asian Americans who are now coming of age and are speaking from their own unique perspectives.

Biracial and Multiracial Asian Americans

The interracial marriage patterns among Asian Americans provide ample evidence of the creation and re-creation of new types of families and identities. Whatever the causes behind these marital trends, they mark tremendous change in the Asian American population. With this in mind, a distinct and growing part of the diverse contemporary Asian American experience are the offspring of Asian and non-Asian interracial unions. Among them are famous golf sensation, Tiger Woods (one-eighth Native American, one-eighth African American, one-quarter white, one-quarter Thai, and one-quarter Chinese), to infamous mass murderer, Andrew Cunanan (white and Filipino). There are no precise numbers showing the number of mixed-race people because the latest census form had no specific category for them. The Census Bureau did, however, conduct one study to find how mixed-race couples chose to identify their children for census purposes. In the 1980 census, it was found that 66 percent of children with one black parent and one white parent were counted as black. For children born to white and Asian parents, just 35 percent were listed as Asian. Other sources of demographic information have also proven to be of little practical use for counting biracial or multiracial individuals. Prior to 1989, for example, the National Center for Health Statistics tabulated the races of children born in the United States from data about the parents' races on birth certificates. A child born to one white parent and one nonwhite parent was generally classified as nonwhite. If neither parent were white, the child was classified based on the race of the father. This became problematic because in 13 to 15 percent of the cases, there was no data about the fathers.[55]

Individuals of mixed-race backgrounds continue to confront and confound American society's rigid racial boundaries. Those who don't fit into a specific category are considered an aberration. This is abundantly clear when looking at the negative social and historical mythologies that have evolved to maintain a marginal status for mixed-race people. Sociologist Cynthia Nakashima (1992), herself a biracial Asian American, vividly describes several biological arguments that viewed mixed-race people as "genetically inferior to both (or all) of their parent races." Nakashima also found sociocultural stereotypes that maintained mixed-race people have severe inferiority complexes and were in a constant state of restlessness and discontentedness.[56] Attempts to deny the existence of mixed-raced people and to categorize them into rigid racial categories continues even today. A major issue for biracial and multiracial Asian Americans, along with mixed race people in general is the social pressure to have to "choose" what group they belong to.

An obvious example of this occurs whenever a person has to fill out a government form, such as the U.S. census. "My first instinct was not to fill it out," explained Theresa Thurmond, whose father is African American and mother is Japanese American. She was told to choose only one racial classification box on her 1990 census form, and no more. She does not remember which box she marked. For Thurmond, the question of which box is an important statement about self-identity.[57] It should be noted that racial categories in the census and the statistics that are gathered are useful data for many federal agencies. Agencies such as the Department of Justice and the Equal Employment Opportunity Commission use race statistics to ensure that states comply with civil rights laws. Calls for a separate multiracial census category have been criticized by some civil rights advocates because it could dilute hard-fought political gains.

According to Nakashima, biracial and multiracial people who are part white are sometimes seen as "whitewashed," are not allowed to discuss their multiraciality, and are not truly seen as a "person of color." Nakashima cites the Japanese Cherry Blossom Festival that prohibits participation from people who are below one-half Japanese American, or if they don't "look" Japanese.[58] This sentiment is confirmed by research on Asian–white college students on the East Coast conducted by Kwai Julienne Grove (1991). Grove quotes one young woman saying, "A lot of times I talk with Asians, I am not a 'real Asian' because I don't look Asian so I don't get discriminated against as an Asian does." Many of the Asian/white respondents in Grove's survey did admit they were able to "float" across racial boundaries and felt relatively more free to choose their identity rather than have it chosen for them. "You can't be quite identified," reported one of Grove's male Asian–white respondents. "I like that because no one else is like you and it frees you to make your own identity. . . . People do not look at you and say, 'Oh, you're Asian, so you must be good at math and science.'"[59] However, conflicts over issues of identity and isolation can be especially strong for individuals of Asian and African American descent who often face racism not only from whites but from other Asians as well. The words of Song Richardson are particularly telling: "I can see them look at me and some don't think I can understand Korean. I hear them making derogatory remarks about the fact that I'm mixed . . . I'll walk into a market and see someone behind the counter who looks like my Mom, and I'll feel a certain affection. But then she'll treat me with complete lack of respect and cordiality. Differently than she would treat a white person who comes into the market."[60]

Attitudes and policies that continue to marginalize mixed-race people are being challenged in a variety of ways. One way is through organizing. This can be seen by the growing number of multiracial or multiethnic organizations emerging across the country, as well as student groups formed on many college campuses. Together these organizations and groups have put pressure on the federal government to create a multiracial category on the 2000 U.S. census. In July 1996 the first-ever multiracial families' march was held in Washington, DC, specifically around the creation of a new census category. Around 200 Americans of mixed-race attended the demonstration carrying signs that read, "I'm proud to be me," "No more other," and "I'll choose my own category."[61]

Another way of challenging strict racial delineations and society's attempts to keep multiracial people invisible is through the arts. One of the best known in this arena is playwright Velina Hasu Houston, daughter of an African American and Blackfoot Native American father and Japanese mother. For years Houston used her artistic skills working toward highlighting, creating, and recreating Asian American multiracial identity. Her highly acclaimed trilogy of stage plays, *Asa Ga Kimishita* (Morning Has Broken), *American Dreams,* and *Tea,* traces the journey of a Japanese war bride married to an African American GI, and her experiences living in Japan and in various parts of the United States. "There's a lot of talk in the media now about interracial relationships," she says. "The funny thing about it is, every time I see it mentioned, it's like everyone in America thinks being multiracial means being black–white. . . . In my world, most of the interracial relationships are Asian and white, or Asian and African American, or Asian and Hispanic." Houston is also an outspoken advocate for a multiracial census category, and has publicly clashed with both African American and Asian American political leaders who want to maintain the status quo. "All of us had been raised by our parents to understand that we were multiracial and that we could not get stuck into a category because it was convenient for somebody else to do so."[62]

This leads to the third way of confronting multiracial marginality and invisibility. Experts agree that it is important for the interracially married parents to discuss racial and ethnic differences openly, and to convey a positive valuation of being biracial or multiracial. "Parents are crucial facilitators of the biracial person's self acceptance," writes psychologist George Kitahara Kitch. "If parents are comfortable talking about race and ethnicity with their biracial and bicultural children and model the resolution of conflicts . . . they can actively cultivate the family as an important medium through which a biracial sense of self develops."[63]

Amerasians

Most biracial and multiracial Asian Americans were born in, or have spent a great deal of their lives in, the United States. They are, for the most, part culturally "American." But there is another group of mixed-race Asians who have their own set of distinctive circumstances. Known as "Amerasians" they are also of mixed racial heritage, but they were born in Asia. When Amerasians come to the United States, they have sharp cultural and linguistic issues not faced by other biracial and multiracial Asian Americans. It has been estimated that between 30,000 and 50,000 Amerasian children were left behind in Vietnam following the U.S. military evacuation from Saigon in 1975. The Amerasian experience in postwar Vietnam was extremely difficult. They were known as "dust children," or half-breeds, harassed by the Vietnamese government because they were seen as offspring of the enemy, and because of their obvious physical differences in a largely homogeneous society.

The photographs of Amerasians begging or selling cigarettes on the streets of Vietnam in the late 1970s brought international attention to their plight. In addition, there were increasing complaints by American fathers who faced tremendous obstacles trying to bring their children to the United States. The Orderly Departure Program in 1980 created the first opportunity for separated families to reunite. Unfortunately, only about 4,500 Amerasians were able to leave Vietnam under this program, and this was through a provision that was established in 1982. It wasn't until the passage of the Amerasian Homecoming Act of 1987, that large numbers of Americans and their accompanying relatives were able to leave Vietnam. Since the early 1980s, 81,500 Amerasians and their family members have immigrated to the United States.

Some Amerasians hope to find their fathers once they arrive in the United States, but they are usually disappointed.

Tanisha Terry was one of the lucky ones. She was born in Vietnam and was just a baby when her father, George Terry, left for the United States with plans to send for his daughter and her mother. This proved more difficult than expected as the Vietnam conflict escalated and the situation became even more complicated. Tanisha's mother married another American serviceman and sent Tanisha to live with her grandmother. Then Tanisha's mother left Vietnam just before the fall of Saigon in 1975. It was 10 years before her mother could sponsor Tanisha and her grandmother to the United States. As Tanisha grew older she became more and more determined to find her father. She fortunately discovered a copy of her father's birth certificate and a partial social security number. A private investigator was hired in 1994 and relatives of George Terry were soon found in Alabama. Tanisha learned that her father moved to Germany, and sent him a letter in early December. "Dear Mr. Terry," the letter began, "While you were in Vietnam, you met a women and together produced a baby girl you named Tanisha. After the war you never had contact with her again. If possible I'd like that to change. I am Tanisha." Terry returned to the United States just before Christmas to meet the daughter he hadn't seen in over 22 years. "I never forgot her," Terry said tearfully. He was particularly thankful to be reunited with his daughter because he suffers from serious heart condition. "I'm just glad I've lived long enough to see this day. I never want to lose her again."[64]

Tanisha's story is heartwarming but, unfortunately, all too rare. Unlike other biracial and multiracial Asian Americans in the United States, Amerasians do not often have family support systems. Kieu-Linh Caroline Valverde's article, "From Dust to Gold: The Vietnamese Amerasian Experience" (1992), describes how Amerasians have a double-double burden when they come to the United States. Their first double burden comes from being both refugees and biracial. Amerasians faced the same hardships encountered by refugees suddenly resettled into a new environment, but their needs—particularly around mental health issues—are different from those of "standard" refugees. The second double burden is the negative reaction against Amerasians by both the Vietnamese and non-Vietnamese American communities. Amerasians confront a particular type of hostility from members of the Vietnamese community in the United States. Many Vietnamese Americans assume that the mothers of Amerasians were bar girls and prostitutes, and that Amerasians themselves are cheap lowlifes. The antagonism against Amerasians among Vietnamese Americans often drives them away from the community, and they try to seek relief in mainstream society. What most find instead are more stereotypes as well as adaptation problems. Valverde describes the case of one black Amerasian who was rebuffed by Vietnamese men because of her race and rejected by African American men because she was so culturally different.[65]

Amerasians have been coming to the United States since the early 1980s, and media attention was given to many of them at that time because they were children. Today, as adults, their plight has all but been ignored. Because many Amerasian children were not given any formal education in Vietnam, their educational, social, and economic adjustment to the United States has been particularly acute. Ostracized by Vietnamese Americans and mainstream society who both want to forget the Vietnam War, many Amerasians have found solace in each other's company. Valverde found a need for Amerasians to develop a "third culture" for themselves that acknowledges and accepts their unique multiracial status. Some Amerasians have emerged to become role models for other Amerasians. They include Mary Xinh Nguyen, who was Revlon's Most Unforgettable Woman for 1990, and Tuan Le, a former star defensive back on the Stanford University football team. "This list is growing," Valverde writes. "Amerasians are finding strength to help themselves and each other, as this multiracial group comes of age.[66]

Gay and Lesbian Asian Americans

The Asian American gay and lesbian experience is not new, but has only recently been openly and thoughtfully discussed. Homosexuality has existed in Asian countries for centuries, yet sexuality is seldom, if ever, talked about in traditional Asian American families.[67] In her study, "Issues of Identity Development among Asian American Lesbians and Gay Men" (1989), Connie S. Chan found only nine of thirty-five interviewees told their parents about their sexual orientation. Chan attributed "Asian cultural factors" as a major reason for this low rate of "coming out."[68] Another example of the hidden nature of homosexuality in the Asian American community can be seen in the groundbreaking feminist anthology, *Making Waves* (1989). The anthology was written by, for, and about Asian American women, but the only essay that didn't include the author's full name was the one about Asian American lesbians. Ironically, the essay's author, "Pamela H.," wanted to remain anonymous even though she was arguing that Asian American lesbians were an "emerging voice" in the Asian American community.[69] Attention to Asian American gays and lesbians has come a long way in recent years, and is no longer a taboo subject. For example, in 1994 the Japanese American Citizens' League (JACL) national board of directors adopted a resolution supporting same-sex marriages. The issue sparked a great deal of controversy from a conservative faction of the organization. The faction tried to rescind the board's decision at the JACL national convention, but its attempt failed for lack of votes.[70] A letter to the JACL national board and members signed by a coalition of 15 Asian Pacific American gay and lesbian groups from across the nation thanked the organization for its stand. "Recognizing that same-sex relationships are a matter of civil rights is indeed to understand the importance of expanding in today's society," the letter said. "It is encouraging efforts such as yours that give us hope that we can work together on common issues to achieve a much fairer and more tolerant world in which we will all benefit."[71]

That same year, *Amerasia Journal*, the leading scholarly publication for Asian American Studies, dedicated an entire volume, entitled "Dimensions of Desire," on gay, lesbian, and bisexual identities and orientations. The issue was lauded for presenting important and provocative articles on matters never openly discussed before. The introductory article in this volume by Dana Y. Takagi cautions against rigidly categorizing the Asian American and gay and lesbian experiences and identities as if they are one and the same, or easily interchangeable. "[O]ur search for authenticity," Takagi writes, "will be tempered by the realization that in spite of our impulse to clearly [de]limit them, there is perpetual uncertainty and flux governing the construction and expression of identities."[72] Attempts to limit, or categorize, a specific identity is a major issue for biracial Asian Americans, who are constantly asked to "choose" one identity over another. Likewise, Asian American gays and lesbians are also asked to choose between their Asian American and sexual identities and loyalties.

The issue of "choosing" was quite prominent in the roundtable discussion, "In Our Own Way," published in the same *Amerasia Journal* volume. In this discussion, four Asian American lesbians described in great detail their experiences of homophobia in Asian American communities, as well as racism and tokenism in the gay and lesbian communities. "Those of us who are gay people of color are often forced to choose between the gay culture and people of color culture," said Zoon Nguyen, "The point is that we have to choose and we just can't be who we are."[73] Increased visibility and activism of Asian American gays and lesbians since the 1970s have also served to slowly, but surely, break the barriers of the kind of forced marginalization just described. Gil Mangaoang's autobiographical article, "From the 1970s to the 1990s: Perspective of a Gay Filipino American Activist," highlights the early "schizophrenia" he felt between his political and social identities that needed to be reconciled. "I began to understand that the discrimination and homophobia I perceived were two sides of the same coin and, that in fact, there were similarities of oppression," Mangaoang wrote. "I had to take responsibility for defining what my life was to be a gay Filipino American man and I have found that process of liberation is a continuous one." Mangaoang believes the environment for Asian American gays and lesbians is better and less isolated today than in the 1970s. This is because more Asian Americans are openly accepting their sexual orientation and established organizations have been formed to support them.[74] Huong Nguyen is another Asian American who came to the realization she had to confront the contradictions around her. She is the 22-year-old ROTC cadet at the University of California at Los Angeles who gave up her ambition to be a military surgeon when she submitted a letter to her commanding officer admitting she is a lesbian. Under the military's "don't ask, don't tell" policy, Nguyen could have kept her lifestyle a secret and continued in military service, but this was something she did not want to do. "The military teaches you leadership," Nguyen said. "In order to be a good leader, you need to be honest, and by lying to them, I felt I was not being a good leader." The ROTC immediately placed her on a leave of absence, pending her discharge.[75] Still another prominent gay Asian American activist is J. Craig Fong, the West Coast regional director for the Lambda Legal Defense and Education Fund (LLDEF), the largest legal services organization for the gay and lesbian community. A 1981 graduate of the University of Pennsylvania Law School, Fong worked as the Immigration Project Director for the Asian Pacific American Legal Center in Los Angeles for four years before joining Lambda. The switch from one organization to another was not a difficult one for Fong because he sees gay and lesbian civil rights issues being no different from civil rights issues for other groups. "I feel very close to the Asian Pacific Islander community," Fong said. "I'm also a gay man. And this community means a lot to me . . . I can link communities that normally don't talk to one another [o]r that are not familiar with one another. That's an enormous opportunity."[76]

Among these linkages are several common issues. Among the most serious are HIV/AIDS and hate violence. Researchers have acknowledged relatively low incidence of HIV/AIDS among Asian Americans, and this has led to a general sense of unconcern and even myths of genetic immunity among Asian Americans.[77] The recent death of Siong-huat Chua, founder of Boston Asian Gay Men and Lesbians, one of the first gay and lesbian support groups, served to bring greater attention to the realities of HIV/AIDS in the Asian American community.[78] Community activist Ignatius Bau has been working to educate the community on the risks and impending dangers of this disease. He cites an estimate by San Francisco HIV Prevention Planning Council that 37 percent of the Asian American gay men are living with HIV, and warns this high rate of HIV seroprevalence means that there may very well be a sudden increase in AIDS in the near future. One of the most important aspects of Bau's work is getting HIV prevention materials out to specific Asian American homosexual and heterosexual target audiences. This includes translating information into the various Asian languages, getting them published in widely circulated ethnic newspapers, and announced on radio stations and cable programs that serve a predominantly Asian audience.[79] A study of 334 Vietnamese men and women in Orange County, California, conducted by Cuong Quy Huynh and Geraldine V. Padilla (1996), found that the most effective routes of communication about HIV/AIDS was through the Vietnamese media (i.e., newspapers and television) and through personal networks (i.e., family, friends, co-workers). The findings were similar to an earlier study of the Latino community and the effectiveness of HIV/AIDS education.[80]

Hate violence described in Chapter 5 is not limited to race but also extends to sexual orientation. A recent report published by the California State Attorney General's office (1996) found 69.3 percent of hate crimes were related to the victim's race or ethnicity, 18.1 percent were related to sexual orientation, and 12.5 percent were related to religion.[81] One of the most brutal incidents of anti-gay violence occurred in the affluent Ssouthern California community of Laguna Beach where Loc Minh Troung, a Vietnamese American, was viciously beaten. Troung suffered severe brain damage as a result of the attack, has not been able to return to work, and for a time had to live in a supervised residential care facility. The senseless attack on Troung rallied both Asian American and gay activists who worked to ensure that the perpetrators were arrested and convicted. The two assailants, Jeffrey Michael Raines and Christopher Michael Cribbins, both pled guilty to committing felonies but denied the anti-gay hate crime charge. However, their denials were contradicted by prosecution witnesses who testified that Raines and Cribbins bragged about "wanting to beat up some fags" prior to meeting and then assaulting Troung. Raines is serving a ten-year prison sentence for attempted murder, but Cribbins received only a one-year prison term and five years of probation for assault. Truong did file a civil suit against his assailants, along with one of their friends who stood by and watched the beating, and was recently awarded $1.1 million for medical costs and "pain and suffering."[82]

While there are common interests in many civil rights issues for Asian American and gays and lesbians, there was one major issue that created a tremendous amount of antagonism and friction. In the spring of 1991, the Lambda Legal Defense and Education Fund and the New York City Lesbian and Gay Community Services Center made plans to feature the controversial Broadway play *Miss Saigon* as the centerpiece of both of their fund-raising events. Members of the Asian Lesbians of the East Coast and Gay Asian Pacific Islander Men of New York immediately complained about the fund-raisers and threatened to organize demonstrations if they were not called off. The Lesbian and Gay Community Services Center agreed to cancel its fund-raiser, but Lambda refused to do the same because it had already invested money into the event.[83] The Lambda snub infuriated Asian American gay and lesbian groups and made them all the more active with the broader national Asian American protest against *Miss Saigon* discussed in Chapter 6. Lambda has had an uneasy relationship with Asian American gays and lesbians since that controversy, and this fact was not lost to J. Craig Fong when he was hired by the organization. "[The fundraiser] was distinctly a lack of cultural sensitivity," he admits. "Everyone affiliated with the organization now knows it and acknowledges it. And the truth is, like anything else when you're working across communities and across cultures, it's about learning." Fong is aware of the fact that Lambda has recognized the need to diversify the organization, adding: "I think they realized it was to their benefit to have an Asian American at the helm of their West Coast office."[84]

For all the activism, organization, and high-profile role models, the biggest personal issue for Asian American gay and lesbians is still "coming out" to parents. This and other chapters have described the pressures, control, and expectations of Asian American parents. Conformity is highly valued in many Asian American families, while being "different" or "independent" is not. This has led many Asian and non-Asian Americans to assume that Asian American parents would be much less tolerant and homophobic than other parents, and this is why many Asian Americans feel they must stay in the closet. This stereotype, however, is not necessarily true. "I don't think any group of people is more or less homophobic than the other," says Zoon Nguyen. "Mom and Dad will not disown you, though there are some who do; but then there are lots of white families who have also disowned their gay kids." What may be true is the strong sense of mutual dependency and obligation fostered in Asian American families, and this makes it extremely difficult for sons and daughters to even contemplate coming out and taking a risk at losing family relationships. "Our families are important," Nguyen explains. "I could never cut them out of my life. That's me, I am an extension of my family." Similarly, Christy Chung admits when she came out to her father, she did it with "respect" for him. "He'll love me forever and he knows . . . (but) I would never tell anyone on his side of the family. It's out of respect for his family, his position in the family. . . . I don't feel like it's my place to upset that balance. And I don't feel I need to."[85]

Like many other parents, one of the first reactions of Asian American parents when they learn about their son or daughter's sexual orientation is to blame themselves. The other major reaction is a sadness that comes with the realization that the long-term plans and expectations they had for their child may not come to pass. "It was the thing of disbelief, horror and shame and the whole thing . . . (t)hat she didn't turn out the way we raised her," explained one Japanese American mother. "The grieving process took a long time. Especially the thing about not being a bride. Not having her be a bride was a very devastating change of plans for her life. . . . I didn't know how I could fit into her life because I didn't know how to be the mother of a lesbian."[86] While these reactions are typical, others are quite surprising. Maria, an Asian Indian lesbian, came out to her father and was amazed when he told her he sometimes had feelings for men. "I think this sharing really strengthened the bond between us," Maria gladly admits.[87]

The Asian American gay and lesbian experience affects not only the individuals but also their families. Whether "out" or not, family relationships are invariably altered in one form or another. Asian American gay and lesbians and their families must be willing to re-create a new kind of family experience that includes a different set of expectations. This is by no means an easy task. "I would say what is probably the best lesson to be taken away from this, whether you're straight or gay, Asian or not, is that finding your identity is an exercise in great courage," says J. Craig Fong. "However you want to slice it, it's an exercise in courage (for) all of us to find, nurture, cultivate, and ultimately adopt the identities and beliefs that make us up as human beings."[88]

CONCLUSION

Non-Asian Americans often mistakenly assume that Asian Americans are all essentially the same, that they are ruled by some rigid and omnipresent cultural or Confucian ethos that binds them together. This chapter has highlighted some similarities, but has concentrated on the wide variety and diversity found in Asian American families and identities. In addition, these distinct family and identity structures are constantly changing, evolving, and reacting to external forces that affect them. This chapter calls for a recognition of the racial, ethnic, class, gender, generational, linguistic, national, and sexual differences that exist within what is known as "Asian American." This, of course, does not mean there is no basis for unity. But unity cannot be forged by ignoring differences, and the presumption of "sameness" is dangerous whether imposed externally by society, or perpetuated internally from within a group. Unity comes only with embracing differences in the particulars, while at the same time keeping in mind the broader issues diverse people have in common. The following chapter on political empowerment will focus on how issues of unity for Asian Americans are forged and maintained.

ENDNOTES

1. Mary Ann Schwartz and Barbara Marliene Scott, *Marriages and Families: Diversity and Change* (Englewood Cliffs, NJ: Prentice Hall, 1994), pp. 39–41.
2. Laura Uba, *Asian Americans: Personality Patterns, Identity, and Mental Health* (New York: The Guilford Press, 1994), pp. 27–28.
3. Walter R. Allen, "The Search for Applicable Theories of Black Family Life," *Journal of Marriage and the Family* 40:1 (1978): 117–129.
4. Ronald L. Taylor, "Black American Families," in Ronald L. Taylor (ed.), *Minority Families in the United States: A Multicultural Approach* (Englewood Cliffs, NJ: Prentice Hall, 1994), pp. 19–24.
5. Maxine Baca Zinn, "Adaptation and Continuity in Mexican-Origin Families," in Taylor (ed.), *Ibid.*, pp. 70, 75.
6. Robert Staples and Alfredo Mirande, "Racial and Cultural Variations Among American Families: A Decennial Review of the Literature on Minority Families," *Journal of Marriage and the Family*, 42:4 (1980): 887–903.
7. Stanley Sue and Harry Kitano, "Stereotypes as a Measure of Success," *Journal of Social Issues* 29 (1973): 83–98; and Harry Kitano, "Japanese-American Mental Illness," in Stanley Plog and Robert Edgerton (eds.), *Changing Perspectives on Mental Illness* (New York: Holt, Rinehart & Winston, 1969), pp. 256–284.
8. Pyong Gap Min, "Korean Immigrant Wives' Overwork," *Korean Journal of Population and Development* 21 (1992): 23–36, cited in Pyong Gap Min (ed.), *Asian Americans: Contemporary Trends and Issues* (Thousand Oaks, CA: Sage Publications, 1995), p. 222.

9. D. D. Godwin and J. Scanzoni, "Couple Consensus During Marital Joint Decision-making: A Context, Process, Outcome Model," *Journal of Marriage and the Family* 51 (1989): 943–956; Pyong Gap Min, "The Korean Family," in Charles H. Mindel, Robert W. Habenstein, and Roosevelt Wright, Jr. (eds.), *Ethnic Families in America* (New York: Elsevier, 1989), pp. 199–229; and Morrison G. Wong, "The Chinese American Family," in Mindel et al. *(eds.) Ethnic Families in America,* pp. 230–257.

10. Betty Lee Sung, *The Adjustment Experience of Chinese Immigrant Children in New York City* (New York: Center for Migration Studies, 1987), pp. 186–195.

11. Min, *Asian Americans,* pp. 222–223.

12. Young I. Song, *Silent Victims: Battered Women in Korean Immigrant Families* (San Francisco: Oxford Press, 1987), pp. 133–134.

13. *Ibid.,* p. 95.

14. Nazli Kibria, *Family Tightrope: The Changing Lives of Vietnamese Americans* (Princeton, NJ: Princeton University Press, 1993).

15. Tara Shioya, "For the Lys, America Is an Ongoing Journey," *San Francisco Chronicle,* December 9, 1994.

16. *Ibid.*

17. Stanley Sue, "Mental Health Policy," in *The State of Asian Pacific America: Policy Issues to the Year 2020* (Los Angeles: LEAP Asian Pacific American Policy Institute and UCLA Asian American Studies Center, 1993), pp. 79–94.

18. Uba, *Asian Americans,* pp. 119–120.

19. *Ibid.,* pp. 89–118.

20. Marcus Lee Hansen, *The Problems of the Third Generation* (Rock Island, IL: Augustana Historical Society, 1938).

21. Donna Nagata, *Legacy of Injustice: Exploring the Cross-Generational Impact of the Japanese American Internment* (New York: Plenum Press, 1993).

22. Uba, *Asian Americans,* pp. 97–107.

23. *Ibid.*

24. Joe R. Feagin and Clairece Booher Feagin, *Racial and Ethnic Groups,* fourth edition (Englewood Cliffs, NJ: Prentice Hall, 1994), p. 6.

25. Cited in Victor G. Nee and Brett de Bary Nee, *Longtime Californ': A Documentary Study of an American Chinatown* (Boston: Houghton Mifflin Company, 1974), pp. 384–385.

26. Jean Phinney, "Stages of Ethnic Identity Development in Minority Group Adolescents," *Journal of Early Adolescence* 9 (1989): 34–49.

27. Quoted in Felicia Paik, "Say Anything," *A Magazine,* February–March 1995, p. 34.

28. Quoted in "Asian American Women Struggling to Move Past Cultural Expectations," *New York Times,* January 23, 1994.

29. Snehendu B. Kar, Kevin Campbell, Armando Jimenez, and Sangeeta R. Gupta, "Invisible Americans: An Exploration of Indo-American Quality of Life," *Amerasia Journal* 21:3 (Winter 1995–1996): 25–52.

30. Ngoan Le, "The Case of the Southeast Asian Refugees: Policy for a Community 'At-Risk,'" in *The State of Asian Pacific America: Policy Issues to the Year 2020,* pp. 167–188.

31. Ruben G. Rumbaut, "Mental Health and the Refugee Experience" in T. C. Owen (ed.), *Southeast Asian Mental Health: Treatment, Prevention, Services, Training and Research* (Rockville, MD: National Institute of Mental Health, 1985), pp. 433–486.

32. Le, "Policy for a Community 'At-Risk,'" pp. 179–180.

33. Sue, "Mental Health Policy," pp. 84–85.

34. Uba, *Asian Americans,* p. 199.

35. *Ibid.,* p. 205.

36. Trudy Narikiyo and Velma Kameoka, "Attributions of Mental Illness and Judgments About Help Seeking Among Japanese American and White Students," *Journal of Counseling Psychology* 39:3 (1992): 363–369.
37. Quoted in Katherine Kam, "A False and Shattered Peace," *California Tomorrow,* Summer 1989, pp. 8–21.
38. Quoted in *Ibid.,* p. 21.
39. Quoted in Ben Charny, "Mental Health Center Targets the Asian Community," *Oakland Tribune,* October 17, 1994.
40. Bill Lann Lee, "Yung Wing and the Americanization of China," *Amerasia Journal* 1:1 (1971): 25–32; Ruthann Lum McCunn, *Thousand Pieces of Gold* (San Francisco: Design Enterprises, 1981); James W. Loewen, *The Mississippi Chinese: Between Black and White* (Cambridge, MA: Harvard University Press, 1971); Barbara M. Posadas, "Crossed Boundaries in Interracial Chicago: Pilipino American Families Since 1925," *Amerasia Journal* 8:2 (1981): 31–52; and Karen Leonard, *Ethnic Choices: California's Punjabi-Mexican Americans* (Philadelphia: Temple University Press, 1991).
41. Bok-Lim Kim, "Casework with Japanese and Korean Wives of Americans," *Social Casework* 53 (1972): 242–279; Kim, "Asian Wives of U.S. Servicemen: Women in Shadows," *Amerasia Journal* 4:1 (1977): 91–116.
42. John Conner, *A Study of the Marital Stability of Japanese War Brides* (San Francisco: R & E Research Associates, 1976); and Aselm Strauss, "Strain and Harmony in American-Japanese War-bride Marriages," *Marriage and Family Living* 16 (1954): 99–106, cited in Teresa K. Williams, "Marriage Between Japanese Women and U.S. Servicemen Since World War II," *Amerasia Journal* 17:1 (1991): 135–154.
43. See Raymond A. Joseph, "American Men Find Asian Brides Fill the Unliberated Bill," *Wall Street Journal,* January 25, 1984; and Venny Villapando, "The Business of Selling Mail-Order Brides," in Asian Women United (eds.), *Making Waves* (Boston: Beacon Press, 1989).
44. Joan Walsh, "Asian Women, Caucasian Men," *Image,* December 2, 1990, pp. 11–17.
45. Harry H. L. Kitano, Wai-Tsang Yeung, Lynn Chai, and Herbert Hatanaka, "Asian-American Interracial Marriage," *Journal of Marriage and the Family,* 46 (1984): 179–190. Also see Harry H. L. Kitano and Lynn Chai, "Korean Interracial Marriage," *Marriage and Family Review* 5 (1982): 75–89; Harry H. L. Kitano and Wai-Tsang Yeung, "Chinese Interracial Marriage," *Marriage and Family Review* 5 (1982): 35-48.
46. Sharon M. Lee and Keiko Yamanaka, "Patterns of Asian American Intermarriage and Marital Assimilation," *Journal of Comparative Family Studies* 21 (1990): 227–305.
47. Wen-Shing Tseng, John McDermott, and Thomas Maretzki, *Adjustment in Intercultural Marriage* (Hawaii: The University Press of Hawaii, 1977).
48. Quoted in Barbara Kantrowitz, "The Ultimate Assimilation," *Newsweek,* November 24, 1986, p. 80; Betty Lee Sung, *Chinese American Intermarriage* (New York: Center for Migration Studies, 1990). *Note:* "Intermarriage" is a generic term referring to either interracial or interethnic marriage. "Intermarriage" is often used interchangeably with "outmarriage."
49. Larry H. Shinagawa and Gin Y. Pang, "Marriage Patterns of Asian Americans in California, 1980," in Sucheng Chan (ed.), *Income and Status Differences Between White and Minority Americans* (Lewiston, NY: The Edwin Mellon Press, 1990), pp. 225–282.
50. Charles F. Westhoff and Noreen Goldman, "Figuring the Odds in the Marriage Market," in J. Gipson Wells (ed.), *Current Issues in Marriage and the Family* (New York: Macmillan, 1988), pp. 39–46.

51. Shinagawa and Pang, "Marriage Patterns of Asian Americans," pp. 269–270.
52. Colleen Fong and Judy Yung, "In Search of the Right Spouse: Interracial Marriage Among Chinese and Japanese Americans," *Amerasia Journal* 21:3 (1995): 77–98.
53. Larry H. Shinagawa and Gin Y. Pang, "Asian American Pan-Ethnicity and Intermarriage," *Amerasia Journal* 22:2 (1996): 127–152.
54. *Ibid.*, p. 30.
55. "Interracial Children Pose Challenge for Classifiers," *Wall Street Journal,* January 27, 1993.
56. Cynthia L. Nakashima, "An Invisible Monster: The Creation and Denial of Mixed-Race People in America," in Maria Root (ed.), *Racially Mixed People in America* (Newbury Park, CA: Sage Publications, 1992), pp. 162–178.
57. Quoted in Samuel R. Cacas, "New Census Category for Multiracial Persons?" *Asian Week,* July 15, 1994.
58. Nakashima, "An Invisible Monster," pp. 173–174; and Meredith May and Mai Hoang, "Crossing Color Barriers a Tough Path for Asians," *Oakland Tribune,* February 12, 1995.
59. Quotes in Kwai Julienne Grove, "Identity Development in Interracial, Asian/White Late Adolescents: Must It Be So Problematic?" *Journal of Youth and Adolescence* 20:6 (1991): 617–628.
60. Quoted in Angelo Ragaza, "All of the Above," *A Magazine,* 3:1 (1994): 76.
61. Donna Abu-Near, "Multiracials Want Own Category," *San Francisco Examiner,* July 21, 1996.
62. Quoted in Jan Breslauer, "Hues and Cries," *Los Angeles Times,* July 7, 1991, Calendar Section, pp. 3, 66, and 70.
63. George Kitahara Kitch, "The Developmental Process of Asserting Biracial, Bicultural Identity," in Root (ed.), *Racially Mixed People in America,* pp. 304–317.
64. "Daughter Finally Finds GI Dad," *San Francisco Chronicle,* December 24, 1994.
65. Kieu-Linh Caroline Valverde, "From Dust to Gold: The Amerasian Experience," in Root (ed.), *Racially Mixed People in America,* pp. 144–161.
66. *Ibid.*, p. 161.
67. Recent publications focusing on same-sex eroticism in Asia include Rakesh Rattti (ed.), *A Lotus of Another Color: An Unfolding of the South Asian Gay and Lesbian Experience* (Boston: Alyson Publications, 1993); Wayne R. Dynes and Stephen Donaldson (eds.), *Asian Homosexuality* (New York and London: Garland Publishing, Inc., 1992); Bret Hinsch, *Passions of the Cut Sleeve: The Male Homosexual Traditions in China* (Berkeley: University of California Press, 1990); Tsuneo Watanabe and Jun'ichi Iwata, and translated by D. R. Roberts, *The Love of the Samuri: A Thousand Years of Japanese Homosexuality* (London: Gay Men's Press, 1989); and Peter A. Jackson, *Male Homosexuality in Thailand: An Interpretation of Contemporary Thai Sources* (Elmhurst, NY: Global Academic Publishers, 1989).
68. Connie S. Chan, "Issues of Identity Development among Asian-American Lesbians and Gay Men," *Journal of Counseling and Development* 68 (September–October 1989): 16–20.
69. Pamela H., "Asian American Lesbians: An Emerging Voice in the Asian American Community," in Asian Women United (eds.), *Making Waves,* pp. 282–290.
70. Gerard Lim, "JACL Formally Adopts Same-Sex Marriages," *Asian Week,* August 12, 1994.
71. "Support for JACL Decision" printed in *Asian Week,* August 12, 1994.
72. Dana Takagi, "Maiden Voyage: Excursion into Sexuality and Identity Politics in Asian America," *Amerasia Journal* 20:1 (1994): 1–18.
73. Quoted in Trinity Oronda, "In Our Own Way," *Amerasia Journal* 20:1 (1994): 137–147.

74. Gil Mangaoang, "From the 1970s to the 1990s: Perspective of a Gay Filipino American Activist, *Amerasia Journal* 20:1 (1994): 33–44.
75. Quoted in Alethea Yip, "ROTC Rebel," Asian Week, February 23, 1996.
76. Quoted in Carlos Mendez, "A Fighter for Gay Rights," *Asian Week,* July 22, 1994.
77. Terry S. Gock, "Acquired Immunodeficiency Syndrome," in Nolan W. S. Zane, David T. Takeuchi, and Kathleen N. J. Young (eds.), *Confronting Critical Health Issues of Asian and Pacific Islander Americans* (Thousand Oaks, CA: Sage Publications, 1994), pp. 247–265.
78. Daniel C. Tsang, "Founder of First Gay and Lesbian Asian Group Succumbs to AIDS," *Asian Week,* September 2, 1994.
79. Ignatius Bau, "APAs and AIDS: We Are Not Immune," *Asian Week,* January 5, 1996.
80. Cuong Quy Huynh and Geraldine V. Padilla, "Vietnamese Knowledge and Attitudes about HIV/AIDS," a paper presented at the Thirteenth Annual Meeting of the Association for Asian American Studies in Washington, DC, May 29–June 2, 1996.
81. California Department of Justice, *Hate Crimes in California, 1995* (Sacramento, CA: Division of Criminal Justice Information Services, 1996), Table 1, p. 7.
82. Daniel C. Tsang, "Jury Awards Vietnamese American Bashing Victim $1.1 Million Sum," *Asian Week,* March 24, 1995.
83. Yoko Yoshikawa, "The Heat Is on 'Miss Saigon' Coalition: Organizing Across Race and Sexuality," in Karin Aguilar-San Juan (ed.), *The State of Asian America: Activism and Resistance in the 1990s* (Boston: South End Press, 1994), pp. 275–294.
84. Quoted in Mendez, "A Fighter for Gay Rights."
85. Quotes in Ordona, "In Our Own Way," pp. 142–143.
86. Quoted in Alice Y. Hom, "Stories from the Homefront: Perspectives of Asian American Parents with Lesbian Daughters and Gay Sons," *Amerasia Journal* 20:1 (1994): 19–32.
87. Maria, "Coming Home," in Ratti (ed.), *A Lotus of Another Color,* pp. 204–212.
88. Quoted in Mendez, "A Fighter for Gay Rights."

8

THE FINAL FRONTIER: ASIAN AMERICAN POLITICAL EMPOWERMENT

VISIBILITY AND INVISIBILITY

The Asian American population is the fastest growing segment in the United States, and they have excelled in science, technology, education, and business. Yet, for all these achievements, Asian Americans have a strange presence when it comes to political influence and political power relative to other ethnic groups. The most recent controversy has been the media attention on overseas Asian governments, corporations, and individual power brokers who have contributed millions of dollars to political candidates allegedly attempting to influence U.S. policy decisions. Much of the focus has been centered on John Huang (among others), the former vice chair of the Finance Committee of the Democratic National Committee (DNC), who resigned after questions about his role in raising illegal political campaign contributions by foreign Asians. The DNC hired an auditing firm to investigate this controversy and anyone with an Asian surname suddenly became a suspect. Thus, a dark shadow has been cast on Asian Americans who have a legal right to contribute to the political candidates and parties of their choice. For example, attorney Anthony Ching was told that his $5,000 contribution to President Clinton's reelection campaign would be "invalidated" if he did not cooperate with the investigation. Ching was so insulted he demanded his contribution be returned. "I don't think many people, including the Democratic Party, understand the difference between Asian American and Asian," Ching said angrily. That same day Ching received another call from the DNC inviting him to buy tickets for Clinton's reelection inauguration. "I found it ironic and humorous."[1]

The Organization of Chinese Americans (OCO) and the Japanese American Citizens' League (JACL) quickly organized a press conference denouncing the way the audit was being handled. "They aren't going to say they are going after Asian Americans, but their process focuses on . . . the Asian American community," said Bob Sakiniwa, the Washington representative about the JACL. He was particularly concerned that the DNC's investigation of individuals who attended any Asian American political event and who contributed less than $2,500 would serve only to discourage any further particiation by Asian Americans. Tensions over the racialization of the issue became even more heightened when the March 24 cover of *National Review* magazine featured an illustration of President Clinton, Mrs. Clinton, and Vice President Al Gore all with exaggerated slanted eyes and buck teeth. This prompted U.S. Senator Daniel K. Akaka (D-Hawaii) to lash out in anger. "Some irresponsible publications, in the interest of sensationalism, are obviously more than willing to conflate racist stereotypes with modern standards of objective journalism," Akaka said on the Senate floor. "The President, Mrs. Clinton, and the Asian American community are owed an apology for this gross affront to decency and taste."[2]

Despite the recent spate of negative visibility on political donations, Asian Americans have generally been considered quite invisible in American electoral politics. Until recently, relatively little attention has been paid to Asian Americans because of their small numbers and image of being apolitical. Both public commentators and political scientists have again used a cultural argument to explain why Asian Americans seem so lacking in political interest. In his book, *Asian Power and Politics* (1985), Lucien W. Pye argues Confucian concepts of political power are distinct and inconsistent with Western concepts. According to Pye, Westerners search for personal identity and autonomy, whereas Asians are more accepting of benevolent authority.[3]

While culture may be a factor in determining political behavior, Asian American nonparticipation in mainstream politics can just as easily be explained by a history of institutional racism and discrimination that served to segregate Asian Americans from the center of political life in the United States. Beginning with the Naturalization Act of 1790, which stated that only "free whites" were eligible for naturalization and citizenship, Asian Americans were denied the right to vote or run for political office until after World War II. Despite a history of institutional barriers that inhibited Asian American participation in electoral politics, it would be wrong to say that Asian Americans have been apolitical. Asian Americans have not been silent in their attempts to gain equal rights that were denied to them in the United States. This was done primarily in the formation of organized self-help groups and through legal redress.[4]

However, it is true that Asian American involvement in mainstream electoral politics has been at best mixed. Numerous studies on Asian American participation in electoral politics have shown low voter registration rates relative to the general population. These studies have generally concluded that the high percentage of foreign-born among the Asian American population is the primary factor for low voter registration rates and, thus, low voter participation. For example, Don Nakanishi (1985–1986, 1986) and Grant Din (1984) found the registration rates in Los Angeles County and San Francisco were both over 60 percent. However, the percentage of registered Japanese Americans in Los Angeles was 43 percent, for Chinese Americans 35.5 percent, Filipinos 27 percent, Koreans 13 percent, and Vietnamese 4.1 percent. Similarly, registration rates for Japanese Americans in San Francisco was 36.8 percent and 30.9 percent for Chinese Americans. In a more recent study of Asian American voting patterns in Oakland, California, Albert Muratsuchi (1990) found citywide voter registration rates to be 67.4 percent, while Japanese and Chinese Americans were just 41.8 and 22.6 percent, respectively.[5]

One study that does adjust for noncitizenship found that 77 percent of California Asian American citizens were registered to vote compared to 87 percent for whites. This study by Carol Uhlander, Bruce Cain, and D. Roderick Kiewiet (1989), also found that of those Asian Americans who were registered, only 69 percent actually did vote, compared to 80 percent for whites and 81 percent for African Americans.[6] In an update of his previous work, Grant Din (1993) found that the percentage of Chinese American registered voters in San Francisco increased from 30.9 percent to 40.2 percent. Din attributes this increase to two successful voter registration drives in 1991, which registered almost 6,000 new voters, 90 percent of whom were Chinese Americans. Although the voter registration drives were important, Chinese Americans, who were 34.3 percent of the voting-age population in San Francisco, were still only 21 percent of the registered voters.[7]

Other studies have found that when Asian Americans do vote, they tend to vote in racial and ethnic terms. An exit poll of 2,000 Asian Americans in the San Francisco Bay Area, conducted by David Binder and Catherine Lew (1992), asked respondents how they would vote if they had to choose between two equally qualified candidates in an election in which one is an Asian American and the other is not. The study found 74 percent said they would more likely choose the Asian Pacific American. Similar results were seen in another exit poll in the San Francisco Bay Area in 1994 conducted by Larry H. Shinagawa.[8] These findings correspond with exit polls in Monterey Park, California, conducted by John Horton and his researchers in 1988 and 1990.

Monterey Park, known as the "First Suburban Chinatown," is the only city in the continental United States with a majority Asian American population. The exit polls came up with some interesting results. First, they confirmed low voter turnout participation among Asian Americans. Although Asian Americans represented over 50 percent of Monterey Park's population, they made up only a little over a third of the people who voted. Second, the exit poll showed a strong pattern of ethnic voting among Asian Americans. The established Chinese American candidate and eventual top vote getter in each election, Judy Chu (1988) and Sam Kiang (1990), captured a very high percentage of the Asian American vote. Chu received 89 percent of the Chinese and 75 percent of the Japanese American vote in 1988, while Kiang received 90 percent of the Chinese and 69 percent of the Japanese American vote in 1990. Lastly, Horton found that the most interesting finding from the exit poll was the relatively high percentage of cross-ethnic voting. Chu received 35 percent of the Latino and 30 percent of the white vote in 1988, while Kiang received 30 percent of the Latino and 40 percent of the white vote. Horton concluded that even with the strong Asian American support, neither Chu nor Kiang could have won their respective elections without a broad-based coalition.[9]

This sentiment was echoed and expanded by political scientists Roy Christman and James Fay (1991, 1994), who surveyed all 459 cities in California looking for Asian American representation. The two came up with some very interesting conclusions. First, Christman and Fay argued that Asian Americans are not as underrepresented in electoral politics as many might think. In 1994 there were 48 Asian Americans out of 2,468 city council members in California. This represents just 2 percent of elected city officials, which is a very low figure considering Asian Americans represent nearly 10 percent of California's population. This statistic, however, tells only half the story. According to Christman and Fay, "Asian politicians tend to get elected in large and medium-sized cities with above-average Asian populations, so they represent over three million Californians, or almost ten percent of the state's residents." Second, Christman and Fay emphasize the fact that Asian Americans are elected not because of a massive voter turnout of Asian Americans, but through the support of white, African American, and Latino voters. They cite the fact that only two Asian Americans were elected from areas in which a majority of voters were Asian Americans. Christman and Fay predicted Asian Americans will increase their numbers and clout as long as they continue to pursue coalition-building strategies.[10]

This chapter focuses on Asian American politics through both nonelectoral and electoral empowerment efforts. It will begin with the history and evolution of Asian American political activism. Next, this chapter will look at Asian American empowerment from the 1970s to the 1990s. Third, this chapter will focus on structural barriers to Asian American political participation, with particular emphasis on bilingual voting rights and redistricting efforts. Lastly, this chapter will discuss alternative voting strategies in the 1990s that may serve to enhance Asian American political clout in the future. The Asian American community can be, and has been, divided along many lines. What are the points of unity? How can they be sustained? What are its limits? These and other questions will be addressed in this chapter.

HISTORY OF ASIAN AMERICAN POLITICAL ACTIVISM

Asian American involvement in mainstream politics has been a continually evolving phenomena. Social segregation and political disenfranchisement of Asian Americans prior to World War II severely limited the ability of Asian Americans to advocate for their rights. As a result, several forms of alternative political expression and empowerment were created. The early Asian American political empowerment can be divided into four generally sequential phases: (1) mutual aid societies; (2) homeland politics; (3) early civil rights organizations formed by U.S.-born Asian Americans; and (4) the Asian American movement of the late 1960s and early 1970s.

The first and most natural phase for the first wave of Asian immigrants in the United States was the creation of mutual aid societies. These societies were primarily intended for economic survival and the maintenance of community, but were also a source of political unity. Leaders of these groups protested to federal, state, and local authorities over anti-Asian hostility and also hired attorneys to challenge discriminatory laws. The Chinese had a complex network of mutual aid societies known as "huiguan," which included organized kinship, language, village, region, and occupational networks. The dominant force in the Chinese American community was the Chinese Consolidated Benevolent Association (CCBA), also known as the Chinese Six Companies, because it was the umbrella organization for six "huiguan." Japanese immigrants organized almost exclusively around the prefectural or regional association known as "kenjinkai." The umbrella organization among Japanese immigrants was the Japanese Association of America (JAA), which was formed in 1908 and was closely tied with the Japanese consulate in the United States. Unlike the Chinese and the Japanese, mutual aid societies for Koreans and Asian Indians were heavily influenced by religion. The first Korean mutual aid organization, the Friendship Society, was formed in San Francisco in 1903, and it was not long before Korean churches became the focus of Korean immigrant life. The first Sikh temple in the United States was built in Stockton, California, in 1912, and served as main center for religion and mutual aid assistance for the early Asian Indian immigrants. The earliest Filipinos to the United States, the Pensionados, were young men from elite families who were sent abroad in the early 1900s for their college education. They tended to organize themselves into fraternal organizations that emphasized maintaining cultural ties and activities. Later, as the "Pinoys," or Filipino workers, arrived in large numbers to the United States, they found unity by organizing themselves around labor issues. In 1933 the Filipino Labor Union was formed, and in 1936 the American Federation of Labor granted a charter to the California Mexican-Filipino Field Workers Union Local 30326.[11]

A second phase of political empowerment for the early Asian immigrants involved appealing to their own homeland governments for help. This, however, provided very minimal success. During the late nineteenth and early twentieth centuries, most Asian countries were extremely weak and could do little more than lodge complaints to the U.S. State Department. For example, the government in China at the time was facing extreme hardships created by war, famine, foreign intrusion, and economic instability. China could only watch as the anti-Chinese sentiment expanded in the United States and the 1882 Chinese Exclusion Act was passed. On the other hand, the Japanese government enjoyed relatively high international prestige and respect following its rapid industrialization and militarism in the early 1900s. Vehement protests by the Japanese government over attempts to completely exclude Japanese immigrants carried a great deal of weight with the U.S. State Department. This led to the negotiation of the 1907 "Gentleman's Agreement," which served to limit—rather than eliminate—Japanese immigration. At the same time, however, the Japanese government was powerless against states' rights and unable to stop the passage of California's 1913 and 1920 Alien Land Acts. Korea, India, and the Philippines were all under the colonial control of foreign governments at the turn of the century, and their abilities to act on behalf of their overseas nationals were practically nonexistent.[12]

Asian American studies scholar L. Ling-chi Wang writes, "Confronted by racial oppression and stripped of any political rights in the American democratic system, Asian immigrants of all classes saw their mistreatment in the United States as a direct outcome of the powerlessness of their homeland governments."[13] Not surprisingly, Asian immigrants in the United States actively supported modernization and independence movements abroad. In particular, Chinese, Korean, and Asian Indian immigrants closely followed the political events in their home countries and often raised large sums of money to support favored political leaders. It is interesting to note that most of the Japanese and Filipinos in the United States were not particularly active in homeland politics compared with other Asian groups. Unlike other Asian groups at the beginning of the twentieth century, the Japanese population was dominated by American-born Japanese who were U.S. citizens, and who never set foot in their parents' homeland. As a result these second-generation Nisei were far more preoccupied with being recognized as loyal Americans. In the case of Filipinos, they were officially American "nationals" and felt they belonged in the United States despite the often harsh treatments they faced. However, Filipino nationalism was clearly expressed during World War II when Japanese militarism spread to the Philippines.[14]

The third phase of political empowerment utilized by Asian Americans emerged with the coming of age of a second generation of Asian Americans. The early Asian American civil rights organizations that were created at this time were primarily concerned with improving their own economic opportunities, social lives, political influence in the United States, as well as establishing an identity separate from their parents. As early as 1895, a small group of American-born Chinese in California founded the Native Sons of the Golden State, which was intended to fight for citizenship rights. The group renamed themselves the Chinese American Citizens Alliance (CACA) in 1915, and its leaders were decidedly assimilationist-oriented, concentrating on confronting discrimination by urging Chinese Americans to engage in politics. In 1935, the organization began publishing *The Chinese Digest,* the country's first English language Chinese American newspaper. At the same time, however, because of the wartorn crisis in Asia, the upstart CACA worked closely with the established Chinese Consolidated Benevolent Association (otherwise known as the Chinese Six Companies) in supporting China in its time of need.[15]

By far the largest cohort of second generation Asian Americans at this time were the Japanese American Nisei, and the vast majority of young Nisei regarded themselves as Americans first. They enrolled in the Democratic and Republican parties, and founded patriotic groups like the American Loyalty League. In 1930 delegates from several of these groups formed the Japanese American Citizens' League (JACL), to this day the community's most important organization. It should be noted that the JACL's relationship with the established first-generation (Issei) leadership was quite paradoxical. On the one hand, the first JACL leaders were only in their twenties and early thirties and were still closely aligned with the Japanese Association of America. For example, the JACL chose to remain silent on the issue of Japanese militarism in Asia. On the other hand, JACL leaders were also sensitive to discrimination and stressed that total allegiance to the United States would overcome prejudice. Indeed, one of the requirements for membership in the JACL was American citizenship. In 1940 the JACL published a statement that clearly expressed its loyalty to the United States : "I am proud that I am an American citizen of Japanese ancestry. . . . Because I believe in America, and I trust she believes in me, and because I have received innumerable benefits from her, I pledge myself to do honor to her at all times and all places; to defend her against all enemies, foreign and domestic; to actively assume my duties and obligations as a citizen, cheerfully and without any reservations whatsoever, in the hope that I may become a better American in a greater America."[16] Their loyalty would be tested after the bombing of Pearl Harbor in December 1941 and President Roosevelt's Executive Order 9066 in February 1942.

Politics within Asian American communities during the Cold War era between World War II and the early 1960s were also highly influenced by events in their home countries. In particular, there was considerable repression and suspicion against Chinese Americans following the 1949 Communist revolution in China. This antagonism increased when the People's Republic of China sent troops to support North Korean Communist forces against the U.S.-backed South Korea government in 1950. At the beginning of the Korean War (1950–1953), many Chinese Americans feared they might be forced into internment camps just as Japanese Americans had been less than a decade before. Established Chinatown leaders actively worked to assure the U.S. government that Chinese Americans were loyal allies, formed anti-Communist organizations across the nation, and worked to persecute those who deviated or challenged their authority. Needless to say, Asian Americans remained extremely low-key for fear of being branded disloyal and a Communist.[17]

Things changed dramatically during the tumultuous civil rights era of the 1960s and 1970s. Civil rights demonstrations, protests against the Vietnam War, student unrest, urban riots, and the rise of ethnic and feminist identity were all part of the cultural milieu during this important period in U.S. history. This was the broader context for the development of the fourth phase of Asian American empowerment that was led by a new post–Cold War generation, and was commonly referred to as the Asian American movement. This phase of Asian American empowerment was a tremendous leap from the efforts that preceded it, and its defining event was the student-led "Third World Strike" at San Francisco State College (now University) in 1968–1969. The Asian American movement was much more critical and deliberately confrontational. The young Asian Americans were heavily influenced by the black power movement and their forceful challenges to racial and economic inequality in the United States. In addition, these Asian American activists rejected the established community institutions for what they believed was their accommodation to the U.S. government and their self-serving attempts of social control over the community. According to L. Ling-chi Wang, "young Asian Americans challenged the dominant ideology, relentlessly attacked established organizations—such as the Chinese Six Companies and JACL—fought for community services for the poor and disadvantaged, demanded civil and political rights for all Asian Americans, and pressured major universities to establish Asian American Studies programs."[18] San Francisco State student groups like the Intercollegiate Chinese for Social Action (ICSA) and the Philippine-American College Endeavor (PACE) were instrumental in starting numerous civil rights and service projects in their respective communities.[19]

The second significant distinction between the Asian American movement and previous political empowerment efforts was the call for the establishment of Asian American Studies programs and the beginning of a pan-ethnic Asian American political movement. Karen Umemoto's essay, "'On Strike!' San Francisco State College Strike, 1968–1969: The Role of Asian American Students" (1991), describes the new movement's efforts to build a coalition grounded not only on individual ethnic experience but also on the common experiences and shared interests of Asians in the United States. The lead student organization in this regard was the Asian American Political Alliance (AAPA), which was formed mainly by Japanese American women. AAPA was more clearly committed to unifying the various Asian American ethnic groups into one consolidated political body than ICSA and PACE, and was more ideological rather than service-oriented. The demand for Asian American studies was not only a way to help Asian Americans to learn about their own history but was also part of a broader strategy of social change. "The focus of the strike was a redefinition of education, which in turn was linked to a larger redefinition of American society," Umemoto writes. "These activities were rooted in and also shaped more egalitarian relationships based on mutual respect. While this doctrine was not always fully understood nor always put into practice, it was the beginning of a new set of values and beliefs, a 'New World Consciousness.'"[20]

The third significant distinction between the Asian American movement and earlier political activism is the fact that student activists recognized they had to band together with other students of color and supportive white students if they wanted to achieve their goals. In the fall of 1968 ICSA, PACE, and AAPA joined with Black Students Union (BSU) and Mexican American Students Confederation (MASC), to form a multi-ethnic coalition known as the "'Third World Liberation Front" (TWLF). November 6, 1968, marks the first day of the longest sustained student strike in U.S. history. The TWLF at San Francisco State led a shutdown of the campus that lasted for five months and called for dramatic changes in the school's education policies. Among the most important student demands was for the college to institutionalize an Ethnic Studies program.

The intensity of the San Francisco State strike captured the attention of the entire nation, and students at other colleges began organizing and making similar demands. Not surprisingly Asian American student organizations began to spring up on college and university campuses throughout California. However, because a large majority of Asian Americans lived in California, the visibility of Asian American student involvement appeared to decline as protests on college campuses rapidly expanded outside of the state. This is not to say that Asian Americans student groups were not active outside of California. According to historian William Wei (1993), Asian American student organizations were active on college campuses in the early to mid-1970s throughout the United States. On the East Coast, Asian American Political Alliance groups were founded at Yale and Columbia. In the Midwest, Asian American student groups were formed at the University of Wisconsin (Madison), the University of Illinois (Chicago), the University of Michigan (Ann Arbor), and Oberlin College (Ohio).[21]

It is clear that the Asian American movement was a profound turning point in Asian American history. The most obvious accomplishment of the San Francisco State strike was the establishment of the first School of Ethnic Studies in the United States, which included Asian American studies. But there were other outcomes as well. Umemoto states that the strike was a spark for a new generation of young Asian American political activists, many of whom continued to make an impact after they graduated from college. Some returned to the community to start social service agencies and focus on grassroots organizing efforts. Others went on to obtain advanced degrees and have moved into mainstream positions of power and influence in business and government. Still others became involved in electoral politics in the belief this is the best avenue to create social change. Umemoto found after interviewing scores of individuals who participated as student activists during the late 1960s and early 1970s, that "(a)lmost without exception, those interviewed affirmed a deep commitment to the basic values and beliefs forged during their days as students active in the strike; many traced their convictions to the period of the strike itself."[22]

ASIAN AMERICAN POLITICAL EMPOWERMENT, 1970s–1990s

The student-led Asian American movement of the 1960s and 1970s was the beginning of what seemed to be an impressive emerging force in American politics. Asian Americans were suddenly very active on a variety of fronts. For example, the creation of the School of Ethnic Studies at San Francisco State inspired student leaders to fight for other Asian American studies programs on college campuses throughout California and across the United States. More recently, Asian Americans also organized around a variety of civil rights, community, and cultural rights issues. High profile, often nationwide, mobilizations were organized in support for redress and reparations for Japanese Americans interned during World War II, workers' rights, immigrant rights, welfare rights for the poor and elderly, fairness in the media, as well as protests against anti-Asian violence. Some political pundits boldly predicted that Asian Americans were finally on the verge of assuming a prominent role as a unified political interest group much like European American ethnics and African Americans. This speculation was based on recent political successes, the rapidly growing population, and upward mobility of Asian Americans.[23]

Unfortunately, increasing numbers and upward mobility have also turned out to a be double-edged sword for Asian American politics. L. Ling-chi Wang argues that the rapid growth of the Asian American population also brought with it great diversity, which is extremely difficult to unify. He acknowledges that the new Asian immigrants since 1965 differ considerably from the earlier waves of immigrants. Today affluent Asian immigrants are resented for bringing over capital, starting businesses, and purchasing luxury cars and expensive homes in exclusive neighborhoods. They also perpetuate the image of the successful "super minority" or "model minority" that overshadows the struggles of the poor Asian Americans and Asian immigrants and refugees. In addition, many of the well-to-do Asian immigrants have no understanding of the historical struggle of Asian Americans in search of political empowerment. With this in mind, Wang has taken an interesting position on John Huang and the controversies surrounding his political fund-raising practices described at the beginning of this chapter. Wang is not oblivious to the racist anti-Asian sentiments fueling the hostile media attention on the issue, but he also believes a clear distinction must be drawn between those who have a genuine concern with empowering Asian Americans and those who just want to buy influence. "John Huang himself has never, to my knowledge, identified himself with any community cause," Wang wrote in a scathing editorial published in *Asian Week*. "Asian Americans should be angry with him and denounce him for using Asian Americans as a cover to channel foreign money for purposes other than advancing the rights and welfare of Asian Americans. . . . He is more interested in buying influence for his clients, both domestic and foreign."[24]

Wang clearly points out important factors and divided interests that make unified Asian American political empowerment "doubly difficult." Despite these events, others have insisted that Asian Americans can be mobilized into a solid political force. In her book, *Asian American Panethnicity: Bridging Institutions and Identities* (1992), Yen Le Espiritu acknowledges the great diversity within the "Asian American community," but describes the process, construction, and maintenance of pan-ethnicity as a fundamental political process. Some scholars have examined the primordial (cultural) and instrumental (interest group) nature of ethnic unity as the reasons why various ethnic sub-groups *voluntarily* form political blocks, but Espiritu concentrates on external factors that work to forge alliances between diverse peoples. One of the external factors Espiritu discusses is the role of the state in distributing resources and privileges based on ethnic and racial similarities and differences. A good example of this is seen in the decennial U.S. census. As described in Chapter 7, a variety of government agencies now rely on the U.S. census count to ensure civil rights laws are being upheld, as well as to determine political boundaries and representation. In the past, however, the census was often more effective at excluding individuals and groups instead of including them. "The census classification of ethno-racial groups has been problematic," Espiritu writes. "[T]he categories have been arbitrary and inconsistent—often reflecting the Census Bureau's administrative needs rather than the population's perceptions of meaningful cultural and racial differences."[25] She describes in detail attempts by the Census Bureau before the 1980 and 1990 survey counts to simply lump Asian American groups into one group, and calls by Asian Americans for a more accurate and detailed count. It is ironic that because the Census Bureau treated Asian Americans as a homogenous group, diverse Asian American groups had to respond as a one group to express their individual identities.

A more direct example of external factors creating the pan-ethnicity described by Espiritu is the response to anti-Asian violence. Chapter 5 of this book provides ample background on anti-Asian violence and briefly described organizations such the National Asian Pacific American Legal Consortium (NAPALC) that was formed to address the issue. Espiritu argues that Asian Americans are very aware of the fact that the general public does not usually distinguish Asian American subgroups. This reality naturally leads to what Espiritu calls "protective pan-Asian ethnicity" or "reactive solidarity." She emphasizes that anti-Asian sentiment and violence are the most significant issues unifying Asian American groups across ethnic, class, generational, as well as political lines, and has forged a pan-Asian consciousness.[26] It is important to note that pan-ethnic movements often have a short life span due to the fact they are often circumstantially and spontaneously created. The maintenance of a pan-ethnic movement, however, is an act of volition by a group of people dedicated to creating a condition, as well as an organization, that can sustain and revive the issue at hand. The 1982 killing of Vincent Chin in Detroit, Michigan, continues to be a seminal moment in Asian American history because a variety of organizations have emerged to keep Chin's memory and the issue of anti-Asian violence alive.[27]

Since the 1960s politicians and social critics have called for a "color-blind" society in which all people are judged by the content of their character and not by the color of their skin. This notion is obviously appealing, but it cannot be denied that the United States continues to be a highly racialized society. "The continuing importance of race and the persistence of racial lumping in American society suggests that, at present and in the immediate future, Asian Americans cannot—and perhaps should not—do away with the notion of pan-Asian ethnicity," Espiritu writes. "Pan-Asian unity is necessary if Asian Americans are to contest systems of racism and inequality in American society—systems that seek to exclude, marginalize, and homogenize them."[28] This does not mean to say that Asian Americans are merely victims of a racist society and can only react to the negative situations that confront them. Indeed, Espiritu argues that the "bridging" the diverse elements within the Asian American community is very much a creative process, not just a reactive one. Nonetheless, the internal divisions and separations within the Asian American community are significant and they are most apparent in mainstream electoral politics. Asian American involvement in electoral politics has never approached the type of success achieved by certain European ethnic groups (e.g., Irish and Italians), African Americans, and Latinos.

Asian Americans in Electoral Politics

Ask almost anyone in the United States to name five currently serving Asian American elected officials outside of Hawaii, and you will most likely get a quizzical look. If you're from the Pacific Northwest you'd probably know about Gary Locke, the newly elected governor of Washington, the first Asian American elected governor in the continental United States. Others might mention U.S. Senator Daniel Inouye, but he can't be counted in this informal poll because he hails from Hawaii. Those from California might cite longtime secretary of state, March Fong Eu, but she resigned her position in 1994. Others might mention U.S. Congressman Norman Mineta (D-San Jose), but he retired in 1995 after 21 years of service. Those from the East Coast might know S. B. Woo, former lieutenant governor from Delaware from 1985–1989, but he is currently out of politics after an unsuccessful campaign for the U.S. Senate in 1992. One of the brightest young Asian American political stars was Mike

Woo, but he was defeated in his election bid for mayor of Los Angeles in 1993, and he is also out of politics.

Yet, according to the *1996 National Asian Pacific American Political Almanac*, there are over 300 Asian American and Pacific Islander elected officials in the United States, including its territories (e.g., American Samoa and Guam).[29] According to the *Political Almanac*, the largest number of Asian American elected officials come from the state of Hawaii. Not surprisingly, the state with the second largest number of Asian American elected officials is California (see Table 8-1). The first Asian American elected to the U.S. Congress was Dalip Singh Saund, an Asian Indian farmer from the Imperial Valley of California. He was elected in 1956 and was reelected in 1958. Unfortunately, he had to resign his position in the middle of his second term because of ill health. When Hawaii was granted statehood in 1959, decorated World War II hero Daniel Inouye was elected the state's first U.S. representative, and businessman Hiram Fong was elected to the U.S. Senate (along with former governor Oren Long, who is not Asian American). No other Asian American outside of Hawaii served in the U.S. Congress until Norman

Table 8-1   Asian American Elected Officials of 50 U.S. States, 1996

State	Total
Hawaii	146
U.S. Senators (2)	
U.S. Representatives (1)	
State Governor (1)	
State Senators (19)	
State Representatives (34)	
City Mayors (4)	
City Councilmembers (27)	
Judges (58)	
California	129
U.S. Representatives (2)	
State Representatives (1)	
State Treasurer (1)	
City Mayors (9)	
City Council members (26)	
Judges (90)	
Washington	31
State Representatives (2)	
City Mayors (2)	
City Councilmembers (12)	
Judges (15)	

Table 8-1 *continued*

State	Total
Texas	14
City Mayors (2)	
City Councilmembers (4)	
Judges (8)	
New York	11
State Representatives (1)	
City Councilmembers (1)	
Judges (9)	
Arizona	6
State Representatives (1)	
City Mayors (1)	
Judges (4)	
Massachusetts	5
City Mayors (1)	
City Councilmembers (2)	
Judges (2)	
Colorado	3
State Senators (1)	
City Mayors (1)	
Judges (1)	
Illinois	3
City Councilmembers (1)	
Judges (2)	
Michigan	3
City Mayors (1)	
City Councilmembers (1)	
Judges (1)	
Nebraska	3
City Councilmembers (3)	
Oregon	3
State Senators (2)	
City Councilmembers (1)	
Utah	3
State Representatives (1)	
Judges (2)	

Table 8-1 *continued*

State	Total
Alaska City Mayors (1) City Councilmembers (1)	2
Minnesota City Mayors (2)	2
Ohio City Councilmembers (1) Judges (1)	2
Pennsylvania Judges (2)	2
Nevada Secretary of State (1) Judges (1)	2
Kansas City Mayors (1)	1
Maryland Judges (1)	1
Missouri City Councilmembers (1)	1
New Jersey City Councilmembers (1)	1
Oklahoma City Mayors (1)	1
Tennessee City Councilmembers (1)	1
Vermont Judges (1)	1
Virginia Judges (1)	1

Source: Don T. Nakanishi and James S. Lai (eds.), *1996 National Asian Pacific American Political Almanac,* seventh edition (Los Angeles: UCLA Asian American Studies Center, 1996), p. 20.

Mineta, the former mayor of San Jose, California, was elected in 1974. Two years later, California elected former San Francisco State University president S. I. Hayakawa to be its U.S. senator. Hayakawa served only one term in office, but he remains the only Asian American elected by a mainland state to serve in the U.S. Senate. In 1978, another Japanese American, Robert Matsui from Sacramento, was elected to Congress. For years the highest ranking Asian American state official in California was Secretary of State March Fong Eu, who was elected in 1974, but she resigned her position to serve as ambassador to Micronesia in 1994.

The 1990s has shown a remarkable flurry of activity for Asian Americans in electoral politics, especially in California. It is interesting to note that almost all of the Asian Americans elected to state and federal office in the 1970s and 1980s were Democrats, but in the 1990s many are Republicans. Jay Kim, a Republican businessman and mayor of the Los Angeles suburban town of Diamond Bar, became the first Korean American elected to Congress in 1992. That same year Nao Takasugi, also a Republican businessman, became the first Asian American elected to California's state assembly since 1978. In 1994, Matthew Fong, son of former California secretary of state March Fong Eu, became California's highest ranking Asian American officeholder after he was elected state treasurer. In contrast to his mother, who is a Democrat, the younger Fong is a Republican. On the local level Tony Lam, a restaurant owner, became the first Vietnamese refugee elected to public office when he won a city council seat in Westminster, California, otherwise known as "Little Saigon" in 1992 (city council seats are officially nonpartisan). The following year, Michael Guingona of Daly City and Chris Villanueva of Vallejo became the first Filipino American city council members in their respective cities. In 1994, San Francisco elected Mabel Teng and Alameda County (Oakland) elected Wilma Chan supervisors in their respective counties. Even unsuccessful Asian American candidates generated a great deal of attention. Mike Woo ran an aggressive campaign for mayor of Los Angeles in 1993, and Ted Dang gained national notoriety for his surprisingly strong bid for mayor of Oakland in 1994. In November 1996, Gary Locke, a son of Chinese immigrants, became the first Asian American to be elected governor in the continental United States. Locke campaigned successfully as a liberal Democrat, supporter of gay and abortion rights, but tough on crime and a fiscal moderate in a state where Asian Americans represent less than 6 percent of the population. It is also interesting to note that two Asian Americans have been elected to Oregon's state senate and two have been elected to Washington's state assembly. There are actually two Asian American mayors in each of the states of Minnesota, Texas, and Washington. In addition, there is at least one Asian American mayor in the states of Alaska, Arizona, Colorado, Kansas, Massachusetts, Michigan, and Oklahoma.

Despite these successes, there are still concerns over the lack of participation among Asian Americans in the electoral process. Their major concerns are focused around the issues of representation and empowerment. Representation means having Asian Americans elected to political office who will ideally serve as advocates for the Asian American interests. It should be said that just because an Asian American is an elected official does not necessarily mean he or she will be a voice for Asian American interests. Nonetheless, political representation is still an important goal. For example, Daniel Inoyue, Norman Mineta, and Robert Matsui were all instrumental in the passage of redress and reparations legislation through the U.S. Congress that was eventually signed into law in 1988 by then President Ronald Reagan. In contrast to representation, empowerment means having a unified community of interest that can formulate a political agenda, mobilize around specific issues, and pressure their Asian American or non-Asian American political representatives to act on the community's behalf. Asian Americans leaders are particularly concerned about the lack of involvement among Asian American voters because it only serves to undermine the group's political empowerment.

Who Votes, Who Does Not, and Why

As discussed at the beginning of this chapter, overall Asian American voter registration rates and participation in electoral politics has historically been low relative to other major ethnic groups. This can be seen in a 1994 report by the Field Institute that showed Asian Americans in California represented 10 percent of the state's population, but only 6 percent of the registered voters, and only 4 percent of the actual voters.[30] The main explanation for this phenomenon is the high proportion of immigrants in the Asian American population who are currently ineligible to vote. However, this historical situation may be changing and changing fast. In their recent article, "Becoming Citizens, Becoming Voters: The Naturalization and Political Participation of Asian Pacific Immigrants," (1996) UCLA professors Paul Ong and Don Nakanishi highlight signs that may indicate potential growth in both the numbers and activism of Asian American voters. Ong and Nakanishi acknowledge there is a high percentage of Asian American adults (55 percent) who are not currently citizens but, at the same time, there is also a high rate of naturalization. Length of residence in the United States, age when they immigrated (young immigrants naturalize at a higher rate than older immigrants), education level, and English language proficiency are cited as key factors that positively influence immigrants to become U.S. citizens.

Although Asian immigrants have a high rate of naturalization, they continue to have a low overall rate of voter registration. Interestingly, however, Ong and Nakanishi found that Asian American naturalized citizens who immigrated to the United States *before* 1975 have among the highest voter registration rates of any group, including U.S.-born Asian Americans. Conversely, Asian American naturalized citizens who arrived to the United States *after*

Table 8-2   Voter Registration and Turnout Rates by Nativity and Ethnic Group ,1994

Group	% Registered to Vote	% of Registered Who Voted in 1994
Non-Hispanic White		
U.S.-Born	69	73
Foreign-Born	68	78
Overall	69	73
African Americans		
U.S.-Born	61	63
Foreign-Born	58	78
Overall	61	63
Latinos		
U.S.-Born	53	62
Foreign-Born	53	74
Overall	53	64
Asian Americans		
U.S.-Born	56	78
Foreign-Born	49	74
Overall	53	76

Source: Paul Ong and Don Nakanishi, "Becoming Citizens, Becoming Voters: The Naturalization and Political Participation of Asian Pacific Immigrants," in Bill Ong Hing and Ronald Lee (eds.), *Reframing the Immigration Debate,* (Los Angeles: LEAP Asian Pacific American Policy Institute and UCLA Asian American Studies Center, 1996), Table 7, p. 299.

1975 have among the lowest voter registration rates. In addition, Ong and Nakanishi also cited 1994 figures that show the overall percentage of Asian American registered voters was low, but this is contrasted by other figures that show the percentage of Asian American registered voters who actually voted was higher than any other group (see Table 8-2). From this data it may not be unrealistic to think that political participation among immigrant Asian Americans will increase as they age and become more settled. "Whether Asian Pacific Americans become a major new political force in American electoral system is nearly impossible to predict with any precision," Ong and Nakanishi cautiously conclude. "This period will be important to witness and analyze because of the extraordinary challenges and opportunities . . . for Asian Pacific Americans in seeking realization of their full potential as citizens and electoral participants."[31]

When Asian Americans do vote, what political party do they support? Unlike other racial minority groups like African Americans and Latinos who overwhelmingly vote Democratic, Asian American party loyalty is mixed. This

trend was first described by Don Nakanishi (1986, 1991) in his analysis of registered voters in Monterey Park, California. Nakanishi and his researchers
found that in 1984, 43 percent of Asian Americans were registered Democrats,
31 percent registered Republicans, and 25 percent declined to state. In a follow-up study in 1989, 35 percent of Asian American registered voters in Monterey Park were Democrats, 37 percent were Republicans, and 26 percent
declined to state. Lack of group and political party unity is further evidence of
the diversity in the Asian American community, but it is also a significant reason why Asian Americans have historically been ignored and lacked solid political clout.

   In recent years the Republican party has been very aggressive in bringing
Asian Americans into its ranks and, in particular, encouraging them to run for
office. "We're trying to get more involvement in general activity with the
Republican Party," explains Dennis See, a Republican insider who is in charge
of the party's Asian American outreach efforts. "Asian Americans need to gain
political experience at all levels. . . . That includes experience as candidates
and voters, but also experience as campaign workers and precinct leaders."[32]
In the 1988 presidential election, 54 percent of Asian American voters supported the Republican George Bush/Dan Quayle ticket compared to 44 percent who voted for the Democrat Michael Dukakis/Lloyd Bentsen ticket. In
1989 the Republican National Committee opened a special Asian American
Affairs Office, and President Bush proceeded to appoint an unprecedented
number of Asian Americans to high-level management and advisory positions.
Among the most well-known appointments were Elaine Chao, who was first
brought in as deputy secretary at the Department of Transportation and was
later asked to head the Peace Corps; Wendy Gramm (who is married to U.S.
Senator Phil Gramm from Texas) to chair the Commodity Futures Trading
Commission; Julie Chang Bloch as ambassador to Nepal; and Patricia Saiki to
head the Small Business Administration. When President Bush was preparing
for his reelection campaign in 1992, he dispatched Vice President Quayle to
speak in support of Asian American candidates running for elected office,
attend local Asian American–sponsored fund-raisers, and speak out against
anti-Asian violence. All these efforts had tangible results. In the summer of
1991, an Asian American–sponsored political rally in Orange County attracted
an estimated 60,000 enthusiastic Asian American supporters.[33] Indeed, one of
Bush's biggest fund-raisers was Zachariah Zachariah, an Asian Indian physician from Florida, who collected nearly $2 million from Asian Americans. It
was clear that Bush and the Republican party had the loyalty of many Asian
Americans. According to one national presidential election exit poll, Asian
Americans supported Bush over Clinton by a 55 to 29 percent margin in 1992,
while 16 percent voted for Ross Perot. This is in stark contrast to the overall
election results in which Clinton won 43 percent of the vote, to 40 percent for
Bush, and 19 percent for Perot.[34]

Despite the Republican defeat in the 1992 presidential election, many inside the party believe Asian Americans have found their home. "Asian Americans are in many ways a natural constituency for the Republican Party," beams Dennis See. He argues that the Republican pro-business and limited government intervention agenda are positions that appeal to many Asian Americans. It should come as no big surprise that Asian Americans, being a generally middle-class community, are attracted to the Republican party. See believes that Southeast Asians and many Chinese Americans also vote Republican because of the party's image of being anti-Communist. But several recent surveys and exit polls on how Asian Americans vote provide some very interesting details and serve to further demonstrate the group's complexity and diversity. In the voter-rich state of California, Asian American Democrats cite two other surveys that suggest that Asian American support for Republicans is soft and could go either way. One statewide poll by the Voter News Service in 1992 showed Asian Americans supporting Bill Clinton 45 percent to 40 percent for George Bush, and 15 percent for Ross Perot.[35] A more detailed study in that same election conducted in northern California by David Binder and Catherine Lew showed Asian Americans strongly supported Clinton over Bush by a 53 to 37 percent margin, with 9 percent going to Perot. Binder and Lew also reported that 49.2 percent of Asian Americans surveyed said Democrats were the political party that cares the most about their needs, compared to just 23.1 percent who said Republicans cared the most.[36]

The trend in California that began in 1992 continued into the 1994 election season. An exit poll by the *Los Angeles Times* found 48 percent of the Asian American respondents said they were Democrats, while 32 percent said they were Republicans, and 20 percent said they were Independents or declined to state. Another exit poll in northern California conducted by Larry H. Shinagawa found that among first-generation Asian Americans who responded to the survey, 61.6 percent were Democrats, 24.0 percent were Republicans, and the rest were Independents or declined to state. The differences were even more stark among Asian American voters who were at least second generation in the United States. Over 70 percent of at least second-generation Asian Americans who responded to the poll said they were Democrats, while only 17.9 percent said were Republicans.[37]

In 1996, the National Asian Pacific American Legal Consortium (NAPALC) sponsored a three-region exit poll to gather data on Asian American voting patterns during that presidential election year. A total of 4,650 exit polls were counted from the San Francisco–Oakland Bay Area, Los Angeles County, and New York City. In all three areas Asian Americans strongly supported Bill Clinton over Republican challenger Bob Dole. In San Francisco and Oakland, 83 percent of Asian Americans polled voted for Clinton, while 9 percent voted for Dole, and another 9 percent voted for someone else or declined to state. In Los Angeles County, 53 percent of

Asian Americans voted for Clinton, 41 percent for Dole, and 4 percent for Ross Perot. New York City results showed 71 percent supported Clinton, 21 percent voted for Dole, and 2 percent went for Perot. These findings differed considerably from the widely cited Voter News Service (VNS) poll that showed 48 percent of Asian Americans voting for Dole, 43 percent for Clinton, and 8 percent for Perot. The VNS poll is sponsored by a consortium of the major television networks and print media sources, but was heavily criticized for surveying only 170 Asian Americans nationwide out of a total sample size of about 16,000 voters. VNS's poll was also conducted without bilingual workers or materials, which biased its sample toward educated, American-born, and English-proficient Asian American voters. The NAPALC exit poll was significant precisely because it offered polling forms in different languages and had multilingual poll takers available. "The primary reason we wanted to do the survey was to monitor the need for bilingual assistance," said Karen Narasaki, executive director of NAPALC. She is sure that the use of bilingual materials and surveyers are the primary reasons for the stark variation in poll findings.[38]

STRUCTURAL LIMITS TO POLITICAL PARTICIPATION

The 1996 NAPALC exit poll may provide evidence of the continued need for bilingual ballots to insure Asian American participation in electoral politics. Bilingual ballots are particularly important given the large Asian American immigrant population. According to the 1990 U.S. census, 29.8 percent of Asian Americans between ages 18 and 64 did not speak English "very well." This figure goes up to 40.9 percent when looking specifically at foreign-born Asian Americans between 18 and 64, and goes down dramatically to just 3.3 percent for U.S.-born Asian Americans 18 to 64 (see Table 8-3). It should be no surprise that these figures differ between Asian American groups. For example, 53.1 percent of foreign-born Korean Americans between 18 and 64 do not speak English "very well," which is slightly higher than the 50.3 percent of foreign-born Chinese Americans between 18 and 64 who have difficulty with English. These figures are quite high compared to other Asian American immigrant groups in which English is fairly common in their native countries. Just 22.2 percent of foreign-born Asian Indians and 23.7 percent of foreign-born Filipino Americans between 18 and 64 do not speak English "very well." With these statistics in mind, Asian American political organizers have been vocal advocates for translating election materials and voter registration information into a variety of languages.

In the summer of 1992, Asian Americans helped lobby Congress to approve a 15-year extension to the bilingual provisions of the Voting Rights Act of 1965. In addition, changes were made in the act that required bilingual ballots be provided in counties where more than 10,000 residents speak the

Table 8-3 Percentage of Asian Americans Who Do Not Speak English "Very Well,"
Ages 18–64

Group	U.S.-born	Foreign-born	Total
All	1.2	37.0	4.2
Asian or Pacific Islander	3.3	40.9	28.7
Asian American	3.3	40.9	29.8
Chinese	4.7	50.3	38.3
Filipino	3.0	23.7	17.3
Japanese	3.1	47.9	18.0
Asian Indian	2.0	22.2	18.4
Korean	2.3	53.1	42.3
Vietnamese	3.6	52.8	45.8
Cambodian	3.8	48.8	43.7
Laotian	3.6	50.8	44.9
Hmong	1.6	48.0	37.3

Source: U.S. Bureau of the Census, *1990 Census of the Population, Asians and Pacific Islanders in the United States* (Washington, DC: Government Printing Office,. 1993), CP-3-5, Table 3.

same foreign language and are not proficient in English. This is an dramatic improvement from the previous benchmark of 5 percent of the total voting population. This earlier standard was extremely difficult to achieve for some of the Asian American ethnic groups with numerically fewer numbers, especially for those in densely populated areas like Los Angeles County. Under the prior guidelines, an ethnic group would need to have 450,000 persons speaking the same foreign language before they would be eligible for bilingual ballots.[39] Another important bilingual voting rights case occurred during the summer of 1994 in New York City. In this incident the Asian American Legal Defense and Education Fund (AALDEF) organized a campaign to convince the Board of Elections to provide bilingual ballots with candidates' names translated into Chinese. The New York City election officials at first refused to comply and tried to argue there was simply not enough room on the standardized ballot machines to translate candidates' names. But AALDEF's effort was backed by a U.S. Department of Justice Civil Rights Division ruling that New York City's noncompliance was in violation of the bilingual assistance provisions in the federal Voting Rights Act. The Department of Justice agreed with AALDEF that a candidate's name is one of the most important items of information sought by voters when casting a ballot. This is because voters get election information that is translated, but become confused and frustrated when the actual ballot is not translated. AALDEF executive director Margaret Fung admits the case was only a partial victory because the entire ballot will not be translated, but the decision could open the doors for other municipalities to translate candidates' names into other Asian languages. The long-term goal continues to be full translation of the entire voter ballot.[40]

A second recent political empowerment strategy used by Asian Americans is redistricting. Redistricting is the highly politically charged process of redrawing, or reapportioning, state and local political districts that follows each decennial census count. The process has taken on special significance with the rapid growth of the Asian American population and its desire to influence redistricting decisions. Elected officials have historically divided geographically concentrated ethnic groups into several different districts, which has served to weaken each group's political power and influence. When a community of interest is maintained in one political district, that community's strength is enhanced because a political representative is accountable to that community. The Civil Rights Act of 1965 prohibits the fracturing of communities and the dilution of communities through the redistricting process. However, it hasn't been until just recently that Asian Americans have begun to be active players in the redistricting process. According to Leland T. Saito (1993), the inspiration for these challenges came from the 1990 Federal 9th Circuit Court of Appeals decision in the case of *Garza* v. *County of Los Angeles*. This precedent-setting class action lawsuit proved that Latino political strength had been undermined through the systematic process of dividing them into separate districts. The Los Angeles County supervisorial districts were redrawn following the court's ruling and a Latina, Gloria Molina, was elected to represent a district in which the majority of the population was Latino. Also on the heels of the Garza decision was the formation of the Coalition of Asian Pacific Islander Americans for Fair Reapportionment (CAPAFR), which marked the first time such a broad-based Asian American redistricting effort had been made. For logistical reasons, CAPAFR divided itself into two ad hoc groups, one from Northern California and another in Southern California. At the same time, both groups were unified for two main purposes. The first purpose was to create a network of individuals and organizations to gather and exchange information. The second purpose was to collect and present demographic information at state hearings that were to begin in December 1990.[41]

Saito highlights one of CAPAFR's successful organizing efforts, which took place in the San Gabriel Valley area of Southern California. Located in this eastern region of Los Angeles County are several cities with large Asian American populations. CAPAFR's goal was to keep these cities in one state assembly district and not have them divided into three different districts as was done in the 1981 redistricting. CAPAFR achieved its goal because it was able to work amiably with the San Gabriel Valley Latino Redistricting Committee on a plan that would not threaten any established Latino elected officials or districts. Asian Americans and Latinos also wanted to work cooperatively on voter registration and bilingual ballot efforts that were fundamental issues for both of these largely immigrant population groups. "Asian Americans and Latinos understood that the political clout of both groups supporting one set of redistricting plans for the region would increase the possibility of the legislature adopting the plan," Saito writes. "Most important, they also knew that if Asian Americans and Latinos were pitted against one another, both groups could end up losing."[42] Saito acknowledges that Asian Americans were the newcomers to the redistricting process and had much to learn. Latinos in the region were the ones who had the political experience, the established organizations, and held all of the major elected offices in the region. The newly created 49th Assembly District now has a 28 percent Asian American population, the highest concentration of Asian Americans in California. This is not a majority, but it does create recognizable constituency, and a potential base for political empowerment. In the long run, as the Asian American population in the San Gabriel Valley continues to grow, they will hopefully benefit from the cooperation that began with this initial redistricting effort.

The redistricting effort in the San Gabriel Valley was relatively smooth for what is usually a highly contentious process. Another example can be seen in the hotly contested redistricting effort that took place in Oakland, California. In 1993 Asian Americans successfully worked with Latinos to create two city council districts that contained an Asian American (District 2) and Latino (District 5) plurality. This effort marked a significant achievement in Oakland especially since African Americans and whites have dominated the city's political agenda for decades. Since 1980 the Asian American and Latino populations that have nearly doubled while African American and white residents comprise a declining—though still predominant—portion of the city's ethnic mix. Together Asian Americans and Latinos made up close to 30 percent of Oakland's population. The three areas with the largest concentration of Asian Americans in Oakland were Chinatown, New Chinatown, and China Hill. Chinatown is the traditional merchant center of the Asian American community, while New Chinatown is an area populated by many less affluent Asian immigrants and refugees. China Hill, on the other hand, is the area for mostly middle-class and American-born Asians. All three areas were divided into three separate city council districts in the 1980 redistricting.

The Asian American–Latino redistricting proposal was one of seven presented to the Oakland City Council. The Niagara Democratic Club (NDC), an African American political interest group presented its own proposal, which continued to keep Chinatown, China Hill, and New Chinatown in three different districts. "Votes on the council mean everything in the world, especially economically," said NDC president Geoffrey Pete. "People say 'you're being divisive' but I am just looking out for our own interests. I would expect nothing less from any other group."[43] The greatest resistance against the Asian–Latino redistricting plan came from whites in District 2. The city council member representing District 2 at the time, Mary Moore, declared she was "standing up" for Oakland's white people and warned of a white backlash if her district were tampered with.[44] Two District 2 "community leaders" also claimed that District 2 was being "nuked" and "napalmed" by the redistricting process. The use of absurdly inflammatory words by Moore and her supporters shocked Asian Americans in the city council audience. The macabre references to weapons of mass destruction used by the United States military against Asians only added insult to injury.[45] Weeks of tense and racially charged debate during the redistricting process eventually ended on July 20, 1993, when the Oakland City Council approved a redistricting plan that dramatically altered two of the seven city council districts. The city council adopted a plan that linked Chinatown, New Chinatown, and China Hill into a redesigned District 2. The decision climaxed a six-month organizing effort by Asian American and Latino advocates, many of whom had been untested in citywide politics, but who were driven by the belief that the city's mandatory, once-a-decade process of remapping voting lines to follow population trends provided a chance to solidify an ethnic power base.

The coalition efforts of Asian Americans in Oakland and in the San Gabriel Valley provide evidence of an increased desire to engage in mainstream electoral politics. While similarities exist between Oakland and the San Gabriel Valley cases, it is the differences that are particularly worth noting. The first difference is the fact that the coalition effort in Oakland was led by Asian Americans. Asian Americans in Oakland were the ones who had the slightly larger population, relatively more political experience, and clearly demonstrated economic resources. In the San Gabriel Valley, on the other hand, the Asian American population is far less compared to Latinos, and they were the self-described newcomers to the political process. The second difference is that Asian Americans and Latinos are both minority groups in Oakland, each representing less than 15 percent of Oakland's population. A coalition of Asian Americans and Latinos was a genuine necessity for both groups to gain political recognition, representation, and power. In the San Gabriel Valley, on the other hand, Asian Americans and Latinos are the majority population, and their coalition appeared to be more based on ideology and practicality, rather than genuine necessity. Latinos dominate the state and federal elected offices and the number of Asian American registered voters was too small to really threaten a solid Latino candidate, but the strong record of Asian American contributions to political campaigns makes them an attractive partner in politics.[46] Third, the Asian redistricting effort in Oakland was actually more complicated than in San Gabriel Valley because of the broad demographic mix and relatively even spread of African American, white, and Asian American/Latinos in Oakland. Far more conflict, struggle, and compromise erupted in Oakland because the political rights of one group are often seen as undermining the rights of another. In the San Gabriel Valley, Latinos and Asian Americans are the two dominant populations in the San Gabriel Valley, with whites not really being a factor and African Americans being almost absent.

NEW POLITICAL STRATEGIES

Despite these victories described above, does redistricting ensure Asian American political unity, representation, and empowerment? The victory in Oakland was somewhat of a mixed bag. Although Asian Americans represent a slight majority of the residents of District 2, they only represent less than 17 percent of the prospective voters. Whites still dominate the registered voter rolls at 44 percent, with African Americans at 32 percent. Oakland's Asian American community realized that after finishing the historic and often brutal power struggle, the battle is far from over. Shortly after winning the redistricting battle, their attention was turned to finding a suitable candidate who could represent the Asian American community. The consensus first choice for the Asian American Redistricting Task Force was Oakland School Board member, Wilma Chan. Chan was an experienced elected official with positive name recognition and a broad constituency, who had close ties to Oakland's progressive left-of-center political establishment. Most importantly, Chan had lived in District 2 for a number of years and had a long history of neighborhood activism. However, Chan declined the invitation to be an Oakland City Council member and instead opted to run for an open Alameda County Board of Supervisors' seat, which she eventually won. Without a solid candidate, Asian American activists in Oakland scrambled to find someone who was both willing and qualified to run for the District 2 council seat. It was at this time the fragile coalition of Asian American ethnic, business, neighborhood, and social services that united over redistricting began to split apart.

One faction, dominated by Chinatown business interests, firmly supported running an Asian American candidate who they said could serve as a role model and to begin the process of grooming a cadre of future Asian American political leaders willing to throw themselves into the political forefront. The candidate of choice for this group was Lily Hu, the president of the Oakland Chinatown Chamber of Commerce, who became the first person to announce her candidacy for the District 2 seat. An immigrant from Taiwan, Hu came to the United States as a student in 1974 and moved to the Bay Area in 1979. On the other hand, neighborhood, social service, and non-Chinese Asian American leaders wanted to support a candidate who would be responsive to the broader Asian American community needs. Their candidate of choice was environmental lawyer, John Russo, an Italian American from Brooklyn, New York, who had moved to Oakland just four years earlier. An "unashamed liberal," Russo was an early supporter of the creation of an Asian district and had a long history of community involvement. Russo also acknowledged that he would not have declared himself a candidate if Wilma Chan had decided to run because their politics were similar and they shared the same volunteer base.

On June 7, 1994, Russo swept the election collecting 4,585 (66.8 percent) votes compared with just 2,277 (33.2 percent) for Hu. A detailed look at the precinct breakdowns in this election is important to better determine how the three heavily Asian areas of Chinatown, New Chinatown, and China Hill voted. The overall city turnout for this election was 36.4 percent, but the turnout rates in Chinatown and New Chinatown were much smaller at just over 22 percent. The voter turnout in China Hill was about the same as the rest of the city, but this is probably due to the fact that this area is generally more affluent and contains more second- and third-generation Asian Americans than the other two areas. Hu had the most success in Chinatown, only limited success in New Chinatown, and was badly beaten in China Hill. Election results showed no evidence of unity among the most concentrated Asian areas in the newly configured "Asian" district. In the end, the most interesting race in Oakland turned out to be hardly a contest at all; but it was an important political lesson for some leaders in the Asian American community. Russo's victory was not completely unexpected because he was virtually assured of capturing the high turnout non-Asian areas of the district. Indeed, outside of Chinatown, New Chinatown, and China Hill, the percentage of voter turnout was in the mid to high 40's range, and Russo's margin of victory was generally 70 percent or more. Still, Oakland Chinatown leaders were hoping for a more impressive showing.

A Reevaluation Is Needed

In recent years political pundits boldly predicted that Asian Americans were finally on the verge of assuming a prominent role as a unified political interest group much like European American ethnics and African Americans. But as described above, the rapid growth of the Asian American population also brought with it great diversity that is extremely difficult to unify. The crushing defeat of Lily Hu shows that Asian Americans still face a long and winding road for full political participation. The ethnic, class, nativity, and generational diversity among Asian Americans make it extremely difficult for a single candidate to galvanize the entire Asian American community.

Several lessons about Asian American political participation can be learned from the Oakland experience. First and foremost, it is essential to develop and groom qualified Asian American candidates. This means encouraging individuals who know the political process, who have demonstrated leadership abilities, and who have a history of involvement with various Asian American communities on a multitude of levels. Oakland School Board member Wilma Chan was almost everyone's initial choice for District 2. She had all of the above qualities, and many political insiders believe she would have won the District 2 seat whether it was redistricted into an "Asian" district or not. Second, Asian Americans cannot rely solely on themselves for political empowerment. With a group as diverse as Asian Americans in a city as diverse as Oakland, coalition politics is still the most important strategy for a political candidate. Some European ethnic groups and African Americans have had political success in areas where they are clearly the dominant population of both the residents and the voters, but this is not the case for Asian Americans. Hu understood this fact intellectually, but her power base was still extremely narrow, ill-defined, and did not expand.

This leads to the third important lesson from Oakland's District 2 election results: Asian Americans may need to move beyond relying on just the political experience of others, especially African Americans, and must be willing look at other empowerment strategies in order to succeed in the political arena. In Lani Guinier's provocative book, *The Tyranny of the Majority* (1994), she focuses on the Voting Rights Act of 1965, and the political empowerment strategies that came after it. According to Guinier, "first generation claims" were the initial lawsuits in the 1970s brought by civil rights groups that worked to eliminate barriers to voting, such as polling taxes and literacy tests. But once African Americans could vote, the southern states redrew the district lines so that African Americans remained in the political minority. In what Guinier calls "second generation civil rights activism" came strategies to redistrict political boundaries that would ideally assure the election of racial "minority" representatives.[47] For the most part Asian Americans have followed these same lines. Calls for the expansion of the bilingual provisions in the Voting Rights Act of 1965 and voter registration drives can certainly be considered "first generation claims," and they have been important elements in Asian American political empowerment. The recent emphasis on redistricting by Asian Americans is obviously part of "second generation civil rights activism."

Guinier is particularly critical of redistricting strategies because she argues it has simply not lived up to the goals it was expected to achieve. The Oakland experience shows that redistricting by itself is an important, but only a partial solution to the problems of Asian American political participation, representation, and empowerment. In addition, following the U.S. Supreme Court's recent *Miller v. Johnson* (1995) ruling against racially conscious redistricting, this type of empowerment strategy may no longer be an option.[48] One of the more interesting ideas Guinier advocates is the notion of cumulative voting, which gives citizens the same number of votes as there are seats available. In Oakland there are eight city council seats (seven districts and one at-large) and so each voter would get to cast those votes any way he or she chooses. This includes spreading out the votes or using all eight votes for one candidate. Guinier contends this model creates greater opportunities for cooperation and representation of substantial minority viewpoints, even though the majority still gets most of the power.

The cumulative voting process is quite controversial and relatively rare, but is already being used to elect councils in cities as diverse as Peoria, Illinois, Cambridge, Massachusetts, and Almogoro, New Mexico. The U.S. Justice Department under President George Bush signed more than 30 cumulative voting settlements with local governments, and corporations use cumulative voting to ensure representation of minority shareholders on boards of directors. In addition, another voting strategy known as single-transfer voting (STV), also called "preference voting," has been used in New York's school board elections. STV allows voters to rank the candidates in order of preference. Once a candidate receives a "threshold" of votes to be declared a winner, any additional votes would automatically shift to the second favored choice until he or she receives the necessary votes to be elected. A study by the Asian American Legal Defense and Education Fund (AALDEF) on preference voting found that seven of eleven candidates identified as Asian American won seats. The AALDEF study also found that successful Asian American candidates had formed coalitions with one another as well as with non-Asian candidates which worked to increase their chances for victory.[49] Cumulative and preference voting plans are currently being discussed in Oakland as part of its citywide Charter Review. These ideas are generating support among many lawmakers in Oakland because they will end the need for district elections and will reduce the costs of elections by eliminating the need for runoffs. The discussions going on right now in Oakland may very well be in effect by the time the city must draw new district lines in 2003.[50] If this change does take place, further study of Asian American political empowerment in Oakland will most definitely be in order.

CONCLUSION

This chapter has shown the difficult road to political participation and empowerment for Asian Americans. The increased diversity among Asian Americans has clearly made it very difficult to maintain a strong political presence. At the same time, however, there are numerous signs that progress is slowly being made. First, there has been a noticeable increase in the number of immigrants who are applying for U.S. citizenship because of the current backlash against immigrants that includes calls for limiting the number of legal immigrants to the United States, proposed restrictions on immigrant rights, and a rise in anti-Asian violence. With U.S. citizenship comes the right to vote, and Asian American immigrant and civil rights activists are working to register new citizens to vote almost immediately. This leads to the second sign of progress—increased emphasis on voter registration and bilingual ballot drives. Among the findings of the 1996 NAPALC exit poll was the high percentage of first-time Asian American voters. First-time voters made up 33 percent of the Asian American voters in Los Angeles, 20 percent in the San Francisco Bay Area, and 18 percent in New York. Poll analysts believe the combination of voter registration drives and availability of bilingual ballot materials were key to encouraging greater voting participation among Asian Americans.[51]

Another recent sign of the increased political awareness and participation by Asian Americans can be seen on college campuses across the country. The 1968 student strike at San Francisco State sparked the establishment of a small number of Asian American studies programs in a few colleges and universities, but today Asian American students are clamoring for more. In 1993, over 200 Asian American students at the University of California at Irvine, occupied the administration building and demanded an audience with the president. They were protesting the lack of an Asian American studies program in the school, which has a 43 percent Asian American student population. In 1994, Asian American students at Stanford University, who represent about a quarter of the student population, also protested the lack of Asian American studies courses. At UC Berkeley, Asian American students have become exceptionally active in student politics. In 1995 the *Pacific News Service* reported that Asian Americans controlled over half of the university's student senate and held many of the top administrative positions including student body president. Andrew Wong boasts of being a Republican student body president in a historically liberal campus, and has future plans of becoming a congressman. He is very much a reflection of the diverse Asian American political sentiments described in this chapter. Asian American students outside of the West Coast are also becoming active. Asian American students at Northwestern University, Princeton, Columbia University, among others, have also protested the lack of commitment to Asian American Studies on their campuses.[52]

Still another another sign of the emergence of Asian American activism can be seen in the creation of new initiatives intended to increase political participation. In San Francisco, newly elected County Supervisor Mable Teng asked the city attorney's office to draft legislation that would allow noncitizens with children in public school to vote in citywide school board and community college trustee elections. Her proposal was immediately ridiculed as "lunacy" by one local politician, but is an idea that won't go away. New York City has allowed noncitizens to vote in local school board elections since 1970 and this has not caused any problems, says Virginia Busti, co-director of the New York School Board Task Force. "Why not allow them [noncitizens] to vote?" she asked. "Their children are in the system, and this gets them involved." More recently, the idea has been gathering momentum and there are attempts to gather the necessary 10,500 signatures necessary to get an initiative on the local ballot. If passed, the new voting plan would greatly affect most of the 123,989 adult noncitizens in San Francisco.[53] Despite their differences, political participation and empowerment are fundamental issues for Asian Americans if they want to truly participate on a level playing field in the political arena. In order to do this, Asian Americans must find their issues of unity, come together as a group, learn to work with others, and aggressively assert their rights and aspirations. All of these actions will further serve to increase the visibility of Asian Americans, and will be another step beyond the "model minority."

ENDNOTES

1. Quotes from April Lynch and Marc Sandalow, "Spotlight on Asian Americans," *San Francisco Chronicle,* March 12, 1997; and Bert Eljera, "DNC Investigates APA Contributors," *Asian Week,* January 3, 1997.

2. Quotes in Frank Wu, "Fundraising Investigation Targets APA's," *Asian Week,* March 7, 1997; and "From the Senate Floor," Senator Daniel Akaka's statement in the U.S. Senate on March 20, 1997, published in *Asian Week,* March 28, 1997.

3. Lucien Pye, *Asian Power and Politics: The Cultural Dimensions of Authority* (Cambridge, MA: Belknap Press, 1985).

4. Roger Daniels, *Asian America: Chinese and Japanese in the United States since 1850* (Seattle: University of Washington Press, 1988); and Bill Ong Hing, *Making and Remaking Asian America Through Immigration Policy, 1850–1990* (Stanford, CA: Stanford University Press, 1993).

5. Don T. Nakanishi, "Asian American Politics: An Agenda for Research," *Amerasia Journal* 12:2 (1985–1986): 1–27; Don T. Nakanishi, "UCLA Asian Pacific American Voter Registration Study," sponsored by the Asian Pacific American Legal Center, 1986, p. 21; Grant Din, "An Analysis of Asian/Pacific American Registration and Voting Patterns in San Francisco" (Masters Thesis, Claremont Graduate School, 1984), pp. 75, 85; and Albert Y. Muratsuchi, "Voter Registration in the Oakland Pacific American Communities: An Agenda for the 1990s" (San Francisco: The Coro Foundation, 1990), p. 10.

6. Carol Uhlander, Bruce Cain, and D. Roderick Kiewiet, "Political Participation of Ethnic Minorities in the 1980's," *Political Behavior* 11:3 (1989): 195–231.

7. Grant Din, "A Comparison of Chinese American Voter Registration in 1983 and 1992," a paper presented in San Francisco at "The Repeal and Its Legacy, a Conference on the 50th Anniversary of the Repeal of the Chinese Exclusion Acts," November 13, 1993.

8. David Binder and Catherine Lew, "Asian/Pacific Vote '92: An Analysis of the Northern California Asian/Pacific Islander Vote" (Oakland, CA: Larry Tramutola & Associates, 1992); and Larry H. Shinagawa, "Asian Pacific Electoral Participation in the San Francisco Bay Area: A Study of the Exit Poll Results of the November 8, 1994 Elections for the Cities of Daly City, San Francisco, and Oakland" (San Francisco: Asian Law Caucus, 1995).

9. John Horton, *The Politics of Diversity: Immigration, Resistance, and Change in Monterey Park, California* (Philadelphia: Temple University Press, 1995), Chapters 5 and 6.

10. Roy Christman and James Fay, "Growing Clout of Asians in California," *Sacramento Bee,* June 29, 1994; and Roy Christman and James Fay, "A New Electorate Gains Power," *Los Angeles Times,* November 4, 1991.

11. Sucheng Chan, *Asian Californians* (San Francisco: MTL/Boyd & Fraser, 1991), pp. 76–91.

12. Ronald Takaki, *Strangers from a Different Shore: A History of Asian Americans* (Boston: Little, Brown and Company, 1989), pp. 197–212.

13. L. Ling-chi Wang, "The Politics of Ethnic Identity and Empowerment: The Asian American Community Since the 1960s," *Asian American Policy Review* 2 (Spring 1991): 43–56.

14. Takaki, *Strangers from a Different Shore*, pp. 357–378.

15. Harry H. L. Kitano and Roger Daniels, *Asian Americans: Emerging Minorities*, second edition (Englewood Cliffs, NJ: Prentice Hall, 1995), p. 27; and Takaki, *Strangers from a Different Shore*, p. 258.

16. Cited in Kitano and Daniels, *Asian Americans: Emerging Minorities*, p. 64.

17. Takaki, *Strangers from a Different Shore*, pp. 415–416.

18. Wang, "The Politics of Ethnic Identity and Empowerment," p. 50.

19. Karen Umemoto, "On Strike! San Francisco State College Strike, 1968–1969, The Role of Asian Amerian Studies," *Amerasia Journal* 15:1 (1991): 3–41.

20. *Ibid.*, p. 4.

21. William Wei, *The Asian American Movement* (Philadelphia: Temple University Press, 1993), pp. 24–7.

22. Umemoto, "On Strike!" p. 36.

23. "An Emerging Political Force," *Los Angeles Times*, December 22, 1992; L. A. Chung, "The Year of the Asian American," *San Francisco Chronicle*, October 31, 1992; Susumu Awanohara, "Spicier Melting Pot: Asian Americans Come of Age Politically," *Far Eastern Economic Review*, November 22, 1990, pp. 30, 32–36; and Stuart Rothenberg, "The Invisible Success Story," *National Review*, September 15, 1989, pp. 43–45.

24. Ling-chi Wang, "Foreign Money Is No Friend of Ours," *Asian Week*, November 8, 1996.

25. Yen Le Espiritu, *Asian American Panethnicity: Bridging Institutions and Identities* (Philadelphia: Temple University Press, 1992), p. 113.

26. *Ibid.*, pp. 134–160.

27. *Ibid.*, pp. 164–165.

28. *Ibid.*, p. 175.

29. James S. Lai (ed.) *1996 National Asian Pacific American Political Almanac* (Los Angeles: UCLA Asian American Studies Center, 1996).

30. Cited in *Ibid.*, p. 187.

31. Paul Ong and Don Nakanishi, "Becoming Citizens, Becoming Voters: The Naturalization and Political Participation of Asian Pacific Immigrants," in Bill Ong Hing and Ronald Lee (eds.), *Reframing the Immigration Debate* (Los Angeles: LEAP Asian Pacific American Policy Institute and UCLA Asian American Studies Center, 1996), pp. 292–293.

32. Quoted in John J. Miller, "Asian Americans and the Republicans: A Natural Fit or a Party in Turmoil?" *Asian Week*, September 16, 1994.

33. Howard Hong, "Asian Americans Welcome Bush with Open Arms," *Asian Week*, June 21, 1991.

34. John J. Miller, "Asian Americans Head for Politics: What Horse Will They Ride?" *Asian Week*, April 7, 1995. Reprinted from the March–April 1995 issue of *The American Enterprise*.

35. *Ibid.*

36. Binder and Lew, "Asian/Pacific Vote '92," pp. 7–8.

37. "State Wide Exit Poll," *Los Angeles Times*, November 10, 1994; and Shinagawa, "Asian Pacific American Electoral Participation in the San Francisco Bay Area," p. 116.

38. Althea Yip, "Asian Votes Shift to the Left," *Asian Week,* November 11, 1996.

39. Stewart Kwoh and Mindy Hui, "Empowering Our Communities: Political Policy," *The State of Asian Pacific America: Policy Issues to the Year 2020* (Los Angeles: LEAP Asian Pacific American Public Policy Institute and UCLA Asian American Studies Center, 1993), pp. 189–197.

40. Samuel R. Cacus, "NYC Civil Rights Group Scores First Victory on Bilingual Voting Rights," *Asian Week,* June 20, 1994; and Samuel R. Cacus, "NYC Agrees to Translate Candidates' Names into Chinese on Voting Ballots," *Asian Week,* September 2, 1994.

41. Leland T. Saito, "Asian Americans and Latinos in San Gabriel Valley, California: Ethnic Political Cooperation and Redistricting 1990–1992," *Amerasia Journal* 19:2 (1993): 55–68.

42. *Ibid.,* p. 61.

43. Quoted in David Cogan, "Oakland's Stormy Redistricting Fight," *East Bay Express,* May 28, 1993.

44. Steve Stallone, "White Noise," *The Bay Guardian,* July 21, 1993.

45. William Wong, "Unseemly Tactics in Redistricting Fight," *Oakland Tribune,* July 16, 1993.

46. Saito, "Ethnic Political Cooperation," p. 64.

47. Lani Guinier, *The Tyranny of the Majority* (New York: The Free Press, 1994), p. 7.

48. On the last day of its 1994–1995 term, the U.S. Supreme Court struck down a Georgia redistricting plan that led to increased African American representation in Congress, setting a strict new judicial test for the way race can be used in drawing legislative districts. In its 5–4 decision, the Court found that Georgia's creation of three black-majority congressional districts violated the rights of white voters. See *Miller v. Johnson,* 115 S.Ct. 2475 (1995).

49. Tito Sinha, "P.R. Elections in N.Y.C.: Effects of Preference Voting on Asian-American Participation," *National Civic Review* 83:1 (Winter–Spring 1994): 80.

50. David K. Li, "Rarely Used Voting Style Advocated," *Oakland Tribune,* November 27, 1995.

51. Yip, "Asian Votes Shift to the Left"; and Annie Nakano, "Asian Americans Vote Big," *San Francisco Examiner,* December 15, 1996.

52. Kristina Lindren, "UC Irvine Asian-American Studies Demanded," *Los Angeles Times,* April 23, 1993; Dexter Waugh, "Stanford Lacks Asian American Studies," *San Francisco Examiner,* February 25, 1994; Lisa Margonelli, "Asian Activists Give UC Berkeley Politics a New Spin," *Pacific News Service,* Stories Issued the Week of January 2–6, 1995; and Ronald Kim, "The Myth and Realities of Ethnic Studies," *Asian Week,* February 16, 1996.

53. William Carlsen, "Teng Voting Plan Faces Criticism," *San Francisco Chronicle,* February 7, 1996; and Alethea Yip, "S.F. Initiative Seeks Vote for Noncitizens," *Asian Week,* May 3, 1996.

CONCLUSION: COMING FULL CIRCLE

VISIBILITY AND INVISIBILITY

Asian Americans are no longer a silent minority. All demographic projections call for the continued growth of the Asian American population, and this will help bring greater attention to this extremely diverse pan-ethnic group. Attention to Asian Americans, their issues, and their experiences is not merely a numbers game, nor something that will spontaneously occur. It is very much a result of combined efforts by Asian American scholars, journalists, artists, and community activists who together continue to bring an awareness of Asian Americans into the national forefront. It is the multifaceted process of population growth, research, *and* social activism that will move Asian Americans from being a mostly invisible entity to a visible force that must be recognized. This book has shown that the Asian American experience is a highly complex combination of many different experiences that defy easy explanation, that goes far beyond traditional race relations theories and the simple model minority stereotypes.

There is no doubt that each of the previous chapters and the issues raised deserve more attention and detail than can be provided in just one book. Fortunately, new research studies about the contemporary Asian American experience is continually being published and are adding to the information already available. At the same time, however, there are also a number of important issues that were not directly addressed in this book. This is due to both their relatively recent emergence and lack of sufficient research on the issues at this time. For example, research on the contemporary Asian American rap and hip-hop youth culture is only beginning. It is only a matter of time before it receives the attention it deserves. The constantly changing nature of who and what constitutes Asian America, and the issues that must be faced, are definitely an ongoing challenge. One way I have attempted to confront this challenge is to center this book on the new thinking in Asian American studies, as an academic discipline, and on the Asian American movement, as a political force. Both have undergone a great amount of self-examination in recent years, and fundamental to this has been a critique of the basic assumptions about the pre-1965 Asian American experience and its applicability to the post-1965 Asian American experience.

Both can clearly be seen in "paradigm shifts" described by Shirly Hune in the introduction of this book. Hune called for race relations in the United States to be viewed beyond the simple black–white paradigm of the past. New thinking on race relations looks more broadly to include today's multiracial reality, along with important class and gender factors that cut across racial lines. Within this, relations between various racial groups is seen as extremely fluid with periods of relative harmony as well as periods of bitter conflict, depending on the social, political, and economic conditions at the time. The new paradigms Hune described also acknowledge the very real diversity among Asian Americans, the willingness of Asian Americans to fight against injustice (agency), and the significance of the immigrant experience for both foreign-born and native-born Asians in the United States.

BEYOND THE MODEL MINORITY

The key question must now be asked: What is the future for Asians in America? Some have suggested that the future for Asian Americans is bright. As a group they will be much more successful at assimilating socially, culturally, and politically into the American mainstream. This perspective also maintains that there will be more acceptance of Asian cultures and that anti-Asian sentiment will decline as the population of Asians in America grows.[1] There are, however, ample reasons to believe these projections may be overly optimistic and simplistic.

First of all, the optimistic outlook is solidly based on the old European immigrant analogy paradigm that sees race and ethnic relations as linear and progressive (i.e., things will always get better over time). This is a paradigm that Hune argues needs to be changed. Many examples in this book show that race relations fluctuate over time and context. For example, the insecurity in the United States created by global economic restructuring has helped to propel increased anti-Asian sentiment and "Asian-bashing" across the nation. Economic instability has historically been powerful fodder for increased social conflict, racial antagonism, and hostility toward immigrants.

Second, the optimistic outlook understates the impact of the continued flow of immigrants and capital from Asia to the United States. On one hand, this will be an overall benefit to the U.S. economy. At the same time, however, large numbers of diverse immigrants are also a double-edged sword for Asian

Americans. New immigrants and refugees quickly became the source of great animosity among many in the general American public. The affluent Asian immigrants are resented for their wealth and education, while poorer immigrants and refugees are resented for receiving welfare benefits and other government supports. In addition, the image of the perpetual foreigner and the stereotypes that go with large immigrant populations will continue to be reinforced among many non-Asians. This does not deny that there will indeed be a large segment of second-generation Asian Americans who will be more assimilated than their first-generation parents. Unfortunately, as we often saw in the book, many non-Asians can't tell the difference between an immigrant and an American-born Asian, nor do they care about the distinctions.

Third, the overly optimistic projection overlooks the relative lack of political representation and empowerment among Asian Americans. According to the United States Commission on Civil Rights (1992), "This lack of political empowerment leads the political leadership of the United States to overlook and sometimes ignore the needs and concerns of Asian Americans."[2] The lack of political power on the national level can also leave Asian Americans vulnerable to broadly targetted attacks. Historical examples include harsh laws limiting immigration from Asia, as well as the massive forced relocation of Japanese American citizens during World War II. More recently, this can be seen in the investigations into illegal political contributions by a few wealthy Asian influence peddlers, and its potential chilling effect on Asian American participation in electoral politics. Many Asian Americans have expressed deep concern that attention to these investigations is scapegoating Asians and Asian Americans rather than focusing on the more fundamental issue of campaign finance reform.[3]

NEW DIRECTIONS IN ASIAN AMERICAN STUDIES

The optimistic projections into the future of Asian America are not totally incorrect, but they must be examined openly and critically. As an academic discipline, Asian American studies must change and grow in order to keep up with the continual change and growth of Asian America itself. Essays by Asian American scholars Chalsa Loo (1988), Michael Omi (1988), Lisa Lowe (1991), Keith Osajima (1995), and Sau-Ling Wong (1995) stand out as important works addressing this concern for the future. Loo's provocative, "The 'Middle-Aging' of Asian American Studies," calls for the maturation of Asian American studies. She borrows from renown psychologist Erik Erikson's eight stages of human development and focuses her attention on stage seven, "Generativity versus Self-Absorption and Stagnation." According to Erikson, this stage generally occurs between ages 25 and 65—which is quite appropriate since Asian American studies was "born" in 1969. This stage is primarily concerned with turning outward from the self and establishing and guiding the next generation. With regard to Asian American studies, Loo writes, "We must care for the welfare of our collectivity, exceed the limitless bounds of creativity, and prepare a second generation to be more courageous, risk-taking and bold than ourselves."[4]

Omi's essay, "It Just Ain't the Sixties No More: The Contemporary Dilemmas of Asian American Studies," agrees with Loo's interest in generativity. However, he warns that the second generation of Asian American scholars, activists, and artists will not, and should not, be clones of their predecessors. Omi recalls a conversation with a colleague who said the people involved in the social activism of the 1960s were greatly influenced and shaped during this unique period of history. The colleague emphasized that although it is important to pass the lessons learned to succeeding generations, it is impossible to re-create these experiences to succeeding generations. "While acquainting students with our collective 'buried past' and stressing the need for them to be political participants, we should not expect to create them in our image," Omi writes. "We need to start exploring some new directions."[5] The process of exploration may be transformative, but it will not be easy." The key to continued growth of Asian American studies, he believes, is to develop a conceptual framework to analyze the contemporary Asian American experience.

This new conceptual framework is advanced by Lowe's seminal essay, "Heterogeneity, Hybridity, and Multiplicity: Marking Asian American Differences." Lowe describes the need for Asian Americanists to look beyond the dominant "modernist" perspective in social sciences and the humanities that posits society has an inherent and consistant underlying order that can be studied and understood. Lowe offers a "postmodern" analysis that reveals the complexity of Asian American life and warns against an overreliance on traditional thinking. "In the 1990s, we can diversify our political practices to include a more heterogeneous group and to enable crucial alliances with other groups—ethnicity-based, class-based, gender-based, and sexually-based," she writes. "I want to suggest that essentializing Asian American identity and suppressing our differences . . . risks particular dangers: not only does it underestimate the differences and hybridities among Asians, but it also inadvertently supports the racist discourse that constructs Asians as a homogeneous group, that implies we are 'all alike' and conform to 'types.'"[6]

Lowe's analysis is sharpened by Osajima in his essay, "Postmodern Possibilities: The Theoretical and Political Directions for Asian American Studies." He cautions against focusing solely on differences because he understands political unity is a necessary element for Asian American social, economic, and political empowerment. Osajima calls for an "oppositional postmodernism," that recognizes the need to expand and to incorporate the divergent elements that more broadly make up the new realities of the Asian American experience. This approach harks back to the fundamental position of Asian American studies to develop knowledge to inform political action.

"For Asian American studies, an oppositional postmodernism requires us to pay serious attention to the multiplicity, complexity, and hybridity of the Asian American experience," he writes. "It requires that our analyses not end at the moment of critique, but, attendant to the history of Asian American Studies, also includes ways for turning postmodern analyses into concrete strategies for change."[7]

Another future direction of Asian American studies is to give greater attention to global and diasporic studies. This is not intended to privilege Asian studies at the expense of Asian American studies. Nor is it intended to have Asian Americans reminisce about their "roots," or entertain romanticized visions of a far-off homeland to which they wish to return or visit for the first time. The most important reason for incorporating a global perspective is fully aimed at better understanding, analyzing, and addressing the experiences of Asians in the United States. Wong warns against any possible misplaced intentions of global and diasporic studies in her article, "Denationalization Reconsidered: Asian American Cultural Criticism at a Theoretical Crossroads," and expresses concern over what may happen with an uncritical acceptance of global and diasporic studies. "To Asian Americans the term 'roots' could evoke contradictory meanings: either 'origin,' where one or one's family hails in Asia; or else commitment to the place where one resides," Wong writes.[8] She emphasizes the second meaning should be the future direction for Asian Americanists, because it expands on the ideals on which Asian American studies was founded.

THE NEXT STEPS

These theoretical ideas should be used to help shape a more realistic, desirable, and positive future prospect for Asians in America. This final section draws upon the new directions in Asian American studies and broadly summarizes actions and ideals that are needed to enhance the social, cultural, economic, and political well-being for Asian Americans, and for the nation as a whole.

Speak Out, Act Up

First and foremost, there has been an conscious emphasis in this book for Asian Americans to transition away from their isolation and invisibility. Both Loo and Omi realize that now is time for a new generation of Asian American scholars, activists, artists, and students to assert themselves, step out, and confront the various issues discussed in previous chapters. These issues may be viewed from a very different lens by this new generation. There may be a new set of priorities, and maybe even the emergence of completely new issues altogther. Chapter 7 highlighted issues of changing families, intermarriage, biraciality, and sexuality as examples of areas of interest not often touched upon by earlier Asian Americanists. These all should be seen as important and vital parts of "generativity."

Embrace Diversity and Change

It is up to the new generation to fully and creatively engage the broad diversity that is Asian America. Lowe convincingly argues that diversity is a strength, and denial of the diverse Asian American reality is highly problematic and ultimately self-defeating. Earlier Asian Americanists focused primarily on the experiences of Chinese and Japanese Americans, and to a lesser degree, Filipino Americans. Today, and in the future, there will be much greater attention to Korean Americans, Asian Indian Americans, Vietnamese, Cambodian, Laotian, and Hmong Americans, as well as other emerging groups who also consider themselves Asian Americans. Diversity and multiculturalism are not unique concerns to Asian Americans. They can also be seen across the nation in cities confronting rapid demographic change, and on many college campuses creating a stage on which difference, equality, and community are brought to the forefront. Asian Americans are part of, not separate from, the increasing pluralization of U.S. society. There are, of course, those who fear that diversity and multiculturalism serve only to create conflict and disunity. These fears fail to recognize the generative role that geographically and historically separated communities play when they come together and establish ongoing relations.

Work Together and with Others

The new directions in Asian American studies are part of a broader social/political/academic movement that recognizes we have reached the limits of the monocultural, monochromatic, and individualistic concept of American society. For Asian Americans this means celebrating their distinctiveness, but at the same time, finding the points of unity among themselves and with others. For Osajima, political organizing involves two steps, and both develop when people understand another person's unique struggles, and recognize the areas of shared experience. The first step usually entails forming pan-Asian coalitions that bridge diverse groups of Asian Americans to work on a very specific goal of mutual importance. The second step involves building alliances with others beyond just the pan-Asian group, and is most often based on broader issues such as working for a more just and fair society. A good example of these two steps in action can be seen around the issue of anti-Asian violence. Asian American activists skillfully rallied to raise awareness on increasing anti-Asian violence, and through these efforts eventually joined forces with other groups to confront the broader issue of rising hate violence in the United States.

Think Globally, Act Locally

It is vitally important that Asian Americans recognize the powerful influence of globalization, or "transnational" interaction, on their lives. This can be seen in many areas such as global economic restructuring, changing patterns of immigration and settlement, and the emergence of new Asian American communities detailed in the beginning of this book. This also includes the fluidity of material culture (i.e., films, books, food, etc.) and the shifting family patterns across national boundaries. Within this, Wong discusses the distinctions between diasporic and domestic perspectives in the contemporary and future Asian American experience. Her emphasis on "roots" meaning a commitment to where one resides shows that attention to globalization must include a local (or domestic) focus for political action. The protests against the motion picture *Rising Sun* brought a great deal of attention to the potential serious consequences for Asian Americans when a global economic issue is sensationalized by the popular media. In short, Wong believes that thinking globally is a significant mode for better understanding the issues confronting Asians in the United States.

CONCLUSION

This book has provided a broad overview and a basic groundwork for greater understanding of the contemporary Asian American experience. The extensive use of real-life examples, personal profiles, and theoretical concepts in this book highlight the dynamic complexities that problematize the simple notion of Asian Americans as the "model minority." No one can predict the future with any authority. However, enlightened individuals and groups can make informed choices about their future, rather than blindly have the future determined for them.

The issues discussed are fundamental to the Asian American experience, and they will continue to emerge and redevelop in the future. Also fundamental is the need for Asian Americans to work together and with other groups. Asian Americans, like all other Americans, cannot continue to live in either self-imposed or externally contrived isolation.

Asian Americans must be willing to enter what African American philosopher, theologian, and activist Cornel West calls "the public square." West writes: "We must focus our attention on the public square—the common good that undergirds our national and global destinies. The vitality of any public square ultimately depends on how much we care about the quality of our lives together."[9] Today the United States is in the midst of a new period of globalization abroad and pluralistic democracy at home. This requires, among many things, greater attention to societal restructuring, self-examination, and negotiation. This period also calls for clear and thoughtful dialogue, historical awareness, and a willingness to listen to diverse populations and ideas as we contemplate the future. Asian Americans are an essential part of this process.

ENDNOTES

1. Pyong Gap Min (ed.) , *Asian Americans: Contemporary Trends and Issues* (Thousand Oaks, CA: Sage Publications, 1995), pp. 279–280.
2. U. S. Commission on Civil Rights, *Civil Rights Issues Facing Asian Americans in the 1990s* (Washington, DC: Government Printing Office, 1992), p. 190.
3. See Emil Guillermo, "Asian Americans Have Become Political Pariahs," *Oakland Tribune,* May 22, 1997; and Phil Tajitsu Nash and Frank Wu, "Asian-Americans Under Glass: Where the Furor over the President's Fundraising Has Gone Awry—and Racist," *The Nation,* 24:12 (March 31, 1997): 15–16.
4. Loo, "The 'Middle-Aging' of Asian American Studies," in Gary Y. Okihiro, et al. (eds.), *Reflections on Shattered Windows: Promise and Prospects for Asian American Studies* (Pullman, WA: Washington State University Press, 1988), pp. 16–23.
5. Michael Omi, "It Just Ain't the Sixties No More: The Contemporary Dilemmas of Asian American Studies," in *ibid.,* pp. 31–36.
6. Lisa Lowe, "Heterogeneity, Hybridity, Multiplicity: Marking Asian American Differences," *Diaspora* (Spring 1991), pp. 24–44.
7. Keith Osajima, "Postmodern Possibilities: The Theoretical and Political Directions for Asian American Studies," *Amerasia Journal* 21:1&2 (1995): 79–87.
8. Sau-Ling C. Wong, "Denationalization Reconsidered: Asian American Cultural Criticism at a Theoretical Crossroads," *Amerasia Journal* 21: 1&2 (1995): 1–27.
9. Cornel West, *Race Matters* (Boston: Beacon Press, 1993), p. 6.

BIBLIOGRAPHY

ABATE, TOM. "Heavy Load for Silicon Valley Workers." *San Francisco Examiner* 23 May 1993.

ABELMAN, NANCY and JOHN LIE. *Blue Dreams: Korean Americans and the Los Angeles Riots.* Cambridge, MA: Harvard University Press, 1995.

Abu–Near, Donna. "Multiracials Want Own Category." *San Francisco Examiner* 21 Jul. 1996.

Act of 14 Jul. 1870. Stat. 16.256.

AKAKA, DANIEL. "From the Senate Floor." *Asian Week* 28 Mar. 1997.

ALLEN, WALTER R. "The Search for Applicable Theories of Black Family Life." *Journal of Marriage and the Family* 40:1 (1978): 117–129.

ALMIROL, EDWIN B. *Ethnic Identity and Social Negotiation: A Study of a Filipino Community in California.* New York: AMS P, 1985. "

ANWAR, YASMIN. "UC Berkeley Puts to Rest Tenure Suit." *Oakland Tribune* 9 Jan. 1996.

AOKI, GUY and PHILIP W. CHUNG. "'Rising Sun,' Hollywood and Asian Stereotypes." *Los Angeles Times* 3 May 1993.

APPLEBAUM, RICHARD P. and GARY GEREFFI. "Power and Profits in the Apparel Commodity Chain." *Global Production: The Apparel Industry in the Pacific Rim.* Edna Bonacich et al., eds. Philadelphia: Temple University Press, 1994. 42–62.

"The Asian American Dream?" *A Magazine* 2:3 (Dec. 1993) 70.

Asian American Students Association of Brown University. "Asian American Admission at Brown University." 11 Oct. 1993.

"Asian American Women Struggling to Move Past Cultural Expectations." *New York Times* 23 Jan. 1994.

Asian Immigrant Women Advocates. Letter and Press Release. 20 Mar. 1996.

Asian Pacific American Education Advisory Committee. "Asian Pacific Americans in the CSU: A Follow–Up Report." Aug. 1994.

ASIMOV, NANETTE. "A Hard Lesson in Diversity." *San Francisco Chronicle* 19 Jun. 1995.

—. "Single Standard for Admissions at Lowell High." *San Francisco Chronicle* 28 Feb. 1996.

ASIMOV, NANETTE and TARA SHIOYA. "A Test for the Best Public Schools." *San Francisco Chronicle* 21 Jun. 1995.

AWANOHARA, SUSUMU. "Spicier Melting Pot: Asian Americans Come of Age Politically." *Far Eastern Economic Review* 22 Nov. 1990: 30+.

AWANOHARA, SUSUMU and *Jonathan Burton.* "More Money than Votes." *Far Eastern Economic Review* 29 Oct. 1992: 29+.

BANFIELD, EDWARD. *The Unheavenly City.* Boston: Little, 1970.

BANKS, SANDY. "UCLA Is Cleared in Bias Case." *Los Angeles Times* 27 Aug. 1993.

BARRINGER, HERBERT R., ROBERT W. GARDNER, and MICHAEL J. LEVINE, eds. *Asian and Pacific Islanders in the United States.* New York: Russell Sage Foundation, 1993.

BAU, IGNATIUS. "APAs and AIDS: We Are Not Immune." *Asian Week* 5 Jan. 1996.

—. "Immigrant Rights: A Challenge to Asian Pacific American Political Influence." *Asian American Policy Review* 5 (1995): 7–44.

BECKER, GARY S. *Human Capital: A Theoretical and Empirical Analysis,* second edition. Chicago: University of Chicago Press, 1980.

BELL, DAVID. "An American Success Story: The Triumph of Asian Americans." *New Republic* Jul. 1985: 24+.

BENEDICT, RUTH. *Race: Science and Politics.* New York: Viking Press, 1959.

Berestein, Leslie. "Nursing Home Rule Starts War of Words." *Los Angeles Times* 27 Feb. 1995.

BINDER, DAVID and CATHERINE LEW. "Asian/Pacific Vote '92: An Analysis of the Northern California Asian/Pacific Islander Vote." Oakland, CA: Larry Tramutola & Associates, 1992.

BONACICH, EDNA. "The Social Costs of Immigrant Entrepreneurship." *Amerasia Journal* 14:1 (1988): 119–128.

BONACICH, EDNA, et al., eds. *Global Production: The Apparel Industry in the Pacific Rim.* Philadelphia: Temple University Press, 1994.

BONACICH, EDNA and IVAN LIGHT. *Immigrant Entrepreneurs: Koreans in Los Angeles.* Berkeley and Los Angeles: University of California Press, 1988.

BONACICH, EDNA and JOHN MODELL. *The Economic Basis of Ethnic Solidarity: Small Business in the Japanese American Community.* Berkeley and Los Angeles: University of California Press, 1980.

BOUVIER, LEON and PHILLIP MARTIN. *Population Change and California's Education System.* Washington, DC: Population Reference Bureau, Inc., 1987.

BOYD, MONICA. "Oriental Immigration: The Experience of Chinese, Japanese, and Filipino Populations in the United States." *International Migration Review* 10 (1976): 48–60.

BRAND, DAVID. "The New Whiz Kids." *Time* 31 Aug., 1987.

BRESLAUER, JAN. "After the Fall." *Los Angeles Times* 13 Jan. 1991, Calendar Section.

—. "Hues and Cries." *Los Angeles Times* 7 Jul. 1991, Calendar Section: 3+.

BROWNING, E. S. "A New Chinatown Grows in Brooklyn." *Wall Street Journal* 31 May 1994.

BUAKEN, MANUEL. "Life in the Armed Forces." *New Republic* 109 (1943): 279+.

BUNZEL JOHN H. and JEFFREY K. D. Au. "Diversity or Discrimination? Asian Americans in College." *The Public Interest* 87 (Spring 1987): 56.

BUTTERFIELD, FOX. "Why Asians Americans Are Going to the Head of the Class." *New York Times Magazine* 3 Aug. 1986: 19–24.

CACAS, SAMUEL R. "Accent Discrimination Case by Five Filipino American Security Guards Is Settled." *Asian Week* 10 June 1994.

—. "Fall River Trial Ends with Murder Conviction." *Asian Week* 23 Sep. 1994.

—. "Language Rights Hotline Established." *Rafu Shimpo* 8 Feb. 1995.

—. "New Census Category for Multiracial Persons?" *Asian Week* 15 Jul. 1994.

—. "NYC Agrees to Translate Candidates' Names into Chinese on Voting Ballots." *Asian Week* 2 Sep. 1994.

—. "NYC Civil Rights Group Scores First Victory on Bilingual Voting Rights." *Asian Week* 20 Jun. 1994.

—. "Vietnamese American Man Charges Police Brutality in Defense Trial." *Asian Week* 30 Sep. 1994.

California Attorney General's Asian Pacific Advisory Committee. *Final Report.* Dec. 1988.

—. Dept. of Justice. *Hate Crimes in California, 1995.* Sacramento: Div. of Criminal Justice Information Services, 1996. Table 1, p. 7.

CAPLAN, NATHAN, MARCELLA H. CHOY, and JOHN K. WHITMORE. *Children of the Boat People; A Study of Educational Success.* Ann Arbor: University of Michigan Press, 1991.

CAPLAN, NATHAN, JOHN K. WHITMORE, and MARCELLA H. CHOY. *The Boat People and Achievement in America: A Study of Economic and Educational Success.* Ann Arbor: University of Michigan Press, 1989.

CARLSEN, WILLIAM. "Teng Voting Plan Faces Criticism." *San Francisco Chronicle* 7 Feb. 1996.

CARREA, JOHN WILLSHIRE. *New Voices: Immigrant Students in U.S. Public Schools.* Boston: National Coalition of Advocates for Students, 1988.

CASS, DANIELLE. "Unfriendly Skies' Slurs Launch Suit." *Oakland Tribune* 27 Oct. 1994.

CAUDILL, WILLIAM and GEORGE DEVOS. "Achievement, Culture and Personality: The Case of Japanese Americans." *American Anthropologist* 58 (1956): 1102–1126.

CAVOSORA, RICHARD J. P. "Discrimination Spoken Here." *Filipinas* Jul. 1993: 16+.

Center for Integration and Improvement of Journalism. *News Watch: A Critical Look at Coverage of People of Color.* San Francisco: San Francisco State University, 1994.

"Chamber Declines to Remove Hu." *Oakland Tribune* 24 May 1994.

CHAN, CONNIE S. "Issues of Identity Development Among Asian-American Lesbians and Gay Men." *Journal of Counseling and Development* 68 (Sep.–Oct. 1989): 16–20.

CHAN, SUCHENG. *Asian Californians.* San Francisco: MTL/Boyd & Fraser, 1991.

—. "Beyond Affirmative Action." *Change* Nov.–Dec. 1989: 48–51.

CHANG, EDWARD T. "America's First Multiethnic 'Riots.'" *The State of Asian America: Activism and Resistance.* Karin Aguilar-San Juan, ed. Boston: South End Press, 1994.

—. "New Urban Crisis: Intra-Third World Conflict." *Perspectives.* Shirley Hune et al., eds. Pullman, WA: Washington State University Press, 1991.

CHANG, IRENE. "Asian, Latino Activists Seek Ethnic Harmony at Schools." *Los Angeles Times* 22 Sep. 1991.

CHARNY, BEN. "Mental Health Center Targets the Asian Community. *Oakland Tribune* 17 Oct. 1994.

CHEN, STANFORD. "It's a Matter of Visibility." *Quill* Apr. 1993: 33–34.

CHIA, ROSINA. "Pilot Study: Family Values of American versus Chinese American Parents." *Journal of Asian American Psychological Association* 13:1 (1989):8–11.

CHIN, STEVEN A. "Asians Terrorized in Housing Projects." *San Francisco Chronicle* 17 Jan. 1993.

—. "Garment Workers Fight for Back Pay." *San Francisco Examiner* 16 Feb. 1994.

—. "The World of B. D. Wong." *Image* 5 Sep, 1993: 6+.

"The China Syndrome." *Mirabella* Mar. 1994: 58+.

CHISWICK, BARRY. *Income Inequality.* New York: Columbia University Press, 1974.

CHO, SUMI. "Conflict and Construction." *Reading Rodney King: Reading Urban Uprising.* Robert Goodings-Williams, ed. New York: Routledge, 1993.

CHOATE, PAT. *Agents of Influence.* New York: Alfred A. Knopf, 1990.

CHRISTMAN, ROY AND JAMES FAY. "Growing Clout of Asians in California." *Sacramento Bee* 29 Jun. 1994.

—. "A New Electorate Gains Power." *Los Angeles Times* 4 Nov. 1991.

CHUNG, L. A. "How Asian American Groups Voted." *San Francisco Chronicle* 6 Nov. 1992.

—. "The Year of the Asian American." *San Francisco Chronicle* 31 Oct. 1992.

CHUNG, PHILIP W. "Beyond Asian Chic." *A Magazine* Summer 1994: 22.

"Citizenship Applications Soaring Among Legal Immigrants." *New York Times* 2 Apr. 1995.

CLARY, MIKE. "Rising Toll of Hate Crimes." *Los Angeles Times* 10 Oct. 1992.

COGAN, DAVID. "Oakland's Stormy Redistricting Fight." *East Bay Express* 28 May 1993.

COLIVER, VICTORIA. "Clinton Cuts 'Sweatshop–free' Deal." *Oakland Tribune* 3 Aug. 1996.

"Confucian Work Ethic." *Time* 28 Mar. 1983.

CONNER, JOHN. *A Study of the Marital Stability of Japanese War Brides.* San Francisco: R & E Research Assocs., 1976.

"A Conversation with David Henry Hwang." *Bearing Dreams, Shaping Visions: Asian Pacific American Perspectives.* Linda A. Revilla et al., eds. Pullman, WA: Washington State University Press, 1993. 185–191.

CORLISS, RICHARD. "Pacific Overtures." *Time* 13 Sep. 1993: 68–70.

CRAWFORD, JAMES. *Bilingual Education: History, Politics, Theory, and Practice.* Trenton, NJ: Crane, 1989.

CRICHTON, MICHAEL. *Rising Sun.* New York: Ballantine, 1992.

"D'Amato Apologizes for Spoof of Judge Ito." *Newsday* 6 Apr. 1995.

DANIELS, ROGER. *Asian Americans: Chinese and Japanese in the United States.* Seattle: University of Washington Press, 1988.

—. *Coming to America.* New York: Harper, 1990.

—. *Concentration Camps: North America Japanese in the United States and Canada During World War II.* Malabar, FL.: Robert A. Kreiger, 1981.

—. Concentration Camps, U.S.A. New York: Holt, 1971.

"The Dark Side of the Sun." *Entertainment Weekly* 6 Aug. 1993: 26+.

DARLIN, DAMON. "The East Is Technicolor." *Forbes* 8 Nov. 1993: 318.

DAS, RAJANKI K. *Hindustani Workers on the Pacific Coast.* Berlin: Walter De Bruyter, 1923.

"Daughter Finally Finds GI Dad." *San Francisco Chronicle* 24 Dec. 1994.

DER, HENRY. "Affirmative Action Policy." *The State of Asian Pacific America: Policy Issues to the Year 2020.* Los Angeles: LEAP Asian Pacific American Public Policy Institute and UCLA Asian American Studies Center, 1993. 215–232.

—. "Clash Between Race-Conscious Remedies and Merit: School Desegregation and the San Francisco Chinese American Community." *Asian American Policy Review 4* (1994): 65–91.

DER, HENRY, et al. *The Broken Ladder '92: Asian Americans in City Government.* San Francisco: Chinese for Affirmative Action, 1992.

DIN, GRANT. "An Analysis of Asian/Pacific American Registration and Voting Patterns in San Francisco." Masters Thesis. Claremont Graduate School, 1984.

—. A Comparison of Chinese American Voter Registration in 1983 and 1992." The Repeal and Its Legacy, a Conference on the 50th Anniversary of the Repeal of the Chinese Exclusion Acts. San Francisco. 13 Nov. 1993.

DIVOKY, DIANE. "The Model Minority Goes to School." *Phi Delta Kappan* Nov. 1988: 219–222.

DOYLE, JIM. "High Court Lets English-Only Job Rules Stand." *San Francisco Chronicle* 21 Jun. 1994.

D'SOUZA, KAREN. "Some Foresee Era of Intolerance." *Oakland Tribune* 26 Dec. 1994.

DUKE, LYNNE. "Panel Finds Japan-Bashing, Violence." *Washington Post* 29 Feb. 1992.

DUTKA, ELAINE. "Asian Americans: Rising Furor Over 'Rising Sun.'" *Los Angeles Times* 28 Jul. 1993.

DYNES, WAYNE R. and STEPHEN DONALDSON, eds. *Asian Homosexuality.* New York: Garland Press, 1992.

EFFRON, SETH. "Racial Slayings Prompt Fear, Anger in Raleigh." *Greensboro News and Record* 24 SEP. 1989.

ELJERA, BERT. "DNC Investigates APA Contributors." *Asian Week* 29 Jan. 1997.

—. "Mixed Reactions on Immigration Moves." *Asian Week* 3 Mar. 1996.

—. An Emerging Political Force." *Los Angeles Times* 22 Dec. 1922.

ESPIRITU, YEN LE. *Asian American Panethnicity: Bridging Institutions and Identities* Philadelphia: Temple University Press, 1992.

FALLOWS, JAMES M. *More Like Us: Making America Great Again.* Boston: Houghton, 1989.

FARAUDO, JEFF. "Chow Takes Silver Medal." *Oakland Tribune* 29 Jul., 1996.

—. "Silence Is Golden for Reluctant Hero Chow." *Oakland Tribune* 24 Jul., 1996.

FARQUHAR, KIDOTJ and MARY L. DOI. "Bruce Lee vs. Fu Manchu: Kung Fu Films and Asian American Stereotypes in America." *Bridge: An Asian American Perspective* 6:3 (Fall 1978): 23–40.

FAWCETT, JAMES T. and BENJAMIN V. CARINO, eds. *Pacific Bridges: The New Immigration from Asia and the Pacific Islands.* Staten Island, NY: Center for Migration Studies, 1987.

FEAGIN, JOE R. and CLAIRECE BOOHER FEAGIN. *Racial and Ethnic Relations.* 4th ed. Englewood Cliffs, NJ: Prentice Hall, 1994.

FERRELL, DAVID and K. CONNIE KANG. " 'Rising Sun' Opens to Charges of Racism." *Los Angeles Times* 31 Jul. 1993.

FIMRITE, PETER. "$1 Million Deal in UC Bias Suit." *San Francisco Chronicle* 9 Jan. 1996.

FLYNN, JOHN. "Success the Old Fashioned Way." *San Francisco Examiner* 30 Apr. 1995.

FONG, COLLEEN and JUDY YUNG. "In Search of the Right Spouse: Interracial Marriage Among Chinese and Japanese Americans." *Amerasia Journal* 21:3 (1995): 77–98.

FONG, TIM. "Yamaguchi's Gold Won't Deter Hate Crimes." *San Jose Mercury News* 25 Feb. 1992.

FONG, TIMOTHY P. *The First Suburban Chinatown: The Remaking of Monterey Park, California.* Philadelphia: Temple University Press, 1994.

FONG-TORRES, BEN. "Why There Are No Male Asian Anchors." *San Francisco Chronicle* 13 Jul., 1986, Datebook Section: 51–55.

"4 Face Charges in Attack." *Los Angeles Times* 6 Jun, 1991.

FOX, DAVID. "Neuropsychology, Achievement, and Asian–American Culture: Is Relative Functionalism Oriented Times Three?" *American Psychologist* 46:8 (1991): 877–878.

FREEDBERG, LOUIS. "Citizenship Wave Surprises INS." *San Francisco Chronicle* 13 Apr. 1995.

—. "Feinstein Fails to Limit Legal Immigration." *San Francisco Chronicle* 26 Apr. 1996.

FUJITA STEPHEN S. and MARILYN FERNANDEZ. "Asian American Admissions to an Elite University: A Multivariate Case Study of Harvard." *Asian American Policy Review* 5 (1995): 45–62.

FULWOOD, SAM III. "Japan-Bashing Condemned by Rights Panel." *San Francisco Chronicle* 29 Jan. 1992.

GALBRAITH, JANE. "Group Takes 'Rising Sun' Protest Public." *Los Angeles Times* 7 Apr, 1993.

Garcia v. Gloor. 618 Fed.2d 264, 270 (1981).

Geron, Tomio. "APA Activism, New York Style." Asian Week 5 Apr. 1996.

—. "N.Y.P.D. Settles APA Complaints." *Asian Week* 1 Mar. 1996.

—. "Voter Drives on in N.Y." *Asian Week* 19 Jul. 1996.

GOCK, TERRY S. "Acquired Immunodeficiency Syndrome." *Confronting Critical Health Issues of Asian and Pacific Islander Americans.* Nolan W. S. Zane, David T. Takeuchi, and Kathleen N. J. Young, eds. Thousand Oaks, CA: Sage Press, 1994, 247–265.

GODWIN, D. D. and J. SCANZONI. "Couple Consensus During Marital Joint Decision-Making: A Context, Process, Outcome Model." *Journal of Marriage and the Family* 51 (1989): 943–956.

GONZALES, JUAN L. *Racial and Ethnic Groups in America.* 2nd ed. Dubuque, Iowa: Kendall/Hunt, 1993.

—. *Racial and Ethnic Families in America.* 2nd ed. Dubuque, Iowa: Kendall/Hunt, 1993.

GORDON, MILTON M. *Assimilation in American Life: The Role of Race Religion, and National Origins.* New York: Oxford University Press, 1964.

GOSSETT, THOMAS F. *Race: The History of an Idea in America.* New York: Schocken Books, 1965.

GOTANDA, NEIL. "Re-Producing the Model Minority Stereotype: Judge Joyce Karlin's Sentencing Colloquy in *People v. Soon Ja Du.*" *Reviewing Asian America: Locating Diversity.* Wendy L. Ng et al., eds. Pullman, WA: Washington State University Press, 1995.

GOULD, STEPHEN JAY. "Curveball." *New Yorker* 28 Nov. 1994: 139–149.

"Gouw Gets Warner Bros. to Pull Offensive Cartoon." *Asian Week* 17 Feb. 1995.

"Governor Wilson Vetoes Garment Manufacturers' Joint Liability Bill." *AIWA News* 10:2 (Fall 1994): 7.

GRAHAM, JEFFERSON. "Actor's Chance to Part a Racial and Cultural Curtain." *USA Today* 13 Sep. 1994.

GRAHAM, TIM. "A Letter from the Editor of the Oakland Tribune." *Oakland Tribune* 1 Apr. 1996.

GROVE, KWA JULIENNE. "Identity Development in Interracial, Asian/White Late Adolescents: Must It Be So Problematic?" *Journal of Youth and Adolescence* 20:6 (1991): 617–628.

GUILLERMO, EMIL. "Asian Americans Have Become Political Pariahs." *Oakland Tribune* 22 May 1997.

GUINIER, LANI. *The Tyranny of the Majority.* New York: The Free Press, 1994.

H., Pamela. "Asian American Lesbians: An Emerging Voice in the Asian American Community." *Making Waves.* Asian Women United, eds. Boston: Beacon Press, 1989.

HAMAMOTO, DARRELL Y. *Monitored Peril: Asian Americans and the Politics of TV Representation.* Minneapolis: University of Minnesota Press, 1994.

HAMILL, PETE. "New Race Hustle." *Esquire* Sep. 1990: 77–80.

HAMILTON, DENISE. "6 Accused in Ethnic Fight on Campus." *Los Angeles Times* 18 Feb. 1995.

HANSEN, MARCUS LEE. The Problems of the Third Generation. Rock Island, IL: Augustana Historical Soc., 1938.

"Have Skills, Will Travel—Home." *Business Week* 18 Nov. 1994: 164–165.

HAYS, CONSTANCE. "Asian-American Groups Call for Breslin's Ouster Over Racial Slurs." *New York Times* 7 May 1990.

HEIZER, ROBERT F. and ALAN F. ALMQUIST. *The Other Californians: Prejudice and Discrimination Under Spain, Mexico, and the United States to 1920.* Berkeley and Los Angeles: University of California Press, 1971.

"Helping Asians Climb Through Bamboo Ceiling." *Wall Street Journal* 13 Dec. 1991.

HENRY, SARAH. "Fighting Words." *Los Angeles Times Magazine* 10 Jun. 1990: 10+.

—. "Labor & Lace." *San Francisco Chronicle* 5 Sep. 1993.

HERBERT, SOLOMON J. "Why African–Americans Vented Anger at the Korean Community During the LA Riots." *Crisis* Aug.–Sep. 1992: 5+.

HERRNSTEIN, RICHARD J. and CHARLES MURRAY. *The Bell Curve: Intelligence and Class Structure in American Life.* New York: The Free Press, 1994.

HINCH, BRET. *Passions of the Cut Sleeve: The Male Homosexual Traditions in China.* Berkeley and Los Angeles: University of California Press, 1990.

HING, ALEX. "Organizing Asian Pacific American Workers in the AFL– CIO: New Opportunities." *Amerasia Journal* 18:1 (1992): 141–154.

HING, BILL ONG. *Making and Remaking Asian America Through Immigration Policy, 1850–1990.* Stanford, CA: Stanford University Press, 1993.

HIRABAYASHI, LANE RYO. "Back to the Future: Re-framing Community-Based Research." *Amerasia Journal.* 21:1&2 (1995): 118.

HOLGUIN, RICK and JOHN LEE. "Boycott of Store Where Man Was Killed Is Urged." *Los Angeles Times* 18 Jun. 1991.

HOLMES, STEVEN A. "Survey Finds Minorities Resent One Another Almost as Much as They Do Whites." *New York Times* 3 Mar. 1994.

HOM, ALICE Y. "Stories from the Homefront: Perspectives of Asian American Parents with Lesbian Daughters and Gay Sons." *Amerasia Journal* 20:1 (1994): 19–32.

HONG, HOWARD. "Asian Americans Welcome Bush with Open Arms." *Asian Week* 21 Jun. 1991.

HORTON, JOHN. *The Politics of Diversity: Immigration, Resistance, and Change in Monterey Park, California.* Philadelphia: Temple University Press, 1995.

HOUSTON, VELINA HASU. "It's Time to Overcome the Legacy of Racism in Theater." *Los Angeles Times* 18 Aug. 1990.

"How Los Angeles Reached the Crisis Point Again, Chapter 5." *Los Angeles Times* 11 May 1992, Special Report: T10.

"How to Tell Your Friends from the Japs." *Time* 22 Dec., 1941: 33.

HSIA, JAYJIA. "Asian Americans Fight the Myth of the Super Student." *Educational Record* Fall 1987–Winter 1988: 94–97.

HUDDLE, DONALD. *The Cost of Immigration.* Washington, DC: Carrying Capacity Network, 1993.

HUGHES, BETH. "Ethnic Formula for Success." *San Francisco Examiner* 28 Jan. 1990.

HUNE, SHIRLEY. "Rethinking Race: Paradigms and Policy Formation." *Amerasia Journal* 21:1&2 (1995): 29–40.

HUYNH, CRAIG TRINH-PHAT. "Vietnamese-Owned Manicure Businesses in Los Angeles." *Reframing the Immigration Debate.* Bill Ong Hing and Ronald Lee, eds. Los Angeles: LEAP Asian Pacific American Policy Institute and UCLA Asian American Studies Center, 1996. 195–203.

HUYNH, CUONG QUY and GERALDINE V. PADILLA. "Vietnamese Knowledge and Attitudes about HIV/AIDS." Association for Asian American Studies Conference. Washington, DC. 29 May –2 June, 1996.

HWANG, HENRY DAVID. *M. Butterfly.* New York: Penguin Books, 1988.

ICHIOKA, YUJI. *The Issei: The World of the First Generation Japanese Immigrants, 1885–1924.* New York: The Free Press, 1988.

IGNACIO, ABRAHAM F., JR. and H. C. TORIBIO. "The House of Pain." *Filipinas* Sept. 1994: 19.

"Interracial Children Pose Challenge for Classifiers." *Wall Street Journal* 27 Jan. 1993.

ISSACS, HAROLD. *Images of Asia: American Views of China and India.* New York: Harper, 1972.

JACKSON, PETER A. *Male Homosexuality in Thailand: An Interpretation of Contemporary Thai Sources.* Elmhurst, NY: Global Academic Press, 1989.

JACOBUS, PATRICIA. "Oakland's Council's 'Asian Seat' Not a Sure Thing." *San Francisco Chronicle* 24 May 1994.

JACOBY, RUSSELL and NAOMI GLAUBERMAN, eds. *The Bell Curve Debate: History, Documents, Opinions.* New York: Random House.

JASCHIK, SCOTT. "Affirmative-Action Ruling on Connecticut Called a 'Big Step' for Asian Americans." *The Chronicle of Higher Education* 19 May 1993.

JENSEN, ARTHUR. *Educability and Group Difference.* New York: Harper, 1973.

JENSEN, JOAN. *Passage from India: Asian Indian Immigrants in North America.* New Haven: Yale University Press, 1988.

"Jessica McClintock Just Doesn't Get It." *New York Times* 14 Feb. 1994.

JOHNSON, CLARENCE. "2nd Choice Easily Wins Key SF Job." *San Francisco Chronicle* 28 Mar. 1995.

JORDAN, WINTHROP D. *White Over Black.* Baltimore: Penguin Books, 1969.

JOSEPH, RAYMOND. "American Men Find Asian Brides Fill the Unliberated Bill." *Wall Street Journal* 25 Jan. 1984.

KABRIA, NAZLI. *Family Tightrope: The Changing Lives of Vietnamese Americans.* Princeton: Princeton University Press, 1993.

KAM, KATHERINE. "A False and Shattered Peace." *California Tomorrow* Summer 1989: 8–21.

KANG, K. CONNIE. "No Longer 'Work, Work, Work.'" *Los Angeles Times* 22 Oct. 1994.

KANTROWITZ, BARBARA. "The Ultimate Assimilation." *Newsweek* 24 Nov. 1986: 80.

KAO, GRACE AND MARTA TIENDA. "Optimism and Achievement: The Educational Performance of Immigrant Youth." *Social Science Quarterly* 76:1 (1995): 1–19.

KAR, SNEHENDU B., KEVIN CAMPBELL, ARMANDO JIMENEZ, AND SANGEETA R. GUPTA. "Invisible Americans: An Exploration of Indo-American Quality of Life." *Amerasia Journal* 21:3 (Winter 1995–1996): 25–52.

KARKABI, BARBARA. "Betty Waki: Sharpstown Teacher Devoted to Easing School's Racial Tension." *Houston Chronicle* 24 Apr. 1989.

KARLINS, MARVIN, THOMAS L. COFFMAN, AND GARY WALTERS. "On the Fading of Social Stereotypes: Studies of Three Generations of College Students." *Journal of Personality and Psychology* 13 (1990): 4–5.

KARNOW, STANLEY. "Apathetic Asian Americans?" *Washington Post* 29 Nov. 1992.

—. *Vietnam: A History.* New York: Penguin Books, 1991.

KARNOW, STANLEY and NANCY YOSHIHARA. *Asian Americans in Transition.* New York: The Asia Society, 1992.

KATZ, JESSE and JOHN H. LEE. "Conflict Brings Tragic End to Similar Dreams of Life." *Los Angeles Times* 8 Apr. 1991.

KAUFMAN, JONATHAN. "How Cambodians Came to Control California Doughnuts." *Wall Street Journal* 22 Feb. 1995.

KEMPSKY, NELSON. *A Report to Attorney General John K. Van de Kamp on Edward Patrick Purdy and the Cleveland School Killings.* Sacramento: California Department of Justice, 1989.

KIM, BOK–LIM. "Asian Wives of U.S. Servicemen: Women in Shadows." *Amerasia Journal* 4:1 (1977): 91–116.

—. "Casework with Japanese and Korean Wives of Americans." *Social Casework* 53 (1972): 242–279.

KIM, ELAINE. "Asian Americans and American Popular Culture." *Dictionary of Asian American History.* Chicago: University of Chicago Press, 1986.

—. "They Armed in Self–Defense." *Newsweek* 18 May 1992.

KIM, ILLSOO. *New Urban Immigrants: The Korean Community in New York.* Princeton, NJ: Princeton University Press, 1981.

KIM, PAN SUK and GREGORY B. LEWIS. "Asian Americans in Public Service: Success, Diversity, and Discrimination." *Public Administration Review* 54:3 (May–Jun. 1994): 285–290.

KIM, RONALD. "The Myth and Realities of Ethnic Studies." *Asian Week* 16 Feb. 1996.

KIM, WARREN Y. *Koreans in America.* Seoul: Po Chin Chai Printing, 1971.

KITANO, HARRY. "Japanese-American Mental Illness." *Changing Perspectives on Mental Illness.* Stanley Plog and Robert Edgerton, eds. New York: Holt, 1969.

—. and LYNN CHAI. "Korean Interracial Marriage." *Marriage and Family Review* 5 (1982): 75–89.

KITANO, HARRY H. L. and ROGER DANIELS. *Asian Americans: Emerging Minorities.* 2nd ed. Englewood Cliffs, NJ: Prentice Hall, 1995.

KITANO, HARRY H. L. and WAI-TSANG YEUNG. "Chinese Interracial Marriage." *Marriage and Family Review* 5 (1982): 35–48.

KITANO, HARRY H. L., Wai–Tsang Yeung, Lynn Chai, and Herbert Hatanaka. "Asian–American Interracial Marriage." *Journal of Marriage and the Family* 46 (1984): 179–190.

KITCH, GEORGE KITAHARA. "The Developmental Process of Asserting Biracial, Bicultural Identity." *Racially Mixed People in America.* Maria Root, ed. Newbury Park, CA: Sage Press, 1992. 304–317.

KOTKIN, JOEL. *California: A Twenty-First Century Prospectus.* Denver, CO: Center for the New West, 1996.

KWOH, STEWART and MINDY HUI. "Empowering Our Communities: Political Policy." *The State of Asian Pacific America: Policy Issues to the Year 2020.* Los Angeles: LEAP Asian Pacific American Public Policy Institute and UCLA Asian American Studies Center, 1993. 189–197.

LA BRACK, BRUCE. "Occupational Specialization Among Rural California Sikhs: The Interplay of Culture and Economics," *Amerasia Journal* 9:2 (1982): 29–56.

—. and JAMES S. LAI (eds.) *1996 National Asian Pacific American Political Almanac.* Los Angeles: UCLA Asian American Studies Center, 1997.

LAM, MAY. "Hate Crime Surfaces in Affluent Neighborhood." *Asian Week* 2 Apr. 1995.

LE, NGOAN. "The Case of the Southeast Asian Refugees: Policy for a Community 'At-Risk.'" *The State of Asian Pacific America: Policy Issues to the Year 2020.* Los Angeles: LEAP Asian Pacific American Public Policy Instutute and UCLA Asian American Studies Center. 167–188.

"Leadership Training Wraps Up." *AIWA News* 10:2 (Fall 1994): 3.

LEE, BILL LANN. "Young Wing and the Americanization of China." *Amerasia Journal* 1:1 (1971): 25–32.

LEE, ELISA. "Asian American Men Bare More Than Greetings in 'Double A' Cards." *Asian Week* 11 Nov. 1994.

—. "Martin Luther King, Jr. Scholarship Recipients Depart for Seoul." *Asian Week* 17 Jun., 1994.

—. "Silicon Valley Study Finds Asian Americans Hitting the Glass Ceiling." *Asian Week* 8 Oct. 1993.

LEE, JOANN. "A Look at Asians as Portrayed in the News." *Editor & Publisher* 30 Apr. 1994: 46.

LEE, SHARON M. and KEIKO YAMANAKA. "Patterns of Asian American Intermarriage and Marital Assimilation." *Journal of Comparative Family Studies* 21 (1990): 227–305.

LELAND, JOHN AND JOHN McCORMICK. "The Quiet Race War." *Newsweek* 8 Apr. 1996: 38.

LEONARD, KAREN. *Ethnic Choices: California's Punjabi-Mexican Americans.* Philadelphia: Temple University Press, 1991.

LI, DAVID K. "Don't Stereotype Asians, Panel Tells Journalists." *Oakland Tribune* 1 Aug. 1994.

—. "Rarely Used Voting Style Advocated," *Oakland Tribune* 27 Nov. 1995.

LIAUH, WAYNE. Statement. Roundtable Conference on Asian American *Civil Rights Issues for the 1990s.* U.S. Commission on Civil Rights. Washington, DC. 27 May 1989.

LIGHT, IVAN. *Ethnic Enterprise in America.* Berkeley and Los Angeles: University of California Press, 1972.

LIM, GERARD. "JACL Formally Adopts Same-Sex Marriages." *Asian Week* 12 Aug., 1994.

—. "Lawsuit Over Chinese American HS Enrollment: Class Warfare by the Bay?" *Asian Week* 19 Aug. 1994.

LIN, CHIN–YAU and VICTORIA FU. "A Comparison of Child-Rearing Practices of American Chinese, Immigrant Chinese, and Caucasian-American Parents." *Child Development* 61:1 (1990): 429–433.

LIN, SAM CHU. "Radio Tirade." *Asian Week* 5 Apr. 1996.

LINDREN, KRISTINA. "UC Irvine Asian-American Studies Demanded." *Los Angeles Times* 23 Apr. 1993.

LINDSEY, ROBERT. "Colleges Accused of Bias to Stem Asian's Gains." *New York Times* 21 Jan. 1987.

LOEWEN, JAMES W. *The Mississippi Chinese: Between Black and White.* Cambridge, MA: Harvard University Press, 1971.

LOU, CHALSA. M. Butterfly: A Feminist Perspective." *Bearing Dreams, Shaping Visions: Asian Pacific American Perspectives.* Linda A. Revilla et al., eds. Pullman, WA: Washington State University Press, 1993. 177–180.

—. "The 'Middle-Aging' of Asian American Studies." *Reflections on Shattered Windows: Promise and Prospects for Asian American Studies.* Gary Y. Okihiro et al., eds. Pullman, WA: Washington State University Press, 1988. 16–23.

LOO, CHALSA and DON MAR. "Research and Asian Americans: Social Change or Empty Prize?" *Amerasia Journal* 12:2 (1985–1986): 85–93.

LOUIE, MIRIAM CHING. "After Sewing, Laundry, Cleaning and Cooking, I Have No Breath Left to Sing." *Amerasia Journal* 18:1 (1992): 1–26.

LOWE, LISA. "Heterogeneity, Hybridity, Multiplicity: Marking Asian American Differences." *Diaspora* Spring 1991: 24–44.

LYMAN, STANFORD. *Chinese Americans.* New York: Random House, 1974.

LYNCH, APRIL and MARC SANDALOW. "Spotlight on Asian Americans." *San Francisco Chronicle* 12 Mar. 1997.

LYNN, RICHARD. *Educational Achievement in Japan.* London: Macmillan, 1988.

—. "The Intelligence of Mongoloids: A Psychometric Evolutionary and Neurological Theory." *Personality and Individual Differences* 8:6 (1987): 813–844.

—. "IQ in Japan and in the United States Shows Great Disparity." *Nature* 297 (1982): 222–226.

MAGNER, DENISE K. "Colleges Faulted for Not Considering Differences in Asian-American Groups." *Chronicle of Higher Education,* 10 Feb. 1993: A32+.

MAGWILI, DOM. "Makibaka! Asian-American Artists Should Struggle—and Not Be Afraid." *Los Angeles Times* 13 Aug. 1990.

"MANAA's Official Statement on the Movie 'Rising Sun.'" Mar. 1993.

MANDEL, MICHAEL J. and CHRISTOPHER FARRELL. "The Immigrants: How They're Helping to Revitalize the US Economy." *Business Week* 13 Jul. 1992: 114+.

MANGAOANG, GIL. "From the 1970s to the 1990s: Perspective of a Gay Filipino American Activist." *Amerasia Journal* 20:1 (1994): 33–44.

MANGIAFICO, LUCIANO. *Contemporary American Immigrants: Patterns of Filipino, Korean, and Chinese Settlement in the United States.* New York: Praeger, 1988.

MAR, DON. "Another Look at the Enclave Economy Thesis." *Amerasia Journal* 17:3 (1991): 5–21.

MARCHETTI, GINA. *Romance and the "Yellow Peril": Race, Sex and Discursive Strategies in Hollywood Films.* Berkeley and Los Angeles: University of California Press, 1993.

MARGONELLI, LISA. "Asian Activists Give UC Berkeley Politics a New Spin." *Pacific News Service* 2–6 Jan. 1993: 3.

MARIA. "Coming Home." *A Lotus of Another Color: An Unfolding of the South Asian Gay and Lesbian Experience.* Rakesh Ratti, ed. Boston: Alyson Press, 1993.

"Marine Wins Bars After Fight Over Bias." *San Francisco Chronicle* 19 Mar. 1994.

MARK, DIANE and GINGER CHIH. *A Place Called Chinese America.* San Francisco: The Organization of Chinese Americans, 1982.

MATHEWS, LINDA. "When Being Best Isn't Good Enough." *Los Angeles Times Magazine* 19 Jul., 1987: 22–28.

MATIER, PHILLIP and ANDREW ROSS. " 'Dog' Comment Bites the S.F. Housing Chief." *San Francisco Chronicle* 17 Jul. 1995.

MAY, MEREDITH and MAI HOANG. "Crossing Color Barriers a Tough Path for Asians." *Oakland Tribune* 12 Feb. 1995.

MAZUMDAR, SUCHETA. "South Asians in the United States with a Focus on Asian Indians: Policy on New Communities." *State of Asian Pacific America: Policy Issues to the Year 2020*. Los Angeles: LEAP Asian Pacific American Public Policy Institute and UCLA Asian American Studies Center, 1993. 283–301.

MCBEE, SUSANNA. "Asian Merchants Find Ghettos Full of Peril." *U.S. News and World Report* 24 Nov. 1986.

"McClintock Attacks Free Speech Rights." *AIWA News* 10:2 (Fall 1994): 1+.

MCCORMICK, ERIN. "Filipino Guards Sue Over 'Accent Discrimination.'" *San Francisco Examiner* 15 Apr. 1993.

MCCUNN, RUTHANN LUM. *Thousand Pieces of Gold*. San Francisco: Design Enterprises, 1981.

MCFADDEN, ROBERT D. "Blacks Attack Vietnamese; One Hurt Badly." *New York Times* 14 May 1990.

MCLEOD, RAMON G. "Elderly Immigrants Swell Welfare Roles." *San Francisco Chronicle* 20 Apr. 1996.

MCNAMARA, VICTORIA. "Battling the Bamboo Ceiling." *Houston Post* 31 May 1993.

MCQUEEN, MICHAEL. "Voters' Response to Poll Disclose Huge Chasm Between Social Attitudes of Blacks and Whites." *Wall Street Journal* 17 May 1991.

MELENDY, H. BRETT. "Filipinos in the United States." *The Asian American: The Historical Experience*. Norris Hundley, Jr., ed. Santa Barbara: Cleo, 1977.

MENDEZ, CARLOS. "A Fighter for Gay Rights." *Asian Week* 22 Jul. 1994.

—. " 'Vanishing Son': No Plans to Disappear." *Asian Week* 3 Feb. 1995.

MICKELSON, ROSLYN ARLIN. "The Attitude-Achievement Paradox Among Black Adolescents. *Sociology of Education* 56 (1990): 44–61.

MILLER, JOHN J. "Asian Americans and the Republicans: A Natural Fit or a Party in Turmoil?" *Asian Week* 16 Sep. 1994.

—. "Asian Americans Head for Politics: What Horse Will They Ride?" *Asian Week* 7 Apr. 1995. Reprinted from the Mar.–Apr 1995 issue of The American Enterprise.

MILLER, SUSAN KATZ. "Asian Americans Bump Against Glass Ceilings." *Science* 13 Nov. 1992: 1225.

Miller v. Johnson. 115 S.Ct. 2475 (1995).

MILLS, C. WRIGHT. *The Sociological Imagination*. New York: Oxford University Press, 1959.

MILVY, ERIKA. "Asian American, Berkeley Rep Join Hands." *San Francisco Examiner/Chronicle* 21 Nov. 1993, Datebook Section: 21–22.

MIN, PYONG GAP, ed. *Asian Americans: Contemporary Trends and Issues*. Thousand Oaks, CA: Sage Press, 1995.

—. "Cultural and Economic Boundaries of Korean Ethnicity: A Comparative Analysis." *Ethnic and Racial Studies* 14 (1991): 225–241.

—. *Ethnic Business Enterprise: Korean Small Business in Atlanta*. New York: Center for Migration Studies, 1988.

—. "The Korean Family." *Ethnic Families in America*. Charles H. Mindel, Robert W. Habenstein, and Roosevelt Wright, Jr., eds. New York: Elsevier, 1989. 199–229.

—. "Korean Immigrant Wives' Overwork." *Korean Journal of Population and Development* 21 (1992): 23–36.

—. "The Social Costs of Immigrant Entrepreneurship: A Response to Edna Bonacich." *Amerasia Journal* 15:2 (1989): 187–194.

MINTON, TORRI. "Quiet Marin Confronts Hate Crimes." *San Francisco Chronicle* 29 Nov. 1995.

MORROW, LANCE. "Japan in the Mind of American." *Time* 10 Feb. 1992: 17–21.

MOY, JAMES S. *Marginal Sights: Staging the Chinese in America.* Iowa City: University of Iowa Press, 1993.

MURATSUCHI, ALBERT Y. "Voter Registration in the Oakland Pacific American Communities: An Agenda for the 1990s." San Francisco: The Coro Foundation, 1990.

MYDANS, SETH. "New Unease for Japanese Americans." *New York Times* 4 Mar. 1992.

MYERS, LAURA. "Spelling Bee Sweep." *Asian Week* 7 Jun., 1996.

NAGATA, DONNA. *Legacy of Injustice: Exploring the Cross-Generational Impact of the Japanese American Internment.* NY: Plenum Press, 1993.

NAKANISHI, DON T. "The Next Swing Vote? Asian Pacific Americans and California Politics." *Racial and Ethnic Politics in California.* Bryan O. Jackson and Michael B. Preston, eds. Berkeley: IGS Press, 1991. 25–54.

—. "Asian American Politics: An Agenda for Research." *Amerasia Journal* 12:2 (1985–1986): 1–27.

—. "UCLA Asian Pacific American Voter Registration Study." Sponsored by the Asian Pacific American Legal Center, 1986.

NAKANO, ANNIE. "Asian Americans Vote Big." *San Francisco Examiner* 15 Dec. 1996.

NAKASHIMA, CYNTHIA L. "An Invisible Monster: The Creation and Denial of Mixed-Race People in America." *Racially Mixed People in America.* Maria Root, ed. Newbury Park, CA: Sage Press, 1992. 162–178.

NAMKOONG, FRANCES M. "Stereotyping Is Holding Asian-Americans Back." *Cleveland Plain Dealer* 17 May 1994.

NARIKIYO, TRUDY and VELMA KAMEOKA. "Attributions of Mental Illness and Judgments About Help Seeking Among Japanese American and White Students." *Journal of Counseling Psychology* 39:3 (1992): 363–369.

NASH, J. MADELEINE. "Tigers in the Lab." *Time* 21 Nov. 1994:86–87.

NASH, PHIL TAJITSU and FRANK WU. "Asian-Americans under Glass: Where the Furor Over the President's Fundraising has Gone Wrong—and Racist." *The Nation* 24:12 (31 Mar. 1997): 15+.

National Asian Pacific American Legal Consortium. *1993 Audit of Violence Against Asian Pacific Americans.* 1st Annual Report.

—. *1994 Audit of Violence Against Asian Pacific Americans.* 2nd Annual Report.

—. *1995 Audit of Violence Against Asian Pacific Americans.* 3rd Annual Report.

National Center for Education Statistics. *Digest of Educational Statistics, 1995.* Washington, DC: U.S. Department of Education, Office of Research and Improvement, 1995. Tables 138, 136.

National Science Foundation. *Women and Minorities in Science and Engineering.* Washington, DC: GPO, 1990.

Naturalization Act of 1790, I Stat. 103 (1790).

NEE, VICTOR G. and BRETT DE BARY NEE. *Longtime Californ': A Documentary Study of an American Chinatown.* Boston: Houghton, 1974.

NGIN, CHOR–SWAN. "The Acculturation Pattern of Orange County's Southeast Asian Refugees." *Journal of Orange County Studies.* 3:4 (Fall 1989–Spring 1990): 46–53.

NJERI, ITABARI. "Power Elite Turns Out a Bitter Brew." *Los Angeles Times* 29 Nov. 1991.

NOLTE, CARL. "Racism Charge Over Mariners Sale." *San Francisco Chronicle* 7 Feb. 1992.

Oakland, City of. "Asian Advisory Committee on Crime." Police Dept.: Community Services Div., 1996.

OGBU, JOHN AND MARIA MATUTE-BIANCHI. "Understanding Sociocultural Factors: Knowledge, Identity, and School Adjustment." *Beyond Language: Social and Cultural Factors in Schooling Language Minority Students.* California State Department of Education. Los Angeles: California State Department of Education, 1986. 73–142.

OKAMURA, RAYMOND. "Farewell to Manzanar: A Case of Subliminal Racism." *Counterpoint: Perspectives on Asian America.* Emma Gee, ed. Los Angeles: UCLA Asian American Studies Center, 1976. 280–283.

OKIHIRO, GARY Y. *Margins and Mainstreams: Asian American History and Culture.* Seattle: University of Washington Press, 1994.

OLSEN, LAURIE. *Crossing the Schoolhouse Border: Immigrant Students and the California Public Schools.* San Francisco: California Tomorrow, 1988.

OMATSU, GLEN. "Expansion of Democracy." *Amerasia Journal* 18:1 (1992): v–xix.

OMI, MICHAEL. "It Just Ain't the Sixties No More: The Contemporary Dilemmas of Asian American Studies." *Reflections on Shattered Windows: Promise and Prospects for Asian American Studies.* Gary Y. Okihiro et al., eds. Pullman, WA: Washington State University Press, 1988. 31–36.

OMI, MICHAEL and HOWARD WINANT. *Racial Formation in the United States: From the 1960s to the 1980s.* New York: Routledge, 1986.

—. *Racial Formation in the United States: From the 1960s to the1990s.* 2nd ed. New York: Routledge, 1994.

ONG, PAUL and TANIA AZORES. "Health Professionals on the Front-Line." *The State of Asian Pacific America: Economic University, Issues & Policies.* Paul Ong, ed. Los Angeles: LEAP Asian Pacific American Public Policy Institute and UCLA Asian American Studies Center, 1994. 139–164.

—. "The Migration and Incorporation of Filipino Nurses." *The New Asian Immigration in Los Angeles and Global Restructuring.* Paul Ong et al., eds. Philadelphia: Temple University Press, 1994.

ONG, PAUL and EVELYN BLUMENBERG. "Scientists and Engineers." *The State of Asian Pacific America: Economic Diversity, Issues & Policies.* Paul Ong, ed. Los Angeles: LEAP Asian Pacific American Public Policy Institute and UCLA Asian American Studies Center, 1994. 165–192.

—. "Welfare and Work Among Southeast Asians." *The State of Asian Pacific America: Economic Diversity, Issues & Policies.* Paul Ong, ed. Los Angeles: LEAP Asian Pacific American Public Policy Institute and UCLA Asian American Studies Center, 1994. 113–138.

ONG, PAUL, EDNA BONACICH, and LUCIE CHENG, eds. *The New Asian Immigration in Los Angeles and Global Restructuring.* Philadelphia: Temple University Press, 1994.

ONG, PAUL and SUZANNE J. HEE. "The Growth of the Asian Pacific American Population: Twenty Million in 2020." *The State of Asian Pacific America: Policy Issues to the Year 2020.* Los Angeles: LEAP Asian Pacific American Public Policy Institute and UCLA Asian American Studies Center, 1993. 11–24.

—. "Work Issues Facing Asian Pacific Americans: Labor Policy." *The State of Asian Pacific American: Policy Issues to the Year 2020.* Los Angeles: LEAP Asian Pacific American Public Policy Institute and UCLA Asian American Studies Center, 1993. 141–152.

ONG, PAUL and DON NAKANISHI. "Becoming Citizens, Becoming Voters: The Naturalization and Political Participation of Asian Pacific Immigrants." *Reframing the Immigration Debate.* Bill Ong Hing and Ronald Lee, eds. Los Angeles: LEAP Asian Pacific American Policy Institute and UCLA Asian American Studies Center, 1996. 292–293.

"Opponent Calls Senate Candidate a Japanese Agent." *San Francisco Chronicle* 27 Oct. 1990.

ORONDA, TRINITY. "In Our Own Way." *Amerasia Journal* 20:1 (1994): 137–147.

OSAJIMA, KEITH. "Asian Americans as the Model Minority: An Analysis of the Popular Press Image in the 1960s and 1980s." *Reflections on Shattered Windows: Promises and Prospects for Asian American Studies.* Gary Y. Okihiro et al., eds. Pullman, WA: Washington State University Press, 1988. 165–174.

—. "Postmodern Possibilities: The Theoretical and Political Directions for Asian American Studies." *Amerasia Journal* 21:1&2 (1995): 79–87.

OSUMI, MEGUMI DICK. "Asians and California's Anti-Miscegenation Laws." *Asian and Pacific American Experiences: Women's Perspectives.* Nobuya Tsuchida, ed. Minneapolis, MN: Asian/Pacific American Learning Resource Center, University of Minnesota, 1982. 1–37.

OXFORD–CARPENTER, REBECCA, et al. *Demographic Projections of Non-English-Language-Background and Limited-English-Proficient Persons.* Rosslyn, VA: Inter-America Research Associates, 1984.

Ozawa v. United States. 260 US 178 (1922).

PAIK, FELICIA. "Say Anything." *A Magazine* Feb.–Mar. 1995: 34.

PARK, EDWARD JANG-WOO. "Asians Matter: Asian American Entrepreneurs in the Silicon Valley High Technology Industry." *Reframing the Immigration Debate.* Bill Ong Hing and Ronald Lee, eds. Los Angeles: LEAP Asian Pacific American Public Policy Institute and UCLA Asian American Studies Center, 1996. 155–178.

PASSEL, JEFFERY S. "Immigrants and Taxes: A Reappraisal of Huddle's 'The Cost of Immigrants.'" Washington, DC: Program for Research on Immigration Policy, The Urban Institute, Jan. 1994.

PENG, SAMUEL, et al. "School Experiences and Performance of Asian American High School Students." Paper presented at the Annual Meeting of the American Educational Research Association, New Orleans. Apr. 1984.

PENG, SAMUEL S. and DEEANN WRIGHT. "Explanation of Academic Achievement of Asian American Students." *Journal of Educational Research* 87:6 (1994): 346–352.

PETERSEN, WILLIAM. *Japanese Americans.* New York: Random House, 1971.

—. "Success Story, Japanese-American Style." *New York Times Magazine* 9 Jan. 1966: 20+.

PHINNEY, JEAN. "Stages of Ethnic Identity Development in Minority Group Adolescents." *Journal of Early Adolescence* 9 (1989): 34–49.

PIMENTEL, BENJAMIN. " 'All–American Girl' Stirs Debate Among Asians." *San Francisco Chronicle* 1 Nov. 1994.

—. "One Man's War Against Marines." *San Francisco Chronicle.* 5 Feb. 1994.

PIMENTEL, BENJAMIN and CHARLES BURRESS. "Oakland Tribune Fires Respected Columnist Wong." *San Francisco Chronicle* 26 Mar. 1996.

POPE, LISA. "Asian American Businesses Targeted." *Los Angeles Daily News* 1 May 1992.

PORTES, ALEJANDRO and ROBERT BACH. *Latin Journey: Cuban and Mexican Immigrants in the United States.* Berkeley and Los Angeles: University of California Press, 1985.

PORTES, ALEJANDRO and RUBEN G. RUMBAUT. *Immigrant America: A Portrait.* Berkeley and Los Angeles: University of California Press, 1990.

POSADAS, BARBARA M. "Crossed Boundaries in Interracial Chicago: Filipino American Families Since 1925." *Amerasia Journal* 8:2 (1981): 31–52.

PRESTONOWITZ, CLYDE V. *Trading Places: How We Are Giving Our Future to Japan and How to Reclaim It.* New York: Basic Books, 1989.

"The Push to 'Buy American.'" *Newsweek* 3 Feb. 1992: 32–35.

PYE, LUCIEN. *Asian Power and Politics: The Cultural Dimensions of Authority.* Cambridge, MA: Belknap Press, 1985.

"Questions and Answers on Lowell High Series." *San Francisco Chronicle* 29 Jun. 1995.

"Racist Convicted in Firebombings Faces New Trial." *San Francisco Chronicle* 1 Sep. 1994.

RAGAZA, ANGELO. "All of the Above." *A Magazine* 3:1 (1994): 76.

RANDOLPH, ELEANOR. "In N.Y., the Breslin Backlash: Asians Demanded Ouster after Newsday Tirade." *Washington Post* 8 May 1990.

RATTI, RAKESH, ed. *A Lotus of Another Color: An Unfolding of the South Asian Gay and Lesbian Experience.* Boston: Alyson Press, 1993.

REICH, ROBERT B. *The Work of Nations.* New York: Alfred A. Knopf, 1991.

REILLY, RICK. "Heaven Help Her." *Sports Illustrated* 20 May 1996: 77–78.

REINHOLD, ROBERT. "Buying American Is No Cure-All, U.S. Economists Say." *New York Times* 27 Jan. 1992.

RICHMOND, RAY. "ABC Gives Innovation 'All-American Try.'" *Los Angeles Daily News* 14 Sep. 1994.

RIGDON, JOHN E. "Asian-American Youth Suffer a Rising Toll From Heavy Pressures." *Wall Street Journal* 10 Jul. 1991.

"Rising Toll of Hate Crimes Cited in Student's Slaying." *Los Angeles Times* 10 Oct. 1992.

RIVERA, CARLA. "Asians Say They Fare Better Than Other Minorities." *Los Angeles Times* 20 Aug. 1993.

ROSENBLATT, ROBERT A. " 'Glass Ceiling' Still Too Hard to Break, U.S. Panel Finds." *Los Angeles Times* 16 MAR. 1995.

ROTHENBERG, STUART. "The Invisible Success Story." *National Review* 15 Sep. 1989: 43–45.

RUMBAUT, RUBEN. "Mental Health and the Refugee Experience. *Southeast Asian Mental Health: Treatment, Prevention, Services, Traning and Research.* Tom C. Owen, ed. Rockville, MD: National Institute of Mental Health, 1985. 433–486.

—. "Vietnamese, Laotian, and Cambodian Americans." *Asian Americans: Contemporary Trends and Issues.* Pyong Gap Min, ed. Thousand Oaks, CA: Sage Publications, 1985.

RUMBAUT, RUBEN G. and KENJI IMA. *The Adaptation of Southeast Asian Refugee Youth: A Comparative Study, Final Report to the U.S. Department of Health and Human Services, Office of Refugee Resettlement.* Jan. 1988.

RUMBAUT, RUBEN and J. R. WEEKS. "Fertility and Adaptation: Indochinese Refugees in the United States." *International Migration Review* 20:2 (1986): 428–466.

RUTTIN, TIM. "A New Kind of Riot." *The New York Review* 11 Jun. 1992.

SAITO, LELAND T. "Asian Americans and Latinos in San Gabriel Valley, California: Ethnic Political Cooperation and Redistricting 1990–1992." *Amerasia Journal* 19:2 (1993): 55–68.

SANDERS, JIMY AND VICTOR NEE. "Limits of Ethnic Solidarity in the Enclave Economy." *American Sociological Review* 52 (1987): 745–767.

SANTOS, BIENVENIDO. "Filipinos in War." *Far Eastern Survey* 11 (1942): 249–250.

SAVAGE, DAVID G. "Study Finds U.S. Asians Get More School, Less Pay." *Los Angeles Times* 18 Sept. 1992.

SCHAPIRO, WALTER. "Japan Bashing on the Campaign Train." *Time* 10 Feb. 1992: 23–24.

SCHMIDT, ERIC. "Asian-American Proves Marine Bias." *New York Times* 21 Jan. 1994.

SCHNIDER, BARBARA and YOUNGSOOK LEE. "A Model for Academic Success: The School and Home Environment of East Asian Students." *Anthropology & Education Quarterly* 21:4 (1990): 358–377.

SCHUYLER, NINA. "Asian Women Come Out Swinging." *The Progressive* May, 1993: 14.

SCHWARTZ, MARY ANN and BARBARA MARLIENE SCOTT. *Marriages and Families: Diversity and Change.* Englewood Cliffs, NJ: Prentice Hall, 1994.

"Science Prodigy Mixes Biochemistry, Music and Laughter." *Oakland Tribune* 26 Mar. 1995.

SCOTT, WILLIAM and RUTH SCOTT. *Adaptation of Immigrants: Individual Differences and Determinants.* Oxford: Pergamon, 1989.

SENGUPTA, SOMINI. "Charlie Chan, Retooled for the 90's," *New York Times* 5 Jan. 1997.

SEYMOUR, GENE. "When Simple Isn't Good Enough." *Los Angeles Times* 25 Jul. 1993.

SHIN, EUI-HANG and SHIN-KAP HAN. "Korean Immigrant Small Businesses in Chicago: An Analysis of the Resource Mobilization Process." *Amerasia Journal* 16:1 (1990): 39–60.

SHINAGAWA, LARRY H. "Asian Pacific Electoral Participation in the San Francisco Bay Area: A Study of the Exit Poll Results of the November 8, 1994 Elections for the Cities of Daly City, San Francisco, and Oakland." San Francisco: Asian Law Caucus, 1995.

SHINAGAWA LARRY H. and GIN Y. PANG. "Asian American Pan-Ethnicity and Intermarriage." *Amerasia Journal* 22:2 (1996): 127–152.

—. "Marriage Patterns of Asian Americans in California, 1980." *Income and Status Differences Between White and Minority Americans*. Sucheng Chan, ed. Lewiston, NY: Edwin Mellon Press, 1990: 225–282.

SHIOYA, TARA. "For the Lys, American Is an Ongoing Journey." *San Francisco Chronicle* 9 Dec. 1994.

—. "Recalling Insights—and Slights." *San Francisco Chronicle* 20 Jun. 1995.

SIM, SHARON YEN-LING. "Parent's Wishes and Children's Dreams Are Sources of Conflict." *Asian Week* 2 Sept. 1995.

SIMON, JULIAN L. *Immigration: The Demographic and Economic Facts*. Washington, DC: The Cato Institute and the National Immigration Forum, 1995.

—. "Studies on Immigrants Prove They'd Rather Give Than Receive." Letter to the Editor. *New York Times* 26 Feb. 1994.

SINGH, GURDIAL. "East Indians in the United States." *Sociology and Social Research* 30:3 (1946): 209–216.

Sinha, Tito. "P.R. Elections in N.Y.C.: Effects of Preference Voting on Asian-American Participation." *National Civic Review* 83:1 (Winter–Spring 1994): 80-83.

SONG, YOUNG I. *Silent Victims: Battered Women in Korean Immigrant Families*. San Francisco: Oxford Press, 1987.

SOWELL, THOMAS. *The Economics and Politics of Race: An International Perspective*. New York: Quill, 1983.

—. *Ethnic America*. New York: Basic Books, 1981.

—. *Race and Culture: A World View*. New York: Basic Books, 1994.

STAATS, CRAIG. "Council Candidate Exaggerated Credentials." *Oakland Tribune* 20 May 1994.

—. "Hu and Her Supporters Can't Agree on Stand." *Oakland Tribune* 17 May 1994.

STALLONE, STEVE. "Crossing Lines." *San Francisco Bay Guardian* 8 Dec. 1993.

—. "White Noise." *The Bay Guardian* 21 Jul. 1993.

STAPLES, ROBERT and ALFREDO MIRANDE. "Racial and Cultural Variations Among American Families: A Decennial Review of the Literature on Minority Families." *Journal of Marriage and the Family* 42:4 (1980): 887–903.

"State Wide Exit Poll." *Los Angeles Times* 10 Nov. 1994.

STEINBERG, LAURENCE, et al. "Ethnic Differences in Adolescent Achievement: An Ecological Perspective." *American Psychologist* 47:6 (1992): 723–729.

STEINBERG, STEPHEN. *The Ethnic Myth: Race, Ethnicity, and Class in America*. Boston: Beacon Press, 1981.

STEINER, STAN. *Fushang: The Chinese Who Built America*. New York: Harper, 1979.

STERBA, JAMES P. "Indians in U.S. Prosper in Their New Country, and Not Just in Motels." *Wall Street Journal* 27 Jan. 1987.

STEVENSON, HAROLD W. et al. "Cognitive Performance and Academic Achievement of Japanese, Chinese, and American Children." *Child Development* 56 (1985): 718–734.

STINNETT, PEGGY. "Racism Is in the Air, Literally and Otherwise." *Oakland Tribune* 30 Oct. 1994.

STRAND, PAUL J. and WOODROW JONES, JR. *Indochinese Refugees in America: Problems of Adaptation and Assimilation.* Durham, NC: Duke University Press, 1985.

STRAUSS, ASELM. "Strain and Harmony in American-Japanese War-bride Marriages." *Marriage and Family Living* 16 (1954): 99–106.

"Success Story of One Minority Group in the U.S." *U.S. News and World Report* 26 Dec. 1966: 73–78.

SUE, STANLEY. "Mental Health Policy." *The State of Asian Pacific America: Policy Issues to the Year 2020.* Los Angeles: LEAP Asian Pacific American Policy Institute and UCLA Asian American Studies Center, 1993. 79–94.

SUE, STANLEY and HARRY KITANO. "Stereotypes as a Measure of Success." *Journal of Social Issues* 29 (1973): 83–98.

SUE, STANLEY and SUMIE OKAZAKI. "Asian-American Educational Achievements: A Phenomenon in Search of an Explanation." *American Psychologist* 46:8 (1990): 913–920.

—. "Explanations for Asian-American Achievements: A Reply." *American Psychologist* 46:8 (1991): 878–880.

SUNG, BETTY LEE. *The Adjustment Experience of Chinese Immigrant Children in New York City.* New York: Center for Migration Studies, 1987.

—. *Chinese American Intermarriage.* New York: Center for Migration Studies, 1990.

—. *The Story of the Chinese in America.* New York: Macmillan, 1967.

"A 'Superminority' Tops Out." *Newsweek* 11 May 1987: 48–49.

"Support for JACL Decision." *Asian Week* 12 Aug. 1994.

SURO, ROBERT. "Study of Immigrants Finds Asians at Top in Science and Medicine." *The Washington Post* 18 Apr. 1994.

SUZUKI, BOB H. "Education and the Socialization of Asian Americans: A Revisionist Analysis of the 'Model Minority' Thesis." *Amerasia Journal* 4:2 (1977): 23–51.

SWORD, SUSAN. "New SF Police Chief Is Widely Respected." *San Francisco Chronicle* 9 Jan. 1996.

TAJAMI, RENEE. "Moving the Image: Asian American Independent Filmmaking 1970–1980." *Moving the Image: Independent Asian Pacific American Media Arts.* Russell Leong, ed. Los Angeles: UCLA Asian American Studies Center and Visual Communications, Southern California Asian American Studies Central, Inc., 1991: 10–33.

TAKAGI, DANA Y. "Maiden Voyage: Excursion into Sexuality and Identity Politics in Asian America." *Amerasia Journal* 20:1 (1994): 1–18.

—. *The Retreat from Race* New Brunswick, NJ: Rutgers University Press, 1992.

TAKAKI, RONALD. *Strangers from a Different Shore.* Boston: Little Brown and Co., 1989.

TAYLOR, DANIEL B. "Asian-American Test Scores: They Deserve a Closer Look." *Education Week* 17 OCT. 1990: 23.

TAYLOR, RONALD L. "Black American Families." *Minority Families in the United States: A Multicultural Approach.* Ronald L. Taylor, ed. Englewood Cliffs, NJ: Prentice Hall, 1994. 19–24.

TENBROEK, JACOBUS, EDWARD N. BARNHART, and FLOYD W. MATSON. *Prejudice, War, and the Constitution.* Berkeley and Los Angeles: University of California Press, 1970.

"Tolerance of Bigotry Has Run Out." *Los Angeles Times* 11 May 1990.

TOMLINSON, TOMMY. *Hard Work and High Expectations: Motivating Students to Learn.* Washington, DC: GPO, 1992.

TRUEBA, HENRY T., LILLY CHENG, and KENJI IMA. *Myth or Reality: Adaptive Strategies of Asian Americans in California.* Washington, DC: The Falmer Press, 1993.

TSAI, SHIH–SHAN HENRY. *The Chinese Experience in America.* Bloomington: Indiana University Press, 1986.

TSANG, DANIEL C. "Founder of First Gay and Lesbian Asian Group Succumbs to AIDS." *Asian Week* 2 Sep. 1994.

—. "Jury Awards Vietnamese American Bashing Victim $1.1 Million Sum." *Asian Week* 24 Mar. 1995.

TSENG, WEN-SHING, JOHN MCDERMOTT, and THOMAS MARETZKI. *Adjustment in Intercultural Marriage.* Hawaii: University Press of Hawaii, 1977.

"Tung Case Pries Open Secret Tenure Review." *The Berkeley Graduate* Apr. 1990.

UBA, LAURA. *Asian Americans: Personality Patterns, Identity, and Mental Health.* New York: Guilford Press, 1994.

"UC Berkeley Apologizes for Policy that Limited Asians." *Los Angeles Times* 7 Apr. 1989.

UDESKY, LAURIE. "Sweatshops Behind the Labels." *The Nation* 16 May 1994: 665–668.

UHLANDER, CAROL, BRUCE CAIN, and D. RODERICK KIEWIET. "Political Participation of Ethnic Minorities in the 1980's." *Political Behavior* 11:3 (1989): 195–231.

UMEMOTO, KAREN. " 'On Strike!' San Francisco State College Strike, 1968–1969." *Amerasia Journal* 15:1 (1991): 3–41.

United States. Bureau of the Census. *Characteristics of Business Owners, 1992.* Washington, DC: GPO, 1992.

—. *1990 Census of the Population, Asians and Pacific Islanders in the United States.* Washington, DC: GPO, 1993.

—. *1990 Census of the Population, Social and Economic Characteristics, Metropolitan Areas.* Washington, DC: GPO, 1994.

—. Commission on Civil Rights. *Civil Rights Issues Facing Asian Americans in the 1990s.* Washington, DC: GPO, 1992.

—. Commission on Wartime Relocation and Internment of Civilians. *Personal Justice Denied.* Washington, DC: GPO, 1982.

—. Committee for Refugees. *Cambodians in Thailand: People on the Edge.* Washington, DC: GPO, 1985.

—. *Refugees from Laos: In Harm's Way.* Washington, DC: GPO, 1986.

—. *Uncertain Harbors: The Plight of Vietnamese Boat People.* Washington, DC: GPO, 1987.

—. Dept. of Commerce. *Statistical Abstract of the United States,1995.* Washington, DC: GPO, 1995.

—. *Survey of Minority-Owned Business Enterprises: Asian Americans, American Indians, and Other Minorities.* Washington, DC: GPO, Jun. 1991.

—. Dept. of Education. *The Condition of Bilingual Education in the Nation, 1982: A Report from the Secretary of Education to the President and the Congress.* Washington, DC: GPO, 1982.

—. Office for Civil Rights. "Statement of Findings." (For Compliance Review No. 01–88–6009 on Harvard University.) Washington, DC: GPO, 4 Oct. 1990.

—. Dept. of Justice. Immigration and Naturalization Service. *1993 Statistical Yearbook of the Immigration and Naturalization Service.* Washington, DC: GPO, 1994.

—. *1994 Statistical Yearbook of the Immigration and Naturalization Service.* Washington, DC: GPO, 1996.

—. Dept. of Labor. "Projections of Occupational Employment, 1988–2000." *BLS Monthly Labor Review* Nov. 1989: 51–59.

—. Equal Employment Opportunity Commission. *Annual Report on the Employment of Minorities, Women and Handicapped Individuals in the Federal Government* Washington, DC: GPO, 1990.

—. Federal Communications Commission. "1995 Broadcast and Cable Employment Report." Washington, DC: GPO, 12 Jun. 1996.

United States v. Ronald Ebans 800 F.2nd. 1422 (1986 6th Cir.).

United States v. Bhagat Singh Thind. 261 U.S. 204 (1923).

"Up from Inscrutable." *Fortune* 6 Apr. 1992: 120.

VALVERDE, KIEU-LINH CAROLINE. "From Dust to Gold: The Amerasian Experience." *Racially Mixed People in America.* Maria Root, ed. Newbury Park, CA: Sage Publications, 1992. 144–161.

VAN WOLFEN, KARL. *The Enigma of Japanese Power.* New York: Alfred A. Knopf, 1989.

VARTABEDIAN, RALPH. "Aerospace Careers in Low Orbit." *Los Angeles Times* 16 Nov. 1992.

VILLAPANDO, VENNY. "The Business of Selling Mail-Order Brides." *Making Waves.* Asian Women United, eds. Boston: Beacon Press, 1989.

"Vision for the 21st Century." *Asian Week* 24 May 1996.

VISWANATHAN, VINESH. "Seeing the Person, Not the Color." *San Francisco Chronicle* 17 May 1995.

VIVIANO, FRANK. "Strangers in the Promised Land." *Image* 31 Aug. 1986: 15+.

WACHS, ESTER. "The East Is Hot." *Far Western Review* 23 Dec. 1993: 34–35.

WAIN, BARRY L. *The Refused: The Agony of Indochina Refugees.* New York: Simon & Schuster, 1981.

WALDINGER, ROGER. "Immigrant Enterprise and the Structure of the Labor Market." *New Approaches to Economic Life.* Bryan Roberts et al., eds. Manchester: Manchester University Press, 1985.

WALSH, JOAN. "Asian Women, Caucasian Men." *Image* 2 Dec. 1990: 11–17.

WANG, L. LING-CHI. "Foreign Money Is No Friend of Ours." *Asian Week* 8 Nov. 1996.

—. "Lau v. Nichols: History of a Struggle for Equal and Quality Education." *Amerasia Journal* 2:2 (1974): 16–45.

—. "Meritocracy and Diversity in Higher Education: Discrimination Against Asian Americans in the Post-Bakke Era." *The Urban Review* 20:3 (1991): 202–203.

—. "The Politics of Ethnic Identity and Empowerment: The Asian American Community Since the 1960s." *Asian American Policy Review* 2 (Spring 1991): 43–56.

—. "Trends in Admissions for Asian Americans in Colleges and Universities: Higher Education Policy." *The State of Asian Pacific America: Policy Issues to the Year 2020.*

Los Angeles: LEAP Asian Pacific American Public Policy Institute and UCLA Asian American Studies Center, 1993. 49–60.

WATANABE, TSUNEO and JUN'ICHI IVATA. Translated by Dr. R. Roberts. *The Love of the Samurai: A Thousand Years of Japanese Homosexuality.* London: Gay Men's Press, 1989.

WAUGH, DEXTER. "Stanford Lacks Asian American Studies." *San Francisco Examiner* 25 Feb. 1994.

WAUGH, DEXTER and STEVEN A. CHIN. "Daly City: New Manila." *San Francisco Examiner* 17 Sep. 1989.

WEI, WILLIAM. *The Asian American Movement.* Philadelphia: Temple University Press, 1993.

WEST, CORNEL. *Race Matters.* Boston: Beacon Press, 1993.

WESTHOFF, CHARLES F. and NOREEN GOLDMAN. "Figuring the Odds in the Marriage Market." *Current Issues in Marriage and the Family.* J. Gipson Wells, ed. New York: Macmillan, 1988. 39–46.

"Why They Count: Immigrant Contributions to the Golden State." Claremont, CA: Tomas Rivera Center, 1996.

WILGOREN, JODI. "High Pressure High." *Los Angeles Times* 4 Dec. 1994.

WILL, GEORGE F. "The Lunacy of Punishing Those Who Try to Excel." *Los Angeles Times* 16 Apr. 1989.

WILLIAMS, DENNIS. "A Formula for Success." *Newsweek* 23 Apr. 1984: 77–78.

WILLIAMS, TERESA K. "Marriage Betwen Japanese Women and U.S. Servicemen Since World War II." *Amerasia Journal* 17:1 (1991): 135–154.

WILLIAMSON, B. C. CHANG. "M. Butterfly: Passivity, Deviousness, and the Invisibility of the Asian American Male." *Bearing Dreams, Shaping Visions: Asian Pacific American Perspectives.* Linda A. Revilla et al., eds. Pullman, WA: Washington State University Press, 1993. 181–184.

WILSON, YUMI. "Designer's Largesse Questioned." *San Francisco Chronicle* 16 Feb. 1994.

Yick Wo v. Hopkins. 118 U.S. 356 (1886).

WONG, BILL. "Human Cargo." *Asian Week* 26 Apr. 1996.

—. "Sweatshop Fame." *Asian Week* 21 Jun. 1996.

WONG, DIANE YEN-MEI. "Will the Real Asian Pacific American Please Stand Up?" *The State of Asian Pacific America: Policy Issues to the Year 2020.* Los Angeles: LEAP Asian Pacific American Public Policy Institute and UCLA Asian American Studies Center, 1993. 270–273.

WONG, KENT. "Building An Asian Pacific Labor Alliance: A New Chapter in our History." *The State of Asian America: Activism and Resistance in the 1990s.* Karin Aguilar-San Juan, ed. Boston: South End Press, 1994. 335–349.

WONG, MORRISON G. "The Chinese American Family." *Ethnic Families in America.* Charles H. Mindel, Robert W. Habenstein, and Roosevelt Wright, Jr., eds. New York: Elsevier, 1989. 230–257.

WONG, SAU-LING, C. "Denationalization Reconsidered: Asian American Cultural Criticism at a Theoretical Crossroads." *Amerasia Journal* 21:1&2 (1995): 1–27.

WONG, WILLIAM. "A Disappointing 'All–American Girl.'" *Oakland Tribune* 9 Oct. 1994.

—. "Election Exposes Chinatown Fissues." Oakland Tribune 25 May, 1994.

—. "Loser Helps Winner: What a Concept." *Oakland Tribune* 5 Jul. 1995.

—. "Unseemly Tactics in Redistricting Fight." *Oakland Tribune* 16 Jul. 1993.

WOOD, DANIEL B. "As Korean Americans Become Visible, They Seek Understanding." *Christian Science Monitor* 27 Jul. 1993.

WU, FRANK. "Campaign of Our Own." *Asian Week* 22 Mar. 1996.

—. "Fundraising Investigation Targets APA's." *Asian Week* 7 Mar. 1997.

—. "Push for Citizenship." *Asian Week* 21 Jun. 1996.

YAMAMOTO, J. K. "Cho Watch." *San Francisco Bay Guardian* 7 Dec. 1994.

YANG, CATHERINE. "In Any Language, It's Unfair." *Business Week* 21 Jun. 1993: 110, 111.

YIP, ALTHEA. "Asian Votes Shift to the Left." *Asian Week* 11 Nov. 1996.

—. "ROTC Rebel." *Asian Week* 23 Feb. 1996.

—. "S.F. Initiative Seeks Vote for Noncitizens." *Asian Week* 3 May 1996.

—. "Talk of the Town." *Asian Week* 29 Mar. 1996.

YIP, JEFF. "A Heroic Leading Role for One Asian 'Son.'" *Los Angeles Times* 25 Mar. 1995.

YOO, PAULA. "Troubled Waters." *A Magazine* 1:4 (1992): 14+.

YOON, IN-JIN, *On My Own: Korean Immigration Entrepreneurship, and Korean-Black Relations in Chicago and Los Angeles.* Chicago: University of Chicago Press, 1996.

YOSHIKAWA, YOKO. "The Heat Is on 'Miss Saigon' Coalition: Organizing Across Race and Sexuality." *The State of Asian America: Activism and Resistance in the 1990s.* Karin Aguilar-San Juan, ed. Boston: South End Press, 1994. 275–294.

YU, ELENA S. H. "Filipino Migration and Community Organization in the United States." *California Sociologist* 3:2 (1980): 76–102.

YU, WINIFRED. "Asian-Americans Charge Prejudice Slows Climb to Management Ranks." *Wall Street Journal* 11 Sep. 1985.

ZELNICK, STRAUS. "To Guy Aoki." Letter. 23 Mar. 1993.

ZHOU, MIN. *Chinatown: The Socioeconomic Potential of an Urban Enclave.* Philadelphia: Temple University Press, 1992.

ZINN, LAURA. "To Marketers, Kristi Yamaguchi Isn't as Good as Gold." *Business Week* 9 Mar. 1992: 40.

ZINN, MAXINE BACA. "Adaptation and Continuity in Mexican-Origin Families." *Minority Families in the United States: A Multicultural Approach.* Ronald L. Taylor, ed. Upper Saddle River, NJ: Prentice Hall, 1994. 70-75.

ZINSMEISTER, KARL. "Asians and Blacks: Bittersweet Success." *Current* Feb. 1988: 9–15.

INDEX

Boston Asian Gay Men and Lesbians, 240
Boston Bar Association, 149
Bouvier, Leon F., 74
Boycotts, 133, 164-65
Brando, Marlon, 176
Breakfast at Tiffany's (film), 176
Breslin, Jimmy, 144-45
Bridge on the River Kwai, The (film), 178
Broadcast industry, Asian Americans in, 197
Brooklyn, New York, 48
Brotherhood Crusade, 165
Brown, Brian, 185
Brown University, 96, 97, 100
Buck, Pearl, 176
Buddhism, 53, 80
Bunzel, John H., 98-101
Burlingame Treaty (1868), 11
Bush, George, 108, 266, 267, 276
Business enterprises, Asian-American owned, 49-56
Business necessity, English-only rules as, 126, 127
Business Week, 199
Busti, Virginia, 277
"Buy American" movement, 153

Cain, Bruce, 250
Calderon, Jose, 93
California
    agricultural industry, immigrants in, 11, 12, 13
    Asian American elected officials from, 260
    Asian Americans living in, 41, 42, 47-48
    enrollment trends in higher education in, 101-2
    Proposition 187 in, 36-37
California gold rush, 10, 11
California Mexican-Filipino Field Workers Union Local
    30326, 252
California Post Secondary Education Commission, 101
California State Attorney General, 158
California Supreme Court, 14
Cambodia, refugees from holocaust in, 30
Cambodian Americans, 46, 52-53, 148-49, 221. *See also* South-
    east Asian refugees
Cambodian Community of Greater Fall River, 149
Camino, Michael, 181
Campanis, Al, 145
Campos, Richard, 149-50
Capital
    human, 55, 68
    sources of, 51
Caplan, Nathan, 80-81
Carradine, David, 186
Carrea, John Willshire, 93
Carrere, Tia, 179
Carrying Capacity Network, 37
Carter, Jimmy, 30
Carter, Sarah, 163-64
Casa San Miguel Convalescent Hospital (Concord, Califor-
    nia), 128
Catholicism, 53
Caudill, William, 79
Census, U.S.
    ethno-racial classifications, 234, 235, 236, 258
    1990, 31
Center for New West, 39
Center for Southeast Asian Refugee Resettlement, 144
Chai, David, 111
Chamberlin, Houston, 76
Chan, Charlie (character), 175-76, 199-200
Chan, Cheung Hung, 163-64
Chan, Connie S., 238
Chan, Jackie, 173
Chan, Wilma, 263, 273, 274, 275
Chang, Edward T., 161-63, 167
Chang, Williamson, 192
Change, embracing, 286
Chao, Elaine, 266
Chao, Rosalind, 184, 185
Characteristics of Business Owners, 1992, 51
Chartrand, Bill, 153
Chen, Ed, 124

Chen, Irene Ann, 73
Chen, Joan, 179, 185
Chen, Yaw-Nan, 112
Cheng, Lucie, 55
Cheng, Yung-Chi, 122
Chi, Chao-Li, 183
Chicago, Illinois, 44
Chicano families, literature on, 205-6
Chin, Frank, 218-19
Chin, Vincent, 140-41, 148, 152, 233, 259
Chinatown: The Socioeconomic Potential of an Urban Enclave
    (Zhou), 54-55
Chinatowns, new, 48. *See also* Communities, emerging
Chinese American Citizens Alliance (CACA), 254
Chinese American Democratic Club (CADC), 90
Chinese American Intermarriage (Sung), 229
Chinese American Parents and Teachers Association
    (CAPTA), 92
Chinese Americans, 10, 11, 14, 18-19, 45, 89-90, 254-55
Chinese Consolidated Benevolent Association (CCBA), 252,
    254, 255
Chinese Digest, The, 254
Chinese Exclusion Act (1882), 11, 14, 19, 175, 253
Chinese for Affirmative Action (CAA) reports, 114-16
Chinese Must Go, The (Grimm), 190
Chinese Six Companies, 252, 254, 255
Ching, Anthony, 248
Cho, Margaret, 173, 187, 188
Choate, Pat, 181
Chow, Amy, 72
Choy, Christine, 179
Choy, Marcella H., 80-81
Christ, Carol, 122
Christman, Roy, 251
Chu, Judy, 251
Chua, Siong-huat, 240
Chun, Glen, 91
Chung, Christy, 242
Chung, Connie, 197
Cities, new communities in, 43-46. *See also* specific cities
Citizenship, aliens ineligible for, 14, 15-16
City College of San Francisco (CCSF), 101
Civil rights
    Asian American organizations, 253-55
    gay and lesbian issues, 240-41
    "second generation civil rights activism," 275
Civil Rights Act (1964), 123, 270
Civil Rights Issues Facing Asian Americans in the 1990s, 56, 154
Civil rights movement (1960s), 22, 24, 255
Cleveland Elementary School (Stockton, California), 93-94
Clinton, Bill, 135, 249, 266, 267, 268
Clinton, Hillary Rodham, 249
Coalition Against Anti-Asian Violence (CAAAV), 158
Coalition of Asian Pacific Islander Americans for Fair Reap-
    portionment (CAPAFR), 270-71
"Coalition of Asian Pacifics in Entertainment" (CAPE), 180
Cognitive development, ethnic identity and, 217
Cold War era, 19-20, 254-55
Cole, Gary, 183
College education, 57-59
Color-blind casting, 193-94
Communities, emerging, 36-71
    ethnic entrepreneurship and, 49-56
    settlement patterns, 40-49
    socioeconomic profile and, 56-67
    visibility/invisibility of, 36-40
Community Health Services (San Francisco), 134
Community organizations, participation rates in, 98, 99
Community policing, 159
Community service officers (CSOs), 159
Competition, economic, 152-54
Completion gratification, sense of, 80-81
Confucianism, 53, 80
Connery, Sean, 180
Contractors, sewing, 133
Corbett, Gretchen, 186
"Correspondence" brides, 226
Cost-benefit analysis of immigration, 37-39
Crawford, Angela Rene, 168

314

How the West Was Won (TV), 184
Hu, Harry, 133
Hu, Lily, 273-74
Huang, John, 248, 257-58
Huang, Young Xin, 158
Huddle, Donald, 37, 38
Hughes Aircraft, 111
"Huiguan," 252
Human capital, 55, 68
Hunan Garden incident, 130
Hune, Shirley, 7-8, 282
Hung, Tran Anh, 173
Hunt, Linda, 176
Huynh, Cuong Quy, 240
Hwang, David Henry, 191, 192, 193, 200
Hypergamy, 230
Hyunh, Kim, 158

Ice Cube (rap artist), 166
Identity. *See also* Families and identities, Asian American
   biracial/multiracial Asian American, 234-35, 236
   ethnic, 215-18
   mental health and, 214-15
Illegal immigration, 23, 36-37
Illinois, Asian Americans living in, 42
Ima, Kenji, 93
Immigrants from Asia, 2, 4
Immigration Acts
   1917, 15
   1924, 12
   1990, 23-24
Immigration and Naturalization Service (INS), 4, 16, 37
Immigration Nursing Relief Act (1989), 27
Immigration Reform Act (1965), 2, 5, 22-25, 167, 210
Immigration Reform and Control Act (IRCA, 1986), 23
Immigration reform proposals (1996), 39
Immigration to U.S., 10-13
   anti-immigrant sentiment, 150-51
   Cold War and, 19-20, 254-55
   costs vs. benefits of immigrants, 37-39
   global economic restructuring and, 25-27
   illegal, 23, 36-37
   Immigration Reform Act (1965) and, 2, 5, 22-25, 167, 210
   post-1965, 20-31
   by region or origin (1820-1994), 21
   Vietnam War and Southeast Asian refugees, 27-31
   World War II and, 19
Income, 63-67, 110-11
Indentured servants, 10
Individualism, issue of, 219-20
Indochinese Resettlement Assistance Act (1975), 29
Industrial manufacturing, movement away from developed
   nations, 25
Inouye, Daniel, 259, 260, 264
Institutional discrimination, 14
Integration strategies in public housing, 155-56
Intelligence Quotient (IQ) scores, genetic superiority/inferi-
   ority and, 76-78
Intercollegiate Chinese for Social Action (ICSA), 255, 256
Interethnic marriage, 231-33
Internment of Japanese Americans, 17-18, 186, 217, 218
Interracial marriage, 224-33
Issei, 217, 254
Ito, Lance, 144
Ivy League schools, legacy privileges at, 97-98

Jang, Bong Jae, 164
Japan
   as international military power, 12
   trade imbalance with U.S., 152-54
"Japan-bashing," 152-54
Japanese American Citizens' League (JACL), 149, 153, 174,
   238, 249, 254, 255
Japanese Americans
   anti-Japanese laws and sentiments, 14-16
   homeland politics and, 253
   immigrants, historical experience of, 11-12
   labor force participation of women, 211
   in military, 17-18, 119, 178

relocation during World War II, 16-18, 186, 217, 218
settlement in cities, 45
Japanese Association of America (JAA), 252
Japanese Investigation, The (film), 175
Jensen, Arthur, 76-77, 78
Jessica McClintock Inc., 132-34
Jewish Americans, 73, 82-83, 97, 163
Johnson, Lyndon B., 28
Journalism, Asian Americans in, 195-98
Joy Luck Club, The (film), 179

Kaige, Chen, 173
Kao, Grace, 74
Kar, Snehendu B., 220
Karlin, Joyce A., 163
Kaufman, Philip, 181-82
Keitel, Harvey, 180
Kelloge, Louise, 225
Kelly, Jim, 176
"Kenjinkai," 252
Kennedy, Ted, 39
Kerner Commission report (1968), 162
Khmer Rouge, 30, 221
Kiang, Sam, 251
Kibria, Nazli, 213
Kiewiet, D. Roderick, 250
Killing Fields, The (film), 178
Kim, Bok-Lim, 225
Kim, Elaine, 167, 178, 188, 219
Kim, Helen, 135
Kim, Jay, 263
Kim, Ky Chuoen, 167
Kim, Pan Suk, 113, 114
Kim, Wes, 188
King, Rodney, 1, 160, 162, 163, 166
Kingston, Maxine Hong, 173, 195
Kin Hing, 133
Kitano, Harry, 215, 226-28
Kitch, George Kitahara, 236
Koch, Ed, 145
Korean/African American Dialogue program, 168
Korean Americans
   African Americans and, 143, 160-68
   domestic violence among, 212-13
   immigrants, historical experience of, 13, 19-20
   labor force participation of women, 211
   Los Angeles riot (1992) and, 1, 161, 165-67
   self-employed, 50, 54
   settlement in cities, 45
   types of businesses owned by, 51
Korean War (1950-1953), 19, 254
Kornheiser, Tony, 145
Kung Fu (TV), 185-86
Kusatsu, Clyde, 186, 187
Kwan, Michelle, 2
Kwan, Nancy, 178
Kwoh, Stewart, 195

L. L. Bean, 135
Labor force participation among Asian American women,
   210-11, 212
Labor movement, 13, 127-36
   community-based labor organizing, 130-36
Lam, Tony, 263
Lambda Legal Defense and Education Fund (LLDEF), 240,
   241
Language rights, 122-27
Laotian Americans, 30, 46, 51. See also Southeast Asian
   refugees
Latour, Robert, 148-49
Lau, Fred, 116
Lau, Kinney, 85
Lau v. Nichols, 85-86
Laws. *See also specific legislation*
   anti-Asian, 11, 14-16, 36-37
   anti-miscegenation, 16
Lawyers' Committee for Civil Rights under Law of The Boston
   Bar Association, 149
Le, Ang, 173

Pomona Valley Hospital Medical Center, 125-27
Population growth in U.S., 2-3
Portes, Alejandro, 54
"Postmodern" analysis, 284-85
Post-traumatic stress disorder, 221, 223
Poverty, 63-65, 81, 207-9, 210
Preference voting, 276
Pretowitz, Clyde V., Jr., 181
Princeton University, legacy privileges at, 97-98
Problems of the Third Generation, The (Hansen), 217
Professionals, Asian Americans, 59-63, 112
Proposition 187 in California, 36-37
Protestant work ethic, 53
Pryce, Jonathan, 193
Public housing, move-in violence in, 155-56
"Public square," 287
Purdy, Edward Patrick, 93-94
Push-pull theory, 25, 27
Pye, Lucien W., 249

Quan, Roland, 90, 91
Quayle, Dan, 266
Quon, J.B., 187
Quotas in higher education, alleged, 95-98

Race, Evolution and Behavior (Rushton), 77
Race and Culture (Sowell), 82
Race/ethnicity. *See also specific race/ethnicity*
    enrollment in higher education by, 96
    SAT average scores by, 75
Race relations. *See also* Violence, anti-Asian
    models, 7
    in public housing, 155-56
Racial distinctiveness, 151
"Racial Formation" theory, 7
Racial segregation, 155
Racial stereotyping. *See* Stereotypes, racial
Racial tensions and violence in schools, 91-94
Racism, 76, 154, 216, 218-19. *See also* Violence, anti-Asian
Rainer, Louise, 176
Raines, Jeffrey Michael, 241
Ramirez, Florentino, 125
Reagan, Ronald, 264
Redistricting, 270-73, 275, 280n48
Redwood Curtain (TV movie), 189-90
Refugee Act (1980), 30, 64
Refugee assistance, 64-65
Refugee camps, 30, 221
Refugees, 38. *See also* Southeast Asian refugees
    Amerasians, 189-90, 236-38
    Chinese, 19
Regional distribution, 43
Reich, Robert, 134-35, 154
Relative functionalism, 82-84
Religion, entrepreneurship and, 53-54
Republican National Committee, 266
Republican party, 266-67
Residential area, ethnic identity and, 218
Richardson, Song, 235
Rights, language, 122-27
Right-to-left writing, 84
Rising Sun (motion picture), 287
Rohmer, Sax, 175
Roldan, Salvador, 16
Romance and the Yellow Peril (Marchetti), 175
Rooney, Mickey, 176
Roosevelt, Franklin D., 17, 199, 254
Roosevelt, Theodore, 12
Rose, Cabrito, 125
Rumbaut, Ruben G., 93, 221
Rushton, J. Philippe, 77
Russo, John, 274
Russo-Japanese War (1904-1905), 12

Sacramento, California, anti-Asian violence in, 149
Sacrifices for children's education, 89
Saiki, Patricia, 266
St. Elsewhere (TV), 185
St. Louis Post-Dispatch, 196

Saito, James, 186
Saito, Leland T., 270-71
Sakiniwa, Bob, 249
Salonga, Lea, 189
Sanders, Jimy, 55
San Diego, Asian American communities in, 44
Sand Pebbles, The (film), 178
San Francisco
    Asian American communities in, 44
    employment in local government of, 114-16
    move-in violence in, 155-56
San Francisco Bay Area, settlement patterns in, 48
San Francisco Chronicle/Examiner, 196, 226
San Francisco Housing Authority, 155, 156
San Francisco Laundry Ordinance (1880), 15
San Francisco Police Department, 157
San Francisco State College
    School of Ethnic Studies, 256, 257
    student strike (1968), 6-7, 256, 277
San Francisco Unified School District, 89-90
San Gabriel High School (Alhambra, California), 92-93
San Gabriel Valley, California, 47, 270-73
San Jose, Asian American communities in, 44
San Mateo County, California, settlement patterns in, 48
Sansei, 217
Santa Clara County, California, settlement patterns in, 48
Saund, Dalip Singh, 260
Saxon, John, 176
Scholastic Aptitude Test (SAT) scores, 74, 75
Schools, racial tensions and violence in, 91-94. *See also* Education
Schott, Marge, 102-3
Science, glass ceiling in, 109-12
Scientific racism, 76
"Scotch tape Asian" actors, 176, 193, 194
Seattle Mariners baseball franchise, 153
Seattle Times, 196
"Second generation civil rights activism," 275
See, Dennis, 266, 267
Segregation, racial, 155
Selective attitude toward ethnicity, 217-18
Self-employment, 49-56
Sense and Sensibility (film), 180
Service Employees International Union (SEIU) Hospital and Health Care Workers Local 250, 128
Seto, Patricia, 145-46
Settlement patterns, 40-49
    nativity and geographic distribution, 40-43
    new communities, 43-49
Sewing contractors, 133
Sexual harassment, 120-22
Sexuality, 176, 178, 184-85
Sexual orientation, 238-43
Shankar, Subramonian, 26
Sharan, Kaushal, 146-47
Shimoda, Yuki, 186
Shin, Alan, 224
Shin, Young, 131
Shinagawa, Larry H., 229-30, 231-33, 250, 267
Shivers, Kaia Niambi, 168
Shon, Steve, 223
Siegel, Lenny, 135
Sikhs, 13
Silent Victims: Battered Women in Korean Immigrant Families (Song), 212-13
Silicon Valley, 110, 111
Simcox, David, 74
Simon, Julian L., 37-38
Simpson, Alan, 39
Single Guy, The (TV), 185
Single-transfer voting (STV), 276
Sixteen Candles (film), 176
Slavery, 10
Smith-Mundt Act (1946), 26
Snipes, Wesley, 180
Social Security, 38
Social Security Administration, 37
Socioeconomic mobility, education as means of, 83
Socioeconomic profile, 56-67